THE DEMOCRATIC PHILOSOPHY OF EDUCATION

Other Books
by
HERMAN HARRELL HORNE

THE PHILOSOPHY OF EDUCATION
THE PSYCHOLOGICAL PRINCIPLES OF EDUCATION
IDEALISM IN EDUCATION
FREE WILL AND HUMAN RESPONSIBILITY
STORY-TELLING, QUESTIONING, AND STUDYING

This volume, written by a member of the Faculty of New York University, appeared during its Centennial celebration.

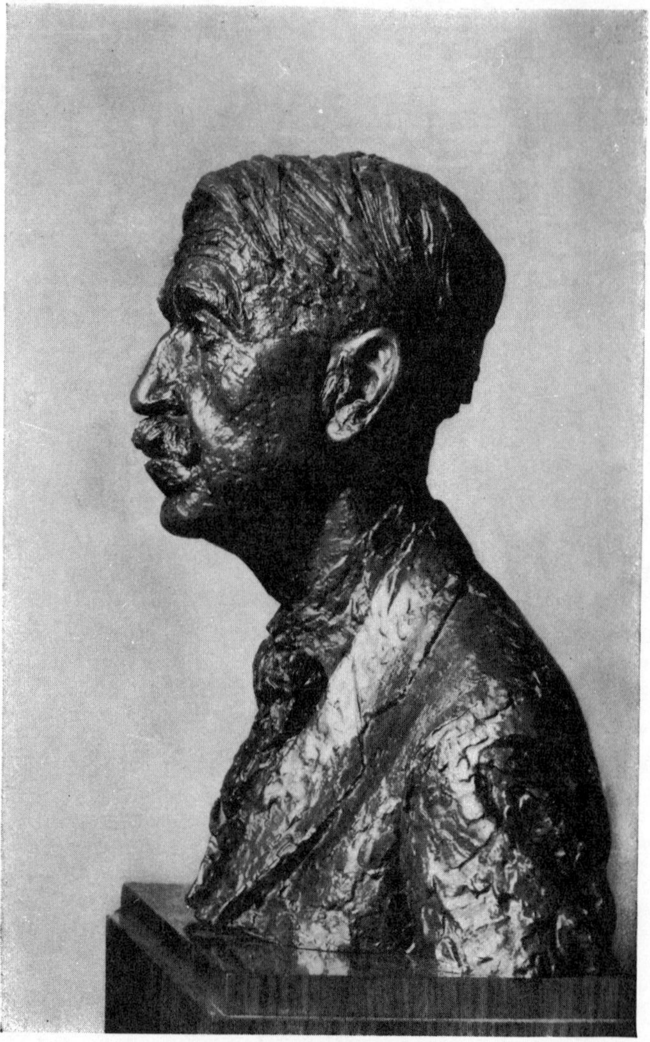

JOHN DEWEY
From the Epstein Bust

THE DEMOCRATIC PHILOSOPHY OF EDUCATION

COMPANION TO DEWEY'S *DEMOCRACY AND EDUCATION*

EXPOSITION AND COMMENT

BY

HERMAN HARRELL HORNE, Ph.D., LL.D.

PROFESSOR OF THE HISTORY OF EDUCATION AND OF THE HISTORY OF PHILOSOPHY AT NEW YORK UNIVERSITY

GREENWOOD PRESS, PUBLISHERS

WESTPORT, CONNECTICUT

Library of Congress Cataloging in Publication Data

Horne, Herman Harrell, 1874-1946.
The democratic philosophy of education.

Reprint of the ed. published by Macmillan, New York.
Includes index.
1. Dewey, John, 1859-1952. Democracy and education. 2. Education--Philosophy. I. Dewey, John, 1859-1952. Democracy and education. II. Title.
LB875.D365H67 1978 370.1 77-27970
ISBN 0-313-20207-9

Reprinted with the permission of Macmillan Publishing Co., Inc.

Reprinted in 1978 by Greenwood Press, Inc.,
51 Riverside Avenue, Westport, Conn. 06880

Printed in the United States of America

10 9 8 7 6 5 4 3 2 1

To Commemorate
The Centenary of the Death of
G. W. F. Hegel, Absolutist,
Of Whom John Dewey, Experimentalist,
Writes . . . . . "acquaintance with Hegel
has left a permanent deposit in my thinking."

PREFACE

The two following letters furnish the background for the composition of this text and suggest its character. The author joins his readers in expressing appreciation of Dr. Dewey's characteristic magnanimity in this matter. He was in Europe at the time the first letter was sent.

NEW YORK UNIVERSITY
SCHOOL OF EDUCATION
Washington Square East
New York City
June 18, 1929

Professor John Dewey,
Columbia University,
New York City.

My dear Dr. Dewey:

Since the appearance of your *Democracy and Education* it has been one of my required texts in our work in the Philosophy of Education in the School of Education of New York University. As a result of a number of years' experience in using this text two impressions have been formed concerning it. These impressions are the result of the students' viewpoint particularly.

The first is that an expository analysis of the main points in the argument is very welcome to the average student. The second is that a contrasting point of view, showing a different type of philosophy from your own, is likewise a stimulus to students in formulating their own viewpoint.

So, for some time the project has been in mind of writing something like a companion volume to your *Democracy and Education* including the two points of exposition and comment. May I inquire whether it would be agreeable to you to have such a volume written? The last chapter in my revised *Philosophy of Education*, contrasting the pragmatic with the idealistic points of view, is an indication in brief of what such a treatment would be like.

May I add that Dr. C. C. Van Liew of the Macmillan Company has been apprised of my thought in the matter and is favorably disposed to the idea, in case you are. And if the idea is approvable by you, may I ask whether you would prefer some different publisher than the Macmillan Company? Their attitude is quite generous in the matter.

May I say in a personal way that the exposition given in my *Philosophy of Education* of the pragmatic views has not been criticized as being in any way unfair or unjust to those views.

It is also a part of my plan to have the volume introduced with the new picture of the Epstein bust of yourself.

There is no particular occasion for hurry in your reply.

Allow me to join your many friends in extending to you the very best wishes for the continuance of your good health through many years of great usefulness.

Yours very cordially,
HERMAN H. HORNE
Professor of the Philosophy of Education

HHH: B

COLUMBIA UNIVERSITY[1]
in the City of New York
DEPARTMENT OF PHILOSOPHY

August 24, 1929.

Professor Herman H. Horne,
New York University,
Washington Square East,
New York City.

My dear Professor Horne:

I am very sorry to be so late in replying to your interesting letter of last June. I hope you have not been hindered in carrying out your plan by my failure to write.

Such a volume as you have in mind would certainly be welcome to me personally, and I have no doubt will be very useful to the educational public. It seems very fitting that The Macmillan Company should publish the book.

Sincerely yours,
(Signed) JOHN DEWEY

JD: JT

This book has been written in accordance with the foregoing plan. For years we have used Dewey's *Democracy and Education* as one of our texts in the Philosophy of Education, because of its importance and influence. Like other readers, our students have found the style difficult. At the same time

[1] Dr. Dewey's reply is published here with his kind permission.

the instructor has had certain views of his own to present that differed notably from those in the text. Consequently a two-fold need has arisen for this work; the first is to understand Dr. Dewey more readily, and the second is to estimate his views more discriminatingly.

Our method is the simple one of following the Dewey text in order and sequence, first with a clarifying exposition, and then with an interpretative and critical comment. In accordance with the review of the argument contained in Chapter XXIV, the contents have been divided into four logical parts, as indicated in the Table of Contents and in the body of the discussion.

Dr. Dewey has exerted a great influence on education both at home and abroad. Dr. Kilpatrick's *Source Book* and Dr. Dewey's *Democracy and Education* are the texts most widely used in our country in the field of educational philosophy.[1] About one-fifth of the former book is drawn from the writings of Dr. Dewey. This situation suggests the significance of Dr. Dewey's educational views at home. Concerning his educational influence abroad, Professor Kandel writes:

> Translations have appeared of practically all of his educational writings. One or more have been published in most of the European languages—French, German, Russian, Hungarian, Bulgarian, Greek, Italian, Spanish, and Swedish—and in Arabic, Turkish, Chinese, and Japanese, while special editions of his earlier works have been published in England. The [foreign] literature about Dewey has been slight, but it is noteworthy that of fourteen articles or books on his educational theory the majority are of recent date, although the first goes back to 1901, when an American student wrote for the doctor's degree in a German university a dissertation on Dewey's doctrine of interest.[2]

Concerning his interest in education and his volume before us, Dr. Dewey has himself written:

[1] Cf. Mack, Henry W., "Comparative Content of Educational Philosophy Text Books," *Education*, December, 1928.

[2] Kandel, I. L., "John Dewey's Influence on Education in Foreign Lands," in *John Dewey the Man and His Philosophy*, Cambridge, 1930, p. 71.

While I cannot write an account of [my] intellectual development without giving it the semblance of a continuity that it does not in fact own, there are four special points that seem to stand out. One is the importance that the practice and theory of education have had for me: especially the education of the young, for I have never been able to feel much optimism regarding the possibilities of 'higher' education when it is built upon warped and weak foundations. This interest fused with and brought together what might otherwise have been separate interests—that in psychology and that in social institutions and social life. I can recall but one critic who has suggested that my thinking has been too much permeated by interest in education. Although a book called *Democracy and Education* was for many years that in which my philosophy, such as it is, was most fully expounded, I do not know that philosophic critics, as distinct from teachers, have ever had recourse to it. I have wondered whether such facts signified that philosophers in general, although they are themselves usually teachers, have not taken education with sufficient seriousness for it to occur to them that any rational person could actually think it possible that philosophizing should focus about education as the supreme human interest in which, moreover, other problems, cosmological, moral, logical, come to a head. At all events this handle is offered to any subsequent critic who may wish to lay hold of it.[1]

It is the opinion of the present writer that the work before us contains the seed thoughts of Dr. Dewey that come to flower and fruitage in his later weightier philosophical volumes.

The views of our author are both warmly admired and keenly criticized. An enthusiastic and eulogistic disciple of Dr. Dewey writes of him and of this work as follows:

We think of Professor Dewey as the most profound and understanding thinker on education that the world has yet known. . . . *The Republic of Plato* may well claim to be regarded as the first of secular books. . . . He is the divine Plato whose thoughts are worthy of God, but whose thoughts about God were contributed in the name of the children as teaching material. No wonder Rousseau called

[1] Dewey, John, "From Absolutism to Experimentalism," in Adams, G. P. and Montague, W. P., *Contemporary American Philosophy*, Vol. II, pp. 22–23, The Macmillan Company, 1930.

this the greatest book on education ever written. It was that until John Dewey wrote his *Democracy and Education*.[1]

If Plato is divine and his thoughts worthy of God, and Dewey is greater than Plato, what follows?

At the unveiling of the Epstein bust of Dr. Dewey (see frontispiece), Professor Kilpatrick used this language:

> As we look to the ancient days for comparisons I see in Professor Dewey the modest sincerity of Socrates, the radical constructive thinking of Plato, the balanced outlook of Aristotle. . . . These [contributions] and more are so conceived as to constitute the most thoroughgoing grasp yet achieved of how civilization is to be placed on a functional and dynamic basis.[2]

This despite the fact that, though Dr. Dewey has a method, he lacks a plan.

But not all voices join in this chorus. Another writes:

> It is from the sociological principles set forth in this chapter and the last that Dewey's *Democracy and Education* is to be appraised. It is based upon and presupposes the sort of philosophy that has just been criticized. Every chapter of Dewey's book expounds the sort of pedagogical theory to which critical reference has just been made. From a dozen points of view he overemphasizes the deliberative, conscious aspect of social life, and in as many ways slurs over the value of habit, drill, and compulsion. The inevitable result is to discount the importance of the social heritage and to pour oil on the already dangerous fire of contemporary individualism. While it is true that the citizens of a democracy need to be taught to think—those of them who have good brains, at least—it is quite as important, especially in the present crisis [1928], that they be taught to revere and obey. It is true that *Democracy and Education* contains some positively constructive theory of very great value, especially the author's exposition of industrial education, which Dewey's followers seem, strangely enough, to have overlooked for the most part. It also contains a valuable half-truth, namely, his emphasis upon constructive thinking. Nevertheless, if the argument of the preceding pages is valid, then it

[1] Moore, E. C., "John Dewey's Contribution to Educational Theory," in *John Dewey the Man and His Philosophy*, Cambridge, 1930, pp. 7, 9–10.

[2] Kilpatrick, W. H., "Remarks at the Unveiling of Dr. Dewey's Bust," *School and Society*, December 22, 1928, pp. 777–778.

> follows that that part of Dewey's theory which has gained the most faddish vogue is dangerous, since its emphasis is in the wrong place. At a critical time its influence has increased, rather than checked, the obsessions of the *Zeitgeist*, and the resulting disorders by which the stability of our modern civilization is most deeply and subtly menaced.[1]

It is evident the reader will need to do some study and thinking on his own account, in doing which we will aid him all we can.

Concerning the difficulty of Dr. Dewey's style of writing, two views may be quoted, one of these being from Dr. Dewey himself. In reviewing the volume by Professor Joseph Warren Beach on *The Outlook for American Prose,* Henry Hazlitt[2] writes:

> An example of the professor's audacity, and of his penetration as well, is his analysis of the style of John Dewey. Dewey has long been revered as our foremost living thinker, and the obscurity of many of his pages is usually attributed to the subtlety of his thought. Professor Beach examines the matter and finds—and, what is more, proves—that this obscurity is to a very large extent simply the result of bad writing. It is not merely lack of elegance, it is "a lack of clearness, a lack of precision," and Professor Beach rewrites a typical passage, supplying necessary transitional phrases and substituting more accurate terms, to demonstrate his point. "I cannot help suspecting," he concludes, "that the writer who is constantly guilty of looseness in expression in detail may sometimes be guilty of looseness of thinking in the large." Quoting Chaucer's question, "And if gold rust, what shall iron do?" Professor Beach regards the case of Dewey as "a plain indication of one of the reasons for the inferiority of American prose writing to that of England and France. It is a simple lack of intellectual discipline."

Far be it from the present writer, having paraphrased not a passage but a volume of Dr. Dewey, to admit that he lacks "intellectual discipline," if there be any such thing, though agreeing that Dr. Dewey is difficult to read and that this difficulty is in part traceable to his prose style.

1 Finney, R. L., *A Sociological Philosophy of Education,* The Macmillan Company, 1928, pp. 478–479.

2 *The New York Sun,* November 6, 1926.

That Dr. Dewey himself is not unmindful of this difficulty, the following quotation will indicate:

> I imagine that my development has been controlled largely by a struggle between a native inclination toward the schematic and formally logical, and those incidents of personal experience that compelled me to take account of actual material. . . . The marks, the stigmata, of the struggle to weld together the characteristics of a formal, theoretic interest and the material of a maturing experience of contacts with realities also showed themselves, naturally, in style of writing and manner of presentation. During the time when the schematic interest predominated, writing was comparatively easy; there were even compliments upon the clearness of my style. Since then thinking and writing have been hard work. . . . It is hardly necessary to say that I have not been among those to whom the union of abilities to satisfy these two opposed requirements, the formal and the material, came easily.[1]

Among the sources of the stylistic difficulty of Dr. Dewey, the present writer would enumerate the following: the use of familiar words with unfamiliar meanings; the use of words with pregnant meanings; the use of long, involved, and highly concentrated sentences (cf. for example, the last but one in the previous quotation, p. x); the development of different important ideas in the same paragraph; and not making it clear when he is stating the views of others and when his own. If one might hazard a few guesses, the associative processes of Dr. Dewey's mind work rapidly, and every topic upon which his rich intelligence turns has for him a wealth of associations, all of which seem, as he writes, to tumble out at once in golden profusion and confusion. Further, that he probably does not write from an outline. And again, that he does not revise what he has once written. For example, let the reader compare the half-page paragraph of three sentences composing the first part of his "Preface" in *Democracy and Education,* with the writer's fifteen shorter sentences in three paragraphs (p. 1 below) giving the main ideas of the same. In addition, Dr. Dewey, like Browning, knows and takes for

[1] Adams and Montague, *op. cit.,* pp. 16–17.

granted in his references as known so much history which his readers do not know and which future followers of his pragmatic educational theories are likely to know less and less.

Let it be distinctly stated that the paraphrase here given is not a substitute for the original; it is only a glass through which the original may be read more easily. Students should continue to wrestle with Dr. Dewey himself. Readers should beware of letting anyone tell them what is on one of his pages.

Dr. Dewey is addicted to the use of italics for the sake of emphasis; the present writer is not, though he has retained the italics of Dr. Dewey in the expositions.

It will be noted that there are some repetitions in the main argument, especially where dualisms are involved. The "comments" reflect the same.

It is the purpose of the "comments" to present the writer's points of view in contrast with those of Dr. Dewey. This contrast centers not so much in practical methods of teaching as in the fundamental philosophy of life. Since the writer holds that idealism conserves all the proper values of pragmatism, he holds that the philosophy of experimentalism alone is one-sided, over-emphasizing method and under-emphasizing content. As Dr. Louise Antz says:

> We are discussing the relative merits of idealism with pragmatism as educational policies. Pragmatism is one of the most-talked-of tendencies in educational thinking because the most-talked-of leader in education is a pragmatist—Dr. John Dewey. But Dewey's pragmatism is essentially a method, not a philosophical system. As a method, it is probably the greatest blessing that has in recent years come to education.[1]

The composition of this book, it may be frankly stated, has given the writer a better knowledge of the text that he has taught many years and a more sympathetic insight into Dr. Dewey's views, though leaving him no less reluctant to accept

[1] Antz, E. L., "Idealism and Pragmatism in Education," *Education*, June 1926, p. 606.

them. The consistent practice of Dr. Dewey's views would in his judgment substitute an impoverished for an enriched experience. Let the reader read, weigh, and decide!

Having said so much already, let this long prefatory bow include the following human interest document (dated May 20, 1931) by one of my students:[1]

REACTIONS TO
DEMOCRACY AND EDUCATION

When I am in my sober senses, I appreciate this "Philosophy" greatly. Its parts fit so neatly and accurately into each other, like the well-planned pieces of an intricate jig-saw puzzle. Not one piece is ill cut. Not one piece left to chance. Not one piece a misfit. It is so precise; it is so rational; it is so scientific. The problem of solving it is so stimulating.

But sometimes, when I am melancholy, or dreamy, or fanciful, when I am in a holiday mood, or perhaps, when I have "experienced" education long and monotonously, a strangely illogical longing and a curiously indescribable hunger arise within me for something beyond and above this philosophy.

Like Sissy Jupe, when I do not "walk upon flowers" in fact, I fain would see them upon my mental carpet. Queerly enough, too, I would now and again feed myself some occasional light pie into which no educational planner has ever had an apportioning finger. Doubtless my mind from the cradle has not been practically formed by rule and line. Doubtless my self-devised pies very often give me mental indigestion. The pragmatists claim to know what is good for me.

Nevertheless I become rather frightened when I see the never-ending regions of education stretching out before me, through which, like Tennyson's *Brook,* I must run on forever.

Is my play always to be work, my work always to be play? Am I never to dance for the pure joy of dancing or to sing with delight with the light-hearted fairy, "Heigh-ho!"? Must I sing to please, to entertain, or like little Tommy Tucker, for my supper, and dance just to make my corpuscles behave?

Is there never an "I" except when I am in company? Has society formed the "I" of me, or in my aloneness is there not still an invisible society of God and me—which can mould me as can millions?

[1] Valentine, Marian Gill. Quoted with permission.

Whence have I come and whither am I going? I have made my entrance. I must make my exit. From where? To what? Who is the Stage Manager, I wonder?

Whenever I approach with such puzzling problems that do not happen to fit into the pragmatic philosophy at present very popular in many noted temples of education, the high priests of the activity programs blandly wave me aside, trusting, perhaps, that I will fade away into the misty realms of the transcendent they so often belittle. Not all the *Artful Dodgers* are to be found in the pages of *Oliver Twist.* All the *twists and turns* of the English language can be used by these orthodox to the bewilderment of the non-conformist!

Many of us to-day accept the pronouncements from the rarefied atmosphere of science in education as uncritically, as abjectly, as the people of ancient Egypt accepted the mandates of the priests of Isis and by so doing display as great an act of faith in this scientific age as ever did any ignorant slave of Pharaoh then.

Does not even science itself, and, above all, the science of education, need its critics? Has not Dr. Millikan himself said that we do not know a thing more precise about atoms than we do about souls and spirits? If then, Matter, Reality itself, can never be fully explained, how then can the reactions of such a complex mechanism as Man, one moreover, animated by a mysterious soul or spirit, ever be completely and adequately foretold, analyzed, defined? How, in the innumerable and unaccountable situations in which matter-plus, or man, moves, can other than some infinite Master-Mind ever be completely and adequately all-powerful in control?

Perhaps I should not, at this modern day, be still pondering with my friend, the Elizabethan, Henry Vaughan, of a "country far beyond the stars." I should be content with *now,* and not worry about the before or the hereafter, say my pragmatic friends.

But this whirling present, this *now,* is so uncertain, so shifting, I timidly reply. My spirit is troubled, "my heart is disquieted within me." There must be a Rock of Ages for my unsteady feet to stand upon. I need beneath me the Everlasting Arms. "Like as the hart panteth after the water brooks," there is within me a thirst for that which is beyond and above the mortal.

The pragmatic philosophy welcomes the astronomer—but not the star-gazer. Must I then return to the Elizabethans for a "glimpse beyond the stars?" Or is there a system of philosophy to which I can refer these very scientific educators that will allow me to believe with the poet Ronsard "that this our little life is but a day in the eternal," and where star-gazing with him I can cry to these earth-bound mortals:

> There is the joy whereto my soul aspires,
> And there the rest that all the world desires,
> And there is love, and peace, and gracious mirth,
> And there in the most brightest heavens shalt thou
> Behold the very beauty whereof now
> Thou worshippest the shadow upon earth.[1]

If there is such a philosophy, I must make it mine.

Because *Democracy and Education* as a text has proved a confusing wilderness of stimulating ideas to many earnest readers these sixteen years, it is hoped by the author that other intellectual travelers than his own students will find this *Companion* a welcome guide. We would not lessen the profit but increase the pleasure in reading this contemporary educational classic.

H. H. H.

New York City,
January, 1932.

[1] Pierre de Ronsard (1524–1585).

TABLE OF CONTENTS

Chapter V

Chapter VI

PART II. DEMOCRACY IN EDUCATION

Chapter VII

Chapter VIII

Chapter IX

THE DEMOCRATIC PHILOSOPHY OF EDUCATION

INTRODUCTION

On Dr. Dewey's Preface

Exposition. This text deals with the application of democracy to education. The ideas implied by a democracy are detected and stated. The aim of social change should be to realize adequately the democratic ideal. We are only nominally democratic. One reason why society is hampered in becoming more democratic is the influence, strange as it may seem, of the theories of knowing and morals we hold. These theories were formulated centuries ago under the influence of non-democratic societies and were suited to those ages. With us they are hold-overs. They need to be critically estimated and modified. What a real democracy in distinction from a nominal one means in reconstructing the aims and methods of our public education we shall see.

The three great influences of modern life are science, industry, and democracy. Our remarkable scientific progress is due to the use of the method of experimentation in studying nature. Our revolutionary industrial changes are due to our science and the mechanical inventions springing therefrom. Our democracy lags behind our scientific and industrial advances. It should catch up with science and industry, indeed it should motivate these in the interest of man.

It is a business of philosophy to assist us in connecting democracy with the interests of science and industry and, further, to show us how education, which is society shaping itself to its future ends, should change both its subject-matter and method to meet the demands of the democratic ideal.

Comment. A few anticipatory comments will be made at this point. They are intended to suggest in a general way the philosophical issues ahead of us. If only a vague notion of what it is all about is gotten at the moment, that will be enough.

According to Dr. Dewey, philosophy should not concern itself with speculations that can not be tested by experience (see what is perhaps his most significant work, *Reconstruction in Philosophy*) but with resolving the conflicts within experience. This is why the treatment of *Democracy and Education* can be called *An Introduction to the Philosophy of Education* (see the sub-title). Such an interpretation of the rôle of philosophy wipes out the distinction in method between science and philosophy. (See his work, *The Influence of Darwin on Philosophy.*) Philosophy becomes the application of the scientific method to the problems of society, it is one with social science. It studies the conflicts in society and resolves them in terms of the social, that is, the democratic, ideal.

This socio-scientific view of the world has doubtful validity. It holds that the universe, in the phrase of James, has "the lid off," is not a closed system, is in the making, is inherently indeterministic, is adventurous, implicating man himself in its real perils; that it is characterized by uncertainty, novelties, creativeness, inventiveness, possibilities, and irregularities; that its order is uninsured, allowing no absolute certainty in science, aesthetics, logic, and ethics; that reality is a process of events in time, everything changing, and change and time being noumenally real; that most problems are falsely stated, implying a non-existent dualism, e.g., the mind-body problem; that the human mind emerges within a social experience, and that values are intelligent interests, religion seeking to make real the potential aspects of the actual.

Such a conception of philosophy is in line with the "Positivism" of August Comte and the "Agnosticism" (no invidious meaning here) of Herbert Spencer. The difference between Spencer and Dewey as regards "the unknowable" is that Spencer writes about it (see his *First Principles*) and Dewey ignores it. This philosophy is also known as "Instrumentalism" because it uses thought not to go beyond experience but as an instrument or tool to find suitable means for ends with experience. Since it subordinates thought to action, it is also called "Pragmatism." Since it locates values within the stream of human experience, it is also called "Humanism." And since it advocates the supremacy of the scientific method, it is also known as "Experimentalism." In educational thinking it would wipe out (and has largely done so in America) the distinction between principles of education and the first principles of education; the latter is the classical philosophy of education. Here we are to see a philosophy of education that raises no questions concerning the transcendent; that is, concerning the general meaning and issues of existence, the nature of reality, the explanation of the cosmos, or the place of man in the universe, and makes no suggestion whatever that education may in any way be concerned with any of these things. Dr. Dewey's conception of philosophy omits, that is, ontology, cosmology, and as generally conceived, religion. Though omitted, they are nevertheless implied. Experimentalism is a form of naturalistic metaphysics. (Cf. Childs, J. L., *Education and the Philosophy of Experimentalism,* New York, 1931, Chap. III.)

Historically speaking, this is not all of philosophy. It is theoretical sociology or politics. It is Aristotle on "Politics," not on "Metaphysics." Philosophy has historically turned over to the various sciences the questions that could be answered by experimentation and experience, and has left for itself the questions that can not be answered positively but only tentatively by the reason, without proof. All the sciences were once philosophical, that is, speculative. Physics was once natural philosophy; chemistry was once alchemy; astronomy was once astrology. The latest subject to pass from philosophy to science is psychology. Logic too is a science.

Ethics and Æsthetics are partly scientific, and partly philosophical. Metaphysics is non-scientific (not anti-scientific) and philosophical, in the sense that its conclusions can not be proven by experience, though they may be outgrowths of thinking about experience. Such metaphysical questions still reserved by that modern philosophy which has the classical background are: What is reality? How is the order of the world to be explained? What may man hope? Is man's origin an accident? His destiny fated? His spirit immortal?

There are some advantages in the author's position; it limits the field of thought, it thereby allows concentration of effort, and it saves much energy that would otherwise go into reflection.

But there is one great disadvantage. Man simply will think about things he can not fully know. There is no such thing as stopping human speculation. Man's curiosity leads him to think out beyond experience. Tell him he should not and he will do so the more. As Kant wrote, in beginning the "Preface" to the first edition of his *Critique of Pure Reason:*

> "Our reason has this peculiar fate that with reference to one class of its knowledge, it is always troubled with questions which cannot be ignored, because they spring from the very nature of reason, and which cannot be answered, because they transcend the powers of human reason" (Müller's Translation).

Furthermore, man's emotions are not satisfied when hemmed in by the order of experience; man wants to worship, to pray, and to praise. And still further, man must act and live. He prefers to do so *sub specie æternitatis.* Deny him this outlook, keep him *sub specie generationis* and his impulses to act are not so broadly motivated as they might be. We want a philosophy of education that will relate our work to man's transcendent as well as his social relationship. And this conclusion may well be based on the nature of man himself and the kind of world in which he lives and must live, that is, on pragmatic, humanistic, grounds. If speculation satisfies an interest of man, it is not good pragmatism to reject it.

PART I

EDUCATION AS A NEED AND FUNCTION OF SOCIETY

CHAPTER I

EDUCATION AS A NECESSITY OF LIFE

1. Renewal of Life by Transmission

Exposition. Living beings are able to maintain themselves as individuals for a period through controlling their environment, and as a species through reproduction. This is the great distinction between the animate and the inanimate world, between a plant or animal on the one hand and a stone on the other.

When we think of "life" or "experience" as something more than physical, it "covers customs, institutions, beliefs, victories and defeats, recreations and occupations." In this sense also life continues through renewal, as is evident in any social group. The means whereby a social group continues itself, renews itself, maintains its ideals, is, in the broadest sense of the term, "education."

Unless there were education in this sense, the characteristic life of the group would cease with the death of the elders. The young must be preserved physically and initiated socially, learning the ways of the elders, if the life of the group is to continue. This is the necessity of education. It spans the gap between the ignorance and indifference of the young and the aims and habits of the social group. As biological life maintains and transmits itself by nutrition and reproduction, so social life transmits itself by education. The young of human beings are so immature and inefficient that even survival requires special pains and tuition. "How much more then is this the case with respect to all the technological, artistic, scientific, and moral achievements of humanity."

Comment. Thus we begin our philosophizing about education with the phenomenon of life. No question is raised concerning the nature of life and the origin of life. The biologists and the philosophers are still working on these two questions. We know the practical difference between a dead body and a living body, the latter having capacities of metabolism and reproduction. But we do not know what makes a cell live or how it came to exist. Herbert Spencer said vaguely that life was the adjustment of internal and external relations. This is not a definition of life, as it purports to be, but a verbal statement of the condition for the continuance of life. Some modern students hold, more specifically than Spencer, that electrical disequilibrium is a condition of life in a cell, an amœba sustaining life until its positive and negative electrical energies neutralize each other.

Concerning the origin of life speculative scientists and philosophers are alike still in the dark. Has life always existed, even in the primitive nebulae, or did it arise as something new on this or some other planet? In either case, what is the explanation? Some scientists have held that the living cell is itself an evolution, perhaps finally becoming alive under conditions of great physical pressure; others, that life on this planet came by way of a meteor from some other planet.

Philosophers have held a number of different views, among them being that life arose as a chance occurrence; that it arose as an absolute necessity under the reign of impersonal physical law; that it arose by creative fiat, or the act of a Supreme Intelligence (Creationism); or, that it arose as a new expression of an immanent Purpose in the world, as a part of the Spiritual Order of the universe.

Now it makes a difference which of these philosophical views we hold. To believe in chance or necessity as the origin of life is to diminish its value. The category of chance is haphazard and the category of necessity is blind. To believe in either a Creator working externally upon dead matter or in an Immanent Purpose working internally through matter is to enhance the value of life. The category of creation and the category of purposeful development alike mean life was intended. If this is the case, then life conscious of itself, as in man, may sense its unity with, and coöperate with, the ultimate Source of things.

Educationally speaking, on the basis of the former alternatives, our pupils are behaving organisms and children of time. On the basis of the latter alternatives, our pupils are,—*in addition,* be it observed—images of their Great Original and children of eternity. Our sense of the dignity of teaching as a profession and life career thus depends considerably on our conception of the origin and nature of life. A thoroughgoing philosophy of education should therefore include the theories of the origin of life.

2. Education and Communication

Exposition. Transmission and communication are practically synonomous terms. Society continues by communication, by passing on; it also exists *in* communication, sharing. The process of possessing things in common is communication. "Likemindedness" is the basis of social unity. Schools though important, are "a relatively superficial means" of forming the dispositions of the immature.

A group of persons is a community when it acts for common ends of which its members are all aware and in which they are interested. Such a consensus or likemindedness, demands communication, or sharing.

Even our most social groups are not yet socialized, not a complete community, for individuals still use one another without reference to the feelings, ideas, and consent of those used.

Communication as the vital sharing of purposes and interests is one with social life and is itself educative. By communication one's experience is enlarged, whether one be the giver or the receiver of the communication. Routine communication may cease to be educative.

The young have to be taught for the sake of the group. This necessity helps to reduce the experience of the mature to communicable and usable form.

Comment. One characteristic of Dr. Dewey's style is to give a familiar word an unfamiliar meaning. We shall have many illustrations of this fact, of which the use of the term "communication" in this section is one. We ordinarily think of "communication" in connection with a note, letter, telegram, etc., whereby some news is communicated by one individual to another individual. Communication is thus a product, *a* communication, and individual. To Dr. Dewey it is a process of sharing common interests, of holding things in common, of transmitting things held in common. It is communicating, involving a group, and so social. It is more like that which some sociologists call "unconscious imitation," which they contrast with "invention."

3. The Place of Formal Education

Exposition. Any social institution, like the home or the school, arose in a very practical way. Thus, religion began in the desire to secure favor from the overruling powers and to ward off evil. Though so arising, the worth of any social institution must now be measured by its contribution to the enrichment of human experience. The institution is made for man. The consciousness of this fact came from having to teach the young.

With savage man, education is largely by transmission and communication; it is informal, without schools. With civilized man, in addition, it has become formal, in schools. "To savages it would seem preposterous to seek out a place where nothing but learning was going on in order that one might learn." Apart from their formal initiations into full membership in the tribe, their learning is direct, by participation in adult activities, or indirect, through dramatic plays.

In civilized societies the social life of the elders is so complex that children can neither participate in it nor playfully imitate it [but cf. aviation toys]. Hence formal schools, with studies and teachers, arise to bridge the gap. They give the training necessary to share effectively in adult activities, they transmit the resources of a complex society, they provide symbolic knowledge.

This formal education, though necessary, has its dangers. The old informal education was personal, practical, and vital; formal education easily becomes remote, unused, and dead. And worse yet: we come to think this outcome is education itself! Thus the symbols of formal education come to replace the social interests of informal and real education.

How to be formally (*i.e.,* by the school as a social institution), yet truly, educated at the same time is one of the hard nuts for an educational philosophy to crack. One's schooling must not interrupt his education, but continue it and supplement it. Not only information and skill but also a social disposition are to be secured. Knowledge and skills have grown so rapidly in the last four centuries that the danger of a split between the school and life was never greater than now.

Comment. Dr. Dewey recognizes that formal education has a necessary place in modern complex society. By this he means that the school as a social institution is justified in civilized society. The education that the school gives is "formal" in the sense that the school is one of the social forms or institutions through which civilization must intentionally transmit itself.

But Dr. Dewey is opposed to educating formally in the school, though the school is a formal social institution. The method of educating within the school should be informal and as nearly like the method of direct social participation of primitive man as possible. We are to educate intentionally in schools as formal institutions by methods as informal and unintentional as living itself. "Formal education" is to be informally acquired.

This is the meaning of the familiar, but vague, phrase, "the school is life." The school is not life in the sense that it is all of life, or in the sense that it exactly mirrors all of life, the bad and the good, but the school is, or should be, life in the sense that the children live and learn adequately, fully, richly, naturally, informally, creatively in school. Our estimate of this method when unsupplemented by more formal procedures will come later.

CHAPTER II

EDUCATION AS A SOCIAL FUNCTION

1. The Nature and Meaning of Environment

Exposition. The title of this chapter means that education is a function of the social environment. The chapter itself discusses the way in which the group educates its immature members. The point of the first section is that the social environment is not composed of people generally but of those to whom one responds, with whom one varies, thereby becoming adapted to one's group.

Our immediate question is then, how do the young assimilate the point of view of their elders? or, how do the elders bring the young into likemindedness with themselves?

The answer in general form is: the elders as a social environment call out certain responses from the youth, *i.e.*, by means of the social S—R, the S being the social group and the R being the responses of its immature members. The situation involves seeing, feeling, planning, believing, in a certain way in order to win the approval of the elders. By this means a certain system of behavior in line with group custom is produced in the young.

The genuine environment of a person is not his surroundings, but those things, near or remote, with which he varies, which really concern him, with which his characteristic activities are continuous. A stick or a stone, strictly speaking, has no environment or medium; a fish's environment is water; while to the astronomer both his telescope at hand and the distant star he is studying are his environment, and to the antiquarian the coin at hand and the remote epoch to which it belongs are his environment, and to the Arctic explorer the north pole is a part of his environment, even if he never reaches it. Thus whatever things sustain or frustrate the activities characteristic of a living being are its environment.

Comment. There are two novelties in this section. One is the use of the situation-response idea as the general mode of explaining how the young of a group become like their elders. This is somewhat "behavioristic." Most sociologists and social psychologists would refer instead to imitation and the influence of example. Dr. Dewey will consistently stress the active element of experience.

The second novelty is the twist given the dictionary meaning of the term "environment," as previously the word "communication." The definition of the term as given would permit us to deny that the doll shop which the business man passed every morning but to which he paid no attention was a part of his environment, and correspondingly to affirm that the London money market was a part of his environment. In general, the things to which a man responds, though remote in space and time, are his environment, while the things to which he does not respond, though at hand, are not a part of his environment. As things distant in time are necessarily conceived without being perceived, it would be easy to stress man's conceptual world as a real part of his environment. This is important in appreciating man in distinction from the fish as being lifted above the particular and the concrete, the here and the now.

2. The Social Environment

Exposition. The social environment is composed not of those by whom one is surrounded but of those with whom one shares experiences. These experiences may be thinking or feeling as well as overt acting. One's experiences are dependent upon the attitudes of others. This condition makes them social. Just as a merchant can not do business with himself, but only with his customers, just as a manufacturer must lay his private plans with his markets in mind, so the activities of every individual must be defined in social terms.

Once again, as in the previous chapter, let us ask just how the social medium or the social environment nurtures its immature members. To answer, consider the rat in the maze or the acquired habits of the domesticated animals. The rat in the maze learns finally the route that brings him to his food. The horse with bit, bridle, vehicle, food, etc., learns to obey. Two things are involved in the learning of the domesticated animals, (1) that human beings are concerned with what they do and (2) that human beings control the natural stimuli which influence them, that is, by creating a certain environment.

Now children learn as do the animals, their actions are modified in the same way. The burnt child dreads the fire. Those things are avoided which will yield painful consequences and those things are done which yield pleasurable consequences.

Thus animals are trained; thus children are trained. But are not children also educated as well as trained? Yes. In training, the desired outer action is secured; in education, the desired inner attitudes, the mental and emotional dispositions of behavior, are also secured. Training may or may not yield these educative results.

How then shall we differentiate the process of training from that of educating? The animal does not share in the social use to which his action is put, the child does. That is the difference between training an animal and educating a child. The trained dog or horse is not a partner in a shared activity; he gets food in consequence. The educated child is a partner in a shared activity; he gets a new interest, a new idea, a new emotion, in consequence.

Now is it not true that in too many cases our children are trained like the lower animals instead of educated like human beings? In such cases the child acquires habits that are useful or agreeable to others by the use of the pleasure and pain stimuli. When children are educated, they share in the common activity; their original impulses are modified; the same ideas and emotions are aroused in them that animate their elders. Thus the mental habits, and not merely the outer acts, are assimilated to those of the group. For illustration, consider the way in which, first in games and then in fact, a boy member of a primitive warlike tribe grows up himself to be a warrior. It is not by being put through the motions of fighting, with his outer successes recorded and failures penalized, but praise or blame attaches to his total performance.

Again, how then does the group assimilate, *i.e.*, educate, the youth? It begins as animals are trained by setting up stimuli to action. This is the first step. The second and completing step is making the youth a sharer or partner in the adult activities, with the result that successes and failures are felt as his very own. Thus he acquires the emotions, beliefs, ideas, even the knowledge which makes him a member of the group. This knowledge is not divorced from his habitual pursuits.

But does not the use of language make it possible for knowledge to be gained directly from another instead of indirectly through sharing activities with another? Not so; all things, even words, gain meaning by being used in a shared experience or in joint action. As this is an important principle, affecting methods of teaching in a fundamental way, we must both explain and illustrate it. Language does tend to become the chief instrument of learning, but it is not exceptional in having its meanings really rooted in activities.

The baby begins with hearing sounds having no meaning, they are just stimuli to a reflex physical response, some soothing, some disturbing. Sounds come to have meaning for him through being uttered in connection with some action in which a number of persons about him share. Thus, the year-old, on being taken out for a ride, has something put on his head and at the same time hears the word, "hat." The same object is used, handled, seen, in different connections, but each time the same sound is heard. The sound of the name of the object gets meaning by the same process as the object itself. The shared experiences is the basis of the shared sound and of the shared meaning. Language is socially meaningful because, and when, based on social experiences.

But surely when pupils learn from books about the discovery of America or from Homer about Hector's helmet whose waving plumes frightened his child Astyanax in its mother's arms, we have language separated from a shared activity. Our pupils certainly can not share in activities that are over and gone irrevocably. But they do, nevertheless. It is not a sensibly perceived activity but it is an imagined activity and no less shared. The imagined activity is not true to history unless it is based on previous perceived activities. Thus, the concrete word "helmet" gets a meaning as "hat" got its meaning, through the sound being heard when the thing was seen in pictures, or better, being made in home or school, or bought at the store and worn. The general name "Greek" acquires a meaning through being heard in connection with different objects or pictures, such as men, statues, marble buildings, ships, and the like. Then, just as a Greek can wear a helmet, so the sounds "Greek helmet" can go together with meaning, and the imagination can re-picture, even with emotion, the brave Hector about to go forth to war removing his helmet with the waving plume which frightened his child, placing it on the ground, and bidding farewell to the little Astyanax and its mother, Andromache, who smiled through her tears. One who understands thus becomes mentally a partner with those who used and saw the helmet. All words are meaningful only when they enter either overtly or imaginatively into a shared situation; otherwise they are sounds acting as pure physical stimuli, but signifying nothing.

Comment. Since Thorndike formulated his "Laws of Learning" on the basis of experimentation with animals, especially with rats, it has become customary to say that children learn as the animals learn. Watson gave us "behaviorism" by studying men as Thorndike studied mice.

It is time to point out that children are not merely little animals, and that while they can learn as animals learn, animals can not learn as children can. Children can and do learn by the "law of effect," viz., that satisfaction in an act leads to its repetition, and annoyance in an act leads to its avoidance. But if children learned only in this way, along with the "exercise" of repetition and the "readiness" to act in a given way, they could become at best only sublimated pleasure-seekers and pain-avoiders, *i.e.,* only attenuated hedonists. The fact is, many unselfish acts of devotion are not motivated by consequences for the self at all but for others. So children must also learn in some other way. This is not to deny that some of the higher animals also may have higher motives than the so-called "Laws of Learning" allow.

The essential difference is not the one indicated in the text, that animals *do not* share in the uses of the activities in which they engage. The essential difference is that they *can not.* Peary's faithful dogs helped him reach the pole; they could not understand what it was all about. The trained elephant on the stage goes through his tricks, his trainer takes the applause, or trains the elephant to behave as though he took it.

The reason for the difference lies in the *superior* brain capacity of the child, especially in his imaginative and conceptualizing ability. It is this basic difference in brain capacity that enables the child to acquire the meaning of abstract qualifying terms, like "Greek." It is this that enables the child to live imaginatively in the past. It is this that especially allows pupils to use not only reproductive imagination, which repeats the past, but productive imagination which modifies perceptual experience and anticipates the unknown future. The hat may be understood by activities that are immediate; the helmet by reproductive imaginative activities one degree removed from the perceived immediate; but Greek sirens and centaurs are understood only by a productive imagination, thrice removed from the immediate activity. In such cases the mind has produced something it has never objectively experienced on sea and land. It is this transcendent reach of the human intelligence to which no behavioristic law of learning can do justice. It allows for creativeness on the part of pupils. It allows for the formation of ideals to govern acts superior to the pleasure-pain stimuli. And it makes it possible for us to regard the mind as more than any kind of physiological organic response. Education is more than training not because children share in social activities and animals don't,—the animals *do* share according to their ability; but because children are children and not animals, and so can share in the experience of their elders. It is because children can think abstractly that it is not necessary that every item of knowledge grow out of some social activity. A child who with sticks learns $3 \times 3 = 9$ does not later have to learn $9 \times 9 = 81$ by the aid of sticks to see meaning in the equation. There may be learning by the use of language in case the language used has meaning based on experience. Every exclusive "experience" or "activity" curriculum today misses this point. Just how much activity is necessary to give language meaning to children varies with the degree of intelligence of the children. The lower the grade of intelligence, the nearer to the animal level it is, the more activity is necessary. This is a practical matter to be determined by the needs of the specific school. Only low-grade intelligences require only an activity basis of learning. And in view of what Dr. Dewey says about imagination, it is a misreading of his theory to suppose that all learning, though it starts on the basis of physical activity, must be kept there.

3. The Social Medium as Educative

Exposition. So far we have seen that the social environment forms the mental and emotional disposition of behavior in the young. This it does by engaging them in activities that arouse and strengthen certain impulses. These activities have certain purposes and lead to certain results.

The activities induced by association with others do not create the impulses, whether of liking or disliking, but furnishes them with their objects. Thus the main texture of disposition is formed, incidentally and indirectly, quite independently of direct schooling. Our lessons should not interrupt our learning. The best that deliberate teaching can do is to give fuller exercise to these impulses and capacities formed out of school, to refine them, and to provide them better objects.

To illustrate how we are formed, educated, without any set purpose, by the social medium of which we are a part, consider the case of the child growing up in a family of musicians. He becomes a musician without so intending. His musical capacities are always being stimulated. His non-musical capacities will hardly be awakened as they would in a different kind of family, say one devoted to the stage. His social recognition in his group depends on his taking an interest in music and becoming somewhat proficient in it; otherwise he is unable to share in the life of the group to which he belongs. Such direct participation in community life constitutes one's indirect or incidental but none the less basic education. Of course it is often very limited in its range of interest. What is outside the activities of the group is not only strange and foreign, it tends to be morally forbidden and intellectually suspected. We shall see presently how this situation helps to define the functions of the school.

To be specific, there are three things that show in a most marked way this so-called "unconscious influence of environment," viz., the habits of language; manners, which are minor morals; and good taste and æsthetic appreciation. The infant thus acquires what is well called his *mother* tongue. Good manners are good breeding. And æsthetic taste grows up naturally in a truly æsthetic environment. In comparison with these authentic and first-hand results of direct experience, conscious teaching is corrective and second-hand.

The deeper standards of value are framed in the same unconscious way by the situations into which a person enters.

This is a fusion of the three preceding things. These standards lie below the level of reflection; we take them for granted without inquiry; we are not conscious of them; and yet they determine our conscious thinking and our decisions as to what is worth while. These low-lying habitudes have been formed in us by the constant give and take of relationship with others.

Comment. In discussing the unconscious influence of environment most sociologists and social psychologists pay more attention to the influence of example, imitation, suggestion, and folk-ways, to use Sumner's term, than does Dr. Dewey. His principle is rather that of the situation-response. The situation provides the objects which stimulate certain capacities to respond and develop, while others, lacking appropriate stimuli, lie dormant. The two lines of approach may come to the same thing in the end but the emphasis is different. Dr. Dewey's emphasis is more naturalistic and behavioristic. He is not a behaviorist, however, for he holds the response is flexible and adaptive, not mechanical.

Further, concerning the results of this process, however analyzed, in addition to the four things specifically mentioned, Dewey himself would add knowledge and skill as engrained in such habitual, social pursuits. Further, two very significant things should be added to complete the list, viz., the phenomenon of self-consciousness, and the habits of the religious life. No individual is without self-consciousness and no society is without religion. We come to self-consciousness through social situations in ways described by J. M. Baldwin, certainly without intending to become aware of ourselves and certainly without being consciously taught that we have a self,—the teaching would be unintelligible unless we first had become aware of ourselves through experience. And such religious feelings, habits, and ideas as are basically ours came to us first through direct participation in the religious life of the group, however much they may have been later modified by direct instruction.

4. The School as a Special Environment

Exposition. It is the social environment then that educates. If the school is to educate, it is to do so as a special social environment. The only way adults can consciously control the education of the young is to control their environment. It is in relation to this environment that they first act, and hence think and feel. There is no such thing as direct education; all education is indirect through controlling the environment. Unless we deliberately regulate the environment of children, they will be educated by chance environments, effectively, no doubt, but not always desirably. A school is an environment expressly made to influence the mental and moral disposition of the young. It is the typical instance of an educative environment.

Under what social conditions do schools arise? Three things are to be noted, viz., (1) the young need to know more than they can learn by daily direct participation in the life of the community, (2) the community itself is so developed that it depends upon the remote in time and space, and (3) the social inheritance is so complex that it can no longer be transmitted by word of mouth but has to be transmitted through written symbols. The school under such social conditions is the necessary agency to teach what community life can not, to make conscious the community's dependence on the remote in space and the distant in time, and to make familiar and meaningful the written symbols as tools for transmitting the racial culture. For example, though speech may be picked up in incidental intercourse, it takes schools to teach us to read and to write, to acquaint us with cosmic rays and the structure of the atom, and to show us our relation to the British, the Germans, the French, the Italians, the ancient Romans and Greeks, and all the others. As compared with the chance environment of life, the chosen environment of the school has three specific functions. These are (1) to simplify the educative environment of children; (2) to purify it; and (3) to give it a representative and balanced social character.

(1) It is necessary to simplify the educative environment of children because our civilization is too complex to be assimilated as a whole. Its complexity is due to the presence of many important elements, such as business, politics, art, science, and religion. The school simplifies this complex social environment by selecting those features of it which are both fundamental and capable of being responded to and shared in by the young, and then by arranging these in a progressive order for successive assimilation.

(2) It is likewise necessary to purify the educative environment since our civilization is not only complex but also in some respects unworthy. Not all the past is to be transmitted. Dead wood is to be cut out. The positively perverse is to be omitted. The undesirable features of the present environment are not to be permitted to influence the mental habitudes of our children. Only the best is to be selected and utilized. Thus the power of the best in society is reënforced. As a society becomes more enlightened, it selects, conserves, and transmits from its existing achievements only those that make for a better future society. The school is society's chief agent for accomplishing this end. The school is society's organ for purifying and idealizing itself.

(3) It is also necessary for the school to provide a balanced and representative social environment, because each individual needs to escape from the limitations of the social group in which he was born. We do not have society, but societies; not a community but communities. Among the societies usually recognized are family, town, state. Among those not so frequently recognized are the business groups, clubs, races, religions, economic divisions, cliques, gangs, Fagin's thieves, jails, labor unions, political parties, guilds of artists, the republic of letters, the learned class.

Each of these groups has aims in common, each exercises a formative influence on the active dispositions of its members.

There are more groups in a single modern city than existed in an entire continent long ago. Cities now are heterogeneous; continents then were homogeneous. Commerce, transportatition, communication, and immigration have made the difference. The United States of America is composed of different groups with different traditional customs. Thus centrifugal forces are set up by different juxtaposed groups.

In the midst of such societites, what is the school as a society itself to do? It must provide something like a homogeneous and balanced environment. It must set up centripetal forces. It creates a new and broader environment by the intermingling of youths of different races, religions, and customs; and by a common subject matter gives all a broader horizon than that visible to any isolated group. "The assimilative force of the American public school is eloquent testimony to the efficacy of the common and balanced appeal" (p. 26).

In making a diverse environment more homogeneous, the school must also integrate the disposition of the individual. His many societies with their many codes subject him to antagonistic pulls; they would give him a split-up personality with different standards of judgment and emotion for different occasions. The school has the office of coördinating the diverse influences of the different societies, and so of steadying and integrating the dispositions of the young.

Comment. One thing we miss at this point is some yardstick, or some standard, by which the school environment is to be simplified, purified, and given social balance. Concerning simplification, which are the fundamental features of our complex society to be selected? Concerning purification, which are the best features of the past racial achievements to be exclusively used? Concerning social homogeneity, what are the objectives to be aimed at, and how are they to be attained? Until these questions are answered, we may understand in a general way the school as a special social environment, but we are not in a position to improve the schools we have. The discussions to come will help us some on these points.

CHAPTER III

EDUCATION AS DIRECTION

1. The Environment as Directive

Exposition. Perhaps a more suggestive title, and no less correct, for the chapter, would be Education As Directing. Directing is one of the special forms which educating takes. Synonymous with directing are "controlling," "guiding." However, the three terms do not mean precisely the same thing. Guidance assists the individual through coöperation, control means some resistance is met, while directing means leading one's active tendencies in a continuous course and not permitting them to disperse aimlessly. Directing is basic, at one extreme it may guide, at another it may control or rule.

It is sometimes assumed that an individual's tendencies are naturally egoistic and anti-social. Under such a view 'control' usually implies the compulsion or coercion necessary to bring the individual to subordinate his natural impulses to public ends. This notion has affected systems of government in both state and school. But it is a mistaken view. With all their interest in going their own way, which may be contrary to the ways of others, individuals are chiefly interested in entering into the conjoint and coöperative activities of others. This makes a community possible. No, control is not compulsion, it is only emphatic directing, and may even be practiced by an individual upon himself.

In the relation of stimulus and response, the response is the activity and the stimulus is its guide. The stimulus and response are adapted to each other, as light stimulates the eye which responds by seeing. The stimulus guides the activity to its own proper end.

Effective directing of an activity does two things, it eliminates unnecessary movements, as when a person learning to ride a bicycle learns what not to do; and it gives sequence of action, as when a boxer so dodges a blow as to protect himself also from the succeeding blow. These two aspects of directing we may call focusing and ordering. Focusing eliminates the unnecessary movement and ordering secures the proper succeeding movement. Focusing is simultaneous and spatial, ordering is successive and temporal.

From this analysis of the nature of directing, two conclusions follow. First, directing is not alone external, it is internal. All directing is *re*directing. In the strict sense, nothing can be forced upon the young or into them. If threats work, it is because the person fears. The young participate in the directing of their own acts. So, economic and wise directing takes into account the existing impulses and habits of those directed.

Second, directing that does not take account of the nature of the person directed but imposes contrary customs and regulations may prove to be short-sighted. Thus, while a threat may prevent a person doing a forbidden thing, at the same time it may later lead him to be cunning and sly, evasive and tricky. These two general conclusions correspond to the focussing and ordering aspects of directing.

Comment. Educating may well be regarded as directing, but the concept of directing is vague unless we know the direction in which the educative process should go. "Education as direction,"—toward what? If a man on the street asks some one to direct him, it can be done only if he knows where he wants to go. The teacher needs to know in what direction to direct the pupil. This involves knowing at least the kind of society the pupil should share in and the kind of character he should have in order to share in society most acceptably. That is, the directing must be toward certain social and personal standards and ideals. Democratic relations in society and an unselfish character might represent the needed social and personal goals of education as directing.

2. Modes of Social Direction

Exposition. These are first, direct and personal, and second, indirect and impersonal, involving the social and intelligent use of things. The former is occasional, the latter is continuous, and in effect more permanent and influential.

In direct control the use of physical force may be necessary, as in snatching a young child away from a fire. Or a harsh and commanding tone may be used. Or direct disapproval may be resorted to. Or shaming, ridicule, disfavor, rebuke, punishment, or, appealing to his love of approbation may be used to secure a different type of action.

In all such cases the danger is that we secure only a physical, not an educative, result. The horse may refuse to drink, the imprisoned criminal may be neither penitent nor less inclined to burglary. The reason is that nothing within the person has been redirected.

Direct control, however, is justified when the person controlled is unable to see the outcome of his impulsive acts. Even he, however, may in harmless instances be left to experiment and to learn for himself what intelligent action under similar circumstances is.

The indirect mode of control is more important, because more permanent. It consists in the way the persons with whom the immature associate make use of things in accomplishing their ends. The social medium itself is the effective agency for directing activity.

We separate too sharply from each other the physical and social environments in which we live, as though things were unrelated to persons and persons unrelated to things. Instead, the social environment is really composed of *persons using things.* The separation of persons and things is objectionable for two reasons, viz., it tends to exaggerate the importance of direct social control described above, and it also tends to exaggerate the importance of intellectual contact with physical things.

Let us show the meaning of indirect social control of the young through the use their older associates make of things.

To begin with, even direct social control involves using things, though only as a means of personal contact, not as a means of associated endeavor. One person can not influence another person without using the physical environment as an intermediary. Such modes of personal influence as a smile, frown, rebuke, warning, or encouragement, involve some visible or audible physical change, such as, facial expression, gesture, or language. Thus, the mother may directly control her daughter by telling her to help or by rebuking her for not helping.

Indirect social control is due to personal associations in common pursuits involving the use of things as means to ends. Thus, the daughter is engaged in the household life by imitation, emulation, and common need,—all of which involve indirect social control. The mother is hunting for a lost object and the child joins in the hunt. Thus, direction is given the activities of the young through their association with elders in the use of things. Such participation in a joint activity is the chief way of forming disposition.

The learning process has been unduly dominated by a false psychology. It has been falsely supposed that we learn *from things;* instead, we learn *from the use of things.* We know what objects are when we know what to do with them. We do not learn by being impressed with the qualities of a thing and then combining these qualities into an idea of the thing. Instead, the meaning of a thing comes from its use. You know a thing when you know what to do with it. You know what a chair is when you know what it is *for.* An orange is more than a set of passively received sense-impressions; it is something to be eaten, to be responded to in a specific way.

The use to which a thing is put is a part of its meaning, and the essential part. Our idea of a thing includes more than the sensations we get from it; it includes also the proper response to be made to it. An act responsive to the meaning of a thing is mental; an act responsive to a thing apart from its meaning is purely physical. Such physical acts occur reflexly, as in response, say, to a sudden unexpected loud noise.

When the meaning of the noise is recognized, *e.g.*, thunder, there is a mental act. Physical responses may lead to training; only mental responses can lead to education. A child bowing automatically in company may be trained; one who bows deferentially is educated.

To be a real member of a social group is to have the same ideas about things which others have, to attach the same meanings to acts which others attach, to have a common mind, a common intent in behavior. Many persons may manufacture a single article, say a pin; if each knows nothing of the work of the others, there is no genuine association; if each knows how his work is affected by others and affects others, then there is a common understanding, genuine association, and the action of each is thereby controlled. This is indirect social control.

Take another illustration. A hungry child cries. If he does not understand the acts of preparation of his food to relieve his distress, he cries more as his discomfort grows. This is a purely physical response. But if he understands, his attitude changes, he takes an interest. His response is somewhat intelligent. His response too is socially directed.

Or still again, a man at some distance wildly waves his arms. If his act means nothing to us, we may stare at him stupidly as at the gyrations of the arms of a windmill; this is a physical response. If his act means something to us, we judge the appropriate thing to do; this is a mental response, it is based on a change in the physical environment, and it is socially controlled.

Recurring to the use of language, as an illustration. It is the great means of social direction. It enables us to act jointly in common situations. But, after all, it is one degree removed from the primary social experience of using things as means to reach common results. Language is meaningful when it is a shorthand mode of reference to earlier experiences which are meaningful. Children understand language because they have minds, and they have minds because they have used such things as tables and chairs as other persons are accustomed to use these things.

Concerning the "modes of social direction," then, we conclude that the fundamental mode is not personal, direct, and "moral," but impersonal, indirect, and intellectual. The personal moral appeal is important in crises. The impersonal intellectual appeal is the basic normal way; it consists in using things in social situations to control responses. And to the power to understand things in terms of the use made of them is mind as a concrete thing. A socialized mind understands the uses of things in shared situations. Mind in this sense is the desirable method of social control.

Comment. Three things are to be noted in connection with these views on the two methods of social control. Of course the question is how the behavior of children is to be directed. The first thing is the probable under-estimation of the importance and the efficacy of direct personal appeal; the second is the probable under-estimation of sensation as a source of knowledge; and the third is the probable under-estimation of the ability of the mind to transcend the physical use of things.

Given sympathy and understanding between the mature and the immature, direct personal guidance requiring obedience, quickly and without floundering experimentation, puts the experience of the race at the disposition of its young members. The experience of the young then becomes a deductive proof of the things taught instead of an inductive discovery. In view of the vast amount of knowledge the race already has acquired and the relatively slight amount of it that any individual can re-discover for himself, and the likelihood that he will make no valuable addition to it at all, direct personal control will probably continue to hold the major, but not the exclusive, place in the educative process. As a test let the reader recall the greater influences that have shaped his life; are they not persons rather than things controlled by persons?

The second matter,—the importance of sensation as a source of knowledge, we begin to realize if we take away our senses one by one. Those born blind can know nothing of light and color by acquaintance, though they may learn much *about* them by description. Those born deaf know nothing of tones and noise. Without a sense of touch, adjustment to one's physical environment could not take place at all and there would be no knowledge of distinct things. Admitting that a thing is best known when it can be used, there is a sensation of the motor elements involved in the use. Nobody wants to separate sensation from use, but it is the sensation and not the use that gives the knowledge, and without sensation there could be no intelligent use. Then too, there are so many things of which our sensations give us the materials of knowledge despite the fact that we can not "use" them at all, like the stars. Through sensation we may know what we do not use, as the articles in a store window, or the apparel of the opposite sex. We do not need to be "sensationalists" like Locke in our psychology to recognize the primary rôle of sensation along with action in acquiring knowledge.

Third, the mind can transcend the physical use of things. Mind may arise in the organism as an aid to manipulation, but it does not remain on this practical level of use. This is seen in the æsthetic experience of contemplating a work of beauty. To produce a thing of beauty, the physical use of things is necessary; to enjoy it, not so. Likewise, in the moral experience of admiring and approving a good deed, there is no physical use made of it. In the religious experience of praise and adoration, no use is being made of the Object, as a fetich-worshipper would constrain his fetich. Even in the intellectual types of experience, the physical use of things is not always necessary; we may know stellar distances in terms of light years without using them. We may respond even to general concepts, as truth-speaking, after they have been developed out of percepts. In sum, the doctrine of indirect personal control through reaction to things tends unduly to limit mental action to the use of material things.

And our general conclusion on this point is that though indirect control has its place, as Rousseau indicated, especially in eliminating the sense of arbitrary commands, direct control has the larger place in the wise guidance of the immature.

3. Imitation and Social Psychology

Exposition. Here are four pages giving us a different conception of imitation from the usual one. It fits in with the preceding points of view and extends them. Two of these conclusions so far are (1) it is absurd and impossible to separate persons and things, and (2) the only way to control persons is by using things. We are not directly related either to persons or to things. We are directly related to persons doing things. Now the usual view of imitation is based on the false notion that we are directly related to persons. And imitation in this sense is the basis of a so-called social psychology.

This psychology bases social control on the imitative instinct, that is, the tendency to copy the acts of others, taken as models. There is no intention here of denying the fact of the tendency to imitate but only of relying upon it as the chief agency of social control, and regarding it as a direct relationship between persons. Really, what is commonly traced to imitation of one person by another is due to common participation by two or more persons in the use of things leading to consequences of common interest. Thus, similarity in action is rather a result than a purpose, and what is called imitation is rather an effect than a cause. We must not put the cart before the horse.

Acts are similar in many cases not because one person imitates another but because the persons are similar, and the situations and their stimuli are similar. Naturally the responses are similar. We do not so much imitate persons as act similarly in similar situations. All persons resent an insult; in this they are alike; there is no imitation about it. Customs are alike in one place because of similar stimuli, including conscious instruction, social approvals, and disapprovals, premiums put upon like-mindedness, and the ostracism of the unlike. Customs in different places are dissimilar because of dissimilar stimuli.

In playing a game, like ball, the players play alike, not to imitate each other but because the game requires it. If one player imitates another, it is done intelligently, observantly, judiciously, as a means of improving his game, not unconsciously to be like somebody else as an end in itself. The imitation of means to chosen ends is a factor in the development of effective action. The imitation of ends is superficial, transitory, stupid; it is being an ape, monkey, parrot, or "copy cat."

Connecting this discussion of imitation with the preceding one of social control we reach the conclusion that behavior is controlled by forming a certain mental disposition, viz., the disposition to understand situations as a means of effective participation in associated activities. It does not take place by forcing a line of action contrary to natural inclinations, or by a process of direct imitation.

Comment. No doubt among strong-minded, intelligent people there is much similarity of action that is not due to imitation. They see the reason for doing as others do. So they bob their hair or shorten their skirts for reasons of convenience or comfort. A wave of student suicides too may be due not to imitation but to similar responses to the sense of disillusionment and futility in living due to increase of knowledge and experience unattached to purpose.

But the text probably understates the case in two respects Children are naturally imitative of elders they know and like and many adults, after all, do engage in unintelligent imitation of ends. Smile at the baby and you get a flickering smile in return; frown and you get a puckered countenance. Put on your hat, take it off, and hand it to a two-year old; he will put on your hat. This is the imitative tendency at work. It is not stupid; it is one of nature's methods of teaching. There appears to be a general native tendency among children to do as their elders do.

Among elders too there is in quantity a great deal of direct imitation. Why such high heels? Why the return to long hair and skirts? And consider the following news item:

LONDON COPIES STYLES SET BY KING AND QUEEN

Copyright, 1925, The New York Times Co.
By wireless to the New York Times.

London, July 24.—Last Tuesday afternoon at the first royal garden party of the season at Buckingham Palace, the King wore a gray top hat and a gray morning suit, while the Queen wore a mauve dress and hat.

Neither the King nor Queen probably realized that they were setting a fashion which would keep the tailors and hatters working overtime, but within the remarkably short space of three days every man and woman who could do so had copied the style of the King and Queen.

This afternoon, when their Majesties entered the gardens to greet 5,000 guests at their second party they saw a veritable sea of gray and mauve. There were hundreds of gray toppers and gray morning coats, while scores of women had copied the Queen's style and wore mauve gowns and hats.

Today's party was one of the most colorful ever seen at Buckingham Palace. A number of Americans were present. As on Tuesday the crowd was representative of diplomacy, the church, art, stage, letters and exclusive society.

The views presented on imitation, like those on direct personal control, are a way of de-personalizing the educative process. But it still remains true that direct personal control of the right sort and the imitation of worthy models taken as examples are among the best, most common, and most influential ways of forming mental and moral dispositions. We can control children directly without being arbitrary and we can imitate our superiors without being slavish. We must continue to be what we want our children to become.

4. Some Applications to Education

Exposition. Of these applications to education of the preceding discussion in this chapter, there are four.

(1) Let us understand that the difference between savagery and civilization is not a matter of native intelligence or of moral sense, it is a difference in the stimuli to which the savage and civilized groups are subjected. A savage reared in the midst of civilization would be civilized, and the child of civilization reared among savages would be a savage. It is the stimuli from their respective social environments that make the difference; the stimuli of a savage group are crude, restricted, limited, inferior; the stimuli of a civilized group are weighted, selected, charged, superior. The savage mind is an effect of backward institutions; the civilized mind is an effect of progressive institutions, of the transformation of natural conditions by prior human efforts.

But let us beware of supposing that civilization consists in things, such as good roads, autos, telegraph, telephone, cable, light, heat, power, and machinery. Not these things, but their uses, are civilization. These things free our time, thus enabling us to acquire and transmit a body of knowledge. Our inventions and our discoveries embodied in our appliances of art prevent the return of the ages of superstition, myths, and infertile imaginings about nature. When our machines are used in the interest of a truly shared or associated life, they become a positive resource of civilization. The highest civilization will utilize for social ends such material resources as it can command. In so far as education may be regarded as the preservation and transmission of the successes of the race in mastering its material environment, it is education that makes the difference between savagery and civilization.

(2) It is not persons, it is things as they enter into the actions of persons in daily life, that educate us, that form us mentally and morally. We are made by the things that we use. The school environment, then, must be equipped with agencies for doing,—with tools and physical materials. Adequate equipment of this kind at present is rare. Pupils should have direct and continuous occupation with things. If at present methods of instruction and of administration do not allow such use of things, let them be modified.

(3) The use of language made by teachers should be more vital and fruitful. This it can be by recovering its normal connection with shared activities in the use of things. So used, language enriches the experience of the present. It leads us to share vicariously in the experience of the past. It enables us, symbolically and imaginatively, to anticipate the future. Language is so significant in life that to be unlettered and uneducated are almost synonymous. No one will doubt our appreciation of the liberal share of language in what is worth while in life, and yet the emphasis upon language as a tool in school has its dangers. In this point our theory and our practice are at odds. We theoretically condemn teaching by pouring in, and yet almost every schoolroom is like a fountain surrounded by little pitchers. We universally condemn learning by passive absorption and then treat our pupils as sponges. We theoretically concede that education is an active and constructive process, and then violate our principle by making it an affair of 'telling' and being told. This is a deplorable situation. And why does it exist? Because of the very thing of which we speak. The doctrine itself that teaching is not telling is merely told, preached, lectured, and written about. To begin to practice the doctrine requires the new school equipment of which we have spoken. "These things ought ye to have done, and not to have left the others undone."

(4) We want in our schools a social and not a bookish spirit. We want our pupils to come to understand the meaning which things have in the life of which they are a part, and not merely be engaged in motor activities and sensory recitations. We want them to acquire a socialized disposition, and not merely a technical ability in algebra, Latin, or botany. And how are these worthy desires to be realized? Once again, by having pupils learn in school as they learn out of school, that is, by sharing in an activity of common concern and value, by the social use of materials and tools. The isolation of learning from the social use of materials is pseudo-intellectual and self-contradictory.

Comment. An educational reformer may have to overstate his case to be heard. In these applications we note the tendency to stress things rather than persons, and to rely on the use of things rather than personal relationships, and to hold thinking down to the manipulation of material. Whereas, really, pupils are persons, teachers are persons, the social use of things depends on the purposes of the persons, and things themselves are known only as the common property of different minds. Incidentally note that the writer condemns writing about the doctrine he is writing about. And teachers of English would be glad to know how the recommendation to use language only in connection with the social use of things would affect their practice.

CHAPTER IV

EDUCATION AS GROWTH

1. The Conditions of Growth

Exposition. Education is growth. The young of today will be the society of tomorrow. As it fashions the young today, so society is fashioning itself tomorrow. Society fashions the young by determining, directing, their activities. This is their growth, and this is their education. Growth, then, is this cumulative movement of directed activities toward a later result.

There is really but one primary condition of growth; it is immaturity. But immaturity has two chief traits, viz., dependence and plasticity. Immaturity, dependence, and plasticity all need to be carefully understood, if we are to understand growth.

By immaturity we mean the power of the organism to grow. It is a force, an ability, something positive, something present. Wherever there is immaturity of life, there are already eager and impassioned activities. Despite the negative prefix, immaturity is not negative, not a mere lack. It is a capacity that acts, a potentiality that is powerful.

It is a common tendency to regard immaturity as negative, as the lack of something. But this is objectionable from two standpoints. It means that children are regarded comparatively instead of intrinsically, and it means that the ideal of education is a state instead of a process. Take the adult as standard, and the child by comparison lacks something. But the child, if he could reply, might well say, take the child as a standard, as an excellent adult authority says, and it is the adult that lacks something. Children are to be regarded intrinsically as well as comparatively; if so, immaturity will appear as somethnig positive.

Again, to regard immaturity as negative is to regard maturity as positive, growing fulfilled, growth accomplished, the standard attained. Thus a static end becomes the educational ideal. But this is futile. Growth goes on; "ungrowth" does not exist. How quickly the adult resents the imputation of having no further possibilities of growth! If he has lost some, the fact is mourned. Past finished achievement is regarded neither as a satisfactory compensation for lost power nor as an adequate manifestation of power. If growing is good for the adult, why regard the child as lacking something because he is not grown? So, immaturity as the condition of growth is positive, constructive.

Dependence, as a trait of immaturity, is likewise a positive power, however absurd it sounds so to speak of it. This, of course, is not meant to deny the helplessness of dependence. But this helplessness is physical, not social. His physical helplessness is thoroughgoing. He is weak, and the strength he has he can not use to advantage. At birth and for a long time thereafter he can not take care of himself, can not keep himself alive. Left alone, he would hardly survive an hour. The young of the brutes are immeasurably his superiors.

But what the human infant lacks physically is compensated for socially. The social powers of the dependent child are positive. The young of the lower animals lack socially what they possess physically; being able to take better care of themselves from birth, their lives are not intimately bound up with the lives of the creatures about them. The young of animals lack the social gifts which human infants possess; human infants lack the physical gifts which the young of animals possess.

But after all, do human infants possess social gifts? Yes. Their helplessness contains a positive element, else no development could ever take place. Their dependence is not impotence but a constructive power to grow. Children are not merely physically present in a social, adult environment, but socially present; they are not merely passive recipients of the influences of social forces, but active social agents. Others are attentive to children, true; but children have the power marvelously to enlist attention. In fact, they are gifted with an equipment of the first order for social intercourse. They vibrate sympathetically. They are sensitive and responsive to the attitudes and acts of those about them. Few grown-ups are equally so. They can not control physical things, they do not so much attend to physical things, so they all the more are interested in and attentive to the doings of people. Their native mechanisms, their impulses, all tend to a flexible and facile social responsiveness.

But are not children egotistic, selfish, and self-centered? How then are they so socially sensitive and responsive? Even if it were true that pre-adolescents are self-centered, it would not disprove the view that they are socially effective; it would only prove that they use their social efficiency in their own behalf. But it is not true that pre-adolescents are self-centered. What is true is that children are engrossed in their own interests, pursuing them directly, not that they are putting these interests above those of others. Adults were once similarly engrossed in ends all their own; having outgrown their childhood interests, adults look back upon them mistakenly as narrow and selfish. Besides, adults have their own engrossing interests which are not those of children. The adult's egoism condemns the child's egoism. Children are socially effective and they are not self-centered.

Thus dependence, being a positive power for engaging in social life, turns out to be a form of interdependence. The danger is that dependent children in becoming independent adults may lose something of interdependence, of social capacity. Independence is self-reliant; it should not become self-sufficient, aloof, indifferent, and insensitive of relations to others. The idea that one can really stand and act alone is an illusion, a form of insanity not yet named, and a fertile cause of much remediable suffering in the world. The independence of adults, like the dependence of children, should be a phase of interdependence.

Following dependence is plasticity, the second of the two traits of immaturity. Plasticity is the specific adaptability of an immature creature for growth; it is the ability to learn from experience, that is, the ability to carry over from an earlier experience something of value in controlling a later experience; thus, it is the power to develop dispositions. The plasticity of an organism is different from that of putty or wax; the latter can take on a change of form in accord with external pressure; the former, while influenced from without, continues to have a bent from within, like persons whose pliability permits them to merge with the group of which they are a part and yet retain their own individuality.

The higher the organism the greater the plasticity of its young. The greater the plasticity of the young, the more things to be learned from experience after birth, the greater the possibility of progress. Consider the chick and the child. What the chick learns in a few hours after hatching the child learns in six months after birth, that is, coördination of motor and visual activities. Paradoxically, this is to the advantage of the child. The chick is limited by the relative perfection of its original endowment; it continues to peck successfully for food. The child is unlimited in progress by reason of the imperfection of its native mechanisms; he must learn to utilize his instinctive reactions, of which he has a greater number than the lower animals; he experiences a multitude of instinctive tentative reactions; his control becomes flexible and varied; in learning one act he learns methods good to use in other situations; he acquires the habit of learning; he learns to learn. Thus he opens up the possibility of continuing progress. The higher the organism the more plastic it is; the more plastic an organism, the greater the possibility of progress.

Looking back then upon immaturity with its two traits of dependence and plasticity, or variable control, we see the importance for human life of human infancy. John Fiske in his *Excursions of an Evolutionist* gave the first systematic exposition of what has come to be called "the significance of prolonged infancy." The human infant remains an infant a longer time than the young of any other creature. This helps both the adults and the young. To the young it means longer dependence, more plasticity, an adequate period of time in which to develop the powers needed in an increasingly complex social life, the acquisition of variable and novel modes of control, and so a further push to social progress. To the adults the presence of dependent and learning infants for years meant a stimulus to nurture and affection; a chief reason for transforming temporary co-habitations into permanent unions; a chief influence in forming habits of watchfulness,—that constructive interest in the well-being of others which is essential to associated life; the introduction, intellectually, of many new objects of attention, stimulating foresight and planning for the future. Thus there was a reciprocal influence between society and infancy, society preserving infancy and infancy transforming society from animality into humanity.

Comment. Rousseau's paradoxical expression, "a grown child," very well suggests the appreciation of childhood found in this section.

In discussing the unending character of growth, rejecting the static ideal of "ungrowth," it would be a reasonable inquiry at this point to ask whether the death of the human individual means the cessation of his growth. A cemetery at the end of life, if that is all, seems static "ungrowth" indeed. It is not enough to reply that society goes on, though the individual ceases to be, for some astronomers tell us death awaits human society too. What then happens to the organic ideal of growth, unless there be immortal progress?

The rejection in the text of the view that children are self-centered must not lead us to the view that all children are unselfish. Some are not. The selfishness of some children, however, may be traced not to themselves but to the poor direction their growth has had. A proper social guidance of their "eager and impassioned activities" might well have led to that social sharing which is the antithesis of selfishness. Whether the admitted natural egoism of the normal child becomes selfish egotism or unselfish interdependent altruism depends on the child's social environment. Our children are what they are made to be until they get old enough to help make themselves. Natively they are neither selfish nor unselfish but socially responsive.

Concerning plasticity, the discussion in the text might well be somewhat more physiological in character. Plasticity is a quality of the nervous system. That is where the habits are located. The plasticity of the nervous system means the possibility through stimulation of forming new neuronic connections which affect later responses. The origin of the nervous system and of its plasticity is one of the fascinating biological problems.

2. Habits as Expressions of Growth

Exposition. It is plasticity that makes possible the acquisition of all habits, including the habit of learning. As growth takes place, habits are formed. As habits are formed, definite dispositions are developed. We have now to consider the salient features of habits. The following diagram will assist us in following the main points.

Growth: Habits
- 1. Motor adaptations
  - 1. Passive accommodation
  - 2. Active
- 2. Intellectual and emotional disposition.
  - 1. Ruts
  - 2. Resources

Habit touches all phases of our life. It means both the acquirement of ease, economy, and efficiency in action and the formation of intellectual and emotional dispositions. The two groups of habits will receive our successive attention.

In the first place, a habit is a form of executive skill, of efficiency in doing, like walking, talking, playing the piano, and such specialized skills as those characteristic of the etcher, the surgeon, and the bridge-builder. The control of the body is of course involved. But the point to note here is that the motor habit involves the control of the environment as well as the control of the body. Natural conditions are used as means to ends. Through controlling the motor organs of the body there is an active control of the environment. The motor habits are not simply ease, deftness, accuracy on the part of the organism. They are that, and more. The value of these qualities lies in the effective control of environment with a minimum expenditure of energy. Walking as a motor habit not only controls the body in a certain way but puts certain properties of nature at our disposal, *e.g.*, the distant becomes present. The thirsty tree must wait for the shower to come to it; the thirsty man can walk to the spring. Consider for yourself how each of the other motor habits mentioned above bring the environment of the body under control.

And this brings us to speak of passive and active motor habits. If we stress motor habits as control of the body, our habits are passive; if we stress motor habits as control of the environment, our habits are active. Of course, passive and active motor habits are only relatively distinguishable, passive habits being somewhat active, and active habits being somewhat passive. Passive motor habits may be illustrated by the way we get used to our surroundings,—to our clothing, our shoes, our gloves; to the atmosphere so long as it is fairly constant; to our daily associates. Such passive habits are cases of *habituation* or *accommodation*.

Now there are three marked traits of such habituations, viz., (1), as stated, they represent changes in the organism rather than in the environment. The organism conforms to the environment, the environment is not made to conform to the organism. As said, this is only relatively true, for our clothing, shoes, gloves, even our atmosphere in buildings, are measurably adjusted to the organism.

(2) We get habituated, accommodated, used to things by first using them. Thus we get used to a strange city. Lacking habituation at first, we experience excessive stimulation (do you remember your first night in a city hotel?) and in consequence ill-adapted response. We get used to the city not by changing the city but by selecting certain relevant stimuli to which to respond, and degrading the irrelevant stimuli, not responding to them any longer, or better, responding to them in a persistent, equilibrated way.

And (3), these passive habits as an enduring adjustment form the background for active habits, for those specific adjustments needed upon occasion. The whole environment is not changed at once; the most of it is accepted, taken for granted, just as it is. Being passively adjusted to the most of the whole makes it possible to become actively adjusted to a part of the whole, that is, make needed changes. Active habits may be the lever but habituation is the leverage.

Now active motor habits, as indicated, involve adapting the environment to the organism. Active habits use the means of the environment to achieve the ends of the organism. The wax conforms to the seal in passive adjustment, the seal is made to stamp the wax by active adjustment. A savage tribe manages to live on a desert plain mainly by passive accommodation, acceptance, acquiescence, putting up with things as they are. A civilized people enters upon the scene, introduces irrigation, brings in other plants and animals that can flourish there, improves the native stocks, and lo! "the wilderness blossoms as the rose." The savage is conformed to his environment; the civilized man transforms his environment to suit himself.

Now education is not infrequently defined as the adjustment of the individual to his environment. And one essential phase of growth is adjustment. But in the light of the preceding discussion it is essential that adjustment be understood as active as well as passive. Education leads to control of means for achieving ends of the organism as well as changes wrought in the organism to enable it to fit into the environment. Education as adjustment not only conforms the individual to the environment but transforms the environment to fit the individual. The transforming power of education is underemphasized; the conforming power of education is overemphasized, this over-emphasis being of a logical piece with the views previously considered that stimulus and response are only externally related and that immaturity and plasticity are negative in character. The environment is no fixity, providing the standard for changes in the organism; adjustment is not just fitting ourselves into fixed external conditions.

So far we have been discussing the executive and motor phase of habit. Now we turn to the view of habit as the formation of emotional and intellectual disposition. Any habit has an emotional phase, it marks an inclination, an active preference, a choice. Habits may bind us but we love our chains. Habits may free us, and then we love our liberty. The point is that the habit does not wait, Micawber-like, for some stimulus to set it off; it reaches for the match. If the expression of the habit is blocked, the inclination behind it passes into uneasiness and craving. Thus our emotional dispositions, our likes, dislikes, and choices are matters of habit.

Our intellectual disposition is likewise a matter of habit. By his habits a man is made an engineer, an architect, a physician, or a merchant. Such sets of habits as these involve not merely skill and desire or inclination but also intellectual acquaintance in each case with certain materials and equipment; an understanding of the situation in which the habit operates; they are based on observation and reflection. Even in unskilled labor some intellectual factors are present, but they are at a minimum precisely because the habits involved are not of high grade. We readily recognize the presence of motor habits in handling a tool, painting a picture, or conducting an experiment, but it is important to note that these same physical processes involve habits of judging and reasoning. Thus intellectual habits penetrate motor habits as forms of skill.

But even more. It is the habits of mind that give significance to the habits of eye and hand; the intellectual habits supply meaning to the motor habits. The more intellect in a habit, the more varied and elastic the use of the habit, and so the more growth. Similarly, the less intellect in a habit, the more monotonous and rigid the habit, and so the less growth. In this connection we meet the phrase "fixed habits." It has two meanings. The one refers to habits with much intellectuality in them; established powers acting as resources; our having a free hold on things. The other refers to habits with little intellectuality in them; ruts, routine ways, with less of freshness, open-mindedness, and originality; things have a fixed hold on us. It is the second of these two views of "fixity of habits" that leads people to identify habits on the one hand with mechanical and external modes of action, neglecting the mental and moral attitudes, and on the other with "bad habits." But, as we have seen, intellectual and moral habits constitute one's aptitude in his profession, and so his habits include more than his use of tobacco, liquor, or profane language.

Now childhood is the friend of fixed habits in the first sense of the term and age is their foe. Our problem is to make habits into resources instead of mechanisms. The difference depends on the amount of intellectuality involved. Cease to think and routine holds sway. Continue a habit condemned by judgment, and it becomes "bad." Routine habits possess us, we do not possess them. They put an end to plasticity, the power to vary. The passage of time marks the lessening of basic organic plasticity, a settling down, an aversion to change, a resting on past achievements, increased difficulty even in thinking. How then shall we stay young, though becoming old? How shall we continue to grow? Only by an environment which invokes the function of intelligence to the maximum.

Thus our habits are expressions of our growth, forming both our motor adaptations and our intellectual and emotional dispositions, both our adaptations and our dispositions having their less valuable, passive, and routine phases and their more valuable, active and resourceful phases.

Comment. Note that the whole process of growth is subsumed under the conception of habit-formation. Even the moral, emotional, and intellectual phases of life are treated as effects of the environment on the responsive organism, as cases of habit. This is accomplished by introducing the conception of "active habits,"—a conception not consistently held to in other portions of the discussion (see p. 395 of the original text). Nevertheless there is an implication that observation, deliberation, judgment, and decision mark the distinction between good and bad habits. Why then the subordination of these acts of intelligence to the concept of "active habits?" It is a naturalistic emphasis which hardly does justice to the value of man's higher powers of mind.

Particularly is this evident if we raise the question whether judgment and decision can change a bad habit into a good one. Apparently not, since the choices and decisions are presented as themselves a part of the emotional disposition which is itself in turn made by habit. This is, of course, the question of man's freedom. Dr. Dewey believes, as we shall see later (see p. 352 of original text), that man should be socially free to express himself in an unrestrained way but he does not maintain that man has freedom of choice.

This appears also in the view just presented that the environment is to secure that full use of intelligence which prevents men from becoming machines, it is the environment that invokes the function of intelligence to its maximum. But can not man invoke his own intelligence? And how is this intelligence-invoking environment to be secured? In short, this whole treatment of habit makes the response and not the respondent responsible.

A protest against the treatment of man's inner life solely from the viewpoint of habit is voiced by Count Herman Keyserling in his article, "The Animal Ideal in America" (*Harper's Magazine*, August, 1929). This ideal is said to be "a high standard of living." The Americans are said to act on the belief "that man is an animal like any other.

> That spiritual initiative and free will play practically no part of his make-up and conduct. The concrete 'habit' stands for the whole of man's vital activity—there is no beyond in the sense of a possible metaphysical or otherwise spiritual reality. And that habit can be explained, determined, and ruled and changed entirely from without by external influences."

3. The Educational Bearings of the Conception of Development

Exposition. "Education is development," it is said; but everything depends on how development is conceived. Our own conception is, and this is our net conclusion, that life itself is development, and that developing, that is, growing, is life. Educationally speaking, this means two profound things, viz., (1) that the educational process has no end beyond itself; it is its own end; and (2) that the educational process is one of continuous reorganizing, reconstructing, transforming. To each of these views special attention will be given.

(1) The educational process its own end. If so, then children are no more to grow like adults than adults are to grow like children. Both children and adults are to grow. Children are to grow in the adult's way, and also in the child's way; adults are to grow in the child's way, and also in the adult's way. Children are not to cease to be children in becoming like adults; adults are not to cease to be adults in becoming like children. What children require that adults commonly have includes executive skill, definiteness of interest, specific objects of observation and thought, the use of their

powers to transform their environment, thereby occasioning new stimuli to redirect and develop their powers in coping with scientific and economic problems. What adults require that children commonly have includes sympathetic curiosity, unbiased responsiveness, and openness of mind. A child is to be regarded intrinsically, and not merely comparatively; and an adult is to be regarded comparatively and not merely intrinsically. A child is not to be condemned because he is not an adult; and an adult is not to be praised because he is not a child. The adult environment is not to be accepted as a standard for the child. Education as growth is no respecter of age. It is a false idea of growth that it is a movement toward a fixed goal. Growth is an end in itself; it does not have an end.

Three fallacious ideas we rejected; their three educational counterparts we now reject. They are all connected with a false idea of growth. They are as follows:

(*a*) We rejected the idea that immaturity was privative; we reject the failure to take account of the instinctive or native powers of the young. Natural instincts should not be disregarded; neither should they be treated as nuisances, as obnoxious traits either to be suppressed or brought into conformity with external standards. Conformity is no aim; it leads to uniformity. What is distinctively individual in a young person should not be brushed aside, or regarded as a source of mischief or anarchy.

(*b*) We rejected the notion of a static adjustment to a fixed environment. We reject the failure to develop initiative in coping with novel situations. We are to induce interest in the novel, without aversion to progress, without dread of the uncertain and the unknown.

(*c*) We rejected the rigidity of habit. We reject an undue emphasis upon drill and other devices which secure automatic skill at the expense of personal perception. It is wrong to regard the end of growth as outside of and beyond the process of growing, and so to resort to external agencies to induce movements toward it. Any educational method deservedly called "mechanical" is objectionable, for it brings external pressure to bear to reach an internal end.

In all these respects education has no end beyond itself; it is all one with growing, even as growing is all one with living.

(2) Education as continuous reorganizing. As growth is relative to nothing except more growth, so education is subordinate to nothing except more education. We say tritely: "education should continue and not cease when one leaves school," but miss the point that the purpose of the school is so to organize the powers of growth that continuance of education is insured. Thus the finest product of schooling is, on the one hand, the development of the inclination to learn from life itself and, on the other hand, the re-making of the conditions of life to enable us all to learn as we live. Education means the enterprise of supplying the conditions which insure growth, or adequacy of life. Living has its own intrinsic quality, irrespective of age, and the business of education is with that quality.

Cease then to regard immaturity comparatively and as lacking something desirable. Abandon the practice of supplying the lack by pouring knowledge into a mental and moral hole. Recognize that a living creature lives as truly and positively at one stage as at another, with the same intrinsic fullness, the same absolute claims. Then the youth will not impatiently long to be grown, and the grown will not impatiently regret the lost opportunities and wasted powers of youth. That irony will cease.

A warning here is necessary. In the words of Emerson, "Respect the child. Be not too much his parent. Trespass not on his solitude . . . respect him to the end, but also respect yourself . . . keep his *naturel* but stop off his uproar, fooling, and horseplay." Realize the meaning of life as growth; then a lazy, indulgent, "idealizing" attitude will not be taken toward childhood. Some acts and interests are superficial and are not to be identified with life. Manifestations of interests, surface fooling and phenomena, are to be accepted not as ends in themselves but as signs of possible growth, to be turned into means of development, of carrying power forward. Either to rebuke or to encourage overmuch these superficial interests may lead not to development but to arrested development through fixation. The important thing for parent and teacher is not what the impulses of children have been but what they are going to become.

And do not suppose for a moment that the principle of reverence for childhood and youth makes the path easy for teachers. As Emerson goes on to show, "it requires time, use, insight, event, all the great lessons and assistances of God."

Comment. The doctrine of "education as growth" is one of the most popular and influential advocated by our author. It is well to note particularly the original warning given by him against its misinterpretation. We are not to pay too much attention to superficial interests and we are to see that they lead on. This warning, however, has not been taken by all his followers, and Dr. Dewey has had to repeat it in addresses to the Progressive Education Association and elsewhere. (See Home Edition, *N. Y. Sun,* March 9, 1928.)

And naturally so, for the phrase education as growth is too vague to be a practical guide, even when the statement is added that growth leads to more growth. The trio of famous statements, "Education is life," "life is growth," "education is growth," all sound well and awaken pleasurable emotional states but they do not tell us what to do next. The trouble is we have growths as well as growth; there is a wrong way to grow as well as a right way; there is abnormal growth as well as normal growth; there are schools of crime in which there is much growth of the wrong kind; much life is perverted growth; some education called "new" is arrested growth (against this Dr. Dewey warned in advance). It is not enough to say "education is growth"; we must add, education is growth in the right way. And criteria of right growth must be set up. Teachers must be able to tell when they are directing growth in the right way. Often they can not tell; they only know that their pupils are growing. The very definition of growth proposed is not clear: "This cumulative movement of action toward a later result is what is meant by growth." Is there any action without a later result? What is the "movement of an action"? Could not any Fagin's or Gradgrind's school claim to have "a cumulative movement of action toward a later result"? The definition is not only vague; it is defective in giving us no clear distinction between good education and bad education. All directed action leads on to later results. But which later results are worth while? A head-line in the morning paper says, "Pick-pocket arrested, giving boy 16, lesson." Here is growth, to be sure.

But the difficulty lies deeper. Growth aims at more growth, and education is subordinate only to education. This is the theory. Its weakness is, growth needs a goal. There is no need to mince words at all. Children must be directed in their growth toward something worthwhile in personal and social relations. They must grow up to be something admirable by constantly having admirable models and patterns and associations. Growth must be toward an ideal of human character. This ideal is not the objectionable "idealizing of childhood," it is the unobjectionable idealizing of life itself as the embodiment of worthwhile purposes and patterns. We do not have to be afraid of the word goal. We need a goal to work toward. If it is really valuable, we rarely fully attain it. If we should attain it, another and higher goal should and would straightway take its place. There is no danger of the pursuit of a goal leading to a static life. Let's have a goal for growth, including the admirable features of social and individual living, and omitting the base. This involves having a standard by which to judge growth. We do not lack such a standard.

Really, there is an implicit contradiction in the conception of growth presented in the text. Growth is said to be relative only to growth, and yet the "cumulative movement of action" must be "toward a later result." Now this later result is preconceived, intended, aimed at, anticipated. Otherwise, how could growth be directed toward it at all? And if so, "the later result" is the goal. Then education does have a goal. Why not admit it, declare it, and formulate the goal.

As we shall see later, though it is here claimed that "there is nothing to which education is subordinate save more education," it would appear that education is subordinate to democracy.

The best phrase in the discussion is "adequacy of life" (p. 61). It is proposed as an equivalent of growth. But it is more than an equivalent. It is an equivalent of right growth. "Adequacy of life" involves setting up standards and ends of living. Really, *to live* is *to live for something.*

Another thing. In the discussion "growth" and "development" are used as synonymous terms. "Growth" is defined and then "development" is introduced as a synonym (pp. 59–60). But the two terms are not synonymous, and the discussion unwarrantably profits by using the associations of the term development along with those of growth. At the same time violence is done the equally valuable conception of development. There is a sense in which education is growth directed toward a right end, and there is a sense in which education is properly stimulated development. What is this difference between growth and development?

Growth, strictly regarded, is enlargement of physical organ or mental function; development is marked by the appearance of new functions or powers. By growth the tissue cells multiply; by development they become differentiated and mature. A little oak becomes a large oak by growth; an acorn becomes a little oak by development. A little chick becomes a chicken mainly by growth; an egg becomes a chick by development; it is also true that the appearance of new mental and physical powers as the chick becomes a chicken is by development. A little muscle becomes a large muscle by growth; a muscle appears at all and the possibility of new muscular coördinations, especially of the smaller muscles, comes by development. A little child becomes a big child by growth; a fertilized ovum becomes a child, and a child becomes a physical and mental grown-up by development. To repeat, growth is expansion of living tissue or mental function already present; development is the appearance of new tissue or function. A tennis player grows a larger muscle in one of his arms but develops a new stroke. Adolescence is marked by both growth and development. Wherever mind is present at all, it is likely that the processess of growth and development are never completely sundered from each other. Normally the two processes of growth and development go together, so that full size (growth) and complete differentiation and maturation (development) are both attained at the end of a suitable amount of time. In early life, growth is rapid and development slow; in later stages, development is rapid and growth slow. Prolonged growth and delayed development mean a massive but sluggish individual, soft, and with low powers of resistance. Arrested growth and precocious development mean a small body with small organs though finely organized. In a sense mass is the enemy of organization, and organization is the enemy of mass. Growth without development is burdensome; development without growth is weakness. Nature must be helped to secure the proportionate amount of both growth and development.

But what difference does it make whether a child only grows up or both grows and develops? A great deal. A relatively underdeveloped mind may very well inhabit a grown body, and a relatively developed mind may very well inhabit a poorly grown body. Education is to secure both right growth and right development of both the physical and the mental constituents of experience.

A very significant point is this, that growth is less dependent on internal factors than is development. By and large, growth is from without, development is from within; growth is dependent on external stimulation, development upon internal changes. Thus, by no manner of means can an acorn become a chick, or a chick become a child. Development is in a measure prefigured in the egg as growth is not. Thus development is rather a matter of nature and growth a matter of nurture. And in this sense nature is probably more than nurture.

The question is also important in connection with the coming discussion of "education as unfolding."

CHAPTER V

PREPARATION, UNFOLDING, AND FORMAL DISCIPLINE

1. Education as Preparation

Exposition. Before expanding further our theory of education as growth, we pause in this chapter and the next to contrast it with certain other theories which are as inadequate in nature as they have been influential in practice. And first "preparation."

Education as we hold does prepare for the future but it is not preparation for the future. Here is a close but real distinction. Being a child does prepare for being a man, but the purpose of childhood is a rich childhood and not a preparation for manhood. There is a difference between preparation as a result, which we accept, and preparation as the main purpose, which we reject. Take care of the present, making it as rich and significant as possible, and the future will take care of itself. The future is just the later present. Growing of the right sort is a continuous leading into the future. It is important to prepare for future need, and growing prepares for future need, but the mistake is to make preparation for future need the mainspring of present effort.

We make this mistake when we regard education as a process of getting ready for the responsibilities and privileges of adult life, when children are not regarded as having full and regular standing as members of society; when they are looked upon as candidates, and placed on the waiting list. It is the same conception, only carried a little further, which considers the life of adults as not having meaning on its own account but as being a period of probation preparatory to "another life." We have already criticised the false notion of growth as negative and privative. Evidently this conception of growth as preparation is another form of that same false notion. Instead of repeating our previous criticism, we shall pass on to consider four evil consequences that follow from putting education on this false basis of "preparation."

(1) There is loss of motive power. Children live in the present, not in the future. This is not a defect but an excellence. It is a fact to be utilized, not evaded. To children the appeal of the future lacks all that urgency and body which the appeal of the present has. In dealing with children on the basis of the present, teachers have a real existent leverage; in dealing with children on the basis of the future, involving an unknown what and why, teachers throw away the leverage they have and trust vague chance instead. A loss of impetus is involved.

(2) A premium is put on procrastination. The future is a long way off, lots of time yet, why worry? The present invites to real adventure; its opportunities are at hand; why not postpone preparation and seize fulfilment? Shillyshallying results, with a moral loss, and children get educated by what we reject for them, and schooled by what we accept. Thus their schooling interrupts their education.

(3) An average standard is substituted for an individual standard. Promotions, college entrance requirements, and the like, take the place of a definite, even severe, judgment on the strong and weak points of the individual under instruction. Conventions rule, not individual needs; conventions too about future attainments based on vague and wavering opinion. Attention is deflected from the strategic present to the unproductive future. Inestimable loss results. And the future is not prepared for!

(4) Artificial motives are substituted for real motives. This is done on a large scale. These artificial motives are those of getting pleasure or avoiding pain. These must be hitched on to the appeal of the future to make it work. Rewards are promised, if the prescribed work is done; pains are threatened.

if it is not done. The work thus is done consciously, it is not done as a factor in present living, it is not healthy. Systems of punishment may end by being harsh, impotent, and disgusting. Then the pendulum swings to the opposite extreme of sugar-coating, and pupils are fooled into taking doses of information they do not like.

These then are the four evils that result from neglecting present possibilities in behalf of preparation for a future. In best growth the stimulation resides in the situation with which one is actually confronted.

Comment. We may accept the principle that education is rightly directed growth and reject the principle that education is getting ready to live completely, and yet find a larger place for education as preparation than our author does. The issue squarely joined is whether preparation for the future should be wholly unconscious as an unanticipated outcome of following present interests, or whether preparation for the future may come in properly as a part of conscious motivation. To us it may.

(1) Is not planning for the future a part of complete living in the present? "Children proverbially live in the present." Proverbs are not exact. Children also for brief periods live in the future. They day-dream. They count on what they can do "sometime." They will be engineers or aviators. They can do then as adults do now. Such thoughts of the future are effective motivation too in the present. "There may be a fire sometime; let's have a fire drill and get ready." "You may have a chance to save a person from drowning sometime; let's learn how." "You may want to stop the blood flowing from a wound sometime; let's learn about the tourniquet." "You may want to go to college or secure a position sometime, you'll need your English then." "You will probably have a 'rainy day' sometime; others do; then you'll need your savings bank account." "You want to be an engineer sometime; you must know your mathematics first." And so on. The motto, "Be prepared," stressing the future, seems an excellent one for

Boy Scouts, and works hand in hand with the other one, "Do a good turn daily," stressing the present. It would seem to be a highly abstract and impractical point of view to separate the present entirely from conscious thought of the future.

(2) The view of the text would hardly apply to any type of professional education. Here, "getting ready" is the essence of it, and the only safe thing for society. The license to practice precedes the practice and the license is based on preparation, and conscious preparation. The courses of study are largely prescribed and are based on requirements of the future practice. Rarely would any one for the love of the thing itself apart from the future use to which it is going to be put undertake a course in pharmacy, dentistry, general medicine, surgery, law, engineering, commerce, aviation, or theology. The conscious thought of the future use of the acquired skill or information merges inseparably with any present interest. Mentally the future here is a part of the present. Often present failure is offset by the hope of future success. If it be claimed that professional education is really properly motivated, though involving conscious preparation for the future, then all education may in principle properly contain some conscious preparation for the future. And it remains clear that not every future musician is interested in all the necessary finger exercises, and not every future physician is interested in all of anatomy for its own sake.

(3) We may go further and say not only *may* education include preparation for the future as part of its conscious motivation, but that it *should* do so. There is a future, its character depends in large measure on the character of the present; a part of the importance of the present is its bearing on the future; the present *is* a preparation for the future, willy nilly. The only question would seem to be not whether, but how wisely, to utilize the future in motivating the present. The future has some legitimate claim on the present. We may even say that this is true not only for children and young

people, but also for adults. If one were about to visit a new continent, it however being uncertain whether one would arrive, the journey being perilous, it would nevertheless be the part of wisdom and foresight to ask whether the continent really existed, and what the chances of arrival were; just so the adult is entirely justified in asking concerning "another life," and making such preparation as reason might dictate. Socrates, the father of the intellectuals, does this in Plato's *Phaedo*.

(4) Some doubt may properly be cast upon the principle, grow and you will be prepared, or take care of the present and the future will take care of itself. It all depends upon how one grows and how one takes care of the present. Growth without foresight of probable future consequences of the line of growth, taking care of the present without thought of the future, may well lead to unconscious but very poor preparation for the future. Topsy "growed." It is a definite ideal of character or service to be attained in the future that keeps any pupil from "just growing." The very conception of education as directed growth presupposes conscious, though not anxious, thought of the morrow.

(5) In the view that altogether omits conscious preparation for the future we probably have an over-emphasis on the rights of the individual and an under-emphasis on the rights of society. Agesilaus, the Spartan, when asked what a boy ought to study, replied: "what he will need when a man." Dewey, the modern, replies "what he needs as a boy." Both views are probably extreme. True, the needs of the young have some claims on society; also true, that the needs of society have some claims on the young. The claims of the young on society are their rights; the claims of society on the young are their duties. The young are to learn to live fully by serving effectively. It is not merely what they want but what they ought to want in view of society's needs that must guide their education. Present satisfactions in service, in meeting

the needs of others, anticipate a socialized future and help prepare for it.

Our net conclusion is then that the contrast between education as growth and education as preparation is too sharply drawn. The best growth includes preparation as a part of its motivation.

2. Education as Unfolding

Exposition. In this section we will consider the nature of the conception of education as unfolding and two examples of it, with an appreciation and criticism of each.

There are two conceptions of the nature of education as "development," one of which we accept, the other we reject. The first in that development means continuous growing; the second is that it means the unfolding of the latent powers of the individual toward a definite goal. This definite goal is conceived of as the completion or the perfection of the individual and society. The goal is the perfect man or the perfect society, on earth or in heaven. The ideal is held to be the real and life is the process whereby the real becomes the ideal. But at no point in time does the real become actually the ideal; it is eternally progressing, unfolding, toward it.

It will be noted that this view is widely held among idealistic philosophers, and that it is logically a variant of the view of education as preparation. However, the preparation theory stresses the practicality of life, while the unfolding theory stresses the spirituality of life.

Now why do we reject this view which in different forms has inspired so many thinkers and writers, especially Rousseau, Froebel, and Hegel? Chiefly for two reasons. First, it is still partly a static and not entirely a dynamic view; and second, it is dependent for its practicability upon some intermediary between the ideal and the real. We will briefly consider each of these points.

(1) This view is still partly static because the goal is complete, perfect, and unchanging. It is like a Platonic idea or the usual conception of Deity. All the change, process, growth, progress, development, is in the real, not in the ideal. The real is the growing life we know, the ideal is the objective of our growth. Thus we have a dynamic life that is real and a static goal that is ideal. Not having yet surrendered its unchanging goal, not being willing to allow that all things change, though with much recognition of growth, this view is "the last infirmity of the mind in its transition from a static to a dynamic understanding of life" (p. 66). It still holds that growth is only transitional, lacking meaning on its own account, having meaning only because it is leaving something behind and pressing forward toward something final. Thus an abstract and indefinite and as yet unrealized future is in control. This connotes depreciation of present power and opportunity. We must educate for a present changing earth, not a future unchanging heaven.

(2) This view, to be practical, depends too upon the presence of some intermediary to represent the ideal in the midst of the flux and flow of life. This intermediary is usually, of course, some idea which an adult would like the child to acquire. It is needed as a criterion to approve this bit of unfolding from within as moving toward the ideal and to condemn that act or attitude as moving away from the ideal. But the child is not given the idea outright, for that would not be "unfolding." Instead, the idea is "drawn out" of the child's mind by suggestive questioning or some other pedagogical device, as Socrates taught Meno. The vice of this is that the child appears to have an initiative in thinking which he lacks. Really, he gropes at random after the results wanted, and forms the habit of dependence upon external cues. In such unfolding we have only drawn out what we wanted to draw out and the pupil has experienced no real growth. In the name of unfolding from within pupils have really been subjected to standardization from without. The adult, repre-

senting the infinite, has re-made the child in his own chosen image. He must educate real growing children by guiding the interaction of their present organic tendencies with the present environment without reference to any infinite patterns latent in their make-up waiting to be unfolded. We must surrender these adult ideas of what an infinite goal requires of us.

In the sphere of philosophy there have been two attempts to provide a working representative of the absolute goal, those of Froebel and of Hegel. These two philosophers hold certain views in common concerning the infinite or absolute goal and the method of unfolding toward it. In each case there is held to be a whole of experience. Since human life is necessarily a part of the whole, the character of the whole is somewhat revealed in the part, it is "immanent," implicit, potential, enfolded in the part. Thus the complete and perfect ideal is operative here and now. Development or unfolding is gradually making explicit and outward what is implicit and inward.

By what method is this process of unfolding effected? Here Froebel and Hegel differ, and we will treat them separately, beginning with Froebel.

To Froebel the effective force in securing unfolding is, perhaps strange to say, the presentation of symbols. But Froebel was a mystic, who sensed his unity with the absolute whole, and saw or thought he saw, much more in symbols than most people seem able to see. Like most educators, what he had found good for himself he thought good for others. These symbols, worse yet, were largely mathematical. From the days of Pythagoras numbers had been held by some to contain the secrets of reality. So these symbols, largely mathematical, were held by Froebel to correspond to the essential traits of the absolute, which likewise reside in latent form in the nature of the child. When the symbol is presented and realized, this trait sleeping in the individual is awakened, it is unfolded. Thus the education of the individual is his progress in the sense of his relationship to the whole. Thus, in the kindergarten usage as formulated by Froebel, the ball typifies unity and the circle in which the children gather is a symbol of the collective life of mankind. To the non-mystic it might be only a convenient way of grouping children.

Before criticising these views of a century ago, let us first express our appreciation of the work of Froebel as an educator. He has perhaps done more for the idea of growth than any other single modern educator. Wide-spread acknowledgment of this idea is due to him. This came about through his recognition of the significance of the native capacities of children, through his loving attention to them, and through his influencing in inducing others to study them.

But by way of criticism we must say three things. Froebel had a false notion of development as unfolding, he set up an infinite static goal, and he resorted to symbolism to effect the unfoldment of the finite toward the infinite. A few words concerning each of these weaknesses in Froebel. (1) Development is not the unfolding of a latent principle toward an infinite ideal; it is just growing, without any completed product as a goal to anticipate. There are results of growing but no final result. It is all process without a goal.

(2) There is no goal in Froebel's sense of the term, or in any sense, except as any stage in a process is a product, at once left behind. Froebel's infinite goal, being static, means the arrest of growth as a process. It is a remote goal. In theory it is a state of complete unfoldedness. Nobody has ever directly experienced or perceived such a state. The notion is empty; it can not be intelligently grasped and stated; it is based on a vague sentimental aspiration. In the language of philosophy, the goal, being beyond human experience, is transcendent. The concept of it is *a priori.* We reject transcendentalism, and the *a priori,* Immanuel Kant to the contrary, notwithstanding.

(3) The goal, being transcendental, itself provides no criterion applicable to the guidance of powers. Hence symbols

of it must be used. The transcendental ideal must be connected with the empirical use of symbols. Some of the concrete facts of experience are selected to symbolize the unexperienced ideal. It is impossible, not having experienced the ideal, to select experienced facts to symbolize it. Arbitrariness enters. Romantic fancy seizes on analogies. A scheme of symbolism is settled upon. The scheme thus arbitrarily and romantically settled upon is treated as a system of laws. Then a technique must be invented to make the children comprehend the inner, or transcendental, meaning of the symbols. Adults formulate the symbols; adults devise and control the technique. Thus Froebel's love of abstract symbolism got the better of his sympathetic insight into the nature of children. And witness the paradoxical result: this modern liberator of childhood became the father of "as arbitrary and externally imposed a scheme of dictation as the history of instruction has ever seen" (p. 68).

We pass to Hegel, another transcendentalist, but with a different type of intermediary between the finite we know and experience, and the infinite we do not know and do not experience. In the philosophical scheme worked out by Hegel, institutions take the place of symbols. These institutions are historic, *e.g.,* the state, and they are said to embody the different traits or factors in the whole or absolute. This absolute is the goal of human progress.

We will express a word of appreciation of Hegel's work before criticising it. In one direction, Hegel's philosophy, like Froebel's, is indispensable. Froebel appreciated children; Hegel appreciated institutions. Apart from institutions, there is no valid conception of the process of life. The great collective institutional products of humanity exert a nurturing influence. They are active factors in the intellectual nurture of mind. Neither institutions nor culture are artificial. Institutions are not despotism begotten in artifice and nurtured in fraud. Language, government, art, and religion are a kind of "objective mind." They play a significant part in the formation of individual minds.

There was an important consequence of these valid views of Hegel. The weaknesses of an abstract individualistic philosophy were made evident. Rousseau, for example, had marred his otherwise excellent educational position (education as natural development, not forced, not grafted upon individuals from without) by holding that social conditions are not natural. The idea of "mind" as a ready-made possession of the individual could no longer be held in the light of Hegel's exposition of "objective mind," though in fact the view still survives to plague us.

In the interest of historic fact be it said, however, that these solid institutional views of Hegel, recognized by him as true, were really rediscovered by him. The idea that man was nurtured by the state and the other social institutions was familiar to the Greeks. And Hegel's philosophy of history and society was the culmination of a series of German writers, including Lessing, Herder, Kant, Schiller, and Goethe.

But having said so much in appreciation of Hegel, we must now show the inadequacy of his philosophy as a basis for education. Three criticisms are in order. Hegel held that "the real is the rational"; that, as against institutions, individuals have no right; and that social progress is a matter of "organic growth." A few words concerning each of these.

(1) The absolute mind is reason; it is the goal of the process of unfolding, it realizes itself in human institutions. These institutions, though existing concretely in human experience, must then be arranged in a hierarchy, on a stepladder of increasing approximations to the absolute. Each in its time and place is held to be absolutely necessary, and is thus rational, being an integral element in the total reason. Thus the real is held to be rational, despite all that experience indicates of its irrationality.

(2) As against these real, and so rational, institutions, individuals have no spiritual rights. The personality of the in-

dividual is developed and nurtured by obedient assimilation of the spirit of these existing institutions. Institutions change, states rise and fall, but such changes are the work of the "world-spirit," or the absolute in the temporal process. Ordinary individuals have no share or lot in them. Extraordinary individuals, the great "heroes," as chosen organs of the world-spirit, do influence the course of history. If this type of philosophical idealism unites with the doctrine of biological evolution, as it did in the latter part of the nineteenth century, then still the process of evolution works itself out to its own end, in comparison with which the ideas and preferences of individuals are impotent. Under such a system, education becomes the conformity of the individual to the existent social order; it is not, as we have held, the transformation of individual and social experience.

(3) Then, again, this system makes social progress a matter of "organic growth," instead of, as we hold, a matter of experimental selection. Society itself is conceived as an organism. This conception was devised by some of Hegel's followers to reconcile the claims of the whole and of the individual; it was to meet the objection to the system that, though it magnified the individual in the abstract, it swallowed up the individual in the concrete. It is true that the adequate exercise of individual capacity presupposes social organization. But the conception of society as an organism is objectionable. In the human body one organ, as hand or eye, cannot do the work of another organ and each organ in its own way is essential to the whole. So it was said that in society each individual has a certain limited place and function, requiring to be supplemented by the place and functions of other individuals; thus certain individuals are supposed to perform mechanical operations, while others become statesmen, scholars, and the like. Thus the notion of "organism" is used to give philosophical sanctions to class distinctions. In its educational application this notion again means external dictation instead of growth.

Comment. It would be easy to write at length on Dr. Dewey's rejection of transcendentalism, the *a priori,* and modern idealistic philosophy. We will try to be brief and only suggest lines of reflection without carrying them out.

(1) Though at one time, in the late eighties, Dr. Dewey was an idealist, his thinking is now more in line with French positivism and British empiricism.

(2) His method is not to refute the views he rejects, nor to prove the views he accepts, but, following the pragmatic lead, to show that the consequences of the views he rejects are repugnant to the views he accepts.

(3) He accepts the fundamental view of Heraclitus that all things change; he rejects the fundamental view of Parmenides that nothing changes, as well as the more common view of Plato that things in the sense world change and that realities in the world of the ideas are changeless. It is meant, of course, that logically and by implication he thus accepts and rejects. All these philosophical issues were fought through by the Greeks and Dr. Dewey's pragmatism, like F. C. S. Schiller's humanism, is closely akin to the phenomenalism of the Greek sophists. Our author is a modern Protagoras.

(4) The rejection of an infinite goal of human life, of a supersensible world whose reality is not directly "perceived," does violence to the experience of the mystics, subordinates the conceptual order to the perceptual, and it would revolutionize the practices of the religions of the world in so far as they involve the recognition of a supersensible or spiritual order in prayer and praise. That there is, however, such a system of non-perceptual reality is witnessed alike by the doctrine of ideas in Plato, by the doctrine of the *a priori* forms of thought and the non-experienced thing in itself of Kant, and by the doctrine of subsistence, not existence, of mathematical relations of the modern Platonist, Bertrand Russell. The ideas of Plato, of which the Good is the chief, the categories of Kant, and the mathematical relations of Russell all are held by their authors to be real, yet they are not objects in

space or events in time. This non-spatial, non-temporal, order of realities may very well be "the light that never was on land or sea and yet the master light of all our seeing." There is nothing in our text that disproves its reality, nor can its reality be disproven or proven. Our philosophy, whether Heraclitean or Platonic, whether positivistic or idealistic, whatever it is, involves an intellectual venture akin to faith.

(5) Having rejected any infinite goal of life, it is logical to reject the symbols of Froebel, and the institutions of Hegel as representing that goal, or manifesting its nature in time. In principle any mediary whatsoever would similarly be rejected, including the Demi-urgos of Plato or the Logos, the word, of the Neo-Platonist. Nothing human has any infinite meaning, there is nothing in any transcendent world that does or can manifest itself in our order of perceptual experience. The Hindu doctrine of the avatars, the Christian doctrine of the incarnation, would have no basis in fact. Things are what they seem, symbolizing nothing transcendent, manifesting nothing eternal. There is no infinite ideal, how then could it become real in time and space? Our purpose in pointing out these considerations is to show that the philosophy of education which proposes in word to enrich human experience may really impoverish it in fact.

(6) Now concerning education as unfolding, it is important to recognize an indisputable element of truth in it. A child is a potential man; under no conceivable conditions is the human infant capable of becoming a lower animal really, or a plant, of course. Why not? Because of his implanted nature, his potentialities, which predestine him to belong to *genus homo,* though reared like Romulus and Remus by a she-wolf. The kind of human creature he becomes depends on his environment, but he becomes a human creature through his native heredity. To this he is destined by circumstances and predestined by the germ-cells which constitute his essence. Here is first an enfolding, then an unfolding that is inescapable. Many hold the inspiring view that this native original being

is a potential image of the divine, and that this image should unfold in accordance with the model of perfect manhood. This view may be rejected; it has not been disproven. There is much to commend it.

(7) Since the kind of man one becomes is dependent on his environment, though not the fact that he becomes a man, it is clear that the social institutions which shape him do prefigure his character. In this way the institution is prior to the new man and shapes him, though posterior to the old man and shaped by him. Human institutions, thus growing with man, do reveal past human nature and do prefigure future human nature. Study then the institution, if you would know the man. So did Plato in *The Republic.* But if Carlyle is right in saying that the true *Shekinah,* or divine symbol is man, then the institution which reveals man likewise has the significance of the *Shekinah.* In this case the institution is not merely a selection made experimentally by society. It is a way to make man, having something of the meaning of the universe in it. The only way to refute this argument is to deny any *Shekinah* whatsoever.

(8) Now concerning symbols. We are constantly using them; we need them; they are educative. The flag of one's country is a symbol, to regard it merely as a piece of bunting is derogatory. The star and crescent, the hammer and sickle, are symbols; they mean by association more than they are in themselves. The square and compass, the triangle, the scimitar, are symbols; they mean much to the initiated that others miss. The double triangle, the seven-branched candlestick, the church spire, the cross, are symbols, for the meanings of which men have lived and died. All pins, badges, medals, and regalia are symbols. Life without symbols would be only bare and factual. Some symbols are intended to have only temporal significance; others are intended to have a supertemporal significance. Both kinds of symbols appear in Froebel's system. Particular symbols of his, originating for

personal or local reasons or such as are beyond the grasp of children, may prove ineffective. But the principle of symbolism cannot be discarded without loss. And to deny the whole can be symbolized, say by a sphere, is to beg the question. In this connection it may be recalled that Pestalozzi held the theory of education as unfolding, "like a tree," without using symbols either of the infinite ideal, or of institutions embodying it.

(9) Students of the pragmatic philosophy of education should have a third set of categories. We know the "static" and the "dynamic." We are taught to prefer the dynamic as progressive to the static as non-progressive. They need to know the "organic," which combines the static and the dynamic. The view that nothing changes or should change is static; the view that all things change or should change is dynamic; the view that some things do and should change and some things do not and should not change is organic The reactionary holds static views; the radical holds dynamic views; the conservative holds organic views with emphasis on the static; the liberal holds organic views with emphasis on the dynamic.

The pragmatic criticisms of the idealistic philosophies of Froebel and Hegel mistakenly treats those philosophies as static; they are really organic. The whole system of reality is organic. Human society is becoming so. Progress toward the infinite goal is without limit and no "arrest of growth" is implied. In mathematics an asymptote approaching its limit is not "arrested" in its directed movement because it is said to reach its limit at infinity. If the infinite goal is an absolute self-consciousness, embracing all experience of value, can a finite individual progressing through infinite time toward that fulfillment be said to be "arrested" or limited in his growth? The concept of progress, unfolding, toward the infinite is an organic, not a static category. The finite changes and is dynamic, the changeless infinite containing the changing finite is both static and dynamic, it is organic. As Plato said, "time is the moving image of eternity."[1]

Our net result is that there is much more in the conception of education as unfolding and in the idealistic philosophies of education held by Froebel and Hegel than our author allows. Froebel and Hegel may be studied with profit by those educational philosophers who want to see reality steadily and see it whole. It is very true that the doctrine of education as unfolding must not be interpreted to mean that the environment is ineffective save as stimulation (Hegel warns against this) or that the process of unfolding is only individual and not social (Froebel warns against this). We unfold in accordance with human nature and in accordance with physical and social environment and possibly in accordance with an immanent and universal plan.

3. Education as Training of Faculties

Exposition. In discussing this now familiar topic, the following plan which the reader should note will be followed: first, exposition of the view; second, its classic formulation in Locke; third, criticism of the view, together with our own views on the same question; fourth, the distinction between general and special education.

First, this theory holds education is a training of the faculties or powers of the mind. It is the same theory as "formal discipline." It has had great vogue, even from the days of Plato, who used mathematics to train the mind in abstract thinking. Until recently it was a commonplace of educational theory and of psychology. The powers or faculties of the mind needing to be trained are such things as perceiving, retaining, recalling, associating, attending, willing, feeling, imagining, thinking, etc. The theory holds that education shapes these powers by exercising them upon the material presented. This material is external, whose value consists in

[1] For recent similar views, cf. Northrop, F. C. S., *Science and First Principles,* The Macmillan Company, 1931.

the exercise it provides the general mental powers. (These powers as a matter of fact are purely and simply the *results* of growth; they are the creations as by-products of other activities and agencies.) The theory regards these powers as the direct and conscious *aims* of instruction. There are a definite number of such powers to be trained, like the strokes in golfing. Education should train them directly. These powers are already there in some untrained form; they are inborn; they are trained, refined, and perfected by constant and graded repetitions. This matter of training through exercise is "discipline," and the power so trained is said to be "disciplined"; and this power is universally available and applicable, hence it is "formal"; whence the theory of education or the training of the faculties is also known as that of "formal discipline."

Second, John Locke (d. 1732) gave classic expression to this theory. The important thing for education is the exercise or practice of the faculties of the mind till they become thoroughly established habits. The analogy constantly employed is that of a billiard player or gymnast who develops automatic skill. Even the faculty of thinking can be formed into a trained habit only by repeated exercise in making and combining simple distinctions for which, thought Locke, mathematics especially should be used.

Locke's statements fitted well into the dualism of mind and matter of his day. In accordance with this view, mind and matter are two things; the outer world presents the material or content of knowledge through sensations passively received; the inner world of mind has all ready its own powers or faculties; knowledge results if the mind divides and unites things as they are divided and united in nature itself. This scheme appeared to give due weight to the subject matter of knowledge while insisting that the end of education is the formation of the person's mental powers. In asserting that all material is received from without, it is realistic; in putting the final stress upon the formation of intellectual powers, it was idealistic. In asserting that the individual can not generate any true ideas on his own account, it was objective and impersonal; in placing the end of education in the perfecting of certain mental faculties, it was individualistic. The generations following upon Locke accepted this distribution of values. By it the educator was provided with the definite task of knowing the faculties, exercising them repeatedly, and grading the exercises.

Third, in estimating this theory, let us note at the outset in appreciation that it has a correct ideal: the creation of specific powers of accomplishment as one outcome of education. Training does mean that one can do important things with greater ease, efficiency, economy, and promptness. Such an outcome is really due to the habits produced by an educative development. The theory of formal discipline makes the fundamental mistake of taking a short cut; it tries to train faculties which do not even exist except as the results of growth.

Specifically, there are five objections to this theory of education as a training of the faculties, viz., (1) the supposed original faculties are mythological; (2) training is not achieved by exercise; (3) the more specialized the training the less transferable it is; (4) the theory is dualistic; and (5) mental powers are really the results of native, active tendencies, being occupied with subject-matters. As the theory we are rejecting is important and widely held, we will give special attention to each of these points and at the same time present our own view of the unity of mind and matter and the origin of mind.

(1) There are no such original mental powers as observation, recollection, willing, and thinking, waiting to be exercised and so trained. There are instead a great number of original native tendencies, or instinctive modes of action, based on the original connections of neurones in the central nervous system. Thus there is an impulsive tendency of the eyes to follow and fixate light; of the neck muscles to turn

toward light and sound; of the hands to reach and grasp and turn and twist and thump; of the nasal apparatus to make sounds; of the mouth to spew out unpleasant substances, to gag, to curl the lip, and so on indefinitely. When something in the throat makes one cough, the obnoxious particle is ejected and so the succeeding stimulus is modified. When the hand touches something hot, it is impulsively, not intellectually, snatched away, and the withdrawal alters the hot stimulus, and the need of the organism for relief is met. Thus the control of the environment is effected. All our first sensations,—seeing, hearing, touching, smelling, tasting, are of this kind. They are not mental, intellectual, or cognitive, and no repetitious exercise could make them so. In sum, these native tendencies are (*a*) indefinitely large in number and subtly interwoven, not few and sharply distinguished, and (*b*) they are responses to environmental change that in turn change the stimuli and so bring about other responses, not intellectual powers at all requiring only exercise for their perfecting.

(2) The training of our impulsive activities is not achieved by exercise, as one strengthens a muscle by practice. Instead of exercise it is by (*a*) selection and (*b*) coördination that the native tendencies are trained. (*a*) Selective response and training are identical. The primary reactions of the human infant are usually too diffused and general to be of much practical use. The elimination of the useless responses and the retention of the responses useful in utilizing the stimulus is the training. Thus, when the eye is stimulated, the responses adapted to reaching, grasping, and manipulating the object are selected. It is true that every stimulus brings about some change in all the organs of response, but we ignore the unadapted ones. (*b*) The different factors of the response must be specifically coördinated, *i.e.*, the connection must be made between the stimulus and the appropriate response, and further, between a situation containing many stimuli and the appropriate complex response. Thus, the

stimulus of light is coördinated with grasping, but not if the object which emits the light is also hot. Thus, too, the object is given a name which as a stimulus evokes both an auditory and vocal response. Thus, our original impulsive activities, through selection of responses based on use, and through suitable coördination of responses, gradually effect the adjustment of the organism to its environment.

(3) The more specialized the training, the less transferable the skill to other modes of behavior, *i.e.*, the less educative it is. What does a pupil acquire in studying his spelling lesson? The orthodox theory of formal discipline says that, in learning to spell those particular words, he acquires an increase of powers of observation, attention, and recollection, which may be employed whenever these powers are needed. As a matter of fact he acquires nothing of the kind. The more he notices verbal visual forms and nothing else, the less he notices anything except verbal, visual forms. His ability to note distinctions even in geometrical forms may not be increased, to say nothing of his ability to observe in general. His scope of coördination is too limited. The ability secured to observe and recall verbal forms is not available for observing and recalling other things, is not "transferable." This is the type of practice to which the theory of formal discipline led. There was an undue emphasis upon the training of narrow specialized modes of skill. Thus we have the paradox that the training of the general powers of the mind ("general" because applicable to many situations equally) was too specific (because of the limited scope of the coördinations in training).

But, departing now from such a limited practice, the scope of the coördination may be extended. In noticing and fixating the forms of words, connections with other things may be noted too, such as the meaning of the words, the context in which they are habitually used, their derivation, their classification, etc. In this case the context is widened, varied stimuli are coördinated with various responses, and so the ability acquired is available for the effective performance of other acts. There is no "transfer" but there is a flexible coördination. The two ways indicated in learning to spell are like using pulley weights in a gymnasium and engaging in a game. The one is uniform, mechanical, specialized, rigid; the other is varied, flexible, general, elastic. The former is the typical product of formal training and is objectionable; the latter is the typical product of education or growth and is acceptable, securing initiative, inventiveness, and readaptability. It is not economy in learning to begin with tennis if golf is one's objective. To be an expert in tennis does not make one an expert golfer. But tennis may help golf if it reveals an aptitude for fine muscular coördination or if the same kind of muscular coördination is involved in each. General vigor is a good thing but it must be applied in specific ways. So, though there is no training of the faculties, there is general as well as specific training in responses, and the general is preferable, being more widely available.

(4) The fundamental fallacy in the theory of education as the training of the mental powers or faculties is its dualism or separation of mind and matter, or division between the individual and the world, or separation of activities and capacities from subject matter. There is no ability to see in general but only to see specific things; there is no ability to hear in general but only to hear specific things; there is no ability to remember in general but only to remember specific things. There being no such general powers apart from the subject matter involved, to talk about training such is nonsense. The mind is just a specific way of responding to a specific material situation and so can not be trained apart from the situation in which the organism functions.

(5) The mental powers are not original; they are the organized results of the occupation of native active tendencies with certain subject matters. This applies to such abilities as observation, recollection, judgment, and æsthetic taste. A man can not observe by "willing" to observe, and there is no observing "faculty," but observation is a natural result of

having something to do which requires for success the intensive and extensive use of eye and hand. It is a consequence of the interaction of sense organ and subject matter. And it varies with the subject matter. If we want our pupils to observe and to remember, and we do, the first thing is to determine what we want them to observe and to remember, and why.

Let us repeat that in answering this question the criterion is social. We want the pupil to be socially-minded, to observe, remember, and judge those things which are significant in life and which make him a competent member of his group. Botanists, chemists, engineers may become good observers because they have such subject matter. Formal disciplinarians may instead set their pupils to observing carefully the cracks in the wall or to memorizing words in an unknown tongue.

Fourth, as we recur to the last point in our opening plan of this section, the special education of mind, involving narrow coördinations, which we have decried, and the general education of the mind, involving broad coördinations, which we have advocated, are not to be confused with so-called special, *i.e.*, professional, education and general, *i.e.*, liberal, education. Though any transfer of function or power is miraculous and impossible, there is possible a broad, flexible, general education of the mind due to activities involving the coördination of many factors. Again, the criterion is social. A technological education, commonly called special or professional, may really be broad and general, if it is connected with human activities having social breadth; and a literary education, commonly called liberal and broad, may be narrow and special, if its activities are kept sundered from their social settings. The chief obstruction in correct practice to securing the desirable general training of the mind is the isolation of subject matter from a social context.

Concerning the term "general" in the educational field, it has three meanings which we have discussed in this chapter and which must be kept distinct from each other. (1) There are the so-called "general" inborn powers of the mind; these we reject. (2) There is a "general" education of the mind, based on broad coördinations; this we advocate. (3) There is a so-called "general" education—liberal, literary, artistic, or religious in character, which we reject if it is disconnected from broad social human activities and which we accept if it is so connected.

Likewise the term "specific" or special has been used in three connections in this chapter which may be confusing unless classified. (1) There is a specific and narrow training given the so-called general mental powers by the formal disciplinarians; this we reject. (2) There is the doctrine of specific, not general mental abilities, which vary with the situations in which they function, and yet, if broadly trained by wide coördination, allow flexible responses; this we advocate. And (3) there is specific or special education, technical or professional in character, which, if made broadly human, is desirable. Unless these distinctions are kept in mind, we shall appear to be accepting in one part of the discussion what we have rejected in another.

Comment. This fair statement of the main views of the theory of education as a training of the mental faculties is familiar to students of educational theory. It is interesting to note in this connection that the theory of formal discipline is based by Bode not only on the notion of mental faculties but also on the notion of soul-substance.[1] The latter discussion goes deeper into the philosophical foundations of the question.

A recent illustration of the disciplinary theory of education, which, of course, still lives, appears in the autobiography of Calvin Coolidge. He writes (*Cosmopolitan*, August, 1929): "When Greek was begun the next year I found it difficult. It is a language that requires real attention and close application. Among its rewards are the moving poetry of Homer,

[1] Bode, B. H., *Conflicting Psychologies of Learning*, Boston, 1929.

the marvelous orations of Demosthenes, and *in after life an increased power of observation*" (Italics ours).

Concerning the historical reference to John Locke as a formal disciplinarian, it should be said that, though common, this view is not wholly justified. There are theories held by Locke which are inconsistent with formal discipline. For example, he wrote: "But the learning pages of Latin by heart, no more fits the memory for retention of anything else than the graving of one substance in lead makes it [*i.e.*, the lead] the more capable of retaining firmly any other characters."[1] Locke himself rejected the "discipline" he received at Westminister and at Oxford. He opposed the writing of Latin themes. He rejected the faculty psychology upon which the theory rests (See "Faculty" in Baldwin, Dictionary of Philosophy), along with innate ideas. Memory is treated as a gift, hardly subject to improvement. His notion of the mind as "a blank sheet of paper," or as "wax," does not fit the notion of discipline. If we may use terms without stopping to define them, we might say of Locke that as to aim he is a social realist, and as to means he is now a sense realist, now a naturalist, and now to a degree a disciplinarian. He is more disciplinary in his theories of physical and moral than of intellectual education. Perhaps Francis Bacon (see his Essay, "Of Studies") would illustrate the disciplinary theory better than Locke.[2]

Concerning the criticisms passed upon the theory, it may be remarked that the language: "nonsense," "miraculous and impossible," "cracks in the wall," is perhaps stronger than the facts allow, and that the substitute theory of the unity of mind and matter is neither quite clear nor proven. It is quite true that the theory of education as the training of inborn general powers by means of exercise is not held by modern educational psychologists. But the transfer of training is still admitted, and must be, as a matter of fact. The theory,

[1] Locke, *Some Thoughts Concerning Education*, § 176.

[2] Cf. Hodge, F. A., *John Locke and Formal Discipline*, Ph.D. thesis, University of Va., 1911. Cuff, Sister Mary Louise, *The Educational Theory of John Locke*, Washington, D. C., 1923.

however, of the transfer is not a matter of agreement, whether by the physiological "identical elements" of Thorndike, or the physiological "flexible response" of Bode (which is based on Dewey), or by the psychological "presence of ideals" of Judd and Bagley. It is noteworthy that the doctrine of the transfer of training gives us back in lesser amount what the rejection of the theory of formal discipline takes away,—"lesser" because something is lost in the transfer. We are still permitted to speak of education as training, only it must be a training of the responses, not of the faculties.

Concerning Dr. Dewey's view that the mental functions are the results of growth through selection and coördination of responses be it said that this is a behavioristic statement of the year 1916. It is "behavioristic" but not behaviorism,—to divide a hair,—because the former type of response is flexible and adaptable, while the latter is inflexible and mechanical. Bode makes much of this. Really, however, if the response is only physiological, and not psychical,—and this is the meaning of both Dewey and Bode, little would seem to be gained by calling it flexible and purposeful instead of inflexible and mechanical. In each case the neurones are alone responsible for whatever takes place.

And here comes the final comment, which concerns the philosophical foundation of Dr. Dewey's views, viz., the unity of mind and matter, of the individual and the world. He rejects dualism in all its forms. He is a monist, not of the idealistic, or agnostic, but of the naturalistic type. In this view awareness is not distinct from the stimulus or situation of which we are aware. The knower and the known are both inseparable constituents of the same naturalistic process. This view is neither particularly clear nor is it proven. In fact, the latest thorough student of the question pronounces in favor of dualism.[1] For ourselves, if there is to be a reduction of dualism to unity, it would have to be a unity of experience, a known unity, a conscious unity, an all-embracing

[1] Lovejoy, A. O., *The Revolt against Dualism*, New York, 1930.

unity, and hence some form of idealism. Intelligence that concludes less than this must perforce think meanly of itself. The origin of mind would not then be in the by-products of the native tendencies to action but in the very nature of the one central reality of all. Man is not simply an organism with flexible responses; he is a self originating in a Self.

Of course a thinker must, like others, use the language that is available. But it is interesting to note that Dr. Dewey uses forms of expression which are inconsistent with his theory. For example, he writes: "It is consequently futile to set up even the ulterior development of faculties of observation, memory, etc., unless *we have first determined* what sort of subject matter we wish the pupil to become expert in observing and recalling and for what purpose. And it is only repeating in another form what has already been said, to declare that *the criterion here must be social.*"[1] (Italics ours.) The way in which the idea is expressed, *i.e.*, implying a mind separate from response, is not consistent with the idea expressed, *i.e.*, denying a mind separate from response.

We may now bring this lengthy discussion to a close by remarking that on the individual side the important thing in Dr. Dewey's thought is the interaction of present organic activities with the present environment, and on the social side is the sharing of group activities. This is the height and the depth of his educational thinking.

[1] *Democracy and Education*, pp. 77–78.

CHAPTER VI

EDUCATION AS CONSERVATIVE AND PROGRESSIVE

In Chapter IV Dr. Dewey places primary emphasis on the present; in Chapter V he rejects emphasis on the future; in Chapter VI he rejects emphasis on the past.

Having the title of Chapter VI in mind, education as formation, as recapitulation, as retrospection, is conservative; as reconstruction, is progressive. Dr. Dewey rejects education as conservative and accepts it as progressive.

1. Education as Formation

Exposition. In contrast with the view of education as formation about to be presented, let us first of all state our own view again. Education is indeed formative of the mind. This view was propounded in our chapter on education as growth, and in our discussion of the mental faculties. Both mental and moral character are formed by education. The formation consists in the selection and coördination of native activities. The formation is *of* native activities *through* native activities for the utilization of the subject matter of the social environment. Thus it is a process of reconstruction, of reorganization. It is a reorganization of something within by means of response to something without.

In contrast the other view of education as formation now to be presented, depends upon something operating from *without*. It is the subject matter which is presented from without. When properly presented it forms the mental and the moral disposition. To instruct the mind is to construct it, to build it, by setting up certain associations or connections between its contents. This theory rejects the ideas of unfolding, of faculties, and of their training.

As in the other cases, we will study this theory through an historical representative. The best is Herbart (d. 1844). Though he gave psychology a new foundation in "metaphysics, mathematics, and experience," his own psychology, mainly intellectualistic, is now largely out of date, yet necessary to an understanding of his educational views. He rejected the theory of innate mental faculties. The soul is endowed with the single power of reaction. Various realities act upon it and it in turn reacts upon them. In so doing various qualities are produced. These different qualities are called presentations (Vorstellungen). They persist, if not above, then below the threshold of consciousness, driven there by new and stronger ones. The interaction of these various presentations, some submerged and some not, some old and some new, form various arrangements and associations. These arrangements are the so-called faculties—attention, perception, memory, and thinking. Thus, when old presentations rise to greet and combine with new ones, we have perception. Even the sentiments are so derived. To illustrate, when the independent activities of presentations reënforce each other, we have pleasure; when they pull different ways, there is pain. It is evident how mechanical and how like physics these conceptions are. The mind, apart from its original capacity of reaction to realities that act upon it, is wholly a matter of its contents. The mind is its "furniture," the various arrangements formed by the various presentations.

There are three educational implications of this doctrine of mind. (1) The kind of minds pupils have depends on the kinds of materials presented to them. Proper minds are formed by the presentation of proper educational materials. What a power schooling becomes!

(2) The character of the earlier presentations is all important. They control the apperception of the new material presented. The new reënforces the old. The business of the teacher is then two-fold, to lay the foundation and to build on them the superstructure; that is, to present the proper

material first and then to arrange the later material so that it may be assimilated by the earlier. In the conception of unfolding, the future goal is in control; here the past, in the form of prior presentations acting as an apperceiving mass, is in control.

(3) There is a uniform method of instruction. First, there is "preparation,"—the awakening into special activity the older presentations which are to assimilate the new ones. Second, there is the central step of presentation of the new material. Third, there is the assimilation of the new by the old and of the old to the new by means of comparison, abstraction, and generalization. Fourth, there is the application of the newly formed content to some task. These steps of instruction are uniform, applicable to all subjects for all pupils of all ages. How apparently simple!

Before criticizing these views, let us appreciate the great service of Herbart. He has particularly influenced method and subject matter. He has done more than any other educational philosopher to bring to the front the problem of the materials of study. He made attention to *content* all important. As to method, under his influence teaching ceased to be routine, accident, casual inspiration, or subservience to tradition. Method became a conscious problem, with a definite aim and procedure. Vague and mystic generalities, ultimate ideals, speculative and spiritual symbols vanished.

Yet Herbart missed the true educational way. He ignored the existence of active and specific functions in the living pupil,—functions which are developed, redirected, and combined as they are occupied with their environment. Herbart is "the schoolmaster come to his own." Only a pedagogue would hold that the mind consists of what it has been taught, and that the importance of what has been taught consists in its availability for further teaching. The weak points in the system match the strong ones. This philosopher says much of the duty of the teacher to instruct but little of the privilege of the pupil to learn; much of the influence of the intellectual environment but little of the influence of the social environment in which pupils share in common experiences; too much of the possibilities of conscious method and too little of the rôle of vital, unconscious, attitudes; much of the old and past and little of the novel and unforeseeable, much of assimilation of externally presented material and little of interaction of native tendencies with the environment. "It takes, in brief, everything educational into account save its essence,—vital energy seeking opportunity for effective exercise."

Comment. Lest a wrong impression of Herbart be gathered from these criticisms of his theory of education as formation, it should be remembered that Herbart held that "the human soul, strictly speaking, develops from itself even each simple impression"[1] (being a pluralistic realist), that he recognized the influence of the family, the life outside of school, and the age of the pupil; that he observed the individual differences and the varying needs of each of his pupils, that he stressed the need of studying children before teaching them, and that he has described his own pupils working, playing, teasing, growing, enjoying life, changing activities frequently, questioning and being developed in all these ways. From such things one concludes there are other trends in Herbart's theory than passivity and mental formation from without.

Furthermore, it is noticeable that Herbart's description of the way the powers of the mind arise through the soul's reaction to the realities that act upon it is remarkably similar to Dr. Dewey's description of the way these same powers of the mind arise through the selection and coördination of the organic responses to stimuli. The two differences are that Herbart is more psychological and intellectualistic and Dewey more physiological and voluntaristic. Accordıng to Herbart the soul is passive until acted upon and then it is reactive;

[1] Herbart, Johann Friedrich, *Pädagogische Schriften,* 2 Bände, herausgegeben von Dr. Otto Willman, Verlag, Leopold Voss, Leipzig, 1880, Vol. 1, p. 322.

according to Dewey the organism in its environment is active as well as passive.

Furthermore, all good expository teaching (as well as public speaking and argumentation) does refer new ideas to old similar ones, does present new material clearly, does combine the new material, does reach general conclusions and practice applications. Dr. Dewey's text may itself be very well taught by the use of Herbart's own four steps of clearness, association, system (generalization), and method (application). It can probably be better taught by Herbart's four steps than by Dr. Dewey's own five steps of reflective thinking (see chapter XII). And there is no denying that Dr. Dewey's own five steps may be used formally and methodically in the hands of unskillful teachers.

It is of course not fashionable now to say a good word for some of the fundamentals of Herbart, and we ourselves are far from accepting his pluralistic realism, his intellectualism and his determinism, but it is still true that knowledge of certain subject matters is important, that Herbart's method is one efficient way of securing such knowledge, that knowledge is one of the sources of interest, and that knowledge and interest combined do greatly influence the conduct which begets character, and that, whatever his method, the teacher's influence is great. Of course other supplementary and modifying things are also true.

Whether Herbart's view of education as formation is entirely out of date may be judged by the following quotation from a modernist book by a leading contemporary humanizer of knowledge: "If we are courageously to meet and successfully to overcome the dangers with which our civilization is threatened, it is clear that we need *more mind* than ever before. It is also clear that we can have indefinitely more mind than we already have if we but honestly desire it, and avail ourselves of resources already at hand. Mind, as previously defined, is our conscious knowledge and intelligence, what we know and our attitude toward it—our disposition to increase our information, classify it, criticise it, and apply it. It is obvious that in this sense the mind is a matter of accumulation and that it has been in the making ever since man took his first step in civilization.''[1]

2. Education as Recapitulation and Retrospection

Exposition. Recapitulation and retrospection go together. They form one theory, not two. Recapitulation refers to the content of the theory and retrospection to the attitude of mind it cultivates. Recapitulation is retrospective. The theory of recapitulation developed in Germany mainly among the followers of Herbart. In its detailed and consistent form it has had little currency elsewhere. But the attitude and the idea of retrospection, which underlies the theory of recapitulation, has had such an immense influence, especially upon higher instruction, that the whole theory, even in its extreme formulation, is worth examination.

The theory of recapitulation is based on an analogy. There is a so-called law of biogenesis, formulated by the biologist, Ernst Haeckel, which says that the growth of the body of the individual repeats the past growth of the race; ''ontogeny repeats phylogeny.'' The theory of recapitulation says that likewise the growth of the soul of the individual repeats the past growth of the soul of the race. It might be called the ''law'' of psychogenesis: soul culture parallels biological growth and repeats race culture. And it is the business of education to see that the recapitulation is correctly done. Thus, the child for a time is in the stage of savagery; his vagrant and predatory instincts are to be so interpreted; while in this stage education should nurture his soul on the culture originating in the racial step of savagery,—myths, folk-tales, song, and the like. Then, the pastoral stage is passed through, followed by all the succeeding stages of racial, social evolution. By the time the child is old enough to take part in contem-

[1] Robinson, J. H., *Mind in the Making*, p. 206, New York, 1921.

porary life, he has arrived at the present epoch of culture. A vast, vague, and seductive theory, by following which the bright mind of G. Stanley Hall [not mentioned by name] was led astray.

Before examining the theory of recapitulation, note that it regards education as essentially retrospective; that it looks primarily at the past, naturally at its literary products; and that it regards mind as adequately formed only when it is patterned on the spiritual heritage of the past. This suggests one of its limitations at the outset.

Let us first disentangle from their misleading contents two factors of truth in this joint theory. (1) It is true on the biological side that an infant starts with an assortment of impulsive activities, howsoever obtained. In character these activities are originally blind, conflicting, casual, sporadic, and unadapted to their immediate environment. Of course he had ancestors; but that is not to say he has just these tendencies because he had just those ancestors. (2) It is true on the cultural side that it is the part of wisdom to utilize the products of past history. No one denies this. But there are two ways of utilizing the products of the past. One is to take them as retrospective standards and patterns for the present; this we reject. The other is to take them as *present* resources for the future; this we acccept. So used, the results of prior experience may prove of indefinitely great value. Past literatures, if now possessed and used, are a part of the present environment.

Having now extracted the kernels of truth from the theory, let us proceed to show (1) that its biological basis is fallacious, and also leads to a misuse of heredity; and (2) that making the records and remains of the past the main material of education is a mistake.

(1) The biological basis of the theory of recapitulation is fallacious. While the embryonic growth of the human infant undoubtedly preserves some of the traits of lower forms of life, in no respect is it a strict traversing of past stages. Ob-

viously if the present growth only repeated the past stages, no evolution could have taken place; each new generation would simply have duplicated its predecessors. Only by the entrance of short-cuts and alterations in the prior scheme of growth has it been possible for development to take place. One biologist reports: "The history of development . . . offers to us . . . a series of . . . efforts to escape from the necessity of recapitulating, and to substitute for the ancestral method a more direct method."

Education should take its cue from this point of view. Its aim should be to facilitate such short-circuited growth, to liberate the young from reviewing, and retraversing, and dwelling in, an outgrown past. The educational advantage of immaturity is that it makes this possible. The young live in an environment of civilized men; to ignore its directive influence is to abdicate educationally.

Now concerning the use and misuse of heredity. It is a misuse of heredity to assume that past life has predetermined the main traits of an individual, or that these traits are practically unalterable, or that heredity and environment are opposed in influence, or that environment is inefficacious. The right use of heredity recognizes the basic fact that the individual has a given equipment of native tendencies, however produced or derived; that these tendencies are the capital of the educator; that he cannot work with what is not there; that a study of these native aptitudes and deficiencies is a preliminary necessity; that inherited deficiencies constitute a limit to education; but especially that heredity does not predetermine the future uses of one's original endowment. The fact that some property is an inheritance does not predetermine its future use; the problem is to make the best use of it. The educator can not use what the educand lacks, but he can use to different ends what the educand has. It is wasteful and irritating to try to make something out of an individual which he is not naturally fitted to become. But, except in the case of the imbecile, and even in the case of the stupid, the inherited capacities are more varied and more potential than we as yet know how to utilize properly. The first step is to know the inheritance, the subsequent—and important—step is to furnish the environment that will put it to work in the best way.

The relations of heredity and environment in the educability of the individual may be illustrated by spoken language. By heredity one has vocal organs, auditory sense-receptors, and connections between the two. Without this outfit, no conversation is possible. But one may have the complete outfit and still be unable to converse, if brought up in a dumb environment, or able to converse in one language only, if he has heard only one. Heredity determines that he may speak, but not that he shall speak or what he shall say. The heritage from the past is thus usable in, but not determinative of, the present.

(2) Making the records and remains of the past the main materials of education is a mistake. That this is true specifically in the case of the recapitulation of past culture-epochs supposed to correspond with the stage of development of those taught, we have just seen. It is also true generically. The products of the past are not the main materials of study. For a number of reasons the view that they are is indefensible; it divorces the products of past growth from the process of present growth; a study limited to past products will not help us understand the present; cutting the vital connection of present and past, it tends to make the past the glorious rival of the present, and the present a futile imitation of the past; it makes culture an ornament, a solace, a refuge, an asylum, an escape mechanism from the crudities of the present; having turned its back on the present for the past, it has no way left of bringing home to the present the spoils of the past.

All this is not to reject the study of the past, a knowledge of whose heritage is of great significance when, if, and as, it enters into the present. The function of educational subject matter is to keep the educational process alive, and in ways which make it easier to keep it alive in the future. But it is only in the present that we can really live. The present is what life is in leaving the past behind, it is more than a temporal sequence, more than a product of the past. What the past offers is to be used to ripen the crudities of the present. So used, the past is a source of suggestion to solve the present problem, a resource of the imagination, adding a new dimension to life. It is the present which generates the problems, which sends us searching the past for solutions, and which supplies meaning to what we find. Minimize present living and growing, and your future goal becomes remote and empty, and you turn for comfort to the imagined refinements of the past. Be adequately sensitive to the needs and occasions of the present, and you will have the liveliest interest in its development. The past as another and disconnected world is little; as the past *of* the present it is one mode of directing movement.

Comment. The war of opinion between the biological hereditarian and the sociological environmentalist goes steadily, not merrily, on. The two things now seem fairly clear, viz., first, that the environment affects the heredity itself and thus the two forces are not competitive but coöperative, as Dr. Dewey suggests, and the second, that our heredity contributes more to our making than does our environment. A recent scientific study of the question concludes: "Neither the extreme hereditist nor the extreme environmentalist is correct; but the contribution of heredity is several times as important as that of environment.

"Heredity and environment vary in their relative importance in relation to specific or general traits. From the data it was seen that heredity was about five times as significant as environment in determining I.Q. differences between twins, while for weight heredity was only about twice as potent in its causal effectiveness as environment. Emotional qualities were not quantitatively tested, but it is probable that in respect to these qualities heredity would be found to be from two to five times as potent as environment."[1]

Concerning Dr. Dewey's view that the culture which consists in a knowledge of the past apart from some present problem is only an unwarranted refuge, opinions will differ. Knowledge of any kind may be a good on its own account. The fact that some individuals are interested in acquiring impractical knowledge and enjoy the possession of it may be an adequate justification for it. Yet in either case no present problem is being solved by such knowledge, unless "the problem" be one of complete living or finding intellectual satisfaction. And if this is the problem, there can be no such thing as a disconnected past. The issue is squarely joined on the pragmatic principle of instrumentalism, viz., that knowledge is only a tool, without being a self-justifying end in itself.[2] For example, consider the following words of Amiel, the introspective professor of Geneva: "Moreover, to know satisfies me, perhaps even better than to possess, to enjoy, to act. My strongest taste is for watching, understanding, contemplating. And the theory needs to be universal, panoramic, spherical; it refuses to be shut up in a special case."[3] Shall we say that such knowledge to Amiel was not of value? It is possible that pragmatism is not broadly practical enough in limiting culture to use in problem-solving. In speaking of the cultural, especially the literary products of man's history, Dr. Dewey writes: "Their value lies in their use to increase the meaning of the things with which we have actively to do at the present time" (p. 93). Shall we add: "and in satisfying man's natural desire to know?" Palmer's rhythmic prose translation of Homer's *Odyssey* hardly increases "the meaning of the things with which we have actively to do at the present time," but for some persons it is a pure joy to read. Ex-

[1] Hirsch, N. D. M., *Twins: Heredity and Environment,* Harvard University Press, 1930.

[2] Cf. Powys, J. C., *The Meaning of Culture.* Martin, E. D., *The Meaning of a Liberal Education.*

[3] Philine, tr. *Van Wyck Brooks,* Houghton Mifflin Company, 1930.

perience would be immeasurably poorer if all knowledge had to be used in facing a present issue instead of simply enjoyed for its own sake.

There is still another way of justifying man's study of the past; not for its practical utility, nor yet for the satisfaction of knowing, but for the development it affords the self of man. It is the Hegelian educational doctrine of *Selbst-Entfremdung.* By going far afield, the self leaves its limited quarters behind, becomes at home in the big foreign world, finds itself there too, and then returns a larger self to its native place. Only by estranging oneself from one's little self can one find one's larger self. By compassing the past one may better realize oneself. Such personal idealism is in striking contrast with pragmatism. Which is the larger and truer view?

3. Education as Reconstruction

Exposition. We now come to the most famous section in the book. It is the conception of education most widely accepted and heralded by the disciples of Dr. Dewey. It is marked off from all the rejected conceptions, viz., education as preparation, as unfolding, as formal discipline, as external formation, and as recapitulation. The accepted conception is that education is the continuous reconstruction of experience. It is the result of the ideal of growth. The end of education is the direct transformation of the quality of experience, and this end is always immediate. Living is to enrich its own perceptible meaning. This is its chief business. Age makes no difference to this end, whether infancy, youth, or maturity; the learnings then and there are the values.

How is the meaning of an experience increased? By perceiving more of its connections and consequences. Our experience consists of the activities in which we are engaged. Of some of the connections of these activities we are aware; of others we are unaware. And experience is educative, *i.e.,* its meaning is increased, when we become more aware of that of which we were unaware, when the unperceived connections become perceived. The activities of the young begin impulsively, they are blind, they do not know what they are about, they do not know their interactions with other activities. The process of becoming aware of these interconnections of experienced activities is education.

For example, the child and the candle, or the scientist in his laboratory. The child does not begin by knowing that the attractive candle flame is hot and will burn. He reaches and learns. Henceforth he has knowledge. The activity of reaching for the flame has gained meaning. To that extent he has become educated. The scientist before his flame in the laboratory is still a child, and only a child, in his method of learning. He too does certain things, thereby making perceptible certain connections between heat and other things, of which previously he may have been ignorant. So there results knowledge of combustion, oxidation, light, and temperature. The flame has acquired more meaning, more intellectual content. And note, having learned, he can now *intend* consequences instead of just letting them happen.

So the increased perception of meaning leads on to better control. Having learned connections, one can better anticipate them, getting ready for beneficial consequences, preferring to omit undesirable ones.

This is the essential conception of education which may now be summed up in a technical definition as follows: Education *"is that reconstruction or reorganization of experience which adds to the meaning of experience, and which increases ability to direct the course of subsequent experience" (pp. 89–90,* italics ours). The words reconstruction or reorganization are defined by the ideas of increasing the present meaning of, and directing the subsequent course of, experience. Nothing additional is meant.

Now this fruitful reorganization of experience is both personal and social. As personal it transforms the individual;

as social it transforms society. These two are phases of one and the same process, though discussed separately.

A genuinely educative activity for the individual is neither a capricious activity, nor yet a routine activity. Making fine distinctions we may say that caprice is *dis*continuous activity; routine is contin*ued* activity; while education is continu*ous* activity.

To explain, beginning with caprice. In capricious or aimless and random activity, one does not care what happens; he lets himself go, he neglects connections, he avoids associating the consequences of his act with the act itself. While great activity is customarily frowned upon as willful mischief or carelessness or lawlessness, its true source is not recognized and the true remedy not supplied. Its true source is maladjustment with surroundings and its true remedy is having a purpose of one's own, being led to see the connection between one deed and another, having the answer connected with the method used to reach it. It is a mistake to trace caprice to the isolated disposition of the youth. Look for it rather in that maladjustment coming from external dictation, or being told, or from the failure to connect results with processes, as though the whole thing to the pupil were a trick or kind of miracle. Children are not born capricious; they are made so.

Routine, automatic activity, is better than caprice. It at least increases skill to do a particular thing up to a certain point. So far it is educative. But its weakness is that it does not lead to perceptions of new bearings and connections; and so it limits rather than widens the horizon of meanings. And worse yet, it becomes disastrous at some critical moment when in our changing environment a new issue is faced. A uniform way of acting can not maintain a balanced connection with our changing world.

Turning to the idea of education as the transforming of society, we note that a capricious activity suits no society, that a routine activity suits in a way static society, and that a continuous or educative activity fits a progressive society. Static societies make the maintenance of established custom their measure of value. They fill the immature with the spirit of the social group. Education here is a sort of catching up of the child with the aptitudes and resources of the social group. We have ourselves spoken in this vein in our earlier chapters. This was intended only as a simplified, not a complete conception of education. We do not now reject it entirely but supplement it. Progressive or dynamic communities endeavor to make the future adult society an improvement on their own. Thus, they shape the experiences of the young not to reproduce current habits but to form better habits. It is not a new idea that the education of the young may be consciously used to eliminate social evils and to realize the better hopes of man. But we are doubtless even yet far from realizing the potential efficacy of education as a constructive agency for improving society. Progressive education in developing children and youth may also develop the future society of which they will be the constituents.

What a contrast between this idea of education as the continuous reconstruction of experience and the one-sided ones previously criticised! There the process and the end were different, here they are identical. There it was present preparation for a remote future, or present unfolding in accord with an absolute goal, present discipline for future use, or present formation in accord with an external pattern, or present recapitulation in accord with a remote biological or cultural past. Here present, continuous, reconstructive, *i.e.*, educative, experience is its own end. All education resides in having such experience. Such experience indeed occupies time, but its later period only completes its earlier, bringing to light connections involved but hitherto unperceived, and so revealing its meaning. The experience as a whole establishes a bent in disposition toward the things possessing the revealed meaning. The process is all and it is a process of growth in the perception of the meaning of experience of the interconnections of the activities taking place between the organism and its environment.

Comment. Here we meet the range of Dr. Dewey's educational philosophy, with its limits. There is no doubt of its penetrating and suggestive and valuable qualities. Its weakness is not so much in what it says as in what it omits. We will confine ourselves briefly to some salient observations.

(1) In the reconstruction of experience which is both personal and social, the existence of a self is implied but not stated. The self is the subjective side of the experience, the environment is the objective side. The self has the experience. The self is aware of the meaning of the experience. The growth in the meaning of experience involves a growth in the self of man. The self is the conscious centre of experience which feels values, evaluates, and consciously responds. It is an emotional, judgmental, and ethical self. Being the centre of experience the greatest human value attaches to the self. The conception of experience without the self is impersonal. In the reconstruction of experience it is really the self that is being reconstructed, the self in relation to other selves and the intervening physical world. Thus a more comprehensive conception of education would seem to be that it is the cultivation of personalities in relation to each other and their world. Introducing the concept of the self allows certain additional considerations to come into our philosophy of education.

(2) The implication of the discussion is that while the active adaptation to a dynamic environment is accepted, the passive adaptation to a static environment is rejected, unless it be admitted as a temporary historical expedient in backward societies. Now it is possible that static elements help control even dynamic societies, as the bed and the bank of the stream direct its flow. Thus, among the static elements in a dynamic society may be mentioned the constant and unchanging need for thoughtfulness, just regard for the rights of others, unselfishness, the recognition of fact as fact, and the making of

progress through experimentation. That is, certain principles are changeless even in a changing world. Toward these education may very well take a passive, an absorptive attitude, which indeed, in turn, will modify the active conduct and character. That is, the experiences of the self and of the world experienced may very well contain both static and dynamic elements. For this synthetic view we may, following Hegel, very well use the term "organic." Man's adjustment to his world should be not simply dynamic, but organic, embracing both the static and the dynamic.

(3) The emphasis in the discussion on perception and activities, and the illustrations given, show that the reconstruction contemplated is primarily intellectual and practical, not emotional and æsthetic. The logical reason for this probably is that the æsthetic experience is not primarily practical; it is primarily joy in an experience for its own sake, intrinsic not instrumental. The pragmatic theory is primarily practical. But the worth of beauty and the value of its pure enjoyment demand a place for it in man's educative experience. In a later connection (Chapter XVIII) we shall see that Dr. Dewey recognizes the intrinsic value of certain experiences, without, however, harmonizing such recognition with his pragmatism. Similarly, in his "Quest for Certainty" the "consummatory" experiences are not a part of instrumentalism.

(4) The result and the process of the educative experience are held to be identical. This is, if not self-contradictory, both somewhat vague and incomplete. It is vague because the configuration of fact and the corresponding pattern of our language distinguish between process and product, purpose and result, means and end. True, Emerson can write:

> Till the traveler and the road become one
> With the errand to be done.

But this is commonly thought of as mythical pantheism, at the utmost remove from the practicality of pragmatism. In contrast with the identification of process and result, it might very well be that some perfect life once lived, or conceived as having lived, or some ideal of a perfect life to come, personal and social, might very well be the goal or the conceived end of a process now used as means. This would not detract from the reality of the process but it would give it ultimate direction. Without some such conceived end, the conception of result-process remains vague, and its guidance is difficult.

And also, the conception that the process is identical with the product is incomplete. It assumes that the process is all the reality there is, and that all reality is temporal in character. These are large assumptions indeed and run counter to much good philosophical thinking, both of other days and of to-day.[1] Are the principles of the process also in process? Eddington says that Einstein does not deny absolutes; he only affirms they are harder to find than had been thought.[2] All-devouring space, not time, would seem to be one of them. Mathematics has its unchanging limits as well as its changing curves. Plato has his unchanging concepts as well as his changing sensations. We ourselves have an unchanging centre of reference in ourselves; in a sense, though changing, we remain the same. Now the recognition of this non-temporal or eternal aspect of experience makes it impossible for us to regard the process, even when including its own product, as the sum of reality. And our education, to be complete, must consequently adjust us to the whole of reality of which we are a part. Our education would then be viewed as progress in the consciousness of our relation to the whole of reality of which the process is indisputably a part. Our definition might run: *Education is the increasing realization of the temporal and eternal values of life.*

[1] Cf. Whitehead, A. N., *Process and Reality.*
[2] Cf. Eddington, A. S., *The Nature of the Physical World.*

PART II

DEMOCRACY IN EDUCATION

CHAPTER VII

THE DEMOCRATIC CONCEPTION IN EDUCATION

Hitherto we have been concerned, for the most part, with education as it may exist in any social group. But there are different kinds of social groups; some aim to perpetuate their own customs; others aim to change for the better. Education differs according to the type of group in which it operates. These differences concern the spirit, material, and method of education. Ours is a social group with the ideal of change. What educational practice is suitable for it? This is our next question.

1. The Implications of Human Association

Exposition. There are several, viz., we do not have "society" and "community," but "societies" and "communities"; the connotation of the term society is better than its denotation; there are two criteria of the value of group life,—the sharing of interests within the group and between the groups; and the relative failure of any group life that lacks internal and external reciprocity of interest. Of each of these ideas a brief exposition will be given.

We have society in name and societies in fact. Of every large social unit there are many lesser units,—political, industrial, scientific, religious. There are political parties, social sets, cliques, gangs, corporations, partnerships, kinship groups. In many states there are diverse populations, languages, religions, moral codes, and traditions.

Meantime the terms "society" and "community" *connote* unity, a sharing of purpose and welfare, loyalty to public ends, and mutuality of sympathy. But they *denote* the bad as well as the good—criminality, business exploitations, grafting politics. Each of these bad types of society yet has enough of the praiseworthy qualities of "society" to hold it together,—"honor among thieves." Thus the terms "society" and "community" are ambiguous; on the one hand they are eulogistic, *de jure*, and on the other hand they are reprehensible, descriptive, *de facto*. Any group will socialize its members, and socialization is education, but the value of the socialization depends on the habits and aims of the group.

How then shall we measure the worth of any given mode of social life? By two criteria or standards,—the sharing of interests within the group and coöperative intercourse with other groups. These criteria are found by extracting the desirable traits of existing communities. They may then be used to criticize the undersirable traits and to suggest improvements. Tried by these tests a criminal band fails and the right kind of family life succeeds. The criminal band is held together within mainly by a common interest in plunder, and is isolated without from other groups. The right kind of family life shares material, intellectual, æsthetic, and personal interests within and coöperates with business, school, cultural, and political organizations without. The education given by a band of criminals is partial and distorted; that given by the right sort of family is broad and balanced.

Let us apply the first criterion, that of reciprocity of interest within the group, to a despotically governed state. By contrast it will help us to realize the desirable type of society. For such a government it may be said that there is some common interest between the governors and the governed. The bond of union is not merely one of coercive force, as Talleyrand recognized in his saying that a government could do everything with bayonets except sit on them. The real difficulty with such a government is not simply that it appeals to the sense of fear and the hope of reward, but that these motives are isolated from other capacities. These latter cease to operate on their own account and become the mere servants of attaining pleasure and avoiding pain. Lacking an extensive number of common interests, the governors become masters and the governed become slaves. Such a separation into a privileged and underprivileged class prevents social unification.

Among the evils affecting the superior class are a sterile culture, a showy and artificial display of art, luxurious wealth, over-specialized knowledge, fastidious manners, unbalanced intellectual stimulus, and explosive action. Among the evils affecting the lower class are likewise the lessening of the meaning of experience, the tendency for action to become routine, the acceptance of controlling purposes from others, the lack of understanding of, and interest in, their own socially serviceable activities.

Plato defined a slave as one who accepts from another the purposes controlling his conduct. This condition may obtain where there is no slavery in the legal sense, as in modern industrial societies. Even our own alleged "scientific management" may contribute to it. Too often it is restricted to movement of the muscles, forgetting the man and his fellow-workers, who should see the technical, intellectual, and social relationships involved in what they do. Only so can the division of labor demanded by efficiency in production be saved from a mechanical routine. When industrial workers do not understand what they are doing, and industrial captains do not attend to the human factors in industry, there results for each class an absence of mind and a corresponding distortion of the emotions. Intelligence may have become acute in the production and marketing of goods, but is blunted in its perception of human relationships. Such is despotism, in politics or in industry, within a group.

Turning now to our second criterion, that of inter-group reciprocity of interest, the lack of it is deadening, its presence is vitalizing. Isolation of one group from another makes for the rigid and formal institutionalizing of life, for static and selfish ideals. To the savage, lacking group intercourse, devoted to his own customs, the alien and the enemy are naturally synonymous. The exclusiveness of gang or clique breeds its anti-social spirit. In the same way we may have isolated families, schools, economic classes, learned classes, even nations. In contrast, reorganization and progress come through wider relationships between groups. Foreign contacts reconstruct custom. An alert and expanding mental life depends on enlarging our contacts with nature, and even more with man. Erect barriers, hem off classes and peoples from each other, and you get contraction; demolish barriers, make connections between classes and peoples, and you get expansion. So it has ever been in human history. Even in war we seek an enemy and find a man. Travel, commerce, and the native arts of rapid communication, have done much to connect classes and peoples; it remains, however, to secure the full intellectual and emotional significance of this physical annihilation of space.

Comment. This section gives us the heart of Dr. Dewey. It is his message, this sharing of common interests. He does not insist on all classes becoming one class. He does insist on each class having a community of interests, and all classes having reciprocity of interests. Just how much the emphasis does mean to him appears from his own address at the celebration of his seventieth birthday, in the course of which he said: ". . . there is nothing so important in life as the free unobstructed communication of ideas and experiences and their transmission from one to another, without any kind of restriction, censorship, or intimidation—legal, political, or extra-legal . . . the most inexpensive, the most easily attained source of happiness, is found simply in this broadening of intellectual curiosity and sympathy in all the concerns of life."[1]

The practical application of this to education he suggests: education is socialization, and its value is the same as that of

[1] John Dewey, *The Man and His Philosophy*, Harvard University Press, 1920, pp. 176, 179.

the group which does the socializing, and the highest values reside in the most completely socialized group, within and without. He also suggests its application to political and economic groups. But he leaves us to make our own applications to our race questions, our tariff problems, the League of Nations, the World Court, and the problems of disarmament.

The striking and characteristic thing here is that human associations, while implying sub-human contacts with nature, do not imply superhuman contacts of any kind. The beloved community is composed of only human beings. A completely humanized, socialized, experience is all. Any trans-empirical element within social experience is not recognized; yet I acknowledge you whom I have not fully experienced. Any suggestion as to how animals could become men and men could become human is withheld. Here is a negative and a contractive element in this finely humanistic philosophy. It has left us one barrier between man and his world,—the forbidding barrier of non-communion and non-sharing with reality as a whole. The whole of reality is not socialized as human experience is. The thought stops short. Its own dynamic of a socialized experience might easily push it still forward to completion till man recognized his conscious unity with the All. Thus, the paradox remains of a humanism not fully human, of a pragmatism not completely practical.

2. The Democratic Ideal

Exposition. We come now to the concept which gives part of the title to the whole book. Its fundamental importance is evident. The term "democracy" is used to name the society which meets the implications of the two criteria of greatest social worth just described, viz., full sharing of interests within the group, and free interaction between groups. The one means that the recognition of mutual interests within groups is a factor in social control; the other, that free interaction between groups induces changes in social habit, continuous readjustments through meeting new situations. These two consequences of the two criteria, viz., control based on mutual interests and change based on social interactions, are precisely the characteristics of a democratized society. This is the democratic ideal. "A democracy is more than a form of government; it is primarily a mode of associated living, of conjoint communicated experience."

Democracy is not produced by deliberate effort but is sustained and extended by it. The sharing of wider interests and the freeing of personal capacities which characterize a democracy are produced by science and industry. Science commands natural energy and industry applies science. Thus arise manufacturing, commerce, travel, migration, and intercommunication. Thus too, arise a broader community of interest and greater individualization. Stratification of classes would be fatal to a democracy. To prevent this and to continue the democratic results of science applied to industry, intellectual opportunities must be kept accessible to all on equable and easy terms. This is the work of education. The members of a changing democratic society require personal initiative and adaptability, lest they be overwhelmed by changes they can neither control nor understand. Without such equipment on the part of all, the few will appropriate the laborious results of the many. A democratic society must educate all, a stratified society needs to educate only its ruling class.

Thus democracies are more interested in deliberate and systematic education than other communities have cause to be. Of this there is a superficial explanation, affecting government, and there is a deeper explanation, affecting the structure of society. A democratic government repudiates the principle of external authority and rests upon popular suffrage. Those who elect and follow must do so voluntarily and through interest. This means education. But the sharing of interests within groups and between groups means the breaking down of barriers between classes, races, and nations, the elimination of stratification and isolation. This, too, is the work of education. Thus without education the democratic ideal can not be realized. Our subsequent chapters in this part of the whole will be devoted to making explicit the educational ideas implicit in democracy.

Comment. There are at least three kinds of democracy—political, industrial, and social. These are doubtless implied but not clearly distinguished in the text. By political democracy is meant government by "consent of the governed"; in Lincoln's famous phrase, "government of the people, by the people, and for the people." In a representative democracy, such as ours, the people themselves elect their representatives who make and execute the laws.

In an industrial democracy employers and employees share their financial interests. It is somewhat surprising to find that our text traces the origin of democracy to industry (p. 101), despite not finding democracy in industry (p. 98). Perhaps the origin of democracy is to be sought elsewhere than in industry.

In a social democracy different classes have interchanges of thought and action which forward the development of all and hinder the development of none.

Concerning political democracy it should perhaps be emphasized that, as understood today, it involves not merely the consent of the governed but the common participation of the governed, a participation based on a common understanding reached by discussion, and carrying the sense of a common responsibility.[1]

While the discussion recognizes by implication the forms of democracy and the lack of their attainment, perhaps it does not specifically and adequately state the obstacles in the way. Recent critics of democracy, like Walter Lippmann, G. B. Shaw, Irving Babbitt, Emile Faguet, and others, have

[1] Cf. Lindsay, A. D., *The Essentials of Democracy*, University of Pennsylvania Press, 1930. Burns, C. D., *Democracy, Its Defects and Advantages*, The Macmillan Company, 1930.

not failed to do this. Some of these obstacles are the indifference of the voter, the unreliability of the press, the power of propaganda, the inability of the school alone to solve all problems, and self-seeking politicians. It is only education in the broad sense of the socializing influence of all the groupings of man that can begin to cope with these obstacles.

The essential content of democracy is said to be the sharing of interests within groups and between groups, leading to social control based on mutual interest and to progressive change. This may very well be done under forms of political government not called democracies, *e.g.,* England. And it may not be well done in forms of political government called republics. Democracy is thus essentially a spirit, or an attitude, the spirit of understanding, sympathy, and coöperation within social classes and between social classes.

It is possible the very term "democracy" may not be the best by which to name this ideal. Perhaps the ideal is that of humanity and the term should be "Humanism," or, as one of my students once said, "the interdependent living of independent lives." As, in the course of the past changes in human society, primitive savagery became barbarism, and barbarism became civilization, so may civilization become humanism. This term is used here in a social, not philosophical or religious, sense.

This spirit, whether called democratic or humanistic, will show itself in all departments of life,—the political, the social, and the industrial. The name is not so important, it is the thing itself that counts.

There are many indications that the spirit of sharing is lacking in America. We have divisions between economic classes, between races, between religions. We have surviving savagery and barbarism. As between nations, we are often passive spectators instead of active participators. We do not think, feel, or act altogether jointly, or neighborly, with the nations of the world. There is much for education to do.

The ideal of sharing interests does not necessitate racial amalgamation. This is a fatuous rendering of humanism. Neither does it involve all persons being members of one class, the workers or any other. This is a tragic overdoing of the principle of social unity. Democracy is quite consistent with many classes, many groupings, much variety. If we were all equally ignorant, we should not be equal.

And the ideal means sharing between nations, leading to international understandings, sympathy, and joint effort. The nationalistic state as master would go, as servant it could remain. Art, science, and commerce are international.

A democratized society is similar to but not identical with the religious conception of the Kingdom of Heaven on earth. In content the two are similar; in inspiration and motive they are different. The inspiration to the one is human, to the other is divine. The motive to the one is humanitarian, to the other is theistic. The central conception of the one is man, of the other is God. In the one we have brotherhood without universal fatherhood; in the other we have brotherhood because of fatherhood. Man alone, social man, is the maker of democracy, man as an agent of the spiritual principle of the universe is the maker of the other. Democracy is a grand ideal. It lacks and, in the judgment of many, it needs the dynamic of a belief in God who works with man.

3. The Platonic Educational Philosophy

Exposition. The ideal of a democratized society and the function of education therein will be understood better by reviewing some past conceptions. We select three, viz., the Platonic, eighteenth century individualism, and nineteenth century institutional idealism. These three epochs were like our own in one respect,—the social import of education is conspicuous in each.

In dealing with the educational philosophy of Plato, the following matters will concern us: his system, its strength, and its weakness.

(1) The starting point of his system is that the proper organization of society, which he called "justice," depends upon the knowledge of the aim or end of existence, viz., the "good." Lacking such knowledge, man is at the mercy of accident or caprice, has no criterion for deciding rationally between desirable possibilities, and can not properly distribute personal and social activities.

But how is this necessary knowledge of the final and permanent good to be attained? Such knowledge is possible only in a just and harmonious social order. Outside of such a republic in a disorganized and factional society, the mind can not attain a true knowledge, it is distracted by false valuations, it can not attain self-consistency, it is confused by different models and standards. In a just state, the patterns furnished by institutions, customs, and laws are right. The place of the individual in a just society is determined not by birth or wealth or convention, but by his own nature as discovered in the process of education. There are only three types of faculties or powers in the individual's constitution, leading to three corresponding classes of citizens in the state. Thus, (*a*) men whose appetite dominates become laborers and traders, supplying human wants; (*b*) men of courage become the external defenders of the state in war and its internal guardians in peace; (*c*) men of reason, with a capacity to grasp the universal, become the legislators, the rulers of the state. Thus there are three types of individuals and three types of social classes, each with its assigned social function.

Education of this ideal state has as its function the discovery of talent and its training for social use. It proceeds from the right patterns of a just state, based on the knowledge of the unchangeable good. It is the means of maintaining the order and the unity of the whole. Correct education can not initiate the ideal state but it can conserve it once it exists. Such, very briefly, is Plato's educational philosophy.

(2) In appreciation of its strength let us note at once that no one could express better than Plato has done the fact that

society is stably organized only when each individual is performing a function of use to others in accord with his own natural aptitude; that it is the business of education to discover these aptitudes and progressively train them for social use; that the social arrangements have primary educational significance, and that the maintenance of those arrangements depend on the education of the young. In fact, much of what we have ourselves said so far "is borrowed from what Plato first consciously taught the world."

Having briefly characterized and appreciated this great ancient system of educational philosophy, it is now incumbent upon us to point out its weaknesses as we see them.

(3) First, it will be noted that we can not have the ideal state and the proper education without true knowledge, and at the same time we can not have true knowledge without the ideal state and correct education. The circle seems small and hopeless. Plato saw this difficulty, but could extricate himself from it only by the weak suggestion of some happy accident whereby philosophic wisdom and rulership might at some time coincide. If a wise and powerful ruler, having learned even in outline the patterns of true existence, should form a state accordingly, it could then be preserved. The root of this difficulty is that Plato lacked the conception of social progress. Though his educational philosophy is revolutionary, it was none the less in bondage to static ideals. Having made one great social change, he would abolish change. This was because on the one hand he saw that society was unideal, and on the other he held that true reality is unchangeable and that the end of life is fixed. By a *tour de force* society was to be made ideal and then by education kept so. His philosophy breaks down; he could not bring himself to trust a gradually improved education to improve society and a gradually improved society to improve education, and so on indefinitely.

Second, Plato did not know his individual. He had no perception of the uniqueness of the individual, of his incommensurability with others, no recognition that each individual constitutes his own class, no consequent recognition of the definite diversity of the active tendencies of individuals and their combinations. Original capacities are indefinitely numerous and variable. Instead, he gives us only three types of individuals!

Third, in consequence of this lack of recognition of the individuality of individuals, he allowed too few social classes,—likewise three. He missed the indefinite plurality of activities in which a social group may engage. As the classes of individual capacity are limited to three, so the classes of society are limited to three,—the artisan, the soldier, and the ruler. A greater social diversification would have allowed society to change and yet be stable.

Fourth, the net effect of the two preceding weaknesses was the subordination of individuality and the stratification into classes. Plato did not intend to subordinate the individual to the social whole. Lacking the benefits of modern knowledge, he was faced by conditions which he could not intellectually control. So his admirable ideas concerning the discovery and training for social uses of individual natural aptitudes were restricted in their application. Speaking in terms of democracy, Plato's social organization, through no intent but through lack of knowledge on his part, did not utilize the specific and variable qualities of individuals. He made a class, after all, rather than the individual, the social unit. And he made no provision for progressive social change. In such a state education would soon reach a static limit in each class. The wheels go round, but not merrily.

Comment. Speaking further of Plato from the standpoint of democracy, it might have been pointed out that his Republic is an autocratic aristocracy whose ruling class was not elected by the people but self-perpetuating on the basis of natural gifts discovered and trained by education. Furthermore, the laws were not made by the people or their representatives, but by the ruling class. It was a government of the people and for the people, but not by the people.

Also, having in mind the criterion of free interaction between groups, be it said that Plato's Republic had a warlike attitude toward neighboring states. To fight was nobler than to work, as to think and rule was nobler than to fight.

Also, there was no recognition that education for work might be as extensive as that for soldiering or ruling, though different. The virtue of the worker, appropriate to his appetitive nature, was temperance and his skill was acquired by the apprenticeship method.

Thus, on several counts, Plato does not meet the criteria of democracy. However, it should be pointed out that the conception of progress, which he lacked, is not necessarily inconsistent with the idea of an unchangeable good. He lacked the conception of progress for social, not philosophical, reasons. The social history he knew reported the stability of states which he admired, or their decline, which he deplored. But social progress may be made gradually, even in zigzag fashion, toward a goal that is fixed, "eternal in the heavens." Even democracy as the complete sharing of intra-group and inter-group interests, with consequent inherent social control and outward progressive change, may be regarded as a Platonic "idea," eternal in nature, never fully realized or realizable on earth, and yet the goal of an unending progress toward it. Very likely it is just such a thing. In such a case we have an educational philosophy, which is like Plato's in maintaining the fixed and permanent ideal as the goal, and like Dr. Dewey's in maintaining the need for constant and progressive social change, which is unlike Plato in admitting change as necessary, and unlike Dr. Dewey in maintaining the unchangeable character of true reality. This is the synthetic conception which combines the static and the dynamic in what we have called the organic. The sun too bright for us to see is that by which all things are seen.

4. The "Individualistic" Ideal of the Eighteenth Century

Exposition. In presenting this subject we shall deal with the concepts of nature, society, humanity, and education.

It is a far cry from Plato to Rousseau. Still Plato greatly influenced Rousseau, and "nature" still means the antithesis of existing society. But unlike Plato, "nature" now speaks for the diversity of individual talent and the need for its free development. The native environment of man was conceived in extreme cases as non-social or even as anti-social. Faith in nature as both a model and a working power was unrestrained. This faith was strengthened by the advances of natural science. The world was revealed by Newton as a scene of law, of wonderful harmony, where every force balanced with every other. Inquiry freed from prejudice and the artificial restraints of church and state had brought this new natural revelation. Natural law, if freely followed, could accomplish the same results in human relations. There was great enthusiasm for the new freedom of nature.

Society suffered by contrast, especially as it then existed. Social arrangements were thought of as external expedients whereby naturally non-social individuals might secure a greater amount of private happiness for themselves. In existing political organizations it seemed that man's powers were hampered to meet the selfish interests of the rulers. Social evils were held to be due to the corrupting limitations imposed upon man's free powers. The cause of emancipation from man's feudalistic restrictions led to an intellectual worship of nature. An artificial, corrupt, and inequitable social order was to be replaced by a full return to nature. The diagnosis was better than the prescription.

And what would be the result? Here the thought oscillates between the better citizen and the better man, with the latter the favorite. If Rousseau could have had the kind of citizen he wanted, he would probably have taken him. Many saying of his point to the formation of the citizen as ideally the higher. He opposed existing society as forming neither the citizen nor the man. Under those conditions he preferred to try for the latter. It may well be that his endeavor, as embodied in the *Emile,* was simply the best makeshift the conception of the times permitted. In choosing to form a man, he turned to nature. In giving it full swing, a new and better kingdom of humanity would arise. There would be social progress, a wider and freer society, cosmopolitanism. The individual, emancipated from distorting social requirements, would be the organ for a progressive society. The positive ideal was humanity, not the state. Membership in humanity would liberate man's capacities. The anti-social philosophy was a mask of world-citizenship. Extreme individualism was the obverse of a new society as broad as humanity and of man's indefinite perfectibility. It was a gospel heralded with impassioned devotion. But it was visionary!

What part was education to play? An education according to nature was thought to be the first step in securing this more social society. It was to remove limitations of thought and feeling; the internal chains of false beliefs and ideals were to be struck off. Emancipation from the external chains of economic and political limitations would follow in consequence. Again was education trusted to reconstitute society. Such an emancipating education could be intrusted only to "Nature" which was free, not to a society whose institutions were already false and corrupt. To turn such liberating education over to society would be asking society to do the incredible thing of committing self-destruction. No, it must be an education not according to society but according to nature. The goal, the subject-matter, the method of instruction, the method of discipline,—all come from nature. There were no limits to the possibilities of education by means of the natural environment. The view was even held that the mind itself was originally passive, empty, a wax tablet, to be written upon by natural objects. This was the extreme "sensationalistic theory of knowledge" current at the time. The possibilities of education were thus glorified. The natural world of objects was held to be a scene of harmonious truth; so an education dependent on it alone would infallibly produce minds filled with the truth.

So simple, so doctrinaire, so fatuous! The enthusiasm for freedom waned, it became obvious that the theory was weak on its constructive side. To leave everything to nature was to trust to the accidents of circumstances; this is the negation of the very idea of education. Two constructive factors had been omitted, a method of instruction and some positive administrative agency for carrying it on. It was all right for private individuals to proclaim the gospel of "the complete and harmonious development of all the powers" of the mind, and as its counterpart an enlightened and progressive humanity. But they could not execute the plan; for this a definite organization was required. Pestalozzi was one such herald; he experimented; he exhorted philanthropists to follow his example. But even Pestalozzi, impractical as he was, saw that the new education, destined to produce a new society, was dependent on the state, as an institution of present society. The movement for democracy inevitably entered upon a new stage; it became a movement for schools conducted and administered by the public. So arose nationalism in education.

Comment. Dr. Dewey might very well have applied to Rousseau's social and educational theories the two criteria of an ideal human society, viz., the sharing of intra-group relations leading to control based on mutual interests, and the sharing of inter-group relations leading to progressive social change. Rousseau practically had no group. There was an orphan pupil and a whole-time tutor, and there was humanity. The former group is too small; the latter group is too abstract. Under these conditions education as life-sharing could not go on. The early years of life were necessarily spent in preparation for a society that did not exist. Rousseau's theories do not pass the democratic tests, with all his love of freedom and the individual. His freedom was a freedom *from* not *in*, society, and his individual was apart from, not a part of, society.

The suggestion of Dr. Dewey (footnote, p. 109) that there is a neglected strain in Rousseau favoring the citizen rather than the man is valuable and worthy of special investigation. In this vein he wrote an educational program for the state of Poland. Those interested in following up this clue are referred to the writings of that careful Scotch student of Rousseau, W. Boyd.

5. Education as National and as Social

Exposition. In this section we will show how eighteenth century individualism and cosmopolitanism were illustrated in Germany by Immanuel Kant; how these views passed into the nationalism of Fichte and Hegel; what we may learn from this historical survey of Plato, Rousseau, and Hegel; how nationalism and social, or international, interests are in conflict to-day; and what education can do to solve this conflict.

Kant continued some of the educational views of his elder and revolutionary contemporary, Rousseau. Kant was an individualistic cosmopolitan, a humanitarian, and a sympathizer with the cause of the American Revolution. His views stand in sharp contrast with the nationalism that later developed in Germany, due to its struggle against Napoleon for national independence. Kant lectured on Pedagogy during the later years of the eighteenth century. Among the many ideas expressed in his brief treatise on this subject are the following. Education is defined as the process by which man becomes man. The proper end of education is the realization of humanity as humanity. Education is to assist man in his progress from nature to reason. He begins his history, in the race and in the child, submerged in nature, furnished with instinct and appetite,—the germs which education are to develop and perfect. He is not yet the creature of reason, morality, and freedom he is to become. In truly human life man has to create himself by his own voluntary efforts; he has to make himself truly moral, rational, and free. This creative effort is carried on by the educational activities of slow generations. How can it be accelerated? By men consciously striving to educate their successors not for the existing state of affairs but for a future better humanity. Here is the great difficulty. Each generation is inclined to educate its young for the present world. Parents educate their children so that they may get on; princes educate their subjects as instruments of their own purposes. Who educates for humanity? Our reliance must be upon enlightened men in their private capacity. "All culture," he says, "begins with private men and spreads outward from them." Even the subsidy by rulers of privately conducted schools must be carefully safeguarded. With their money goes their plan for their nation, not humanity.

Thus Kant expresses the individualistic cosmopolitanism of the eighteenth century. The development of personality is identified with the idea of progress and the aims of humanity. And there is an explicit fear of the hampering influence on these ideas of state-conducted and state-regulated education. Where Rousseau relied upon nature, Kant relied upon private individuals, to reform humanity. Neither alone, nor both together, are adequate to the task.

There was a greater agency at hand, as realized by Pestalozzi, the state. For state-supported education we are directly indebted to nationalism in politics; and for nationalism in politics we are both directly and indirectly indebted to Napoleon. His conquests led the German states to believe that education was the best means of recovering and maintaining their political integrity and power. They were not mistaken in this belief, as subsequent events demonstrated. Externally weak and divided, internally guided by Prussian statesmen, they were led to develop an extensive and thorough system of public education, universal and compulsory, from the primary school through the university, and to submit all private educational enterprises to the regulation and supervision of a jealous state. Germany was the first country to do this.

There were philosophers both to inspire and to justify the new rôle of the state in making the individual a man. These were Fichte and Hegel. They elaborated the idea that the chief function of the state is educational. They accepted Kant's idea that the private individual is of necessity an egoistic, irrational being, enslaved to his appetites. But they rejected Kant's idea that he is to become moral, rational, and free through his own voluntary effort. Rather is he to submit voluntarily to the educative discipline of state institutions and laws. The chief function of the state is educational, and an education carried on in the interest of the state would accomplish the regeneration of Germany. Thus, within two decades of Kant, individual cosmopolitanism was supplanted by nationalism and supported by institutional idealism. Education became a civic function, and this civic function was identified with realizing the ideal of the national state. Not by nature, nor by individual effort, nor by the influence of private individuals, was the individual to become a member of humanity, a "man," but by the state was he to become a citizen. The state furnished not only the instrumentalities of education but, also, its goal. From its start in the elementary grades to its finish in the university faculties, the school produced the patriotic citizen, the soldier, the future state official; the school furnished the means for defense and expansion, political, military, and industrial. Such was the practice.

Small wonder that the theory followed in the wake of practice; the aim of education became social efficiency; social efficiency was interpreted to mean the subordination of the individual to the state. Thus the state could compete with other more or less hostile states for military and commercial supremacy. So interpreted, education became a disciplinary training rather than a personal development.

But here arose a conflict of opinion. The humanitarian theory of culture as the complete development of personality persisted. But the practice was to subordinate the individual to the state. How reconcile the two? The answer is in the conception of the character of the state as "organic," *i.e.*, the synthesis of the private individual and the public institution. Objective reason is manifested in the state. The isolated individual is nothing; he attains true personality only in and through an absorption of the aims and meaning of organized institutions. What appears to be subordination and sacrifice of self to authority and superiors is really the only means of becoming truly rational. Thus the development of personality as an aim was reached by the subordination of the individual to the existing institution as means. This is the institutional idealism of Hegel, whose weaknesses have already been characterized.

Passing at this point from the conception of education as "national" to its conception as "social," as indicated in the title of this section, we have to note two results that stand out from our brief historical survey of Plato, Rousseau, and Hegel. The first is that the terms "individual" and "social" as applied to education are quite meaningless apart from their context. The conception of education as a social process and function has no definite meaning until we define the kind of society we have in mind. Plato, Rousseau, and Hegel all sought the full realization of the individual within a certain type of society. But Plato's society was stratified and lost the individual; Rousseau's society was nobly and generously conceived but no workable means was provided whereby the individual could reach it. Hegel's society was the national state which again subordinated the individual. If only some means could be provided whereby the individual could attain membership in a society conceived too vaguely by Rousseau and Kant! We think our democratic conception is the answer.

Our second conclusion from our historical survey is an outgrowth of the German experience with nationalism. This experience raises the question, how is the conflict between nationalism and a wider social aim to be resolved? This is one of the fundamental problems of education in and for a democratic society. The social aim of education is not to be identified with the national aim, though it is still frequently so confused.

This confusion in theory corresponds to the existing confusion in the practice of human intercourse. We have both the national and the super-national. The two contradict each other. The idea of national sovereignty in politics has never been so accentuated as now. Each nation lives in a state of incipient war with its neighbors. It is assumed that each nation has interests which are exclusively its own and that it is the supreme judge of its own interests. To question these assumptions is to question the basis of political practice and science, viz., the idea of national sovereignty. On the other hand, national boundaries are transcended by science, commerce, and art. These are largely international in quality and method. They involve interdependence and coöperation between the peoples inhabiting different countries. Thus the narrower and wider spheres conflict. We are not at one in some respects and are at one in other respects. Such a contradiction exacts of educational theory a clearer conception of education as "social" than has yet been attained.

The supreme practical question for democracy in education is, can a national state conduct a fully social educational process? Upon the national state we must rely as our agency. Can it act socially within and beyond its boundaries? If not, a democratic criterion of education can be applied only inconsistently. Let us see what is involved in the question. It has an internal and an external reference.

Internally, our public system of education is to overcome the economic tendencies which split society into classes, some of which are made merely tools for the higher culture of others. The problem must be worked out both negatively and positively. Negatively, education must not itself be actively used to make easier the exploitation of one class by another. Positively, school facilities must be secured of sufficient amplitude to discount the effects of economic inequalities, and to secure for all the wards of the nation equality of equipment for their future careers. More money and more time are particularly needed. Family resources must be supplemented to enable youth to take advantage of the school facilities provided. All the youth must be retained under educational influences until they are equipped to be masters of their own economic and social careers. This involves a modification of traditional ideals of culture, traditional subjects of study, and traditional methods of teaching and discipline. The details involved in this program will be worked out in future chapters. The ideal itself may seem remote of execution, but, except as it increasingly dominates our practice, democracy in education is a farcical, yet tragic, delusion.

Externally, our public system of education is to reconcile nationalism with internationalism. National loyalty and patriotism are to be harmonized with even a superior devotion to the things which unite men in common ends, irrespective of national political boundaries. Again, negatively, it is necessary, but not enough, to teach the horrors of war and to avoid every stimulant to international jealousy. Positively, the emphasis must be put upon whatever binds people together in coöperative human pursuits, regardless of geographical limitations. The full, free, and fruitful association and intercourse of all human beings with one another is primary. National sovereignty is secondary and provisional. This view must be instilled as a working disposition of the mind. This is the meaning of the idea of democratic education previously developed. Such applications as these should not seem remote from our philosophy of education. They are bound up with the very idea of education as a freeing of individual capacity in a progressive growth directed to social aims. A democratic education is to bring classes together in the field of nationalism and bring nations together in the field of internationalism.

Comment. It is noteworthy that the two criteria of democracy are not applied to the conception of education as national. It is, however, sufficiently clear, perhaps, that, in the light of the earlier discussions of political despotism, any form of nationalism that subordinates the individual to the state does not involve the full sharing of mutual interests within the group leading to internal control of the individual and the state. Also, that a nationalistic state is not entering fully and freely into relations with other groups, involving progressive social change. A nationalistic state in as far as it fails to share interests within and beyond the group is not democratic.

Further, it is to be noted that the nationalistic situation has been somewhat changed since the appearance of the book in 1916. Two conflicting tendencies have been manifest, viz., an increase of dictatorship in Southern Europe (though Spain has just become a Republic again) and Western Asia, and an increase of international coöperation among the nations of the world, as shown in The League of Nations, The World Court, International Conferences on Disarmament, etc. The former tendency is anti-democratic; the latter is democratic. On the whole the world has probably moved forward a bit toward democracy in the years since the war. One should read the text with the fact in mind that it was written during the first half of the World War.

As a major matter it may be mentioned that the split of society into races is perhaps even more difficult for democracy in education to overcome than its split into economic classes. The individual, at least, may change his economic status but not his race.

Further, it is to be noted that Dr. Dewey, unlike Plato, unlike Russia, is looking to education to transform human society continuously, not to maintain it in a fixed state after it is transformed, either by a happy accident or by quick revolution.

And, what is of strategic importance, the question propounded is not answered, viz., can a national state conduct an educational process that conveys the full social meaning of democracy? The implications of so doing are definitely stated. What state has done it? What state will do it? What motives will animate any state in trying it? Yet, the hope of mankind is bound up with some such fruition. Some think the animating motives of a transcendent religion must reënforce humanism before such a consummation can be reached. Dr. Dewey has staked out a course for human progress. He has said that failure to follow this course is not democratic. But he has not said he believed that the course would be followed. Least of all has he said that it was in any way predetermined that man should follow the course. He has no faith in the universe or its ground in that sense. But he does imply that man may follow the course, and so he does have faith in the potentiality of the universe, and in the creative intelligence of man.

Dr. Dewey's characteristic use of history will be noted. Why are the educational philosophies of Plato, Rousseau, Kant, and Hegel surveyed? Because by similarities and contrast they throw light on the democratic conception of education and show that terms must be understood in their context. Like these other masters, he is using the term "social" in an appreciative sense, but, unlike them, he means something different by it. To him it is the participation in common interests within groups and between groups. The historical survey helps to clarify a concept. Dr. Dewey does this repeatedly. It illustrates his own notion of how past history functions in the present.

But it may be questioned whether this mode of procedure is pragmatic. The pragmatic procedure finds meanings in consequences. The meaning of a concept lacking sense-imagery is in the sense-effects to which it leads. C. S. Peirce, the first formulator of the pragmatic principle, says: "To say that a body is heavy means simply that, in the absence of opposing force, it will fall."[1] Thus, a concept is defined in terms of the sense-effects to which it leads. And it leads to the future, to consequences. But the historical surveys of Dr. Dewey lead to the past, to antecedents. Concepts are compared with each other. The Republic of Plato never existed. Neither did Rousseau's ideal society. They were never the objects of sense-perception. They were and are and may long remain "ideas." The use of them is not strictly pragmatic, yet fully justified. They represent the left-overs of an intellectualism now rejected, but not altogether discarded.

Further, one may observe concerning these historical surveys that Dr. Dewey has acquired and utilized a type of classical education that his pragmatic educational philosophy barely justifies. Students brought up in accord with his doctrines may find his own references increasingly unintelligible. Without his broad intellectual background, students brought up only on occupational activities and their meanings will read his writing with increasing difficulty. It would probably be better to have Dr. Dewey's education than to have the education his theory provides.

[1] *Chance, Love, and Logic,* p. 47.

CHAPTER VIII

AIMS IN EDUCATION

1. The Nature of an Aim

Exposition. In this section we are to see that the educational aim is within the educational process; that an educational end is not the same as an educational result; that the test of an aim is intrinsic continuity; that the aim gives direction to the activity; and that having an aim is the same as having a mind. These points will seem less vague after they are discussed.

The educational aim is within the educational process. The aim of education we said (Chapter IV) was the continued capacity for growth. This continued capacity for growth can be achieved only in a democratic society. For one can continue to grow only where there is mutual intercourse and social change. To conceive of education as growth is to imply a democratic society. So education is not subordinate to any end outside the educative process. Growth implies democracy. Democracy as an aim is within the process. What concerns us is to remove undemocratic social conditions which put the aim outside the process. When social relations are not properly balanced, some portions of the group will find their aims are externally determined, are means to the ulterior ends of others, are not the free growth of their own experience.

The aim then is to fall within an activity and not to be furnished from without. If furnished from without, there may be a result, but no proper end. If the aim falls within the activity, there is not simply a result, there is also an end, a fulfillment of an aim. When the wind shifts the sands of the desert, there is a result, but no end. When bees gather pollen, make wax, build cells, lay eggs, seal them, brood them, hatch them, and feed them, we have not simply results but ends. The ends in this case may not be due to conscious intention, but they are ends because there was a beginning, a process of transformation, and a true completion. Each prior event leads into its successor, and so on till the process is finished off. If the bees perceived their end in imaginative foresight, as their keeper does, they too would have the primary element in an aim. Thus an aim is a foreseen end.

Now it is the pupils, not merely the teachers, who are to have educational aims. Letting children do as they please is not having an aim; the wind is only blowing the sands about. Letting children do nothing they please is not having an aim; they are working as mechanically as the bees. Children have an aim when they follow a process having intrinsic continuity through to the foreseen end. Three things are nonsense: to talk about educational aims when each act of the pupil is dictated by the teacher, when acts are capricious or discontinuous (though called "spontaneous self-expression"), and when there is no foresight of the outcome of a given activity.

Be it noted that the aim as a foreseen end gives direction to the activity, *i.e.*, influences the steps taken to reach the end. This foresight of the end, or the aim, functions in three closely connected ways, viz., it leads to careful observation of means and hindrances; it helps to order and arrange the means; and it makes possible a choice of alternatives. Having an aim thus means we are not spectators but participators; we intervene. These three influences of the aim or the act may be detected in the attack on the diseases spread by mosquitoes.

We conclude that there is no difference between acting with an aim and acting intelligently. And to act intelligently is to have intelligence and to be intelligent. Mind is precisely purposeful activity controlled by perception of facts and their relationships. To repeat, having an aim, or having a mind, involves foreseeing a future possibility, having a plan for its accomplishment, and noting the available resources and the obstructive difficulties. The capacity to relate present conditions to future consequences and to relate future consequences to present results is mind, or having an aim. Thus, a man is stupid, blind, unintelligent, lacking in mind, just in the degree in which he does not know the probable consequences of his act. A man is imperfectly intelligent when he just guesses the outcome or takes a chance with his luck, or forms plans apart from a study of the actual external conditions and his own capacities. When the mind is absent, the feelings control our acts.

To have an aim, to act intelligently, and to be conscious, all mean the same thing. "Consciousness" is an abstract noun; it comes from the adjective "conscious"; it is not an entity; it does not gaze idly on the surrounding scene; it does not passively receive impressions made upon it by physical things. Rather, consciousness is awareness of what we are about, it is the purposeful quality of an activity, the direction of an activity by an aim, thus keeping activity from being that of an automatic machine. So, to act with an aim is to intend to do something and to perceive the meaning of things in the light of that intent. Such acting has value, it functions in experience.

Comment. The educational aim is said to be within the educative process, and this aim is said to be growth, and growth is identified with the nature of democracy, and democracy is not yet attained. Really, then, the aim is only potentially within the process; it is actually within, so far as growth and democracy are attained; it is actually without so far as they are not attained. Being without in part, and yet being the aim, it is clear the aim is not wholly within the process except in an ideal sense, or with reference to some future fact. This is important as it lenghthens the time enormously between the beginning and the completion of proper fulfillment of the activity, even beyond the span of an individual's lifetime. Thus the end, though foreseen, may be remote, and does not have to be immediate or near at hand. This interpretation loosens up, widens and gives perspective to the doctrine of aims.

One of the three ways in which an aim is said to direct activity is in making a choice of alternatives possible. This is creative intelligence and effective freedom. The question whether a choice of alternatives is possible is not debated, it is asserted; "we intervene to bring about this result or that" (p. 119). The question is related to but not identical with that of "freedom of the will." It is not the will that is free, but the intelligence that is effective in using the better means to attain given ends.

The discussion identifies mind with acting intelligently, and acting with an aim. Two dubious positions are taken in this connection. The first is that "the relative absence of mind means to make our feelings the measure of what is to happen" (p. 121). Now it may well be that feelings measure what is to happen when mind is present as well as when it is absent. An aim is not merely a foreseen end; it is a foreseen end *felt as valuable.* The choice is not merely between means leading to a given end; it is also between ends. And end is so, not merely because it is foreseen, but because it is desired, and, if we are ethical, because it is perceived to be desirable. In the discussion there is implied an unnecessary dualism between the perceiving intelligence and the feeling. In short, the definition of aim as foreseen end omits the feeling aspect.

A second thing. The identification of mind with acting intelligently makes man a participator, not a spectator. As Bacon said: "Men ought to know that in the theatre of life it is only for gods and angels to be spectators." Now there is no doubt about man being a participator. There is doubt about his not being a spectator, "a looker-on in Venice." The question is whether consciousness or knowledge effects changes in its object in every case; if so, man is always a participator and never only a spectator; if not, man is sometimes not a participator, and only a spectator. A few instances will be given that show man is sometimes only a spectator.

In the case of the enjoyment of a work of art, not its production, man's experience is of the spectator type. The object is not changed through knowing it.

In the case of true memory of the past, we are spectators. The knowledge of the past does not change it. There may be false memories, but they can be identified and corrected only by true memories which do not distort their objects.

In the case of true predictions, as of eclipses, the prediction does not make the eclipse come nor change the time of its coming, nor its objective character. Yet astronomers know it is coming.

There is no doubt that in all these cases the mind is active, and may by introspection be aware of its activity, but this is very different from making the mind a trait of activity. This distinction is very important in its bearings on the conflict between idealistic and pragmatic philosophies of life. If all consciousness is brought within the act, we live in a practical, changing, naturalistic world. If some consciousness is other than a phase of action, we may also live in a theoretical, unchanging, and idealistic world. The former view asserts change and denies permanence; the latter view asserts both change and permanence.

2. The Criteria of Good Aims

Exposition. What criteria are involved in correctly establishing aims? In answering this question the results of our discussion of the nature of an aim will be applied. There are three of these criteria, viz., the aim set-up must be (1) an outgrowth of existing conditions, (2) flexible; and (3) it must lead to a freeing of activities. Each of these will be briefly considered.

(1) The aim set-up must be an outgrowth of existing conditions, based upon what is already going on, having regard

to the resources and difficulties of the situation. Educational, and also moral, theories about the proper end of our activities often violate this principle. Such theories assume ends lying *outside* our activities, issuing from some outside source foreign to the concrete situation. This gives rise to the artificial problem of making our activities realize these external ends, as something for which we *ought* to act. Such "aims" limit intelligence, not being the expression of mind in foresight, observation, and the choice of the better among alternative possibilities, but are given ready-made, imposed by some authority external to intelligence, leaving to intelligence only a mechanical choice of means.

(2) The aim set-up must be flexible, capable of alteration to meet conditions, capable of being used to change conditions; it is experimental, and grows constantly as it is tested in action.

Thus aims can not be completely formed prior to the attempt to realize them. As they first emerge, aims are only tentative sketches, hints. Their whole function is to set a mark in advance. If they direct activity successfully, nothing more is required. But in complicated situations, acting upon the aim brings to light conditions which had been overlooked, thus calling for a revision of the original aim. A farmer who framed his plans in complete disregard of what soil and climate permit would violate the first criterion of an aim; he who passively accepts things just as he finds them, not seeking to change them for the better, would violate the second criterion.

An aim established externally is inflexible, rigid, has no working relationship to concrete conditions, is not confirmed, refuted, or altered by the course of action, can only be insisted upon. Such an end is not reasonable under the circumstances; it lacks adaptation; it ends in failure, which then is mistakenly attributed to the perverseness of conditions.

(3) A correctly established aim must always represent a freeing of activities. What does this mean? The aim is an

end in view, the termination of some process. An activity is defined, specified, directed, continued, only by putting before ourselves the object in which the activity terminates. Thus the activity is freed, not being dominated by something foreign to itself. Some homely illustrations will show the meaning. In shooting, the target is not the end in view, but hitting the target; the target is one of the means of taking aim. In rabbit-hunting, the isolated rabbit is not the end in view but doing something with the rabbit, eating it, exhibiting it, selling it. Thus the end is not the object alone but a certain kind of doing with the object. The end is the successful continuing of the activity. Some process is fulfilled that more activity may go on.

In contrast stands the character of an end imposed from without the activity; it is static, fixed, alone worth while, to which the activity is the unavoidable means, having no significance on its own account, a necessary evil. An aim external to the activity leads to the separation of means and end; an aim internal to the activity is both means and end. The divorce of means from end diminishes the significance of the means and tends to reduce it to drudgery. When aims are internal, the distinction between means and end is only a matter of convenience. Every means is a temporary end until attained; every end once achieved becomes in turn a means for carrying activity further. The present direction of an activity is means, its future direction is an end. Thus, the end in view, or the aim, is one of the means of action. To illustrate the separation and the union of means and end. A farmer has to use plants and animals to farm. If he is not fond of plants and animals but regards them merely as means to get something else in which alone he is interested, there is a separation of means and ends; if, however, he is fond of them, the means become significant, each phase of his entire course of activity has its own value, he realizes his end at every stage, the end in view keeps his activity going fully and freely, the end and means become one.

Comment. One thing we miss in this account of the criteria of good aims is the setting up of a worthy standard. It may be implied in the earlier discussion of democracy but it is not said here. An aim may not be good, and yet pass these three criteria successfully. Consider the hold-up man who gets a thrill out of each new "job." This aim is an outgrowth of existing conditions, it is very flexible, and it frees his activities in a certain direction, leading on to further jobs of the same, or a similar kind; yet it is a bad aim because it shows no respect to human rights, or, as Dr. Dewey might say, there is an inadequate sharing of interests. But the point is, we must have a standard in setting up good aims. Take another illustration. A gang of boys engage in "shooting craps" after school; the aim is inherent in the activity; it changes if "the cop" appears; and it frees activities intensely; yet it is not a good aim.

The root of the trouble here is that there is no *ought* in Dr. Dewey's philosophy. (Note the derogatory reference, top p. 122.) Not even the aim of democracy in education and in society is permitted to lay an obligation or claim on human life. For the ought is substituted the intelligent direction of an activity. But, as just shown, this activity may in the nature of the case be bad as well as good. There is reference to the choice of better means and better possibilities, but no criterion of "better," carrying an obligation, is provided. Such a criterion would establish whether the aim is worthy, desirable, valuable.

Let us add, then, at least a fourth criterion for correctly establishing an aim, viz., a good aim is democratizing. We can hardly do less. This establishes a standard, a norm, an ought. It has content. It may even be conceived as being in harmony with an absolute good.

The discussion is motivated by the unnecessary fear of an external aim, which might very well end by proving to be of a liberating kind. There is a difference between what is and what ought to be, between the actual and the norm, between the real and the ideal. The ideal, if rooted in something else than the potencies of the actual or the intelligent desire of the individual, that is, if rooted in the nature of things or in the will of God for man, has the right to regulate the real. An external aim, representing the true and right ideal, may become internal through the change in the individual's attitude toward it.

The admission of such an ideal as regulative and obligatory, serving as a criterion of good aims, does not necessarily conflict with the three other criteria. The right standard, if followed, will improve existing conditions, will lead to flexible applications, and will liberate activities. It is paradoxical but true that he who is bound to the right is free.

Now concerning means and ends. It is held that the distinction between them is only a matter of convenience, a matter of temporal reference; that really, means are ends and ends are means; that consequently there are really no inferior and superior or supreme values. But this position contradicts the admitted situation. It is admitted that the farmer may employ plants and animals of which he is not fond merely as means to get something else in which he is interested. Here then admittedly the means are not ends. Unwelcome and uninteresting means may be used to attain welcome and interesting ends. A bitter medicine may be taken for the sake of one's health. The illustrations apply all through life. It is necessary, not simply a convenience, to separate wanted ends from unwanted means.

But further, the endeavor to merge ends and means, if successful, would logically give us only means and no ends, or means as the only ends. This is the logical intent of Dr. Dewey's philosophy, in which life is a series of changes, one leading to the next, and so on. We call the present change means, and the coming one end. There are no ends in themselves, no final values, no absolute. Man himself is not an end, only a means, an agent of change. So with all the supreme values of life,—health, truth, morality. There are no absolutes.

But consider such an admitted end as democracy. Democracy is an ideal only partially realized. Until it is realized, the end is different from the means, at least in extent. Will it ever be fully realized? If not, it remains an end different from the means, and itself becomes one of the absolutes. If it ever is realized at some remote future, and becomes an attained end, what then? To what does it become a means? Apparently the theory has no answer, since democracy is its highest category. It is more in harmony with human experience and reason to allow a real and not merely a convenient distinction to be drawn between means and ends.

3. Applications in Education

Exposition. There are some needed preliminary qualifications. Educational aims are not peculiar, they are just like the aims in any other directed occupation. Consider the work of the farmer. He has certain things to do, certain resources and certain obstacles. His resources and obstacles have their own structure and operation independently of him. Seeds sprout, rain falls, the sun shines, insects devour, blight comes, seasons change. His aim is simply to utilize and work with these conditions. His foresight of consequences directs his energies from day to day, leading to more careful observation and planning. Suppose he purposed to farm apart from the named conditions. How absurd!

So with parent and teacher. It would be just as absurd for them to set up their own aims as proper objects of the growth of children, getting in the way of the individual's common sense. Such an aim, being imposed from without and accepted on authority, does harm. Aims mean directing an activity, involving observation of conditions, anticipation of consequences, and arrangements of means. Any aim has value only in so far as it assists in carrying on an activity from moment to moment and hour to hour.

Further, education as such has no aims; "education" is an abstract idea. Only persons have aims. And the aims of persons are indefinitely varied, differing with different children, changing as children and their teachers grow. Stated aims, such as we are about to make, will do more harm than good unless they are taken only as suggestions as to how to look ahead for consequences, to observe conditions, and to choose means in the liberating and directing of childrens' energies. As a recent writer has correctly said: "To lead this boy to read Scott's novels instead of old Sleuth's stories; to teach this girl to sew; to root out the habit of bullying from John's make-up; to prepare this class to study medicine,—these are samples of the millions of aims we have actually before us in the concrete work of education."

Bearing these qualifications in mind, there are three characteristics found in all good educational aims, viz., (1) they are founded on the activities and needs of the pupils; (2) they enlist the coöperation of the pupils; and (3) they are specific and immediate, not "general and ultimate."

(1) An educational aim must be founded upon the native and acquired traits of the given educand; these include his original instincts, his own activities, his capacities, his acquired habits, and his needs. The specific powers and requirements of the individual are not to be neglected. They are neglected when uniform aims are propounded. Also, when the aim is preparation for some remote accomplishment or responsibility. Also, when adult interests or adult accomplishments are set up as fixed aims. But aims can not be standardized, all learning happens to a given individual at a given time and place. The accomplishments of adults, their wider perceptions, have their uses, not as aims for children, but as aids in observing and estimating their abilities and weaknesses. Thus, without the artistic accomplishments of the adult, we should be uncertain as to the significance of the draw-

ing, reproducing, modeling, and coloring activities of childhood. But for adult language, we should be blind to the infant's impulse to babble.

(2) An aim must enlist the coöperation of the pupils. *Their* activities are undergoing instruction, *their* capacities are being liberated and organized. The aim must lend itself to methods and environments suited to their activities and capacities. The trials of the methods test, correct, and amplify the aims. A rigid aim is worthless, preventing the use of ordinary judgment in observing and sizing up the situation, preventing recognition of everything not consonant with itself, rendering unnecessary careful attention to concrete conditions.

Externally imposed ends are a vice with deep social roots. These ends are current in the community; the community imposes them on the school authorities; the school authorities impose them on the teachers; the teachers impose them on the pupils. The poor pupils thus receive their aims through a triple, external imposition; they are confused by the conflict between the external aims in which they are taught to acquiesce and the internal aims which are natural to their own experience. And meantime the intelligence of the teacher is not free; he receives his aims from above, laid down by the authoritative supervisor, text-book on methods, or prescribed course of study; he can not let his mind come to close quarters with the pupil's mind and the subject matter. There is no trust in the teacher's experience, no confidence in the pupil's response. The work of both teacher and pupil is rendered mechanical and slavish. The solution is in the democratic criterion; every growing experience has intrinsic significance.

(3) Ends must be specific and immediate, not "general and ultimate." By "general" is here meant "abstract," detached from all specific context, remote. Such an aim throws us back upon teaching and learning as a mere means of getting ready for an end disconnected from the means. In contrast with

such general aims, education is literally and always its own reward; no alleged study or discipline is educative unless it is worth while in its own immediate having.

There is a sense, however, in which the term "general" may be admitted. Every activity, however specific, leads out indefinitely into other things, has its ramified connections, is "general." So long as a general idea makes us more alive to these connections, it is valuable. Such a truly general aim broadens the outlook, stimulates one to take more connections and consequences into account, leads to a wider and more flexible observation of means.

Anticipating our next chapter, and using the term "general" in the acceptable sense here defined, we shall there study certain general aims current in the educational theory of the day. We shall consider what light they throw upon the teacher's immediate, concrete, and diversified aims. There is no need of making a choice between Nature, Society, and Culture as aims, or regarding them as competitors, since they mean simply different ways of looking at the same scene. So, let us have a plurality of stated aims. One statement will supplement another, emphasizing what it slurs over. A plurality of hypotheses is beneficial to the scientific investigator, helping him to see. The views received from different mountain peaks supplement each other; they are not incompatible or competitive.

Comment. How do the three criteria of good aims correspond with the three applications in education? Point for point in the first of each, but not so thereafter. The second and third criteria of "flexibility" and "freeing activity" are merged in the second application of "enlisting coöperation." The preceding discussion of means and end, which is a phase of the third criterion, leads to the third application. Apparently it is not intended that the parallelism should be exact.

A word of comment on the repeated figure that the teacher is like the farmer. Does the farmer then teach or educate the soil? Is there any difference between the cultivation of the soil and the cultivation of man? There is this difference, that the soil does not consciously coöperate in the process of its cultivation while the pupil does, or may, in the process of his education. The pupil is more than a behaving organism, where the implication of the discussion might leave him; he is a self-conscious personality, though immature, and capable of coöperating in the determination of his own ends and means.

A further word needs to be said on the three applications made to education. The educational aim must be truly socializing in its effect, leading to the sharing of interests in a full and free way within groups and between groups. This is implied in the discussion, if not here, then earlier (see p. 96). Unless this is recalled, any successful bandit's school of crime would exemplify rather well all the three applications. The aim to make an efficient criminal would be based on the activities of the pupils, would enlist their coöperation, and would not be preparation for crime but would be participation in crime. Even the accomplishments of the adult criminals might show the significance of the petty thievery of the youngsters. In interest and efficiency one might even contrast such a school with the usual school aiming at good citizenship. But, speaking socially, the interests shared within the gang and between it and other gangs and society at large, would be "partial and distorted"; it would not be a democratic school.

An educational aim should always be an ideal whose fulfillment is willed. If the democratic ideal as stated is not sufficiently comprehensive of all the values of life, it must be supplemented. Much depends upon not only the fact of interest-sharing but upon what interests are shared. The interests shared should be as comprehensive as the worthy experiences of man.

CHAPTER IX

NATURAL DEVELOPMENT, SOCIAL EFFICIENCY, AND CULTURE AS AIMS

1. Nature as Supplying the Aim

Exposition. To repeat, it is futile to try to establish the aim of education. There is none such, no one final aim subordinating all lesser aims to itself. Instead, any number of general aims may be had, all differing, yet all consistent. General aims are only points of view, useful in surveys and estimates. The history of education shows many aims, such as æsthetic contemplation, personal culture, complete development of personality, discipline, encyclopedic knowledge, the substitution of things for words, better methods of language study, complete living, utility, and social efficiency. These aims have been stated at different times and each in its setting has great local value.

The fact of changing social need explains our having so many different general aims, each having specific value. For stated aims are functions of existent social needs. Like laws, they seek alterations in practice. Whatever exists and is accepted requires no special emphasis. Thus, in times of social authority, a demand for individual freedom will arise; in times of individual license, a demand for social control will arise. Three such general aims, all of recent influence, will be discussed in this chapter.

Rousseau's theory of Nature as supplying the aim has both truth and falsity, as we shall see. To him education is a process of development in accord with nature. We saw (Chapter VII) that he opposed the natural to the social When educational reformers are disgusted with current con ventionality and artificiality, they are prone to resort to nature as a standard. Nature is supposed to furnish the law of development; ours to follow nature.

The following words of Rousseau contain as fundamental truths as have been uttered about education, together with a curious twist. "Education we receive from three sources—Nature, man, and things. The spontaneous development of our organs and capacities constitutes the education of Nature. The use to which we are taught to put this development constitutes that education given us by man. The acquirement of personal experience from surrounding objects constitutes that of things. Only when these three kinds of education are consonant and make for the same end, does a man tend toward his true goal. . . . If we are asked what is this end, the answer is that of Nature. For since the concurrence of the three kinds of education is necessary to their completeness, the kind which is entirely independent of our control must necessarily regulate us in determining the other two." "Nature" is defined as the inborn capacities and dispositions "as they exist prior to the modifications due to constraining habits and the influence of the opinon of others."

It would be impossible to say better what is here said; it covers the ground. There are three propositions, viz., (1) the three factors of educative development are, (*a*) the native structure and functional activities of our bodily organs; (*b*) the uses to which these activities are put under the influence of other persons; and (*c*) their direct interaction with the physical environment. (2) Adequate development of the individual requires the consonance of the three factors of education. And (3) the native activities of the organs, being original, are basic in conceiving such consonance.

Let us refer first to the elements of truth in these views of education according to nature. Its positive value lies in its forcibly calling attention to the wrongness of aims which do not to have regard to the natural endowment of those educated.

The structure and activities of the organs furnish the *conditions* of all teaching which is based on the use of the organs.

In particular, Rousseau's general aim enables him to indicate four desirable specific aims and the means for correcting many current evils.

(1) Make health and vigor an aim. Without these, normal development can not be had. Though obvious enough, the due recognition of this fact would revolutionize many of our educational practices.

(2) Respect physical mobility. He says: "Children are always in motion; a sedentary life is injurious." Nature develops the mind by exercising the body. The use of the bodily organs in explorations, handling materials, in plays and games, has an actual part in mental development. We think with hands and muscles as well as with the brain. Rousseau hardly states the case fairly in saying dualistically: "Nature's intention is to strengthen the body before exercising the mind." (Note too his poetical form of speech. Nature really has no "intention.")

(3) Regard the individual differences among children. The native powers differ in different individuals in their intensity, quality, and arrangement. Rousseau says . . . "after we have wasted our efforts in stunting the true gifts of nature we see the short-lived and illusory brilliance we have substituted die away, while the natural abilities we have crushed do not revive."

(4) Note the origin, waxing, and waning of interests. We must strike while the iron is hot. Especially precious are the first dawnings of power; the ways in which the tendencies of early childhood are treated fix fundamental dispositions and condition the turn taken by powers that awaken later. Educational concern with the early years of life is distinct from the inculcation of the useful arts; this distinction dates almost entirely from the time of the emphasis on the principles of natural growth by Rousseau and his followers, Pestalozzi and Froebel. Capacities bud and bloom irregularly;

there is no even four-abreast development. A student of the growth of the nervous system writes: "While growth continues, things bodily and mental are lopsided, for growth is never general, but is accentuated now at one spot, now at another. . . . The methods which shall recognize in the presence of these enormous differences of endowment the dynamic values of natural inequalities of growth, and utilize them, preferring irregularity to the rounding out gained by pressing will most closely follow that which takes place in the body and thus prove most effective."[1]

As one carries out this suggestion and seeks to observe children, it should be noted that their natural tendencies show themselves most readily in their spontaneous sayings and doings, not under conditions of restraint, not when put at set tasks, not when they are aware of being observed. Not all natural tendencies are desirable and all are operative and must be taken into account. Desirable tendencies must have an environment which keeps them active; thus the undesirable ones will be controlled. Many troublesome tendencies are likely to be transitory; do not fixate the child's attention on them by too much direct notice. Not all the impulsive deviations of children from parental standards are evils to be eliminated. Do not attempt to force children directly into the adult mold; in this sense "follow nature." There is much that is true in so doing.

Turning now to the false side of the doctrine of education according to nature, its weakness is the ease with which "following nature" is precisely equal to doing nothing. The natural is at times physical, at times the norm, but it is confusing to let the physical alone be the *normal*. This discounts intelligence in foreseeing and contriving. We are not just to get out of the way and leave it to nature.

Again, Rousseau mistakenly regards the three factors of education, viz., nature, man, and things, as separate and inde-

[1] Donaldson, *Growth of Brain*, p. 356.

pendent operations. He believes there is a "spontaneous development of the native organs and powers, that this development can go on irrespective of the uses to which they are put by man, that this development supplies its own *ends*, and that to this separate education of Nature the education by man is to be subordinated. All this is profoundly wrong. There are not three kinds of education, but three factors in education. There is no separate development; these three factors *must* work together for any one of them to be educative; the development of the organs depends on use; nature supplies the *conditions* but not the *ends* of the development; and there is no subordination of education by Men to the education of Nature. Once again, the process of acquiring language is a model of proper educative growth; the start is from native activities of the vocal apparatus, organs of hearing, etc., which, however, have no independent growth of their own and if left to themselves would not evolve a perfect speech. The babblings of children are indeed the beginnings of articulate language and are not yet language itself nor the *standard* for teaching language. Taken literally, Rousseau's principle would mean this absurdity. The native powers furnish the initiating and limiting forces in all education; they do not furnish its ends or aims.

It is not random and capricious exercise which causes the native activities to develop; it is the uses to which they are put. It is the office of the "education by Men," the social medium, to direct the growth of powers by putting them to the best possible use.

It is true that the native organs give a strong bias for a certain sort of operation, by trying to go contrary to which we may pervert, stunt, and corrupt them. These instinctive activities may be metaphorically called "spontaneous"; but the notion that there really is a spontaneous normal development of these activities is pure mythology.

As a setting for Rousseau's view of education as following nature, four things may be noted. (1) He identified God with Nature; (2) he held that all natural tendencies are intrinsically good; (3) he substituted specific impulses for abstract, mental faculties; and (4) he held to the doctrine of following nature as a political dogma. These matters will be considered in turn. (1) God being one with Nature, the original powers, coming directly from a wise and good creator, are wholly good. God makes the original organs, with their intended uses; man, by interference, makes their actual uses. So the organs furnish the standard to which their actual uses should be subordinated. Any interference with Nature, God's work, by social arrangements, man's work, is the primary source of individual corruption.

(2) Rousseau also passionately asserted the intrinsic goodness of all natural tendencies. This was itself a reaction against the prevalent notion of the total depravity of human nature. It has had a powerful influence in modifying the attitude toward the interests of children. We will not discuss the question whether Rousseau was correct in identifying God and Nature, and on this second point it may hardly be necessary to say that primitive impulses are of themselves neither good nor evil; they become either good or evil according to their uses. No doubt there is mistreatment of instincts; there are neglect, suppression, and premature forcing; such mistreatment is responsible for many avoidable ills. But the moral is not to leave them alone in their alleged native goodness to follow their own "spontaneous development," but to provide an environment to organize them.

(3) Rousseau substituted specific instincts for abstract, mental faculties. Before his day educational reformers had ascribed practically unlimited power to education. All the differences between peoples, classes, and persons were said to be due to differences in education,—in training, exercise, and practice. Originally for all practical purposes there is the same mind in all, meaning the essential equality of all, and the possibility of bringing all to the same level. In protest the doctrine of following nature meant a much less formal

and abstract view of mind. For faculties of discernment, memory, and generalization were substituted specific instincts, impulses, and physiological capacities. These differ from individual to individual,—Rousseau pointed out that they differ even in dogs of the same litter. And this protest was correct, as modern biology, physiology, and psychology witness. Though nurture modify and transform, nature provides the foundation and ultimate resources. Direct educational effort has great significance but it must presuppose the native unlearned capacities.

(4) Following nature was also a political dogma to Rousseau. It meant a rebellion against existing social institutions. Society, as it exists, is bad. It is artificial and harmful. Though everything is good as it comes from the hands of the Author of Nature, "everything degenerates in the hands of man." Though the natural man has absolute value and is a complete integer, civilized man is only a relative unit. Political institutions make a man unnatural. So he turned away from society to nature, holding that it furnishes not merely those prime forces which initiate growth, but also the plan and goal of growth. Two remarks must be made here. The first is that evil institutions do give a wrong education which the best schooling can not offset; but the conclusion is not to educate apart from social institutions but to provide better social institutions in which native powers will be put to better uses. The other remark is, as previously indicated, that Rousseau, versatile and paradoxical as he was, had the idea of a radically different sort of society. It was to be a fraternal society whose end should be identical with the good of all its members, which would be as much better than existing societies as these were worse than the state of nature.

Concerning this first general aim of education according to nature, we conclude that nature alone does not supply the aim, that it supplies the native activities; that these can develop only through social uses that nurture them; that there is consequnetly no necessary conflict between the natural and the social.

Comment. It is said that education has aims but no aim. This is somewhat confusing after what has been said about growth and democracy. Are not these mutually implied in each other? Are they not the foreseen result of the educative process, directing it, leading to observation of conditions and the selection of suitable means? If so, are they not the accepted general aims of education? If not, we might adopt Rousseau's paradoxical style and say the only general aim in education is to have no general aim.

The view is presented that the aims as stated represent needs or lacks in existing society, that whatever exists and is accepted as right does not enter into the statement of the aim. This would seem to be true particularly of progressive societies. Societies with static ideals, as in primitive times and in the ancient Orient, state their aims in terms of recapitulation of the past (Chapter VI). Whatever is, is right, and the function of education is to maintain the *status quo.* So it was with the primitive customs, the Chinese family, the Hindu caste system, the Egyptian priesthood, the Persian militarism; also, as we saw, even with Plato's ideal state. One might say, in order to bring the exceptions under the rule as given, that in these cases the felt need was stability. But stability was what they had, not what they lacked. Aims are stated in terms of value, and in static societies values are conservative, while in dynamic societies values are progressive. In history generally and in the history of education in particular, the conservative periods and values have been more in evidence than the progressive. Without conservation even in dynamic societies there is no result from progress, and chaos rules. And the rapid transition from a static to a dynamic civilization is fraught with great peril, as in modern China. A valuable historical study could be made of educational aims in relation to social and economic conditions.

Though expressing an opinion on the other views of Rousseau, Dr. Dewey does not comment on the view that Rousseau "identified God with nature" (p. 134). Two things here. First, Rousseau did not identify God with Nature and possibly Dr. Dewey does not mean the phrase to be taken literally. Second, if he had done so Dr. Dewey would not have agreed with him. To identify God with Nature is to be a pantheist. Rousseau was no pantheist. He held the particular rationalist view that was one of the trends of thought of his day, viz., that God exists, the Author of Nature but above and beyond Nature, who, however, does not enter into communication with man by means of miracle, special revelation, or prayer. The name of this view is deism, one form of theism, not pantheism. Rousseau was a deist. Thirty of the 444 pages of the *Émile* (pp. 228–258, Everyman's Library) are devoted to an impassioned utterance of these views in the "Confession of a Savoyard Priest." Rousseau makes him say: "To raise myself so far as may be even now to this state of happiness, strength, and freedom, I exercise myself in lofty contemplation. I consider the order of the universal, not to explain it by any futile system, but to revere it without ceasing, to adore the wise Author who reveals himself in it. I hold intercourse with him; I immerse all my powers in his divine essence; I am overwhelmed by his kindness, I bless him and his gifts, but I do not pray to him. What should I ask of him—to change the order of nature, to work miracles on my behalf?" (*Op. cit.*, p. 257.) It is possible Dr. Dewey does not strictly mean that Rousseau "identified God with Nature" but only that he regarded Nature as the work and sole revelation of God.

Neither would Dr. Dewey identify God with Nature. Spinoza does so but Spinoza's philosophy has not "deserted the classical tradition" (*The Quest for Certainty,* p. 56), and Dr. Dewey's has. His universe, as stated in our comment on the preface, is unclosed, in the making, indeterminate, adventurous, aleatory, implicating man in its perils; possessed of uncertainty, novelties, creation, invention, possibilities, irregularities, whose order is uninsured, in which no absolute certainty is attainable in science, æsthetics, logic, or ethics, but a process of real change goes on in time; in which most problems are falsely stated, *e.g.*, the mind-body problem; in which mind emerges within a social experience; in which values are our intelligent likings, and religion makes real the potential aspects of the actual; in which nature is conceived of as inherently neither rational nor irrational but intelligible to man. To quote: "Abandon completely the notion that nature ought to conform to a certain definition, and nature intrinsically is neither rational nor irrational. Apart from the use made of it in knowing, it exists in a dimension irrelevant to either attribution, just as rivers inherently are neither located near cities nor are opposed to such location. Nature is intelligi*ble* and understanda*ble*." (*Op. cit.*, p. 210.) Dr. Dewey has not discussed in print his conception of God, so far as known to me. The term might be retained in his philosophy as an abstract noun covering the traits of potentiality in nature and of intelligence in man.

2. Social Efficiency as Aim

Exposition. In presenting this aim we will show in succession its nature, its relation to "education according to nature," and the two specific aims involved in it, together with the danger lurking in each.

There is a narrow and unacceptable and a broad and acceptable meaning of "social efficiency." Narrowly, it is habituation to social control, subordination of natural powers to social rules. It is true that we must look to society, to the activities and achievements of associated life, to find what efficiency means. But to secure efficiency, that is, the development of power in the individual, his subordination to society in negative restraint is not necessary; the social utilization of his powers is necessary. This leads us to the broader conception of social efficiency.

Broadly speaking, social efficiency is the result of the positive use of native individual capacities in social occupations; it is the socialization of *mind.* Such a socialized mind is actively concerned in making experiences more communicable, in breaking down the barriers of social stratification, in making individuals less impervious to the interests of others. The chief constituent of the socialized mind (because its only guarantee) is intelligent sympathy or good-will, something behind the service rendered by overt acts. The desirable sort of sympathy is more than mere feeling; it is a cultivated imagination for what men have in common, leading to rebellion at whatever unnecessarily divides them. A benevolent interest in others is not an unwitting mask for an attempt to dictate to them what their goal shall be; it is an endeavor to free them to seek and find the goal of their own choice. Life affords a diversity of goods to different persons, and every individual should be encouraged to make his own choice intelligent. Without such a faith, social efficiency, even social service, are hard and metallic things.

Translated into specific aims, as all general aims must be, social efficiency means two things, (1) industrial competency, and (2) good citizenship, each requiring special treatment.

(1) By industrial competency is meant the ability to earn one's living and that of one's dependent children and to manage economic resources usefully instead of for mere display and luxury. The ways in which the means of subsistence, necessary for life, are employed and consumed, profoundly influence all the relationships of persons to one another. An industrially incompetent person is a drag or a parasite upon the activities of others. He misses for himself one of the most educative experiences of life. If he is not trained in the right use of wealth, the product of industry, he may deprave himself and injure others. No scheme of education can afford to neglect such basic considerations. Yet they have been neglected, even scorned, by higher education, and this in the name of more spiritual ideals. Such views are oligarchical.

With a change to a democratic society an education for industrial competency should receive emphasis.

But a grave danger is here. In becoming economically independent, existing economic conditions and standards are not to be accepted as final. The original capacities of individuals should be trained to the point of competency to choose and make one's career for oneself. Democracy requires so much. Definite industrial callings are not to be selected for individuals on the basis of the economic or social status of their parents. It is not only undemocratic, it is imprudent. Too specific training unfits for occupational displacement in a changing industrial order. At the present time new inventions are leading to new industries, new industries revolutionize old ones, occupational readjustment is necessary, and for this a less definite training is an advantage.

But further, and most of all, the present industrial constitution of society is full of inequities. In this respect it is like every society that ever existed. Social control is not to mean the subordination of individual activities to class authority. Wherever it does, differences in economic opportunity dictate the future callings of individuals, and industrial education accepts the *status quo.* The defects of the Platonic scheme, without its enlightened method of selection on the basis of native ability, are unconsciously revived. A narrow industrial education aims to perpetuate unfair privileges and unfair deprivation; progressive education aims to take part in correcting them.

(2) Good citizenship. A synonym is civic efficiency, which is one of the two phases of social efficiency. It is arbitrary to separate these two phases from each other, though good citizenship is vaguer than vocational ability, covering traits running all the way from being an agreeable companion to being effective in politics. Good citizenship denotes the ability to judge men and measures wisely and to take a determining part in making as well as obeying laws. This aim has the merit of protecting us from the notion of a training of mental power

at large. Power must be relative to doing something, and the things that most need to be done involve one's relationship with others.

The aim also must not be understood too narrowly. Civic efficiency includes scientific discoveries, ability to produce and enjoy art, capacity for recreation, and the significant use of leisure. These things are more important than those conventionally associated with citizenship. Security of social progress depends on scientific discoveries, yet a too narrow view of civic efficiency would have excluded scientists at certain periods as theoretical dreamers. Social efficiency in its two phases of vocation and citizenship means precisely the capacity to share in a give and take of experience, covering all that makes one's own experience more worth while to others and that of others more worth while to oneself.

Comment. The term efficiency is used in the discussion to mean power, or the development of power. But another element in the conception is economy in the application of power. The term refers to machines as well as to persons. An efficient machine is one that has maximum production with minimum consumption. A coal furnace, consuming much energy, making but little heat available, is inefficient. A fire-fly, making light practically without heat, is very efficient. A perpetual motion machine would be perfect in efficiency. The efficiency of a machine or person may be increased by increasing production, consumption remaining the same; or by decreasing consumption, production remaining the same; or by increasing production more rapidly than consumption. An efficient person is one who does things or gets things done easily and well. As Dr. Dewey suggests, there must be much of humanity in efficiency to save it from being mechanical.

It is also important to recognize that one may have anti-social efficiency, as in the commission of the perfect or near-perfect crime which leaves no trace or faint trace. There are "expert" criminals, "crack" burglars, etc. They have power, they have success in the application of power, they are efficient. It is not enough to be efficient.

If a personal reference be allowable, perhaps the best comment on Dr. Dewey's interpretation of social efficiency as an educational aim, involving inseparably vocational and civic ability, is his own fruitful membership in human society. A writer of books and articles, giving interviews to reporters, lecturer, teacher, friend, husband, father, chairman of various educational and political committees, educational adviser to China, Mexico, Russia, Turkey, always on the pioneering front of thought and action, during a long life-time of fruitful good-will to man,—here is indeed social efficiency, humanism at its best.

3. Culture as Aim

Exposition. In presenting this topic we will note a limited and a broad conception of culture. In the limited sense of the term, culture grew up in a feudally organized society and refers to inner refinement of personality. Culture means something cultivated, refined, personal, the appreciation of ideas, art, and broad human interests. Culture is opposed to the raw and crude and to natural development when "natural" means rawness. Culture is opposed to efficiency when efficiency is identified with a narrow range of external *acts.*

But the broad view of culture is synonymous with the broad view of social efficiency. These two are not antagonists; at present they should be synonyms. There is something unique, incommensurable, in an individual. Give attention to this, and you have both culture and social efficiency; develop the distinctive quality of the individual and you have both distinction of personality, which is culture, and greater promise for non-material social service, which is social efficiency. Can society be worth serving unless it is composed of significant personalities?

An aristocratic community depreciates the masses. There is a rigid division of superior and inferior. The superior have leisure to develop themselves as human beings; the inferior labor to provide external products. When a democracy talks of social efficiency in terms only of output or product, it is still aristocratic. To separate the aim of cultural education from that of socially efficient education is fatal to democracy. There are moral and ideal meanings in democracy which demand that all culture be efficient and that all efficiency be cultured, that each person have his distinctive capacity developed and that all persons make a social return.

To emphasize by amplifying this point. Narrow efficiency consists in supplying products to others. Narrow culture is an exclusive individual experiment and polish. One's personality is what one is in association with others, in a free give and take of intercourse. This transcends both narrow efficiency and narrow culture. One must have culture to join fully and freely in common activities, which is social efficiency, and one must have social efficiency to expand in range and accuracy one's perception of meanings, which is perhaps the best definition of culture. So true social efficiency is inner as well as outer and true culture is outer as well as inner.

All educational aims must be included within the process of experience, they must be measured by the achieving of a distinctly valuable experience. Measure efficiency by external products alone and it becomes materialistic. Such products are by-products, inevitable and important but still by-products. An industrial education which aims at making persons efficient only in the production and distribution of commodities is external and false. It leads to a reaction in favor of the conception of culture as internal and equally false. The very idea of perfecting an "inner" personality is a sure sign of social division. Such an "inner" fails to connect with others, is incapable in fact of full and free communication. "Spiritual culture" has usually been conceived as something which a man might have internally and therefore exclusively, wherefore it has usually been futile, with something rotten about it.

In line with these suggestions of the unity of the inner and outer aspects of a worthwhile experience, let it be affirmed that he has missed his calling who has efficiency without culture, who in rendering value to others does not realize value for himself. The most valuable sharing is a having, just as the only valuable having is a sharing. Why then hold that one must choose between others and self? Between sacrificing himself in doing things useful for others and sacrificing others in doing things exclusively for oneself, whether building an inner spiritual life or saving one's own soul? Such a division of interests can not last, and the attempt to make it leads to compromise and alternation, trying each course by turns. And here is a tragedy, none greater, that so much of the professedly spiritual and religious thought of the world has accepted and emphasized this dualism of life; it has perfected others at the expense of self, or it has perfected self at the expense of others. The dualism is now too deeply established to be easily overthrown, but away with it! Let education at the present time take this as its particular task: to give us an efficient culture and a cultured efficiency.

Comment. This problem means a great deal to Dr. Dewey. He returns to it again and again. The following quotations will illustrate one of his most recent formulations of it: "But the distinguishing trait of the American student body in our higher schools is a kind of intellectual immaturity. This immaturity is mainly due to their enforced mental seclusion; there is, in their schooling, little free and disinterested concern with the underlying social problems of our civilization. . . . We have got to wrest our general culture from an industrialized civilization; and this fact signifies that industry must itself become a primary educative or cultural force for those engaged in it."[1]

The discussion makes it clear that of all the partly antithetic aims discussed, Dr. Dewey prefers the broad type of social efficiency. He makes social efficiency so conceived

[1] "The Crisis in Culture," *The New Republic,* March 19 (1930).

synonymous with personal culture. Though discussed in the body of the chapter, culture does not appear in the title of the chapter. There is evident a withdrawal of emphasis from the personal.

The elemental question may properly be raised whether at its broadest and best social efficiency is properly a synonym for culture. It may be admitted at once that a cultivated person should give all he can to society. But two things remain. The first is, he can not give all he is to society; and the second is, he can not get all he is from society. He can not give all he is to society, for that centre of consciousness known as the ego, the self, is an unshareable experience. Descriptive words and revealing acts may be shared but another can not feel your feeling, think your thinking, see your seeing. Here is a unique and unshareable residuum. Further, one can not get all he is from society. There is the first hand and extensive contact with things. For this there is no social substitute. Given the contact, society may help interpret its meaning. And the sense of physical fact, the tang of external reality, no society can give. And in the same way if there be super-physical and super-human realities, or reality, the individual consciousness may come into direct communion with it, as James showed,[1] not through any social medium. For these two reasons it seems hardly adequate to regard culture and social efficiency even at their respective best as synonymous.

Note too that Dr. Dewey allows that efficiency without culture has something "inevitable and important" but that culture without efficiency is divisive, unconnected, exclusive, usually futile and "rotten." Apparently in a choice between evils efficiency without culture is preferable to culture without efficiency.

It is very doubtful whether the views of Dr. Dewey as here expressed would logically justify the anchorite, the monk,

[1] Cf. James, W., *The Varieties of Religious Experience,* Lectures XVI and XVII, "Mysticism," New York (1902).

the mystic, the wilderness type of individual experience, or the use of retreats. These all mean a measure of meditation and contemplation divorced from action. Certainly, soul-culture is not the sole culture but it may well be the soul of culture, as culture is admittedly the soul of social efficiency.

Attention should be directed to an inadequate interpretation in the text of the meaning of the term "self-sacrifice." There is a paradoxical meaning in the phrase. When the minister says: "lay self aside and think of others," he does not mean lose yourself in the service of others; he means find yourself by losing yourself in the service of others. It is the lower self that is lost, the higher self is found. "Self-sacrifice" carries a double meaning, one unworthy, one worthful, and its worthful meanings are a paradox. Self-sacrifice in an unworthy service is loss of self-respect and other values of the self. In a worthy sense it means finding the higher by losing the lower; in this sense self-sacrifice is true self-discovery.

There is a recognized type of valuable human experience which admittedly is cultural but only dubiously can be identified with efficiency. It is the æsthetic experience. Here is an end in itself, an intrinsic value, whose enjoyment involves rest and contemplation. But efficiency is a means to an end, having extrinsic value, whose pursuit involves action and direction. Here again the terms culture and efficiency can not be made synonymous, though they are not antagonistic, except in occurring usually at different times.

A synthetic general aim of education might well be: the realization of man's ideal nature. This presupposes the inherited capacities bestowed by nature and involves both personal and social realization, without necessarily identifying the two. It allows for individuality over and above sociality, and it allows for sociality as one medium of self-expression. And, as in the case of the other general aims discussed, it allows itself to be translated into specific aims suitable to time and location.

CHAPTER X

INTEREST AND DISCIPLINE

1. The Meaning of the Terms

Exposition. In this section we will first define interest, then discipline, and then show how they are related.

As ordinarily used there are three meanings of the word "interest," viz. (1) the whole state of one's active development, as one's business, occupation, employment, or pursuit. Thus, a man's interest may be politics, journalism philanthropy, archæology, collecting Japanese prints, or banking. (2) The point at which an object touches, engages, or influences a man, the objective results that are foreseen or wanted. For example, in some legal transactions a litigant has to prove "interest," *i.e.,* that some proposed step concerns his affairs. Again, a sleeping partner in a business has an interest in it, not because he takes an active part in its conduct, but because its success or failure affects his profits and liabilities. (3) The personal, emotional inclination such as, being absorbed, wrapped up in, carried away by, some object. One may "lose himself" or "find himself" in some affair of interest,—the two here mean the same: the engrossment of the self in an object. In taking an interest one is on the alert, cares about, is attentive.

Interest is the attitude taken by a participant rather than a spectator. The spectator is indifferent to what is going on, one result is just as good as another, since each is just something to look at. He is like a man in a prison cell watching the rain out of the window; it is all the same to him. The participant is not so. He is an agent, bound up with what is going on, whose outcome makes a difference to him; so he does whatever he can to influence the issue. He is like a man with an outing ahead watching the rain; though he can not stop the rain, he may postpone his outing. If a man sees in time an auto bearing down upon him, though not controlling its movement, he can at least control his own. The attitude of a participant is thus two-fold, solicitude concerning the outcome, and a readiness to act to assure the better and avert the worse. This double attitude is interest.

Aims as previously discussed and interest are necessarily connected. Interest is one's concern and one's effort; aims are the foreseen results which elicit one's concern and effort. Interest and aim take each other for granted. The facts of the situation,—the activity, its foreseen results, the anxiety concerning them, the disposition to secure or avoid them, are all inseparable, though we name the objective foresight "intellectual," and the subjective personal two-fold concern "emotional and volitional."

Be it noted that interest thus means that the self and the world are engaged with each other in a developing situation. Changes in persons and things are amenable to the activities of the self, and the career of the self is bound up with the movement of persons and things. Personal attitudes have no world to themselves; our desires, emotions, affections, are tied up with the doings of the things and persons about us. There is no purely personal subjective realm separated from the impersonal and objective. The self can be interested only in some activity whose foreseen consequences are welcome or unwelcome. The significance of these views for education will appear in the second section.

Turning from interest to discipline, we may define discipline as the recognition of what one is about and persistence and resourcefulness in its accomplishment. A disciplined person undertakes action intelligently, deliberately, and endures in it despite distraction, confusion, and difficulty. An army or a mind may have disclipline; it means the same in each case; knowing what one is to do, and moving to its accomplishment promptly and resourcefully. Discipline is positive, is trained power, is the power of continuous attention, is power at command; cowing the spirit, subduing inclination, compelling obedience, mortifying the flesh, making a subordinate perform an uncongenial task,—these things are disciplinary only if they tend to the development of power to recognize what one is about and to persist in its accomplishment.

As the meaning of interest rests on the psychology of feeling, so the meaning of discipline rests on the psychology of will. Some activities take time, much time, for completion, as the writing of a book; many means and many obstacles lie between initiation and fulfilment; deliberation and persistence are required. The every day meaning of will is mainly and correctly the conscious disposition to persist in a planned course of action despite distractions and difficulties; the man of strong will is executive, neither feeble nor half-hearted; the weak will is unstable as water.

Thus there are two factors in will; the first has to do with the foresight of results, the end in view, called intellectual above; the second has to do with the depth of hold the foreseen outcome has on the person, called emotional and volitional above. The man of strong will thus foresees and persists. In contrast stand three types of will we may call the obstinate, the weak, and the flabby. The man of *obstinate* or stubborn will is persistent enough but lacks clearness and criticism of his proposed end. The man of *weak* will has deceived himself as to the consequences of his acts; he picks out the agreeable and neglects the disagreeable; called upon to face the disagreeable, he becomes discouraged, complains of hard fate and shifts to another line of action. It may seem strange and paradoxical, but the primary difference between strong and obstinate or weak wills is intellectual—the thinking through of consequences. The man of *flabby* will has the intellectual foresight of consequences, but they do not grip him and engage him in action; his intellectuality is one-sided; he "takes it out" in thinking.

From this account of the nature of interest and discipline, it will be unnecessary to press the point that interest and discipline are not only not opposed to each other, but are actually connected. Interest is requisite for each of the two phases of discipline, viz., the intellectual phase, or the recognition of what one is about in terms of consequences, and the volitional phase, or persistence in accomplishment of what has been intelligently undertaken. To consider each of these phases in succession. Where there is no interest, deliberation concerning what one is about will be perfunctory and superficial. This is why children often do not want to hear or to understand. Parents and teachers complain about this situation, and indeed it ought to be remedied. Punishment for inattention is sometimes resorted to, as one way of arousing interest. It has value if it actually does lead the inattentive child to reflect upon his activities, and to impregnate them with aims; it has no value if by physical means it merely leads the child to act as the adult desires. Interest is necessary to thinking.

It is even clearer that interest is necessary to acting, to persistence in execution. Interest is the depth of the grip the foreseen end has on the one pursuing it. Employers want workmen who are interested in what they are doing. The doctor or lawyer who sticks to his work most conscientiously is not the one who, finding it uncongenial, carries on through a sense of obligation. So discipline, or trained power, in both its intellectual and practical aspects, is an effect of interest.

Comment. Three things must be noted here. The first is that the contrast between the spectator and participant is perhaps overdrawn. The rôle of the spectator is not always passive; he is not entirely indifferent to what is going on; he has an interest in what he is observing. This is even true of the prisoner watching the rain. It is especially true of spectators at athletic contests with favorites of their own; muscles are taut and fatigue results. The spectator is really more than a spectator, he is a restrained participant. The matter involves more than a figure of speech. From the discussion the conclusion is implicit that to be interested one must be a participant, that interest presupposes action; that being a spectator means feeling no interest. This is a dubious conclusion. One may be a participant without immediate interest, and one may be a spectator with immediate interest. That is, the source of immediate interest may be an idea as well as an act. Educationally this is important.

The second thing to note is that interest is so defined here as to include effort within itself. "The difference imaginatively foreseen [in the aim] makes a present difference, which finds expression in solicitude and effort,"—the solicitude and effort being the double attitude of interest. Dr. Dewey has elsewhere gone more deeply into this important question.[1] Here it is enough to point out that there are two kinds of interest, immediate and remote, that effort may be due to a remote as well as an immediate interest, that Dr. Dewey prefers the immediate to the remote type of interest, that in consequence it is possible that the factors of obligation, conscience, and duty play too slight a rôle in his system. When immediate interest in one's work is lacking, and effort lags, the remote interest in doing one's duty, meeting one's obligation, fulfilling the exactions of one's conscience, may spur to renewed effort. The day may be lost or won through the absence or presence of such a remote interest. Thus effort is an effect of an ultimate as well as an immediate interest.

The third thing is the denial of a "purely personal or subjective realm." Now it may very well be true that most interests of most people are bound up with changes in the environment. But there is one interest left over which is not so bound up and clearly marks off a personal subjective realm; it is the interest in interests, the interest in introspection. There is no occasion to deny interests in our ongoing ob-

[1] Cf. *Interest and Effort in Education.*

jective social and physical environment. Neither should we deny the indisputable fact that we are interested in our emotions, ideas, and acts, themselves. Here is something one step removed from the ongoing process, something transcendent, personal, and subjective.

2. The Importance of the Idea of Interest in Education

Exposition. One of the kinds of interest used in education is properly stigmatized. This kind of interest means the effect of an object upon personal advantage or disadvantage. These are separated from any objective developing activity, being reduced to mere personal states of pleasure or pain. This is the use of interest in the second sense of the term mentioned at the beginning of the preceding section exaggerated and isolated. So teachers may attach some feature of seductiveness to otherwise uninteresting material, a bribe of pleasure secures attention and effort. This is indeed "soft" pedagogy of the "soup-kitchen" variety. We are not to find some pleasant bait that may be hitched onto the alien material. Neither are we to resort to arbitrary, semi-coerced effort. And neither are we to regard the material as alien or irrelevant to the normal activities of the pupils. Really, the forms of skill to be acquired and the subject-matter to be appropriated have an interest on their own account. The remedy for lack of interest or sugar-coated interest is to discover objects and modes of action which are connected with the present powers of pupils. Such material engages activity and carries it on consistently and continuously. This is its interest for the pupil. It will be noted that the misuse of the second kind of interest is corrected by the use of the first and third kinds,—an occupation that is absorbing.

Etymologically, the word interest suggests what is *between*, connecting two distant things. The two things may be distant in time as well as in space. In educative growth there is an initial and a completing step of the process, with ground to be covered between; in learning there is the initial step of the present powers of the pupil, and the completing step of realizing the aim of the teacher, with acts to be performed, difficulties to be overcome, appliances to be used between. The *betweens* are interest; only *through* them will the initial activities reach their consummation. The interest is thus "the means whereby the agent achieves his own end."

To sum up so far. If the material lacks interest, to lend it interest by extraneous inducements is condemnable; to discover material that is connected with present powers and purposes, or to realize existing but unperceived connections is simply good sense. Thus the place of interest in education is dynamic.

Among the concrete values of recognizing the importance of the idea of interest in education is that it leads to considering individual children. Each child has his specific capabilities, needs, and preferences. Not all minds work in the same way, even if they do have the same teacher and text. Pupils vary from each other in attitudes taken and in methods of approach and response to the same material. The same material varies in specific appeal to different pupils because of their different natural aptitudes, past experiences, and life-plans. Consider the individual pupil.

But apart from this concrete value, certain general values accrue to our philosophy of education from the facts about interest. These general values we may group under four conceptions: (1) mind; (2) subject-matter; (3) instruction; and (4) discipline. Certain past wrong conceptions of mind and subject-matter have seriously hampered both instruction and discipline. It has been mistakenly held that mind is isolated from subject-matter and is complete in itself; also that subject-matter is something isolated from mind and complete in itself. Instead we should regard mind as the intelligent or purposeful engaging in a course of action into which things enter. There is no dualism between mind and subject-matter; there is only unity and continuity. The dualistic view that mind and subject-matter are separate from each other leads to false views of knowledge, namely, that it is the result of the application of an internal mind to an external subject-matter, or the result of the impressions of an external subject-matter upon an internal mind, or a combination of the two.

(1) In contrast with this dualistic and mystical conception, let us consider the real nature of mind. Its three essential features are response, anticipation, and control. Thus it appears in actual experience. Mind is response to present stimuli, anticipating and controlling possible consequences; it is a name for a course of action intelligently directed. A course of action is intelligently directed when it involves the selection of means for the attainment of ends. A person is intelligent when his activities display the use of means to attain ends. Neither his intelligence nor his activity is a peculiar possession or an exclusive property of himself. He engages in an activity, partakes of it, but other things and other persons help or hinder the outcome. Mind is only one factor in the production of consequences; any other view of it is meaningless.

Let us illustrate these formal statements. Suppose you are not skilled at typewriting or that your machine does not work well. The process of acquiring skill or rectifying the machine uses intelligence. Your aim is to record certain words in a meaningful order. You attend to the keys, to what you have written, to your movements, or to the mechanism. Your attention is centered upon whatever has a bearing on the desired outcome. The foresight of desired ends and the insight into available means constitute mind. This is intelligence. Foresight without insight is abortive intelligence. If typing is a habit, it is not intelligent, and the intelligence is free to consider the topic. Striking the keys at random, regardless of consequence, is blinded intelligence. To be vague as to end and careless as to means is to be stupid or partially intelligent. Whether mind is running the machine or developing the theme, the case is the same. To be intelligent is to be alert in foreseeing the end and concerned with data pertinent thereto.

(2) Subject-matter. What you need to know to accomplish what you need to accomplish is subject-matter. It is whatever helps or even hinders the desired outcome of events. It is not something complete in itself; it is not just something to be learned by applying the mind to it or by impressing the mind with it. Just as, when halted by lack of skill or by some defect in the machine, one "studies" his typewriter, so with any subject in the curriculum. Any fact or truth becomes "a study" when it figures as a factor in a course of events personally engaging. Numbers are an object of study not because they are a part of mathematics but because the accomplishment of our purposes depends on them. To present pupils with a lesson to be learned is artificial and ineffective. Study is effective when the pupil realizes that what he is studying is the way to his objective.

In contrast with this view, in the traditional schemes of education, subject-matter means so much material to be studied, it is divided up into various independent branches, and each branch is complete in itself. Thus we have history, algebra, geometry, and so on throughout the entire curriculum. And, correspondingly, the traditional program of school work consists of "studies," for the day, the month, and even the successive years, marked off from each other, each supposed to be complete in itself—"for educational purposes at least."

(3) Instruction. Growing out of these conceptions of mind and subject-matter, the problem of instruction is two-fold, namely, to find specific, purposeful, and interesting activities; and to deal with things as conditions for the attainment of the ends of these activities. We saw the evils attending the doctrine of formal discipline. These can not be remedied by substituting a doctrine of specialized disciplines; that is, substituting many formal subjects for a few. The root of the error long prevalent in mental training consists in regarding mind as complete in itself, ready to be directly applied to any present material, thus leaving out of account the enlist-

ment of observation, imagination, and memory in directing the movement of things to desirable future ends. The remedy is nothing less than to reform the notion of mind and its training. This means the discovery of typical modes of playful or useful activities, in whose outcome the pupils have something at stake, which, however, can not be carried through without using reflection, judgment, observation, and recollection in the selection of material.

(4) Discipline. The error of regarding mind as complete in itself, like a two-edged sword, has cut two ways in the matter of discipline. It has served as a screen to protect the "disciplinary" subjects from all intelligent criticism, and it has tended to give us a negative conception of discipline. Traditional studies and methods of teaching have been protected from needed revision. In vain was it shown that they were of no use in life, that they did not really contribute to the cultivation of the self, that discipline did not accrue as a matter of fact, that pupils were lax in application and loose in intelligent self-direction. The defense was held impregnable, the subjects were asserted to be "disciplinary," so questions were stifled, doubts were subdued, the subject was removed from the realm of rational discussion, there was no checking up on the allegation, the fault was held to lie with the pupil, his faults could be corrected by more discipline, the cause of the trouble was held to be its remedy, the educator was not responsible. More discipline for lack of discipline!

The tendency, again, was toward a negative conception of discipline. Will or effort was identified with mere strain. A person just will or will not apply himself. The more indifferent and uncongenial the subject-matter, the more discipline of the will, the more acknowledgment of duty. Application just for the sake of application was alone disciplinary. The humorist was right: "It makes no difference what you teach a boy so long as he doesn't like it."

In contrast with this negative view of discipline, we have presented earlier the positive view that discipline and growth in constructive power of achievement are identical, that will means the effort to foresee and realize consequences, that attention to material because there is something to be done in which the person is concerned, resulting in a desirable increase of constructive power, is disciplinary.

Thus we have reviewed the significance of interest for a philosophy of education with special reference to the nature of mind, subject-matter, instruction, and discipline. The first and last word of a genuine theory of interest is that a topic must be connected with the promotion of an activity having a purpose.

Comment. We are glad to acknowledge with gratitude and appreciation such vital and valuable views on so important a topic in the theory and practice of education. These views are basic in the new educational movements. They are helping to transform the old schools and the old education. They are affecting the training of the new type of teacher. They are helping to direct the practice of experimental schools throughout the world.

Still, the truth of a view is not determined by its influence, in which fads and orthodoxies may have their share. There remains a real doubt as to whether the philosophy of mind as presented is the whole truth, whether all subject-matter may be merged into one without distinct branches remaining, whether activities as basic in method may carry all desirable subject-matter, and whether there may not be some valuable discipline and effort apart from immediate interest.

Let us begin by noting that the view of mind here presented (p. 153, bottom) is parallel to the view of education earlier presented (p. 89, bottom). In each case there is a present stimulating situation, a present response, the anticipation of possible results, and the directing of events toward a desired result. The weakness earlier indicated in the proposed definition of education reappears here in the proposed conception of mind. If mind is only the directive quality of events, it is difficult to see how mind could ever become its own object, as in introspection; how it could ever frame metaphysical systems; how it could be the nucleus for either selfhood or personality; or what reasonable grounds for its own permanence in reality it could entertain.

Again, concerning subject-matter, it is a little difficult to appreciate the objections to separate branches of study in view of the increasing specialization of our day and the impossibility of any encyclopedic mind knowing even the rudiments of all learning and the very great advantage to learning of having knowledge classified. Nor is it clear why the demand for the functional acquisition of knowledge should lead to the elimination of separate branches of knowledge. It is, of course, true that ideally speaking all knowledge is part of a single system, that all parts of knowledge are interrelated, that to know any part wholly is to know the whole system, but none of this means that the unity of knowledge excludes various classes of knowledge. We may anticipate increasing recognition of overlapping of prior classifications, as now in astro-physics, and bio-chemistry, but this only involves the better classification of knowledge or the recognition of newer classes, not the elimination of classes.

Again, concerning instruction, one may recognize the vital character of much learning acquired in the prosecution of activities without insisting that all learning be so acquired. Indeed, it may well be doubted whether all desirable learning can be so acquired. When a project sends one to a reference book, what is read is understood independently of the project, though related thereto, and motivated thereby. Much knowledge is acquired by interested reading apart from any playful activity or useful occupation, and an interest in such unused and unusable knowledge—unusable, that is, in play or gainful occupation may well be a sign of genuine and worthwhile culture. Any worthy occupation has a desirable cultural background, but much real culture has no occupational application.

And concerning discipline too, one may recognize that interest leads to effort and yet not be led to deny that effort "through the acknowledgment of duty" may be worthwhile in itself and even lead eventually to interest. At least many wise and true men have so held. Consider Huxley, for example, who wrote to a young man on choosing a profession as follows: "The habit of doing that which you do not care about when you would much rather be doing something else, is invaluable. It would have saved me a frightful waste of time if I had ever had it drilled into me in youth." [1] In a similar vein physicians and psychiatrists, like Dr. Joseph Collins, are telling us that the development of a stable personality depends upon such virtues as obedience, self-denial, and the recognition of authority,—virtues that are alien to the doctrine that discipline comes from doing only what is interesting. The distinguished British scientist, Sir Arthur Keith, is quoted in an interview [2] as saying: "Modern educationalists strive to make the path of learning easy and pleasant for their pupils. As a student of evolution I believe that conscious mental effort has been an important factor in our progress in the past, and one views this modern tendency with some degree of alarm. Fowls thrive best when they have to scratch for their food, and the law applies to human beings in search of mental refreshment."

The basic difficulty with Dr. Dewey's theory of interest is that the activity is by implication always physical. We shall meet other instances of this view. Here the activity is conceived of either as play or as useful occupation. And if the mind is only the directive quality of events, the activities can not be purely mental. Such a view perforce limits knowledge to action and culture to performance and learning to behavior. But just here is the rub. Perhaps interests are not something the self *is*, but something the self *has*. In this case, instead

[1] *Selections from Huxley*, Edited by C. Alphonso Smith, New York, 1912, p. 27.
[2] *The New York Times*, Jan. 20, 1929.

of the interests determining the self, the self determines its interests. In this case the first word in a genuine educational theory of interest would be that interests are one of the many modes of self-expression leading to self-realization and the last word would be that the interesting activity might be primarily either mental or physical. Our author's views on interest fit children better than adolescents and adults.

3. Some Social Aspects of the Question

Exposition. Social conditions, theory, and the school are three links in the chain of cause and effect. The social conditions cause the theory and the theory causes the school, which in turn may slowly change the social conditions. If the social conditions are wrong, theoretical errors result, which in turn show themselves in school practices. The scope and qualities of the activities in which men partake in society or children partake in school fix their fundamental attitudes toward the world, their philosophy of life.

The social aspects of the question of interest and discipline may be summed up in four propositions, as follows: (1) the real nature of interest is displayed in the artistic attitude in contrast with the mechanical on the one hand, and with the æsthetic on the other; (2) there should be no separate laboring class with discipline without interest and no separate leisure class with interest without discipline; (3) there should be correspondingly no separate vocational education without culture and no separate cultural education without vocation; and (4) this social situation is to be remedied by an educational reorganization that combines learning with purposeful activities.

(1) Art truly exemplifies interest. It brings about changes in the world. These changes are both outer and inner, both physical and mental. Physical changes that are not mental are mechanical. Mental changes that are not physical are æsthetic. Our society to-day is characterized by mechanical

changes and æsthetic attitudes, but not by artistic accomplishment combining the two. Mechanical changes carry no enrichment of emotion and intellect, have no ideal reward, lack a full and free expression of interest, do not adequately engage intelligence. Æsthetic attitudes, on the other hand, are introverted, they are an inner refuge of sentiment and fancy. Even the pursuit of science may become a refuge from the hard condition of life instead of a temporary retreat for understanding the present in order to remold the future. Likewise the good word art, which we have chosen to exemplify the ideal of interest, may lose its external reference and become an eccentric fancy or an emotional indulgence. Thus practice and theory fall apart in mutual contempt, the industrial and the fine arts become divorced, efficiency and culture become one-sided, society becomes stratified, and the true nature of interest and mind is narrowed or perverted.

(2) The division between laboring and leisure classes should not exist in the organization of society. The intelligence of the man who labors without leisure becomes hard; the majority of human beings still lack economic freedom; they have a servile status; their pursuits are fixed by accident or necessity, not by a normal expression of their own powers. The intelligence of the man who has leisure without labor becomes soft, luxurious, effeminate, and illiberal. The few who control the many economic slaves manipulate men for non-human ends. Instead, the intelligence of all men should play freely upon the subjugation of the world for human ends.

(3) This objectionable state of human affairs explains our backward educational traditions and clash of aims. Our elementary education is mainly utilitarian; our higher education is mainly disciplinary or cultural, our liberal education is held to be hostile to vocational aims, intellectual matters are isolated from the practical, and knowledge becomes scholastic, academic, or professionally technical.

(4) To improve our social conditions, what most needs to be done is to reorganize our education. Specifically, purpose-

ful activities, intelligently carried forward, necessitating learning in the process of doing, are the basic requisites. Pupils so trained will acquire intellectual and emotional dispositions combining knowledge with practice. It will be slow work, accomplished piecemeal, a step at a time. But the situation challenges. Our present practice is an oscillation between drill exercises without intelligence and the accumulation of knowledge as an end in itself. Such practice accepts the present social conditions as final and perpetuates them. There is no reason for nominally accepting one philosophy and practicing another.

Comment. It is clear that Dr. Dewey is opposed to our present mainly competitive and capitalistic economic order. It is clear that he opposes the division of society into laboring and leisure classes. But it is not clear just what he would substitute therefor. Apparently, a method of solution, that of learning by doing is to be followed in the schools, which will bring its own undefined social reorganization with it in due time.

Several things are to be observed here. The first is that apparently there is no recognition that brain work is labor. Those who control our present economic order are held to belong to the leisure class. Those who produce goods belong to the labor class. But is not this distinction too sharply drawn? Employers may very well be laborers too in the sense of doing useful work. Also, laborers in a democratic society which has compulsory education through the elementary schools are not merely hand workers. They also think, the proof of which is the various labor organizations. Certainly our economic conditions are far from ideal; still, with laboring employers and thinking laborers and various expressions of democracy in industry, such as profit-sharing and consultative committees, the dualism between our economic classes is not so sharp after all.

Again, one may express a doubt about the schools being successful in changing society by reforming themselves. The question of transfer of training from school to society is involved. One often notes the loss of the idealism of school and college in the realism of business or law or politics. Many a political boss left college with ideals of political reform. It is possible the school will always rather reflect social conditions than change them.

But the case is not hopeless. Society may be improved, nevertheless, by adult education of persons who are actually facing the evil conditions; by the slow process of social evolution in meeting changed conditions, or even, *in extremis,* by social revolution. Societies have gradually improved by social evolution, and societies have on the whole improved by revolutions. Societal evolution, like organic evolution, involves the four factors "of adaptation, variation, selection, and transmission." [1]

In general, concerning the social implications of interest and discipline, it is likely that society will always have some work that is drudgery. Even when machines do most of the work, the machines will have to be tended. There will remain in life an element of discipline without interest. There will always be occupations for somebody all the time or everybody some of the time, which are not entirely congenial. They will be done of necessity, if not of high-minded devotion. To this topic we will return in Chapter XV on play and work in the curriculum. Our conclusion is that life, and education as a phase of life, may be interesting if they can, but disciplinary if they must.

[1] Cf. Keller, A. G., *Societal Evolution,* Rev. Ed., 1931, The Macmillan Company.

CHAPTER XI

EXPERIENCE AND THINKING

1. The Nature of Experience

Exposition. In this section we will seek the answer to these three questions, namely, (1) What is experience? (2) What important conclusions follow for education? And (3) What evil results have flowed from the alleged dualism of mind and body?

(1) Experience is composed of two elements, one active, and one passive. The organism does something to the environment; this is the active element in the experience. And in turn the environment does something to the organism, which the organism undergoes or suffers; this is the passive element in experience. Either element may come first in time. But in experience the two elements are peculiarly combined in that the trying leads on to the undergoing or the undergoing leads back in thought to the prior activity or leads on to a new trying. Just activity, like sticking one's finger into the fire, is not experience; just undergoing, like a burnt finger, is not experience; but connecting the burning with the sticking the finger into the fire is experience. There is no experience without this connecting or learning, and there is no learning that does not originate in this way. Only organisms capable of thus connecting antecedent activity with consequent results can have experience. Sticks and stones have no experience. Mere flux and accidents unrelated to their antecedents, without retrospect or prospect, are not experience. The active or the trying element in experience is an experiment to find out what the world is like, and the passive or the undergoing element is instruction, the answer, leading to the connection of things.

(2) The two conclusions from this account of the nature of experience are these: experience, being an active-passive, or a passive-active affair, is not primarily cognitive, or intellectual, but practical; and, the value of an experience lies in connecting its two elements. To be active without noting the consequences, to undergo changes without noting the antecedents,— these sundered elements of experience are without value. The activity and the suffering are primary and practical; the connecting of the two is secondary, though indispensable, and cognitive. The experience is primarily practical, but the value of the experience lies in the cognition. It were futile to try to separate the secondary cognitive function from the primary trying and undergoing of experience. Yet just this vain thing is too customarily done in our schools. Pupils are made theoretical spectators, they are mistakenly supposed to appropriate knowledge by direct energy of intellect, they are denied the fruitful experiences without which there is no cognition, a mythical mind is reared from the irrelevant physical organs of activity, experience is broken into the two fragments of body and mind, and meaning is lost in being separated from its matrix. Instead, mind should be regarded as the connecting of the earlier and the later elements in an ongoing active process.

(3) The evils flowing from mistaking the continuity of mind and body and accepting a dualism between them instead can not be adequately stated, much less exaggerated. Three striking evil effects, however, may be noted, as follows:

(*a*) bodily activity becomes an intruder;
(*b*) bodily activity is used mechanically; and
(*c*) intellectually, things are emphasized at the expense of relations.

Each of these will be considered in turn. (*a*) Bodily activity, being thought to having nothing to do with mental activity becomes a distraction, an evil to be overcome, leading the pupil's mind away from his lesson, a source of mischief. A premium is put on being still, being silent, on uniformity of posture and movement, on a simulation of intelligent interest. The teacher must exact these requirements of the pupils. But the pupil had to bring his body to school along with his mind; there it is a wellspring of energy; it has to do something; inevitable deviations from the oppressive requirements occur; these must be punished by the teacher. Just here is the chief source of the "problem of discipline" in schools. Nervous strain and fatigue for both teacher and pupil result, whence come pupil indifference, explosions, boisterousness, foolery, restlessness, unruliness. Conscientious, quiescent pupils exhaust their energy in suppressing their active tendencies; it becomes a duty not to give free play to the significant and graceful use of bodily powers. The Greeks were wiser; they never attempted to separate mind and body; this was a chief cause of their remarkable achievements.

(*b*) Such bodily activities as have to be employed are used mechanically; that is, they are separated from purpose and the recognition of meaning. The senses become an inlet to the mind; the muscles become an outlet from the mind. The eye is employed to take in what the book, the map, and the blackboard report; the ear takes in what the teacher says. Eye and ear become mysterious conduits conducting information from the external world of matter to the internal world of mind; they are the gateways, the avenues, of knowledge. The eye fixed on the book, the ear open to the teacher's words, are mysterious courses of intellectual grace. In the reverse direction the muscles are pipes carrying knowledge back from the storehouse of internal mind into the external world. Lips, vocal organs, and hands, in speaking, writing, and figuring, reproduce what has been stowed away. The muscles so involved demand training, secured by using them repeatedly in the same way, resulting in an automatic tendency to repeat. The use of eyes to note the form of words irrespective of meaning, the use of muscles to reproduce such words in spelling and reading, is mechanical; the act is isolated from a purpose.

Such reading can not be done with expression; meaning can not be tied on at will. Drawing, singing, writing, mathematics, and science may all be taught mechanically; that is, separating the bodily activity from purpose and the recognition of meaning. Mathematics is so taught when the technique of calculation is unduly emphasized; science is so taught when laboratory exercises are given for their own sake.

In contrast with such mechanical use of the senses and muscles of the body, consider their purposeful, meaningful, organic, and proper educational use. In experiences out of school, eye, ear, and hands do things in a process from which meaning results. Consider the boy flying a kite. Here is a process with a meaning. His eye is on the kite, his hand is on the string. What he sees and feels has significance and thrills. Senses and muscles are no longer inlets and outlets, conduits and pipes; they are organs of use in doing something with a purpose; thus they are sources of knowledge, functional knowledge, growing out of a present situation, and controlling the coming situation. School work should be like a boy flying a kite.

(*c*) Perhaps worst of all, the attempted separation of mind and body leads to the neglect of *relations* and emphasis on *things*. The knowledge of relations can come only through the connecting of the earlier and later phases of experience. If the body is omitted from the process, the mind has nothing to connect; it has only ideas as the wraiths of former experience, the remembered perception of things.

To be specific in this abstruse matter, perception involves judgments, things involve relations; words are not ideas, though easily mistaken for them; and relations are imperceptible without experience as an ongoing, undergoing affair. But the attempted separation of body and mind would give us perceptions without judgments, words without ideas, and relations without experience.

Perceptions involve judgments, things involve relations. It is an error to suppose that the mind can have perceptions without active experience, and that the judgment can then be called upon to combine such perceptions. The perception is itself judgmental, the thing is itself relational, the mind can not work apart from the setting of practical experience. There is no perception of a chair apart from judgment as to its purpose, its distinguishing characteristics, its "period," and so on. There is no perception of a wagon as a sum of its parts apart from the judgment concerning the connection of the parts, the animals it is drawn by, the load it carries, and so on. Perceiving is active and involves the situation of which the thing perceived is a part. The separation of mind and body takes the perception out of its setting in a relational experience.

Words are the counters of ideas but not ideas themselves. The idea is functional in a situation involving bodily activity; the word is the symbol of the idea. Remove the bodily situation, the idea loses its function, and the word alone remains, carrying only the ghost of a meaning. Thus result half-perceptions, dull observation, pseudo-ideas, half-dead mental action, and symbolic verbosity. In vital experiences requiring judgment involving bodily action, words can not take the place of ideas.

It is incorrectly supposed that relationships can be perceived without that conjoint trying and undergoing which constitutes experience, that the mind can grasp relationships if it will only attend, and that mind can attend at will irrespective of the situation. Whence the world is afflicted by another deluge,—that of half-observations, verbal ideas, unassimilated knowledge, a set of catchwords rendering perception obscure and thinking impossible. Questions are not answered, they are disposed of by words, and this in the name of education. In theory there is universal agreement that the discernment of relationships is the genuinely intellectual, hence educative matter. But in practice our schools remove the conditions of such discernment. An ounce of experience is better than a ton of theory, and can generate a ton of theory, but the ounce.

however humble, is necessary before the theory can be grasped.

In sum, experience is experiment and what one learns from it; it is not primarily cognitive but its value lies in the cognitive feature, the connections, in it; and the evils that flow from attempting to separate knowledge from its setting in experience are the disesteem of the bodily activity, the mechanical use of the bodily activity, and the neglect of relations. The net result is that the mind should be employed about physical activities.

Comment. There are three things to be remarked concerning this analysis of the nature of experience, namely, (1) in stressing experience as the interactive relation of the individual to his environment, the analysis as made omits the interaction between the individual and other individuals; (2) the relational theory of mind as presented is questionable; and (3) mental action need not be limited to physical situations.

(1) Our experience is not limited to our physical environment; there is also our social environment and the important thing about our fellows is that, like ourselves, they are personalities, and not just responding organisms. This difference is recognized in Herbart's distinction between experience (*Erfahrung*) and intercourse (*Umgang*). No analysis of experience is complete without this distinction. And no educative process is adequate that does not profit by this distinction and recognize that the pupil learns from the teacher as well as from his own bodily activities and manipulations. From his teacher he may learn kindness, gentleness, sympathy, and love, honesty, self-respect, and reliability, which are characteristic of social situations in distinction from physical activities. In other connections Dr. Dewey emphasizes the social environment and virtues; it should not be omitted from this analysis of experience.

(2) The view is held that mind is the cognitive element within experience which connects the earlier phase of acting with the later phase of undergoing. This is the relational

view of mind, viz., that mind is a relating of events to each other. It will be noted that the cognitive element in experience is held not to be primary but to be the measure of value of an experience. Now two things may be observed here. The first is that this view makes mind depend on the situation rather than the situation depend on mind. When we remember that the situation exists for mind and that mind could have made the situation different, and does do so in controlling the situation, it is not so clear that mind is entirely dependent on the situation. Furthermore, the relational view of mind as stated assigns the value of an experience to cognition. Undoubtedly cognition in connecting effects with their causes enables us to avoid undesirable effects and to secure desirable effects. But the value after all inheres in the desirable quality of the effect, and this is emotional, appreciated, and desired as well as cognitive, appreciable, and desirable. The theory of mind as relational, as cognitive, thus unwarrantably omits the feeling aspect of consciousness.

(3) And still again, the limitation of thinking to experimenting and undergoing is questionable. We do indeed think in terms of experience, but we can also think beyond the limits of experience. Thus Kant could examine the very conditions of all experience. Astronomers can formulate theories of the formation of the earth prior to any experience of man. Chemists knew what missing elements to look for before they were found. Mathematicians can think in terms of the unexperienced fourth dimension. Plato could think of eternal ideas which get only incomplete embodiment in the present world of changing experience. The logician can examine the processes of thought in general, apart from concrete experiential situations. And the introspective psychologist can think his own thinking. In all these ways thinking can transcend the doing and undergoing of concrete experience. Educationally this ability is important in satisfying the desire to know abstract truth and in enlarging man's perspective.

If all thinking is to be a function of experience, the concept of experience must be enlarged to cover Plato's vision of the ideas, Kant's "intellectual perception," and Hegel's absolute Idea. But this conception of experience is far removed from the instrumental theory of ideas held by Dr. Dewey and leads us into idealism instead.

2. Reflection in Experience

Exposition. There are four questions that concern us here, as follows:

(1) What is the meaning of "reflection in experience?" (2) How does reflection differ from trial and error? (3) How does reflection differ from routine and caprice? And, (4) most important of all, what are the general features of a reflective experience?

(1) Reflection or thought, be it noted, is something that takes place within experience; it is the discernment of the relation between what we try to do and what happens in consequence. This is the view presented in the preceding section. Without reflection experience has no meaning. But the amount of reflection is less or more, giving us two types of experience, as follows:

(2) The type of experience with less reflection in it is that of trial and error; the type of experience with more reflection in it is the reflective experience *par excellence.* But there is always some reflection in the trial and error method and there is always some trial and error in the reflective method. The two types of experience can not be sharply distinguished from each other. But we can contrast the two. In the trial and error method we simply do something, and, if it fails, we do something else, and keep on trying till we hit upon something which works, which we then adopt as a rule of thumb measure in later instances. We see *that* a certain action and a certain consequence are connected but not *how;* the links are missing; discernment is gross. The trial and the error method is at

the mercy of changing circumstance. Though reflection improves, we never get wholly beyond the trial and error situation. Our most elaborate thought can never take into account all the connections, can never cover accurately all the consequences, must therefore be tried in the world, and so tried out.

Still, the reflective experience can be marked off from the grosser trial and error method. In it there is a careful survey of conditions, keen observation and analysis of what lies between action and consequence. Cause and effect are bound together. The guess at results is controlled. Better insight makes more accurate foresight. A missing condition may be supplied, superfluous causes leading to undesirable effects may be eliminated. Thus our practical control of experience is extended; action with an end in view becomes possible. Without reflection we have no aims. The infant and the wisest man each has reflective experience, differing only in degree; as soon as the infant begins to *expect*, begins to take one thing as *evidence* of something else to follow, he recognizes a relationship, and so judges, thinks, reflects, infers; the wisest man only refines this simple process, observing more minutely and more widely and selecting more carefully the factors indicative of certain consequences.

(3) Reflective experience, or thoughtful action, once more, is opposed to routine and caprice. Routine follows custom and, like trial and error, omits the connections between act and consequence. Caprice follows the moment and omits the connections between our personal acts and our environment. One looking to the past, one looking to the moment, both refuse to acknowledge responsibility for the future, which reflection accepts.

(4) Now the very important question concerning the general features of a reflective experience. We will begin with an illustration. "As this is written, the world is filled with the clang of contending armies" (p. 171). Now a commanding general is in a position demanding the most serious

reflection, whose outcome is of greatest importance for his country, his soldiers, himself. He must think. The general staff of which he is a member must think. He faces a difficult incomplete situation. He wants to attain a certain objective; this is his strategy. He must study the situation exactly, as it is. He must devise means to utilize what he has in attaining what he desires; this is his tactics. His own strength must not be overestimated, the enemy's strength must not be under-estimated. His thinking must be impartial, objective, not biased by his deep desires. He must utilize all he has ever learned about war. His judgment finally fixes upon a plan of procedure. The order is issued. Success, partial success, or failure results, according to the adequacy and execution of the plan. There will probably be some surprises.

Consider the related case of a much-interested reflective observer in a neutral country. He too faces an incomplete situation; he does not know how the battle will go; but he conjectures. He follows the situation as it unfolds. He anticipates future moves. He is actively on the lookout to see if they occur. If they do, his expectation is proven correct. He experiences some emotional satisfaction in having correctly anticipated the course of events in which he is not a participant.

Consider an astronomer who studies the changing heavens. Will an eclipse occur? When? The present data must be accurately assembled. Mathematical calculations must be exact. Because of the nature of the circumstances, his prediction is practically sure to be verified. His conclusions are checked by those of many others. Allowance is made for the amount of probable error. He acts upon his expectation of the eclipse; apparatus is arranged, perhaps a journey to a place with a clear sky in the expected path of the eclipse is undertaken; some physical conditions are changed. The eclipse occurs and is studied and the act of thought is completed.

All instances of reflection in experience are like these three. Their general features are the same. The four essential steps are (i) the sense of the problem; (ii) the observation of conditions; (iii) the formation of an hypothesis; and (iv) the testing of the hypothesis. A subdivision of the sense of the problem may be made into (1) an incomplete situation, and (2) a conjecture as to the outcome, which after study will take form as the hypothesis, thus giving five steps in a reflective experience. The number of steps appearing in the analysis is not the important thing, but the fact that thinking works in a practical, problematic challenging situation by means of data, hypothesis, and experimental testing.

A few comments upon the outstanding characteristics of reflective experience should be made to increase our sympathetic understanding of it. Thinking always starts with something going on whose meaning lies in what it is going to be. To think about the news of the day is to think about its outcome. To take anything by itself as a complete existence is to take it unreflectively. Reflection about the past is no exception; we think about a past occurrence when we think about what it led to; its leading is its meaning. To fill our heads, like a scrapbook, with this and that item as a finished thing is not to think; it is to be a piece of registering apparatus. "What follows, or followed, as a consequence?" is the question asked when we think. In origin the course of thinking is an actual part of the course of events and is designed to influence the outcome.

Again, and of course, reflection means concern with the issue. So with the general, the soldier, the citizen of the belligerent nations; their concern is direct and urgent. But even neutrals, if they reflect at all, are concerned about the issue, though their concern is more indirect and imaginative. Human nature is flagrantly partisan; we identify ourselves with one outcome of events, desire it, and reject all others. We take sides, if not overtly, then emotionally, and imaginatively.

Behold here a paradox! Thought is both partial and impartial. Partial it is in its origin; impartial it is, or should be, in its conclusions. The occasion of reflection is finding ourselves in a situation; the value of reflection is in keeping ourselves out of the situation. Hopes, desires, and fears may originate, stimulate, and motivate thinking, but should not control it. The mixing of emotion with observation and interpretation means mistakes in calculation. Achieving such detachment is an almost insurmountable difficulty, made possible only by a growth of social sympathies leading gradually to a wide vision. Here is a fact of great significance for education.

Where there is reflection there is suspense, uncertainty, doubt, a problem. Concerning what is finished, completed, assured, there is no need to think. And, the object of thinking is to help us reach a conclusion on the basis of the given.

Further, since thinking faces a problematic situation, thinking is a process of inquiry, of looking into things, of investigating, of seeking. Acquiring is secondary and instrumental to inquiring. All thinking is "original research" with him who carries it on, though everyone else in the world already has found what he seeks; original research is not the exclusive prerogative of advanced students and scientists.

All thinking involves a risk. The invasion of the unknown is an adventure; we can not be sure in advance. Till confirmed by the event, the conclusions of thinking are tentative, provisional, and hypothetical; to assert them as final is dogmatic and unwarranted. The perplexities of the situation suggest certain ways out; we try these ways; if the situation gets darker, we know we are still ignorant; if the situation clears up, we know we have pushed our way out.

The Greeks acutely raised the question: "How can we learn?" They formulated this dilemma: Either we already know what we would learn, or we do not. If we already know, we can not learn, because we cannot learn what we already know; and if we do not already know, we can not learn, because we do not know what to look for, and even if we found it by chance we could not recognize it. This is a nice piece of formal logic. The error is in the imperfect disjunction of the major premise. Really, there are three alternatives, namely, either we know already, or we do not know already, or we are coming to know. In addition to complete knowledge and complete ignorance, we have the twilight zone of inquiry, of thinking, of hypothesis.

It is worthy of note that as long as man followed the Greeks and kept a sharp disjunction between knowledge and ignorance, science made only slow and accidental advance, but, when men recognized the middle ground of doubt, inquiry, conjecture, and exploration, to be confirmed or refuted by later developments, there began a systematic advance in discovery and invention. While the Greek philosophers made knowledge more than learning, the modern scientists make knowledge only a means to learning. Thinking results in knowledge, and the value of knowledge is its use in thinking. Knowledge is retrospective, thinking is prospective. Knowledge is of value in the solidity, security, and fertility it affords our thinking, our dealing with the future. Because we live in an unfinished, unsettled, ongoing world, our main task is prospective.

Returning to the title of this chapter, present experience is the basis of thinking, but thinking, utilizing the results of past experience or knowledge, is the source of control of future experience.

Comment. This chapter contains a re-statement of Dr. Dewey's now famous analysis of thinking. It is not original with Dr. Dewey (see end of following chapter). It appeared previously in his volume: *How We Think* (Boston, 1910). This analysis has greatly influenced all later exponents of Dr. Dewey's thought.[1] No educational applications are drawn in this section, but are reserved for the succeeding chapter.

[1] Cf. particularly, Kilpatrick, W. H., *Foundations of Method* (1925). Columbia Associates in Philosophy, *Introduction to Reflective Thinking*, Boston (1923).

Concerning the steps into which the complete act of thought is analyzed, let us observe (1) that the incomplete situation may be mental as well as physical; (2) that the problem may therefore be intellectual without involving any change in physical conditions; (3) that the hypothesis may therefore not be provable at all; and so (4) that the thinking may therefore be incomplete, but justifiable as philosophy, without attaining the step of tested thought which is science.

As a typical problem of this kind in speculative science consider that of the appearance of the back side of the moon,—an interesting question exciting some curiosity. It is a question of constructing an image without a prior percept, and so intellectual rather than physical. In constructing such an image no advantageous change in physical conditions is possible; we can not move to a place where the back of the moon is visible. Any hypothesis we may form as to its low visibility and mountainous character can not be proven. And so the last step of testing can not be taken. But we can and do think this problem, though the solution is beyond our actual experience. Here then thinking transcends experience, though growing out of it. Without such thinking the speculative element would be eliminated from natural science, and we should never have heard of such views as relativity, space as a form of matter, cosmic rays, universal radiation, and the like; and thereby much direction to practical experimentation would have been lost.

Consider as a typical problem in philosophical thinking that of man's survival of bodily death. Here the incomplete situation is non-physical. The problem is a purely intellectual one, apart from such methods as spiritualism and psychical research may utilize. The hypothesis either for or against may not be proven. No conclusion that is known to be true for some or all classes of men can be reached. Yet, such thinking is natural to man, tends to satisfy an emotional interest, has engaged our keenest intellects from Plato to Kant, and has motivated for good or evil much human conduct. Admittedly the thinking is inconclusive, speculative, hypothetical, philosophical, but it is nevertheless regulative of much human conduct. We act as though it were true, or false, or a matter of indifference. And such action can be justified only by thinking, which in this case is perforce incomplete. As against then the limitation of thinking to experience, we must indicate the indispensable and invaluable function of the thinking that transcends experience. "Reflection *in* experience," yes, and *beyond* it too! For education this conclusion opens for use in addition to experience the realms of the unexperienced and the, as yet at least, unexperienceable. We do not need with Kant to destroy knowledge of the real world in order to make room for faith; neither do we need with Dewey to destroy faith in the transcendent world to make room for knowledge. The world may be infinite in an indefinite number of ways, and man's limited experience may be only a segment of an infinite whole. The warrant for such a conclusion would take us far into pure philosophy.

CHAPTER XII

THINKING IN EDUCATION

1. The Essentials of Method

Exposition. We have just discussed the stages of reflection in experience. We are now to discuss the stages of thinking, or reflection, in education. Naturally they are identical. And the stages of thinking, or reflection, in education give us the essentials of method. What we now need is to see in detail how thinking, or reflection, should go on in education.

It will help us at the start to note that at present there is not the unity in thinking, reflection, or method, in education that should obtain. We manage mistakenly to keep thinking apart from skill on the one hand, and from information on the other. In teaching reading, spelling, writing, drawing, and reciting, we seek the acquisition of skill alone, not skill and thinking. In teaching history and geography we seek the acquisition of information alone, not information and thinking. Then, apart from skill and information, we seek to train thinking. All three ends are accomplished ineffectively. Skill obtained apart from thinking misses the purpose of skill, and leaves the artisan at the mercy of his own routine habits and of the authoritative and unscrupulous control of those who know what they are about. And information obtained apart from thoughtful action simulates knowledge, develops the poison of conceit, hinders further intelligent growth, is deadweight and a mind-crushing load. And the thinking which is not connected on the one hand with skill, or increase of efficiency in action, and, on the other hand, with information, or increase of learning about ourselves and our world, is defective, unattached, formal, and inconsequential.

We do not adequately recognize, in practice at least, the importance of fostering in school good habits of thinking. Apart from certain specialized muscular abilities, all the school can or need do for the *minds* of pupils is to develop their ability to think. But we must understand, as indicated above, that thinking is no abstract matter; it is the method of intelligent learning, the method of intelligent ongoing experience. We talk about the methods of thinking; this is well enough; but the important thing to bear in mind is that thinking itself is method, the method of all fruitful learning. So, to improve method, improve thinking, improve the conditions which require, promote, and test thinking. There is no other way to improve method, whether of instruction or of learning.

So we now raise the question, what are the essentials of method, that is, what are the stages of thinking in an educative process? These are five, as follows: experience, problem, data, hypothesis, testing, to each of which a brief discussion will be devoted.

(1) Experience. The initial stage of thinking is *experience.* This remark ought to be a silly truism but unfortunately it is not. We insist that the initiating phase of thought is an actual empirical situation, and necessarily so. The empirical situation, or experience, means here just what we said: trying to do something and having something perceptibly done to one in return. The first contact with any new material must inevitably be of the trial and error sort; it may be in play or work; the individual must try to do something with material in carrying out his own impulsive activity, noting the interaction between his energy and the material; this is true whatever the age: the child experimenting with his building blocks, or the scientist experimenting with unfamiliar material in his laboratory.

The out-of-school situation is the kind meant. In ordinary life the child meets situations that interest and engage activity. He has something to do, not something to learn; the doing demands thinking, or the intentional noting of connections; learning results naturally.

The most successful methods in formal education go back to the out-of-school type of situation; this is revealed by a careful inspection of school methods; it is true in arithmetic, reading, geography, physics, or a foreign language.

Of course, as noted previously, the empirical situation which initiates thinking should suggest neither routine nor capricious activity. What is suggested should be both new, uncertain, problematic and so not routine, and yet familiar enough to call out an effective response, accomplishing a perceptible result, mentally connected with what was done, and so not capricious or haphazard.

Such experience on the part of the pupils can not be assumed. To suppose that it can is the fundamental fallacy in our methods of instruction to-day. Instead of beginning with a direct personal experience of a situation, we begin with ready-made subject matter of arithmetic, geography, or whatever it may be. Even the kindergarten and Montessori techniques tend to ignore or reduce the immediate crude handling of the familiar material of experience; they are too anxious to get at material expressing intellectual and adult-made distinctions without "waste of time."

Thinking can not be sundered from experience and can not be cultivated in isolation from it, philosophic theory and educational practice to the contrary notwithstanding. Still, the inherent limitations of experience are often falsely urged as the sufficient ground for attention to thinking. Experience is then incorrectly thought to be confined to the senses, the appetities, and a mere material world, while thinking is incorrectly held to proceed from a higher faculty of reason and to be properly occupied with spiritual, or at least literary, things. To illustrate this false antithesis, a sharp distinction is oftentimes made between applied and pure mathematics, the former dealing with physical things and having a utilitarian but not mental value and the latter having nothing to do with physical things and being fit subject matter of thought.

In sum, then, the first essential of method is that the pupil have a genuine situation of experience, that he be engaged in a continuous activity in which he is interested for its own sake.

(2) The Problem. A genuine problem must develop within this situation as a stimulus to thought. What quality of problem does this learning situation involve? That is the most important question that can be asked concerning any experience that would be educative. Does the problem induce the habitual, the haphazard, or the thoughtful type of response?

So genuine and mock problems must be distinguished. A large part of school work consists in the giving of problems, the putting of questions, the assigning of tasks, and the magnifying of difficulties. It might seem as if usual school methods measured well up to the standard here set. Whether they do or not depends upon whether the problems are real or simulated. There are two marks of a genuine problem, as follows:

(*a*) It arises naturally within some situation of personal experience. It is the sort of trying that takes place out of school. It arouses observation and leads on to experimentation. It is not *just* a problem, an aloof thing, existing only to convey instruction in some school subject.

(*b*) It is the pupil's own problem. His own personal experience inherently stimulates and directs his observation of the connections involved in it, leading on naturally to inference and to a testing of this inference. It is not the teacher's problem, not the textbook's problem, not imposed from without, not the assigned external way of getting a required mark, or of being promoted, or of winning the teacher's approval. These two characteristics of a genuine problem, that it be experential and personal, obviously somewhat overlap.

To what extent do current school practices develop reflective habits? Maybe the picture we are about to draw will seem exaggerated and too highly colored. Children do not have real experiences in school and do not deal with genuine personal problems. School conditions are not similar to the everyday life conditions; the latter generate difficulties. The physical equipment of the average schoolroom is hostile to real experience. The premium is put upon listening, reading, and reproducing. Customary school conditions supply no context of experience in which problems naturally arise. Everything in school contrasts with everything out of school. In school the teachers who know the answers ask the questions; out of school the pupils who do not know the answers ask questions. In school, no curiosity; out of school, all curiosity. In the school, seats, desks, books; out of school, active contact with things and persons on the playground and in the home, as the ordinary responsibilities of life are met.

There being a lack of real experience in the school, the problems are artificial. They are a pupil's problem, not a child's problem. His problem is to meet the peculiar requirements set by the teacher; what does he want? What kind of recitation, examination, and deportment, will satisfy him? The pupil is really studying the conventions of the school system; his relation to subject matter is not direct; the arithmetic, history, geography, must all be adapted to the requirements. Thinking becomes one-sided. The waste in carrying over expertness from school to life is lamentable. At its worst, the pupil's problem is not to meet the school's requirements, but to *seem* to meet them, and so avoid friction; thus character itself is undesirably affected.

The remedy? Not improvement in the personal technique of the instructor. The conditions themselves must be changed. Poor technique with suitable conditions is more profitable than excellent technique with unsuitable conditions. To break the gap between school and life, solid material is necessary, more *stuff*, more appliances, more actual doing of things. Where children are doing things, using materials to accomplish purposes, they discuss what they do, they raise questions spontaneously and often, and they advance varied and ingenious solutions. This is thinking in education. It is done by the pupils for themselves, not for the pupils by the teachers.

(3) The Data. The pupil must himself possess the information and make the observations necessary to deal with the problem. The difficulty that has arisen in the pupil's own personal experience can not be dealt with adequately without data. To think effectively one must have resources enabling him to cope with the difficulty at hand. These resources come from experiences. "Think it out for yourself" does not mean "spin it out of your own head," though a "developing" method may make this mistake. One does not think thoughts or with thoughts; he thinks actions, facts, events, and the relations of things.

There is no thinking without a difficulty as a stimulus; still the difficulty may be so great as to overwhelm thinking and lead to discouragement. The perplexing situation must be hard enough to challenge thought and easy enough to allow success. The novel element in the difficulty makes it hard; the familiar element makes it easy. A large part of the art of instruction lies in making the difficulties the right size. Here the teacher functions. How are the data to be obtained? This does not matter so much; the important thing is not how the data are obtained, but that they are needed and are used. The data may come from memory, from reading, from observation, or even from being told. The relative amount of data obtained from each source depends on the specific problem. Data derived from reading and being told come from others; data derived from memory and observation come from oneself. Strange as it may seem, we may have not only too little direct observation but also too much; and again, we may have not only too much reliance on others but also too little.

Direct observation gives vividness and vitality. It is necessary when something about a familiar object has been missed. But direct observation is unnecessary when memory of the same facts is adequate; a well-trained mind is accustomed to go over its past experiences and learn from them. Direct observation is limited too in time and space, and requires supplementation from the experiences of others. Yet, excessive reliance upon others for data derived from reading or listening is objectionable, and especially objectionable is reliance upon others for ready-made solutions.

It is paradoxical but not inconsistent to say that schools supply both too much and too little information,—too much of the type unused in problem-solving, too little of the type used in problem-solving. There is too much information acquired only to be reproduced in recitation and examination. This static cold-storage ideal of knowledge is inimical to educative development; it lets occasions for thinking go unused; it swamps thinking; it provides no practice in selecting what is appropriate; it gives no criterion of selection to follow. On the other hand, too little functioning information is supplied. Resources in books, pictures, talks, are too limited. Information which is real knowledge is the working capital of further inquiry; it is to be used in furthering the student's own purposes; it is not an end in itself, to be heaped up and displayed on occasion. Of such vital information too much cannot be had. Thus the data, whencesoever derived, concern the problem.

(4) Hypothesis. The hypothesis is the suggested solution of the problem growing out of the data. The data are given, already there, assured; they are determined by careful observation and recollection. They define, clarify, and locate the question. They are facts, things already done. These data *arouse* suggestions, inferences, conjectured meanings, suppositions, tentative explanations, in one word, *ideas,* or hypotheses. The data lead to the hypothesis through the aid of projection, invention, ingenuity, devising. The appro-

priateness of the hypothesis is determined only by reference to the data. When we think, the hypothesis is the correlate of the data. The present data can not supply the answer to the question, the proof of the hypothesis. The hypothesis runs beyond the data. It forecasts things to do. In this sense an inference or an hypothesis is always a leap from the known, an invasion of the unknown.

A thought is creative,—an incursion into the novel. A thought is what a present thing suggests that is not present. Inventiveness is involved. The novelty consists in the new light in which the familiar is seen or the new use to which it is put. The material is familiar, the operation is novel. Creative originality consists in putting familiar things to unfamiliar uses; only silly folk identify it with the production of extraordinary or fanciful materials. Take Newton as an example. His material was familiar: sun, moon, planets, weight, distance, Mars, square of numbers. His originality lay in the unfamiliar use to which he put these familiar acquaintances. He could see the same principle at work in a falling apple and a revolving moon; this was the creative aspect of this thought; and lo! the theory of gravitation. And so it is with every scientific discovery, every great invention, every admirable artistic production. Creative thought makes incursions into the unknown by the aid of the known.

Two educational conclusions follow, namely, all real thinking is original, and no real thinking is conveyable. Thinking is original in projecting considerations not previously apprehended. The child of three who finds out what can be done with blocks is really a discoverer. So is a child of six who finds out what he can make by putting five cents and five cents together. These are genuine discoveries, even though already known to everybody else in the world; they are a genuine increment of experience; they are not mechanical additions, but qualitative enrichments. Children experience the joy of intellectual constructiveness, of creativeness, "if the word may be used without misunderstanding." Sympathetic observers of the spontaneity of little children perceive this intellectual originality and are charmed by it. Learning is not storing away what teachers pour into pupils; a classroom is not a place where forty little pitchers gather around a single fountain. Learning is discovering, and school conditions should favor it. It is possible to give even children and youth the delights of personal intellectual productiveness. If done, teachers too would find their own work less of a grind and strain.

No thought, no idea, can be conveyed as such to another. In being told, the quality of an idea is transmuted into that of a fact. The lecturer may express an idea; the auditor gets directly the fact that the lecturer holds that idea; if the auditor gets an idea from the lecturer, he must develop it for himself from within. The communication may stimulate ideas or it may only smother intellectual interest and suppress dawning thought. The pupil really thinks only when he wrestles with the conditions of the problem at first hand, seeking and finding his own way out. To instigate learning the parent or teacher provides the conditions which stimulate thinking, enters himself into the common experience, and takes a sympathetic attitude toward the activities of the learner. In such shared activities the teacher is a learner, and the learner, without knowing it, is a teacher. And the less consciousness there is on either side of either giving or receiving instruction, the better. The pupil devises his own solution, not in isolation, but in coöperation with the other pupils and the teacher. Learning is not reciting correctly. The teacher is neither to supply ready-made "ideas," nor to furnish ready-made subject matter, nor to listen to its accurate reproduction; nor yet to stand off and look on in quiescence, but he is to participate, to share in the conjoint activity. Thus hypotheses develop, awaiting testing.

(5) Testing. The last step of method in an educative experience, in thinking, is testing; that is, the application of the hypothesis, thereby making its meaning clear and discovering

its validity. The term "hypothesis" is here used as synonomous with the term "idea." An idea, or hypothesis, may be an humble guess or a dignified theory, but in any case it is an anticipation of a possible solution, of some as yet unrevealed continuity between an activity and a consequence. The only way to test an idea is to act upon it, to treat it as a guide to further observations, recollections, or experiments. Thus the idea is not final but intermediate in learning, working between a problem and its solution. It is not easy in education to secure conditions which will make the getting of an idea grow out of a problematic situation and then allow for the testing of the idea by its application; such experiences would both widen and sharpen our contacts with the environment.

What are some positive measures adapted to the effectual development of thought? A school equipment of laboratories, shops, and garden, and the free use of dramatizations, plays, and games. These provide opportunities for reproducing life-situations, and so for acquiring and applying ideas in carrying forward progressive experiences. These ideas do not form an isolated island in experience; they animate, enrich, and direct the ordinary stream of experience.

In contrast with such desirable conditions, a peculiar artificiality attaches to much school learning. The subject matter is unreal, even though the students may not call it such; it does not possess the reality of their vital experiences. Instead, it has reality for purposes of lessons, recitations, and examinations, not for daily life. Such unreality in school work has two bad effects: ordinary experience is not enriched and fertilized by school learning, and half-understood and ill-digested school learning weakens the vigor and efficiency of thought.

All educational reformers have in vain attacked the passivity of traditional education. They have attacked drilling material in, as though pupils were hard and resisting rock; they have opposed pouring in from without, as though pupils were containers to be filled or sponges to absorb. But good theory and bad practices have continued.

The application of ideas, where made, has been inadequate. It is good to fix by exercises ideas already learned, but it is not enough. It is good to develop practical skill in manipulating ideas already learned, but this too is not enough. Fixation and manipulation of ideas lack the primary intellectual quality. Thoughts are incomplete, tentative, suggestive, indicative; they are methods of dealing with experience. Till they deal with experience, till tested, they lack full point, full meaning, and reality, tending to segregate in a peculiar world of their own.

Ideas and activities must not fall apart. We have the wrong view of activities as not involving mind because we have the wrong view of mind as not involving activities. It is possible the wrong view of mind as isolated from the world (see Chapter X, Section 2) grew up under social conditions which did not allow thinkers to act upon their ideas, and so threw them back upon themselves and their own thoughts as ends in themselves. At any rate, mind is not isolated from the course of experience, from action upon things and with things; it is not a self-contained, separate realm; on the contrary, be it said again and again, mind really is the purposive and directive factor in a developing experience. "Self-activity" is not merely mental, something cooped up within the head, finding expression only through the vocal organs.

Having a false view of mind, we have also a false view of activities. Instead of an opportunity for the investment of intellect, manual and constructive activities are employed just to acquire bodily skill, or for "utilitarian," *i.e.*, pecuniary, ends. Thus, upholders of "cultural" education, with their false view of an isolated mind, assume that such activities are merely physical or merely professional in quality. When the mind is held aloof from the body, then the body with its activities is held aloof from mind. And lo, the baleful consequences: bodily activities at best are mere external annexes to the mind, necessary for the satisfaction of bodily needs and the attainment of external decency and comfort; not necessary for mentality or the completion of an act of thought; hence, without a place in a liberal education,—one concerned with the interests of intelligence; having a place, if at all, as a concession to the material needs of the masses; but as for invading the education of the élite? Unspeakable!

It is desirable that all educational institutions should give students active pursuits, and, be it noted, that these active pursuits should typify important social situations. But it will doubtless be a long time before all schools function thus. However, this situation should not afford instructors of youth an excuse for folding their hands and persisting in methods which segregate school knowledge. Let every recitation in every subject establish cross connections between the lesson and life. Actual classroom instruction falls into three kinds, with ascending value, viz., disconnected lessons, connected lessons, and lessons connected with life. Disconnected lessons are unrelated to each other and to other subjects. Connected lessons are related to each other, the earlier helping the understanding of the later and the later throwing additional light upon the earlier, the curriculum remaining a little race-course out of sight of life. Lessons connected with life refine and expand out-of-school experience and are themselves motivated and impregnated with the life-like sense of reality. Thus, education is like life,—thinking in education involving interesting activities, developing real problems, requiring data for their understanding, suggesting hypotheses for their solution, necessitating testing for verification. Thus experience is expanded and enriched.

Comment. Here are the new essentials of method, and for this reason deserving of special attention. It will be noted that the chapter has but one section, that thinking in education is identified with the essentials of method, that it is the pupil whose thinking is contemplated, and that, though the body of the discussion has but four steps, the summary has five. We have followed the five of the summary in our exposition as being clearer. Besides, the five-fold division allows a better contrast with the five formal steps of the Herbartians. For convenience of reference we will number our comments.

(1) There is a danger here lest the new five steps become formal as those of Herbart did. Not every "project" is really one. Not every "activity" is interesting and worth while. Not every "problem" is genuine. Not every "hypothesis" is adequately founded in observed data. Not every "application" of an idea is a real test. It would of course be utterly false to the spirit of the new method to formalize it, but that does not keep it from being done by ineffective followers.

(2) Just as teachers have been trained in our normal schools and colleges since the middle nineties in the Herbartian steps, so, for success to crown the use of the new method, teachers will have to be specially trained to use it. In a measure this is taking place and our normal training is shifting its basis.

(3) This brings us to note the contrast between the Herartian and the Dewey steps. Teachers are so constituted that they like to think the new way is not so different from the old after all; thus, they can be loyal to the old and accept the new at the same time; and so not much change after all will be necessary. Teachers are not alone in making such complacent adjustments. Really, the contrast between Herbart and Dewey is fundamental. Herbart is an intellectualist and Dewey is a pragmatist. Herbart believes the idea is primary and Dewey believes the act is primary. Herbart begins teaching by awakening old ideas in the mind of the child; Dewey by noting the activity which engages the child. Herbart teaches by presenting new ideas to the child similar to the old ones; Dewey by assisting the child in defining his problem, if he requires it. Herbart leads the mind on to a comparison of ideas, ending in a generalization; Dewey leads

the child on to study the data of his problem and to form hypotheses. Finally, Herbart seeks an application of a truth already found, Dewey seeks the testing of the validity of the hypothesis by a trial application. In Herbart we think and then act; in Dewey we think between acts. Parallel columns showing these contrasts would be as follows:

Essentials of Method

Herbart	Dewey
1. Preparation	1. Activity
2. Presentation	2. Problem
3. Comparison	3. Data
4. Generalization	4. Hypothesis
5. Application	5. Testing

Students of Herbart will recall he himself had but four steps, named by him, somewhat clumsily, Clearness, Association, System, and Method, corresponding to the last four in the list given above, and that his followers divided the first into two and re-named the others.

These two methods admirably supplement each other; they are usable in different fields. Herbart is effective in the linguistic, literary, historical, and ideational fields; Dewey in the fields of the manual arts and the sciences. Wherever the content of books is taught, Herbart is useful; wherever the manipulation of things is primary, Dewey is useful. Of course, Herbart does not regard the practical as really educative, and Dewey does not regard the theoretical as really educative. Herbart regards the practical as the field for the use of true ideas, Dewey regards the theoretical as a phase of the practical.

(4) For ourselves, while recognizing an important place in constructive activities like dressmaking, preparing a dinner, and minding the baby (to take the illustrations used by Dr. Kilpatrick in his *Foundations of Method*) for the method of Dr. Dewey, we are constrained to acknowledge also that Herbart is not yet supplanted. Herbart does not hold the

mind down to material occupations and allows a place for speculative philosophy. It would be difficult, if not impossible, to teach the history of philosophy, or the philosophy of education, and similar subjects, by Dr. Dewey's method. Dr. Dewey does not teach his own classes by the method he describes, he lectures to them.

(5) The Dewey method does not provide for the systematic and instructional transmission of the social inheritance. Such knowledge from the past as is acquired comes in incidentally in gathering data for the closer definition of the problem and the formulation of the solving hypothesis. This knowledge would indeed be vital and functional, but it would also be fragmentary and *ad hoc.*

(6) It is also possible that the out-of-school type of experience as a model for in-school learning is somewhat idealized. Children out of school do acquire some first-hand knowledge of how things work, how to make things, how nature behaves, and about each other and about games and play, and they do grow. The guide is curiosity and the method is largely trial and error. Children out of school are not the patient problem-solvers the method requires, they give up easily, they change occupations often, they don't carry through always, they gather few data for location problems, their guesses are largely at random. Only a few of them are little Darwins. They usually face concrete situations and they are weak in generalizing. The method recommended is rather poorly exemplified in the experience of children out of school.

(7) The method as defined is not adequately social. This seems a strange thing to say in the light of the social passion of Dr. Dewey. Still, it is true. All the steps can be taken by one pupil with a tutor. Class instruction is not provided for. Group thinking is not stressed. The only social phase of the method is that the activities in which the pupils engage are to typify social situations. Some of these were worked out in the experimental school of Dr. Dewey in Chicago. A group project easily swamps the individuality of some participants.

(8) After all the credit that has been given Dr. Dewey for describing the stages of reflective thinking, it seems ungracious to point out that this formulation is not original. It is just the scientific method used by all experimentalists alike from the days of Galileo to Darwin. All modern texts in logic formulate these steps in practically the same way. For example, an idealist, far removed from pragmatism, formulates the "stages in the inductive process" in this way: "The various sciences have to start with particular facts learned through experience [Stage 1]. . . . The various sciences are occupied, each in its particular field, in the task of discovering order and relation among phenomena that at first sight appear to be lawless and disconnected [Stage 2]. But in carrying out this undertaking our thinking uses every means which will help it toward its desired end. It is often able, after pushing inductive inquiries a little way [Stage 3], to discover some general principle, or to guess what the law of connection must be [Stage 4]. When this is possible, it is found profitable to proceed deductively, reasoning out what consequences necessarily follow from the assumptions of such a general law. Of course, it is essential to verify results obtained in this deductive way by comparing them with facts as actually experienced"[1] [Stage 5]. The novelty in Dr. Dewey's method is not in the five steps, nor in the positivistic and pragmatic limitation of ideas to experience, in which he was anticipated by Auguste Comte and J. S. Mill. His real novelty and originality is in limiting the essentials of educational method to the essentials of scientific method. And this originality, as we have seen, has the defect of its quality. It is strong where education is scientific and weak where education is literary, historical, æsthetic, and spiritual. Of course there should be scientific thinking in the educative process, but education and life are more, much more, than scientific thinking.

[1] Creighton, J. E., *An Introductory Logic,* The Macmillan Company, 1909, p. 206. [Note date. There are later editions.]

CHAPTER XIII

THE NATURE OF METHOD

1. The Unity of Subject Matter and Method

Exposition. The great trio of school topics is subject matter, method, and administration. We shall not deal specifically with the last. The first two have been dealt with in recent chapters, but in association with other matters. It remains to discuss their nature more explicitly. And, in close connection with the preceding chapter, we begin first with method. In this section we shall point out the nature of method, the unity of subject matter and method, the false dualistic philosophy underlying their separation, and the evils that have hitherto followed from separating them.

We begin with some illustrations. Every artist has a technique in doing his work; this is his method. The pianist does not strike the keys at random, he studies them in an orderly way. The actions of piano, hands, and brain are ordered to achieve the result intended. The action of the piano is directed by the player to accomplish the purpose for which a piano is made. A piano may produce a great variety of music, each variety requiring its own technique. And the technique of performance appears only in the performance; it does not exist separately, ready-made, in the musician's hands or brain. The method of playing is one with the playing, it is properly directed or ordered playing. A real *maestro* would have no occasion to distinguish between his contribution and that of the piano. Other illustrations of the unity of technique and activity, of the person and the subject matter, may be found in any sort of smooth-running functions, such as eating, skating, conversing, hearing music, enjoying a landscape, and whole-hearted play and work. Thus, in general, method is the effective way of employing material for an end, and, specifically, "pedagogical" method is the effective way of arranging subject matter for some use. Never is method something outside material. Method is antithetical, not to subject matter, but to random and ill-adapted action.

"But," you say, "there certainly is a distinction between the *what* of experience and the *how* of experience; and is not the *what* of experience subject matter and the *how* of experience method? The food that one eats is certainly not the same as his way of eating it." True, this distinction can be made, and it is useful to make it, but it is a distinction not in existence but in thought. There is really no eating, and no way of eating, without food. And, similarly, there is no seeing, hearing, loving, hating, imagining, without the things seen, heard, loved, hated, imagined. The useful distinction between the *what* and *how* is due to reflection on experience, not to the experience of the *what* without the *how*.

This distinction between the *what* and *how* of experience is made by reflection for the very practical purpose of *controlling* the course of experience. Getting a clear idea of the *how* of experience is an aid in modifying experience. There is no distinction in fact or existence between a plant and its growth, but the way a plant grows best may be detected by watching carefully the growth of several plants under different conditions. The orderly arrangement of the causes of growth is an account of the method of growth. And as a plant grows, so does an experience prosper. There is no way of walking and learning over and above the acts of walking and learning, but there are certain elements in the act which give the key to its control. So the knowledge of method leads to control of the moving unity of experience.

These views concerning the unity of subject matter and method are naturally implied in what has previously been maintained concerning the unity of the mind and the world.

Thinking, we saw, is a directed movement of subject matter to a completing issue, the deliberate and intentional phase of the process. Science means organized material; the organization is due to intelligence; the science is already, so to say, methodized, it is already arranged for effective use. The method is not something added to the organized material to make it usable; it is the way of organizing the material. Science, or organized material, is not a starting point for learning; it is a consummation of learning. When the crude scattered facts of our ordinary acquaintance with animals have been subjected to careful examination, to deliberate supplementation, and to arrangements to bring out connections which assist observation, memory, and further inquiry, we have a systematic branch of knowledge known as the science of zoölogy. When so formulated, the zoölogy has already been learned, has already profited by method. In the case of an individual who comes to learn afresh such already organized material, his method again is not something external; it too is the effective treatment of material, that is, the utilization of the material with a minimum waste of time and energy. By method, material is organized; by method again, organized material is utilized. In neither case is the method a thing apart from the organizing and the utilizing.

It is a false dualistic philosophy which allows the separation of method and subject matter. Dualism is the view that the world of mind and the world of things are two separate and independent realms. Knowing, feeling, and willing are then assumed to belong to the mind, or self, in its isolation, having their own laws of operation irrespective of their objects. These laws are then made the source of distinct method. Dualism is no less absurd than to suppose that men can eat without eating something. Really, the structure and movements of jaws, throat, and stomach are what they are because of the material with which they are engaged. These organs are a continuous part of the very world in which food exists; just so are seeing, hearing, loving, imagining, and the other acts of the mind intrinsically connected with the subject matter of the world; they are not so much independent acts brought to bear upon things as ways in which the environment enters into and functions within experience. In short, experience is not a combination of two realities, mind and world, subject and object, method and subject matter, but it is a single continuous interaction of a countless diversity of energies.

The isolation of method from subject matter in education has led to four notable evils, viz., (1) a neglect of concrete situations, (2) false conceptions of discipline and interest, (3) the making of learning a direct end in itself, and (4) mechanical methods. The first two have previously been noted. We will devote a few words to each of these evils.

(1) Our "methods" are authoritatively recommended to teachers; they have a mechanical uniformity; they are assumed to fit all minds alike; they are not an expression of the intelligent observations of the teachers themselves. Our pupils work under constraint; they lack the direct normal experiences from which observant educators might derive method. There can be no discovery of method without a study of cases. Our school environment should afford directed occupations in work and play. Then it would appear that methods vary with individuals. So our system of instruction and discipline, founded on dualism, leads to the neglect of the case and the concrete, where subject matter and method are at one.

(2) If we begin with the assumption that subject matter and method are separate, there are three ways of bringing them together again, all objectionable, viz., rewards, penalties, and appeal for effort. The subject matter, lacking intrinsic interest, having no inherent method, must be approached indirectly by some artificial excitement, shock of pleasure, or tickling the palate; or, the consequences of not attending to it are made painful; or, the pupil is urged to put forth effort or exert "will power" without any reason being assigned for doing so, unless indeed it be again avoiding unpleasant re-

sults. Thus, discipline is unmotivated by real interest, and interest is artificial.

(3) When subject matter and method are held apart, the subject matter is not used in carrying forward impulses and habits to significant results, it is just something to be learned, and the act of learning is made a conscious end in itself. The pupil's attitude is that of just having to learn. A condition more unfavorable to an alert response would be hard to devise, for frontal attacks are even more wasteful in learning than in war. Neither are students to be seduced unaware into pre-occupation with lessons. They are to be occupied with lessons for real reasons, through perceiving the place occupied by lessons in fulfilling some experience. Then the learning is not for the sake of the learning, but of the doing. Under normal conditions there is some occupation with subject matter which results in learning. Children do not set out consciously to learn to talk; they set out to express their impulses for communication. Children learn normally in consequence of their direct activities. The better methods of teaching a child to read or to cipher follow the same road; they engage his activities and in the process of engagement he learns, his attention is not fixed upon the fact that he has to learn something, and so his attitude is not made conscious and constrained. The act of learning should not be made a direct end in itself.

(4) When mind and material are separated, method tends to be reduced to a cut and dried routine, to mechanically presented steps, to rigid woodenness. Children in many schoolrooms are compelled to go through certain pre-ordained formulæ in reciting in arithmetic or grammar, it being assumed there is one fixed method to be followed, and that if pupils make their statements in a certain form of "analysis," their mental habits will in time improve. Handing out to teachers recipes to be followed has brought pedagogy into disrepute, nothing more so. When, on the other hand, method is a way of managing material to reach a conclusion, there are

flexibility and initiative in dealing with problems, and pupils are encouraged to attack their topics directly, experimenting with promising methods and learning to discriminate between them by their consequences. Separate mind from material, deduce methods from the nature of mind, use such deduced methods to apply the mind to subject matter or to impress the mind with subject matter, and method and subject matter fall apart, and those proficient in subject matter may accuse pedagogy of being futile,—a screen for concealing the teacher's ignorance of his subject.

Comment. There are four things to be noted here, all related. The first is that "the trinity of school topics is subject matter, methods, and administration." It would be more consistent with our sense of values to include the pupils and the teachers in such a list. This again is part of the impersonality of this system.

Again, there is a sense in which the mind is not one with its material environment. When the mind reflects not upon experience, but upon itself, when it introspects, when it makes itself its own object, it is one with itself, but not with its world. At this point the mind has a trait in which it is not one with the direction of material; it transcends its material. This suggests the importance of concepts and abstract thinking as well as the concrete situation.

And again, there is a sense in which method does exist separate from the activity. The pianist does have a technique of playing when not performing, so the golfer, so the surgeon, so the artist, so the teacher. In such cases the technique exists as habits of skill in the nervous system. A given pianist will show the same old technique in performing a new piece. And the same piece will be performed differently by different pianists, showing the same subject matter allows different methods. It would not do to say several methods are one with the same subject matter. So, in the sense of habit, a method may exist separate from the subject matter.

And still again, while no one advocates method as mechanical routine, much good teaching has been done on the basis of the five Herbartian formal steps. They are the classic illustration of method separated from subject matter. There have been Herbartian teachers who did not have false conceptions of discipline and interest and who did not follow the presented steps mechanically, who, however, believing that children are much alike, may have neglected concrete situations, and who, believing that learning is a good in itself, may have made it a direct end. That they were not wrong in believing children are much alike, the succeeding section on "method as general and as individual" will itself show. That they are likewise not far wrong in believing learning is worth while for its own sake will be admitted by those many who enjoy having it even when they do not need to use it.

2. Method as General and as Individual

Exposition. Teaching is an art. The method of teaching is the method of an art, that is, of action intelligently directed by ends. The practice of any fine art has both its general and its individual phases; general, in so far as all artists use a similar technique; individual, in so far as no two artists use identical technique.

The practice of any fine art is neither extemporizing, nor trusting to the inspiration of the moment, nor working hard without direction. Neither, of course, is it following ready-made rules. There are alternatives between these two extremes. The artist combines guidance from others with his own individuality. He studies the methods and results of those successful in the past. Art has its traditions, or schools, which impress beginners, and often take them captive. The methods of artists depend partly upon traditions; they also depend on acquaintance with materials and tools. Thus, the painter must know about canvases, pigments, brushes, and the technique of manipulation. The attainment of this knowledge requires persistent attention to objective materials. The artist studies tradition and materials; he also studies his own successes and failures. Being an artist thus involves the intelligent application of a technique to materials that are known.

Out of the practice of the arts there thus arises the notion of method as both general and individual at one and the same time,—general as a result of past experience, individual in the characteristic use made by each artist of the work of others. The content of general method is supplied by the past, by current technique, by the nature of the materials used, and by the methods of one's own successes. There is a growing body of fairly stable methods for reaching results; past experience and intellectual analysis authorize it; the beginner ignores it at his peril. Ignoring it, his work is only a passing sensation. The innovator who achieves anything enduring utilizes classic methods more than either he or his critics may recognize. True, his method as individual transforms the general method through new uses. General method is power at command for one's own ends. And there is always the danger, as remarked in discussing habit above, that general method will become divorced from individual method, thereby becoming mechanized, rigid and masterful.

Like the arts, like the fine arts, education too has its general and its individual method. This is obviously true in the case of the teacher; it is equally true in the case of the pupil. There is constructive value to the teacher in knowing the psychological methods, even the empirical devices, found useful in the past, if he has acquired them as intellectual aids in handling his own unique experiences. Much depends upon how far the teacher can utilize the experience of others in making his own responses. Of course, when past usages offend his common sense or come between him and the situation in which he has to act, they are worse than useless.

As is the case with the teacher, so also is it with the pupil. His method should be both general and individual. A very important part of his learning consists in becoming master of general methods, that is, of the most efficient ways used by others in getting or advancing knowledge. Standardized methods used by others, especially experts, are of worth if they make his own personal reaction more intelligent; they are harmful if they induce him to dispense with his own judgment. It is lamentable self-deception to suppose that university students, or even primary pupils, can be supplied with models of method to be followed without individual judgment in expounding or acquiring a subject.

But let it not be supposed that method as general is opposed to method as individual. General methods are reinforcements of personal ways of doing things, of individual initiative and originality. Artistic work, be it said again, involves both general and individual method; even the masterly use of an established technique is not enough; there must also be the individual's animating idea.

In the interest of clarity a distinction should be drawn between general method, even the most general, and a prescribed rule. The former operates indirectly, through enlightenment as to means and ends, through intelligent use. The latter operates directly, through conformity to orders externally imposed, strictly regulating action.

How can method be general without being objectionable? without telling us directly what to do? without being a ready-made model? How can a general method be at the same time intellectual? Consider the physician. Knowledge of established modes of diagnosis and treatment is imperiously demanded; nowhere more so. This is general method. But, after all, cases, though alike, are not identical; each is particular, with its own exigencies. Existing practices, however authoritative, have to be adapted intelligently; they indicate what inquiries to set on foot, what measures to try. The physician's individual methods, his personal attitudes, are facilitated by the general principles of procedure, not subordinated to them. Just so, both teacher and pupil require a general method that is intelligently utilized by themselves. Each is to show originality of thought enlightened by the experience of the race.

Previously we demanded originality of thought all the way from the child of three to Sir Isaac Newton. We do so still. Every individual must have opportunity to employ his own powers in meaningful activities. Originality, individual method, mind, all mean the same thing: the quality of purposive or directed action. Action on this conviction will give us more originality. Instead, we often impose an alleged uniform general method upon everybody. To do so breeds mediocrity in all but the very exceptional, and in these it breeds eccentricity. We stifle the distinctive quality of the many, and, save in such rare instances as Darwin, we infect the geniuses with unwholesome idiosyncrasy. General method, unless intelligently and individually used, curses where it might bless.

If this demand for individual originality seems overstrained, exacting more of education than average human nature permits, the difficulty is that we lie under the incubus of a superstition. We have set up the false notion of mind at large, of a general intellectual method that is the same for all. We then mistakenly regard individuals as differing in the *quantity* of mind they possess. Ordinary persons, having less mind, are then expected to be ordinary. Only exceptional persons, having more mind, are allowed to have originality. The average student, not being exceptional, is not allowed to have originality. Then wrong attitudes rest on the fictional notion of a mind in general. "How one person's abilities compare in quantity with those of another is none of the teacher's business. It is irrelevant to his work" (p. 203). Instead, the teacher's work is to employ each pupil's powers in significant activities, in following which he should ultilize general method intelligently and so develop his own originality. Each pupil has incomparable originality.

Comment. The views of Dr. Dewey on method as general and as individual upset general conceptions of method commonly held. Among these is the conception that method is the art of uniting the mind and the subject matter, which presupposes a dualistic position. Another is that "general method" is the set of principles applicable to all subjects alike; to Dr. Dewey there is no such set of general principles; no method is general without being individual, and no set of principles is applicable equally to all subjects. Another is that "special method" is the application of "general method" to a single field, like history, English, or science; this view is somewhat similar to Dr. Dewey's conception of method as both general and individual at the same time, but the difference is that Dr. Dewey would have the individual teacher or pupil work out his individual modifications of general method for himself. In all these respects the Dewey views upset the usual Herbartian views.

But the question remains, has not Dr. Dewey himself in the five steps of a reflective experience provided another "general method," applicable universally in all learning, whose steps require only utilization and not modification in all situations of inquiry? It is the opinion of the present writer that Dr. Dewey thinks that this is precisely what he has done. In that event his own general method is just another competitor with the Herbartian, and the choice between them rests on the relative merits of each, and his own method becomes the very kind of "model" which he rejects. Otherwise, no universality attaches to it, and its significance is lessened by so much.

Another matter of special moment remains. It concerns intelligence testing on a quantitative basis. The text could easily be interpreted to mean that Dr. Dewey is against it. This, however, in the light of his later views, would be a mistake. His conception is that the scientific findings must not alone determine the procedure of teachers, that they are general and always require special consideration before being followed. He writes: "Illustrations may be given of the use of measurements to guide the intelligence of teachers instead of as dictating rules of action. . . . In other schools [than those cited] that have taken over more or less of the work of the juvenile court, truant officers, medical inspectors and visiting nurses, the I. Q. reports are correlated with factors ascertained in these other lines before there is direct use of them. A homogeneous grouping without intervening inquiries approximates dangerously to transforming a theoretical finding into a rule of action."[1] Even so, the positions are not exactly the same. The text rejects what the later view allows. Our educational practice is divided in the same way, some schools rejecting homogeneous grouping based on intelligence tests, some accepting it. Those who reject the homogenous grouping of pupils on the basis of intelligence tests point to (1) the alleged unreliability of the tests; (2) the difficulty of measuring native ability apart from acquired information; (3) the dependence of the results obtained upon the physical and mental conditions of the pupils and upon the attitude of the testers at the time of the testing; (4) the alleged undemocratic procedure of introducing class distinctions on an intellectual basis, leading to an "intellectual aristocracy"; (5) the mutual advantages to slower and brighter pupils of working together, the slower being stimulated by the presence of the brighter, thereby not acquiring "inferiority complexes," and the brighter being made more socialized as they help the slower, thereby not acquiring "superiority complexes"; (6) the lack of sure tests for certain of the most important qualities of life, such as initiative, ambition, and integrity; (7) the unfairness of giving speed tests to the pupil whose mind works slowly but reliably; (8) the unproven assumption that there is a general and measurable intelligence instead of a set of special intellectual abilities; (9) the inadequacy of a measure of only a small segment of the whole child as a basis for his grouping; (10) their em-

[1] Dewey, John, *The Sources of a Science of Education*, New York, 1929, pp. 36–37.

phasis on abstract intellectual ability instead of on well-rounded personality, and their basic false assumption that the purpose of education is the development of the intellect; (11) the parental pressure to get children in the bright groups, and the jealousy between teachers of bright and slow groups; (12) the ignoring of such important factors in child life as home conditions, ability to get along with people, and interest in a subject; and (13) when applied as a basis for college entrance, the unwisdom of excluding from college those who need its training in adaptation most.

On the other hand, those who accept the homogeneous grouping of pupils on the basis of intelligence tests point to (1) the agreement of the experts in the field that the tests are, or can be made, reliable; (2) the practical elimination of the factor of acquired information in the standard tests; (3) the improving technique of administering the tests; (4) the real democracy involved, not in treating unequals as equal, but in treating unequals as unequals; (5) the discouragement coming to slow pupils in having to work with bright ones, and the bad habits bred in bright pupils by being kept at the pace of slow ones; (6) the making of new tests for measuring character and personality traits; (7) the checking of the results of speed tests by those of non-speed tests; (8) the sense of real achievement on the part of slow pupils when they work together without comparing themselves with their intellectual superiors; (9) the moral and social advantage of keeping bright pupils going at full speed ahead; and (10) the real function of the college as the training of intellectual leaders. The issue is still moot.[1]

[1] Cf. Bagley, W. C., *Determinism in Education*, Baltimore, 1925.

Note. The following from our national humorist, Will Rogers, under date of November 21, 1930, has some bearing on the question: "Chicago University came out yesterday with a terrible radical idea. They propose to graduate a student as soon as he knows enough. That shows you that higher education is making progress. It's taken two thousand years to think of such a thing. Heretofore they have made the smart ones stay there four years, just to keep the dumb ones company."

Meantime, the Horace Mann School, Teachers College, New York City, has adopted a new basis for grouping students: the intelligence tests, supplemented by the judgment of a teacher who has had the child for a year, his ability to achieve, and a consideration of his likes, dislikes, and home life. Personal attention is given children who have difficulties.

Despite the reigning differences of opinion, the tests have had wide use. Pupils in public schools in 66 American cities of 30,000 or more population and in 36 cities of 100,000 or more population are given such tests. The present writer is not ready to discard the tests; they are a notable and distinctive contribution to educational science. He accepts the later view of Dr. Dewey and revised practice of the Horace Mann School.

3. The Traits of Individual Method

Exposition. How does individual method differ from general method? General method is composed of the five-fold features of a reflective situation, viz., experience, problem, data, hypothesis, and testing, leading, of course, to a conclusion. These are the most general features of the method of knowing. Individual method, used by teacher and pupil alike, is composed of the specific elements in a person's way of attack upon a problem, his most effective attitudes in dealing intellectually with subject matter. The five general steps are for all; the way they are taken depends upon each.

What are the sources of individual method? Two things: native tendencies and acquired interests and habits. Because these two sources vary with different individuals, their methods will vary from each other. Because individual methods are matters of personal concern, approach, and attack upon a problem, no catalogue can ever exhaust their diversity of form and tint.

In understanding and finding the responses of pupils as they use general and special method, teachers will rely both upon their personal acquaintance with individual pupils and upon information supplied by students of these matters, derived from child-study, psychology, and a knowledge of the social environment.

Among the most important traits of general method are directness, open-mindedness, single-mindedness (or whole-heartedness) and responsibility, to each of which we will give special attention.

(1) Directness. Taking the attitude of directness toward one's problem means that the individual is not menaced by self-consciousness, embarrassment, constraint, or even *self*-confidence, but is immediately concerned only with his subject matter, and is undeflected by concern with side issues. Taking the attitude of directness means that one is spontaneous, naïve, simple and whole-souled in attacking his problem. "Confidence" is a good synonym for directness, denoting as it does the straightforwardness with which one goes at what he has to do, his unconscious faith in the possibilities of the situation, and rising to meet its needs. On the other hand, self-consciousness means the pupil is thinking partly about his problem and partly about what others think of his performance, leading to diverted energy, loss of power, and confusion of ideas. Being self-conscious, however, is not of necessity abnormal. It may be the easiest way to correct a false method of approach or of making one's method more effective, as is seen in the case of golfers, pianists, tennis players and public speakers. Such self-consciousness is occasional and temporary; when effectual, the person merges again into the performance. Self-consciousness is abnormal, however, when one thinks of himself as a separate object, not as a part of the agencies of execution, as when a player strikes an attitude to impress the spectators or is worried by the impression he fears his playing makes on them. Just so, *self*-confidence may be a form of self-consciousness, or even of "cheek," a name for what one thinks about oneself, a con-

scious trust in the efficacy of one's powers. As such it is objectionable.

It violates the trait of directness in individual method if students are made emphatically aware of the fact that they are studying or learning. As already indicated, learning should be a consequence of direct activities. To be aware of the fact that one is studying or learning is not to study or learn; it is to be in a divided and complicated attitude; if persisted in, the pupil acquires a permanent tendency to fumble, to gaze about aimlessly, to look for some clew to action external to the subject matter, resulting in a state of foggy confusion. Instead, children and adults, unsophisticated by "education," confront the situations of life with sureness.

(2) Open-mindedness. This is the attitude of mind which actively welcomes from all sides suggestions and information that will throw light upon the situation needing to be cleared up, that will help determine the consequences of acting this way or that. Intellectual growth means constant expansion of horizons and consequent formation of new purposes and new responses.

This open-minded attitude is all the more needed since partiality, as we saw, is an accompaniment of interest, of sharing, of partaking, of taking sides in some movement. Aims, as we saw, are subordinate to a changing situation as means for controlling it; the situation is not subordinate to aims as finalities; just as a target is not the goal of future shooting but the centering factor in present shooting. Narrow-mindedness may coexist with efficiency in accomplishing unalterable ends, but the worst thing about such stubborn, prejudiced, narrow-mindedness is that mental development, being shut off from new stimuli, is arrested. To be open-minded means to remain childlike; to be closed-minded means premature intellectual old age.

There are foes of the open-minded attitude in school. The two chief ones are the desire for uniform procedure and the desire for prompt external results. Teachers are devoted to uniform procedure because that is the path the teacher's own mind approves, and because too it seems to promise the desired speedy, measurable, and correct results. This zeal for answers leads likewise to forcing and overpressure. In consequence of using uniform, rigid, and mechanical methods and stressing correct answers, alert and varied intellectual interests are smothered and intellectual blinders are put upon pupils. Results can be hurried; processes can not be; they take their own time to mature. There is a kind of passivity, a willingness to let experiences sink in and ripen, which is essential to development. But open-mindedness is not the same as empty-mindedness; true intellectual hospitality is not hanging out a sign saying "Come right in; there is no one at home." Would you work a revolution in teaching? Then, let all instructors realize that the quality of mental process, not the production of correct answers, is the measure of educative growth.

(3) Single-mindedness. This trait of individual method refers to unity of purpose, *completeness* of interest, mental integrity, and absence of suppressed though effectual ulterior aims, of divided attention, of double-mindedness. Single-mindedness is nurtured by absorption in the subject matter for its own sake; it is destroyed by divided interest and evasion.

How does double-mindedness arise? In the conflict between personal urgent desires and the demands of others. When desires can not be directly expressed, they are driven into deep subterranean channels. It is almost impossible entirely to surrender oneself and whole-heartedly adopt the demands of others. Among the possible outcomes are revolt on the one hand, or the attempt to deceive on the other. More frequently, however, one tries to serve two masters, resulting in a confused and divided state of interest, or even in self-deception as to one's own real intent. One master demands conformity, "paying attention to the lesson," or whatever the requirement is. For this master are working the social instincts, the strong desire to please and to win approval, social training, the general sense of duty and of authority, and the apprehension of penalty. Consciously the pupil may think he means to do as directed. For the other master are working the suppressed desires, determining the main course of thought, the deeper emotional responses. The strain of attention to the undesired is irksome, the mind wanders from the nominal subject, devoting itself to its intrinsic interests. Result: a divided attention expressing double-mindedness.

This attitude of divided attention is prevalent both in and out of school. Some of it may be necessary, but its bad intellectual effects should be faced. These are the loss of energy of thought, the fostering of habitual self-deception, the confused sense of reality, the hampering of integrated mental action, the split set up between conscious attention and impulsive desire, the half-hearted dealing with subject matter, wandering attention, furtive transactions with intellectually illicit topics, the failure to regulate response by deliberate purposeful inquiry, the concealment of the most congenial enterprises of the imagination, all resulting in demoralization. Thus the mind becomes divided between public, socially responsible, undertakings and private, ill-regulated indulgences.

There are school conditions favorable to this unhappy division of mind. Some of these are: "stern discipline," external co-ercive pressure, extraneous motivation, schooling treated as preparatory, and emphasis upon drill without thought. The school favors single-mindedness when it provides outlet for thought, emotion, and desire in immediate activities. Thus what is native, spontaneous, and vital in mental reaction gets used and tested, and the habits formed make these qualities more and more available for public and avowed ends.

(4) Responsibility. This trait in the intellectual attitude of the individual means the disposition to consider in advance the probable consequences of any proposed step and deliber-

ately to accept them, not in word only but in deed. We have seen that ideas are methods of bringing about a solution of a perplexing situation, forecasts of results effective in influencing responses. A statement is not really accepted, a suggested truth is not really believed, unless its implications are considered, and its consequences for oneself accepted. Responsibility is thus intellectual *thoroughness, seeing a thing through.* It depends upon a unity of purpose to which details are subordinated, and is manifested in the firm developing of the full meaning of the purpose. It does not depend upon presenting a multitude of disconnected details, and it is not manifested even in "conscientious" attention to externally imposed actions.

In our schools we have intellectual irresponsibility because there is so much acceptance and so little conviction. There is an undue complication of school subjects, there is a congestion of lessons and studies. Among the bad results are worry, nervous strain, and superficial attainment. But the most permanent bad result is the failure to make clear what is involved in really knowing and believing a thing. The standard is severe,—nothing less than acting upon the measuring of one's acquisitions. It would be much better to have fewer facts supposedly accepted and more situations leading to real convictions, involving some identification of the self with the type of conduct demanded by the facts and the foresight of results. Responsibility means to act as one thinks.

Comment. As Plato might say, "the very god of jealousy himself could find no fault" with such morality of the intellect as straightforwardness, open-mindedness, whole-heartedness, and responsibility. Some of the best feats of analysis in the text are done here, especially in presenting the origin and evils of double-mindedness.

A few things, however, are to be noted. The first is the presupposition of the discussion that the individual pupil showing these four traits is engaged in some form of practical and appealing activity. This involves dubious exclusive commitment to the occupational school and the project method. This type of school and this method have their characteristic advantages, but they are hardly adequate to transmit the culture of the race in assimilation of which education largely consists.

The second thing is that these four traits may well be had in other types of school than the occupational, making use of other types of method than the project. That the traits themselves are intrinsically desirable goes without saying.

The third thing is that the distinction between the five steps of general method and the four traits of individual method is not clear. The five steps are said to grow out of the experience of the race, but so also do the four traits. The four traits are said to belong to the intellectual equipment of the individual, but so do the five steps. Really, it would seem that the steps of general method are also individual, and the traits of individual method are also general. Each individual in solving his problem should use the five steps of general method, and every individual in using the five steps of general method should exemplify the four traits of individual method. The net meaning of this is that we should all be direct, open-minded, single-minded, and responsible as we think reflectively. The methods merge. The general method becomes individual, and the individual traits become general.

CHAPTER XIV

THE NATURE OF SUBJECT MATTER

1. Subject Matter of Educator and of Learner

Exposition. The subject matter of the educator is not the same as that of the learner. Neither is subject matter identical with the curriculum. Let us see.

Subject matter is, as we have seen, what one needs to know in order to do what one is interested in doing. In order for a purposeful situation to develop effectively, ideas and a knowledge of relevant fact are necessary. These facts may be observed, recalled, read about, talked about, or acquired in any other way. Such ideas and facts functioning in the development of a situation having a purpose are subject matter.

The materials of school instruction, the studies, comprise the curriculum. It includes reading, writing, mathematics, history, nature study, drawing, singing, physics, chemistry, languages, and so on. The curriculum is supposedly actual subject matter for the educator who has covered it by using it, but it is only potential subject matter for the learner who is beginning to use it. The curriculum becomes subject matter to the learner when, if, and as he uses it in a purposeful activity.

Here we face again the question, What is the teacher's part in the enterprise of education? It is to furnish the environment which stimulates the responses of the pupil and directs the course of his learning. This is *all* the teacher can do. In the last analysis the teacher's work is so to modify stimuli that the pupil's responses—as surely as is possible—will form desirable intellectual and emotional dispositions. What are these stimuli and what is this environment? The curriculum is an intimate part of the answer. The teacher must see that the curriculum becomes subject matter to the learner.

As previously noted too, a social environment is necessary to give meaning to these intellectual and emotional dispositions. This is clear in the case of the informal education of the primitive group; social intercourse carries directly the subject matter to which pupils respond; the young member of the community forms his habits in accord with what his associates do and say. The need for the social environment is, however, no less when instruction becomes formal and deliberate, when curriculum and subject matter become separate.

Even in primitive social groups, some things are learned directly by social participation, and some things are learned indirectly through conscious communication. Among the things directly learned are eating, hunting, making war and peace, constructing rugs, pottery, baskets, etc. Among the things indirectly learned are the meanings precipitated out of the previous experience of the group, being identified with the collective life of the group. They are treasured up in stories, traditions, songs, liturgies, myths, legends, and sacred verbal formulæ. They accompany the primitive rites. These indirect learnings can not be picked up in the daily occupations, so pains are taken to perpetuate them consciously. Special initiation ceremonies are devised for the purpose, performed often with intense emotional fervor. More pains are spent on the consciously communicated, than on the direct, learnings. So arose the distinction between curriculum and subject matter. The curriculum grew out of the subject matter as the transmitted deposit of previous experience.

What took place naturally in the primitive group became more pronounced in the growing complex group. The number of acquired skills and standard ideas deposited from the past and dependent on conscious instruction increased. The content of social life becomes definitely formulated for purposes of instruction. As we saw, the very need to instruct the young that the group life might be perpetuated was the chief urge in developing a curriculum, by studying, extracting, and systematizing the important meanings of the group life. The process of selecting, formulating and organizing the group meanings once started, there is no definite limit to it. The invention first of writing and then of printing gave the operation an immense impetus.

The result? A practical divorce between curriculum and subject matter, between school studies and the habits and ideals of the social group. The bonds originally uniting the two are disguised, the ties are so loosened as to appear non-existent. It is as if the curriculum existed independently on its own behoof, as if study were the mere act of mastering it for its own sake, irrespective of social values. Knowledge for its own sake? Absurd. The tendency to separate curriculum and real social subject matter must be counteracted, for practical reasons. The chief purpose of our theoretical discussion is to recover the lost connection and to show the social content and function of the chief subjects of study. The curriculum must become subject matter again.

Subject matter means properly one thing to the instructor and another thing to the student. The meaning of subject matter to the instructor is twofold, viz., (1) definite standards of culture, and (2) the possibilities inherent in the crude activities of the immature. (1) School studies give, or should give, the standardized meanings of current social life desirable to transmit, the essential ingredients of the culture to be perpetuated. The studies give these meanings in concrete and detailed terms, in organized form, protecting the teacher from indulging in haphazard efforts to find the significant social meanings for himself. There is no question here of getting rid of the curriculum; there is only a question of making it socially vital subject matter.

(2) The subject matter reveals to the teacher the possibilities inherent in the crude activities of pupils. The subject matter is itself the product of past activities. The reactions

of the young are seemingly impulsive and aimless; they require directing stimuli. These stimuli come from the subject matter. What past activities have produced will, under the teacher, stimulate present activities to produce. The more the teacher knows of music, the more possibilities he perceives in the inchoate musical impulses of a child. And so with the other subjects of study. The sciences and the arts are the fruitage of experiences like those of the pupils, involving the same world, and powers and needs similar to theirs. Old organized subject matter is not perfection or infallible wisdom, it is the best at command to further new achievements which may surpass the old. Thus, to the teacher, the studies are working resources, available capital. They really are remote from the present experience of the young.

So the subject matter of the learner is not the subject matter of the adult; neither, indeed, can it be. The subject matter of the adult enters directly into the activities of the expert and teacher; it is formulated, crystallized, and systematized; it is found in books, works of art, etc. All this represents only the *possibilities* of the pupil. He is at the beginning of a process of learning through doing, whereas the adult is at the end. The teacher already knows what the pupil is beginning to learn. Adult subject matter simply can not enter directly into the pupil's activities. A text is one of several expressions of pre-existent knowledge; it is adult subject matter; it is not the beginner's subject matter. Most mistakes made in using texts and similar adult material is due to the failure to distinguish the subject matter of the teacher from that of the learner.

Hence it comes about that the problem of the teacher and the problem of the pupil are radically unlike. In the teaching process the problem of the teacher is the attitude and response of the pupil; the problem of the pupil is the topic in hand. The teacher's attention should not be fixed on the subject matter but on the pupil; the pupil's attention should not be fixed on the teacher but on the subject matter. The teacher should know his subject matter so well that he can use it in directing the responses of his pupil. So, simple scholarship is not enough. The teacher should know the constitution and functions of human nature in the concrete, the characteristic needs and capacities of the student, as well as his subject matter. The teacher's problem is to keep the experience of the pupil moving in the direction of the expert's attainment. Scholarship without the teacher's interest in the growing pupil may actually hinder effective teaching. The teacher's knowledge is both more extensive and better organized than that of the pupil. For this reason mastered subject matter, or scholarship, if taken by itself, may actually obstruct effective teaching. Both in range and in the principles involved, the knowledge of the instructor extends beyond that of the pupil's understanding and interest; in fact, the instructor's knowledge may be as remote from the living world of the pupil's experience as the astronomer's knowledge of Mars is from the baby's acquaintance with his room.

The experience of the beginner is not even organized by the same method as that used by the expert. The experience of the beginner is organized in connection with direct practical centers of interest. For example, take geography. The child's home is the organizing center of his geographical knowledge; his items of information are held together by his own movements about the locality, by his journeys abroad, by the tales of his friends. His subject matter is fluid, partial, and connected through personal experience. But the geographer has developed the implications of these smaller experiences; he organizes his knowledge, not on the basis of relations to his house, his bodily movements, and his friends, but on the basis of relationship which the various facts bear to each other. Thus his subject matter is extensive, accurately defined, and logically interrelated. This contrast between the learning of the beginner and of the expert is practically all-important. Since, however, even the learned should still be learning, the contrast is only relative, not absolute.

Comment. There are four matters of note here, the first not being important. It concerns the use of the term "educator." In the text it is used synonomously with instructor and teacher, especially one who is a master of his subject. The term "educator" might preferably be reserved for those who express important and influential opinions about education. The educator may or may not be a teacher also.

The second point is the important recognition given to conscious tutelage in primitive groups, and to school studies as standards of current culture. This means that a "child-centered" school or curriculum is necessarily one-sided. The child is not isolated from his fellows and from nature. Neither can his cultivation be so. Some phases of "progressive education" in "child-centered schools," neglecting the racial deposit of relations with society and nature, supposedly inspired by Dr. Dewey's theories, have departed radically from both the spirit and the letter of his teaching. His view is neither, on the one hand, that the racial experience is negligible, nor, on the other, that it is to be bodily and totally transmitted, but that it is to be used as stimuli in the growing experience of pupils. And this brings us to our third point.

Is it feasible, practical, possible to use the knowledge of the race only as stimuli to the purposeful activities of pupils? The latter are relatively few and decidedly limited in their carrying power. The deposit of racial experience is vast. We need some larger basic principles than that of the stimulus-response situation on the practical plane. We need the recognition of mental assimilation without a necessary practical application. We need too the recognition of the worth of knowledge concerning social conditions that no longer exist. And we also need the recognition of the worth of knowledge that satisfies individual desire and interest, even if such knowledge lacks present social meaning or present practical use. In this sense knowledge may justifiably exist for its own sake, and truth be its own excuse for being. This view does not eliminate subject matter having current social meanings acquired by practical purposeful activity in typical social situations but it supplements such subject matter. It allows culture for its own sake, even hobbies in learning, and the social transmission of intellectual coinage no longer current for those whose fondness lies that way.

The fourth matter concerns the view that "in the last analysis, *all* that the educator [teacher] can do is to modify stimuli. . . ." Of course the new type of teacher does conceive his rôle as that of modifying stimuli, and providing suitable environment. And of course all teachers have always done this to some extent, even when writing was done on palm leaves and computation was done in the sand. But in a personalistic in distinction from a pragmatic philosophy of education, the teacher not only supplies environment but is environment, not only modifies stimuli but is a stimulus. His contacts with his pupils are not only indirect through a situation he is handling but direct with a person in whom he is interested. And the responses of the pupil are made not only to the stimuli of an impersonal situation but to the stimulus of a personal guide and friend. As usual, the idealistic philosophy does not so much reject as supplement the pragmatic philosophy.

2. The Development of Subject Matter in the Learner

Exposition. So subject matter is not something having value just by itself; it is to help the immature realize the meanings implied in their present experience. How is this to be done? In some way the subject matter is to become organized in the activities of the growing members of the group. Yes, the subject matter is to be developed in the experience of the learner. Three fairly typical stages in its growth may be marked off, as follows: knowledge as intelligent control of activities, knowledge as experienced information, and knowledge as rationalized, which is science. Each of these will receive special attention.

(1) Knowledge as intelligent control. The first form of knowledge acquired by children, and the most lasting, is power to do, how to walk, talk, read, write, skate, ride a bicycle, run a machine, calculate, drive a horse, sell goods, manage people, and so on. Knowledge is not primarily a store of information, it is a way of doing things, as exemplified in the life of the farmer, sailor, merchant, physician, or experimenter. Only in misunderstood education is knowledge regarded as a store of information aloof from doing.

The popular mind retains the connection between knowing and doing which education and academic philosophies have lost. This is shown in several ways. Instinctive acts are adapted to an end; they are popularly regarded, indeed unjustifiably, as a sort of miraculous knowledge. "Ken" and "can" are allied words. "Attention" includes taking care of. "Mind" means obeying one's mother and taking care of the baby. To be "considerate" is to heed the claims of others. "Apprehension" includes the dread of consequences. To display "good sense" is to act as the situation demands. "Discernment" is more than hair-splitting, it is practical insight. "Wisdom" includes the proper conduct of life. In all these ways the popular mind shows the fundamental association of knowledge with intelligent control.

The outcome of this kind of knowledge is familiarity or acquaintance with things. The things we put to frequent use are the things we are best acquainted with, such as chairs, tables, pen, paper, clothes, food, knives, forks,—all on the commonplace level. But even on the specialized level of one's own occupation the principle still holds that the things we use the most are the things we know the best,—the forceps of the dentist, the transit of the civil engineer, the knife of the surgeon, the trowel of the mason, the awl of the cobbler. Employ a thing with a purpose and you enjoy an intimate and emotional sense of acquaintance; the hunter caresses his gun. We can anticipate how the familiar implement will act and react. Thus the familiar things with which we are acquainted through use carry a sense of congeniality, friendliness, ease, and illumination, like the "old oaken bucket," while the things with which we are not accustomed to deal are strange, foreign, cold, remote, "abstract," like the surgeon's cabinet of instruments to the patient.

This primary nature of knowledge indicates to us something to follow and something to avoid in education. We are to set out with situations involving learning by doing. The initial stage of the curriculum should be arts and occupations, for these mean intelligent control in accomplishing ends. Initial subject matter is not scientific truths, not scholastic knowledge; it is a matter of active doing, involving the use of the body and the handling of material. We are to avoid isolating the subject matter of instruction from the needs and purposes of the learner, thus making of it just something to be memorized and reproduced on demand. Practically all our knowledge, except that due to deliberate technical study, is of this first sort.

(2) Knowledge as experienced information. The second stage of the growth of subject matter in the experience of the learner is that of experienced information. In this stage intelligent control of activities is surcharged and deepened through communicated knowledge. The transition from stage one to stage two may be very easy and natural; in fact, the two processes of acquiring intelligent control and receiving information somewhat overlap in time. Purposeful doing includes dealing with persons as well as with things. We learn much from others, who tell us their experiences and the experiences they have been told. To the extent that these reported experiences interest or concern us, their content becomes a part of our experience. The sharing becomes so intimate that the line between "my" experience and "yours" can not be drawn. Your words become stimuli evoking my responses, thereby merging your experience with mine. The ear is as much an organ of experience as the nose, or eye, or hand. Whatever affects the issue of our acts becomes a part

of our experience, be it far or near. The eye reads reports of what it can not see. Whatever accounts, brought to us through the stimuli of the sense-organs, affect our dealings with things at hand become a part of personal experience. In this second stage our experience is widened by communication with others, but the communicated information so affects our responses that it becomes itself personal experience. It is in the practical response of the recipient that transmitted information becomes transmuted into knowledge.

Truly to be informed is to be posted; to have at command materials for dealing effectively with a problem, for making significant both the search and the solution; it is to have something in a doubtful situation to fall back upon as given, settled, established, assured. Informational knowledge is the bridge the mind uses in passing from doubt to discovery; its office is that of an intellectual middleman, using past experience to enhance the meaning of present experience. Knowledge is not communicated; information is communicated; information, though it be knowledge to the giver, becomes knowledge, if it does, to the receiver when it is used by him in modifying his behavior. Brutus assassinated Caesar, the length of the year is 365¼ days, the ratio of the diameter of a circle to the circumference is 3.1415 . . . here is indeed knowledge for others, but to one being told these things for the first time, here is only a stimulus to knowing.

Growing out of this second stage in the development of subject matter in the experience of the learner we have again something to follow and something to avoid in the educative process. What is communicated as information must be organized into the existing experience of the learner. It must grow naturally out of some question of his, and it must fit into his direct experience so as to make it more efficacious and meaningful. Information that meets a felt need, is used, and deepens meaning, is educative. The greater the amount heard or read the better, provided the canons of need and application are met.

It is so easy to theorize, so difficult to practice! In our day there has grown up an imposing, stupendous bulk of communicated subject matter. This is due to extending by inventions the area of intercommunication, to acquaintance with the remote heavens and bygone history, and to the recording and distributing of information by the printing press. On the shelves of our libraries there are rows and rows of books, atlases, cyclopedias, histories, biographies, books of travel, and scientific treatises. So it comes about that most people think of "knowledge" as just the body of facts and truths ascertained by others, and not at all in terms of intelligent control. Even logicians and philosophers have been deceived likewise. They too regard knowledge as a deposit, as a series of statements and propositions, which record past findings. Thus the mind of man is taken captive by the spoils of its former victories. Really, to say it again, knowledge is the issue of active concern with problems, an outcome of inquiry, a resource in further inquiry, a weapon for waging war against the unknown. It is not contained in books or in a course of study; it lives only in the mind of the discoverer.

The schools too, like the populace and the élite, have worshipped at the false shrine of bulky tomes. In the seventeenth century, following Aristotle and Bacon who took all knowledge for their province, the accumulated store was still small enough for men like Comenius to set up the ideal of a complete encyclopedic mastery of it. With the present colossal and still growing bulk, the encyclopedic ideal is obviously impossible. But the educational procedure remains much the same. The "course of study" is largely information, distributed into "branches," subdivided into "lessons," containing cut-offs from the general store. The pupil is expected to acquire a modicum of information in each "branch" of learning, or at least in a selected group of branches. This is the principle of curriculum making from elementary school through college. The only distinction made is that between the easier portions for the earlier years and the harder ones for the later years. So it comes about that subject matter is not worked into the direct experiences of pupils, it swamps them. It forms another and strange world overlaying the world of personal acquaintance. Their sole problem becomes to learn for school purposes of recitations and promotions the constituent parts of this strange world. Second-hand knowledge becomes verbal. Communicated information resolves itself into pure sense-stimuli, sound signifying nothing, calling out mechanical reactions in repeating statements, writing, or doing "sums." And then educators complain of the consequences of the conditions they have themselves accepted, learning that does not enter into character, that does not affect conduct, memoriter work, cramming, Gradgrind preoccupations with facts, devotion to fine distinctions and ill-understood rules and principles. These evils come from identifying knowledge with propositions containing information; they can depart only if communicated information be experienced. Over-consumption and mental indigestion *versus* activity and use is the present educational issue.

(3) Science or rationalized knowledge.[1] This is the third and last stage of growth of subject matter within the experience of the learner. Science is rationalized knowledge, is knowledge in its most characteristic form, is the perfected outcome of learning,—its consummation. Science is what is *ascertained, what* is *so,* undoubted, sure, certain, settled, disposed of; it is that *with* which we think, not that *about* which we think.

Science is an acquired art, not spontaneous; is learned, not native. It consists of all those appliances and methods slowly worked out by the race whereby reflection may be reliably tested. It is the method of dependable inquiry and testing. Thus science is defined in terms of method.

But is not science, according to the current conception, 'organized and systematized knowledge"? And are not the

[1] Note. The arrangement here departs from that of the text. The explanation is given in the *Comment* below.—Author.

two views inconsistent? Not so, when the ordinary conception is properly completed. It is not organization that differentiates science but the *kind* and the purpose of that organization which is secured by adequate methods. To illustrate, a farmer's knowledge is in stage one described above; a chemist's knowledge is stage three. The farmer's knowledge is organized and systematized practically on the basis of relation of means to the ends of securing crops, livestock, etc. Any adequately tested and confirmed, *i.e.* scientific, knowledge of his is incidental. The chemist describes water as H_2O, because it is constituted by two molecules of hydrogen combined with one of oxygen. This description of water is no truer than our everyday conception, and not so available for our ordinary uses, but it is superior from the standpoint of inquiry; it connects the nature of water with that of other things; it indicates to the initiated how the knowledge is reached and how it bears upon the structure of other substances. When subject matter is so organized as to facilitate further discovery, it is science. And such organization is impossible without the appropriate method. Science is science because its method has made it so. For this reason the definition of science must recognize the primacy of method.

Otherwise stated, the characteristic mark of science is not organized knowledge but rationalized knowledge. Science has rational assurance, logical warranty. In it every statement follows from others and leads to others. Its concepts mutually imply and support one another. The terms logical and rational mean "leading to and confirming."

There are certain natural propensities of the human race against whose evil consequences science is a safeguard. We tend to substitute *our* certainty for *subject matter* certainty; credulity is natural; we are made, so to speak, for belief. The mind undisciplined by science is averse to intellectual suspense and hesitation; it likes things undisturbed, settled, and, being prone to assertion, treats them as such without warrant. The measuring rod of truth then becomes congeniality to desire, or common repute, or familiarity with the accepted idea. Ignorance is a great foe to learning, but opinionated and current error, which displaces it, is still greater. Thus a Socrates arises to declare that the consciousness of ignorance is the beginning of wisdom, and a Descartes to say that science is born of doubt.

To approach our need for the discipline of science from a slightly different angle. We naturally tend to cut short the process of testing, we are averse to suspended judgment, we have a predilection for premature acceptance, we are satisfied with superficial and short-visioned applications, we too easily suppose our assumptions have been confirmed. If our assumptions do not work out satisfactorily, we put the blame, not where it belongs—on the inadequacy of our data and thoughts, but on our hard luck and the hostility of circumstance; or, we may even stubbornly cling to our conceptions in spite of their untoward consequences.

In contrast with all this incorrect procedure, data and ideas used scientifically have their worth tested experimentally; in themselves they are tentative and provisional; our errors are revised; our incomplete inquiry is extended.

So science is a safeguard against evils to which the race is prone, and it is an acquired art. Whence follows the unique and invaluable place of science in education. Without initiation into the scientific spirit and method, one lacks the best tools humanity has yet devised for directing reflection effectively, and also fails to understand the full meaning of knowledge, missing the traits that distinguish opinion and assent from authorized conviction.

On the other hand, there are dangers to be avoided in using science in education. The results of science, taken by themselves, are remote and aloof from ordinary experience, they are popularly designated as "abstract." This result is due to the technique used, to the fact that science is not so much a body of knowledge as a way of knowing, the way of using old knowledge to acquire more knowledge. The danger besetting instruction in science is this isolation; it is even greater than that attendant upon presenting other forms of ready-made information described above.

Thus we have seen the three stages in the development of subject matter in the experience of the learner, viz., knowledge as intelligent control, knowledge as experienced information, and knowledge as rationalized, or science. Our next two chapters will present various school activities and studies as successive stages in this evolution of knowledge. Meantime another important aspect of subject matter awaits our attention.

Comment. It will be noted that, in the interest of clarity in exposition, "3" in the text is here brought under "2" as (3) thus indicating that science is the third stage in the development of subject matter in the learner. And "4" will become "3."

At the outset it will assist us in unifying different parts of the theory to note the following parallels between the steps in a reflective experience, or method, and the stages in the development of subject matter in the learner.

Reflection	Subject Matter
1. Activity	1. Knowledge as Control
2. Problem	
3. Data	2. Information to be Used
4. Hypothesis	
5. Testing	3. Science

Thus, method is not apart from subject matter, and science is not so much a systematic body of knowledge as the reliable mode of inquiry.

Here we may note is what appears to be another type of "culture epoch theory." As with the race, so with the individual. First there is learning from personal experience, then from the experience of others, and then a technique is devised, called science, to control experience. But the first continues into the second and the third, and the second likewise continues into the third. Science is the peak of the process, the perfection of knowing. The three stages do not exist separately, though the third may not be reached at all; it is an acquired art.

Again, we note the pragmatic emphasis upon knowledge as control of a situation. This is the only thing in the first stage, and the main thing in the other two stages. In stage two the communicated information does not become knowledge until it is used practically. In stage three, knowledge is used to advance knowledge. We have had and shall have occasion to note that there are other theories of knowledge than the pragmatic, useful as the latter is in connecting knowledge with action. We know and enjoy much that we can not use. We understand and appreciate much that we have not experienced, though something similar has been experienced. We know by experience this side of the moon; we know by reason that the moon is a sphere and has another side, which we have not experienced, and of which we can make no use, except argumentative. The point that pragmatism misses here is that we can know by reason the unexperienced and unexperienceable. And life is much richer because of our ability to transcend experience in some forms of knowledge. We know that an Einstein equation purporting to identify electricity and gravitation has a meaning without experiencing the meaning, and without being able to make any use of the meaning, and certainly without any ability to use the meaning in discovering other meanings. And we marvel at the knowledge we know we lack. We can know some things we can not use in controlling a practical situation.

A third thing. In insisting that information is not knowledge until it is used, the range of knowledge is unduly limited; the valuable distinction between "knowledge of acquaintance" and "knowledge about" made by James is lost. If I am reliably informed that there is a city in Japan called Tokio, I know there is such a city, though I am not personally acquainted with it, and may never be. If the historic statement, "Brutus assassinated Caesar," is not knowledge to the reader but only a stimulus to knowing, but little history is known. We are, however, quite justified in accepting vouched-for historic information as real and genuine knowledge. We do not have to do anything else about it to make it knowledge for us. It may or may not ever prove useful to us in controlling practical experience. We can know what others tell us without testing it for ourselves. Most of our knowledge is of this type. Another's knowledge is my knowledge when it is understood and accepted, even if not applied or made the basis of discovering more knowledge.

Again, a fourth point. Science is assigned the last place in the development of subject matter in the experience of the learner. This whole treatment is from the intellectual standpoint. This treatment is desirably supplemented in the succeeding section on the social aspect of subject matter. Still, something essential is lacking. It is the appreciative aspect of experience. This is introduced in Chapter XVIII, but it needs to be introduced here. Subject matter is more than knowledge, even if all three stages of knowledge are present. It is the appreciation, the valuing, of what is known. It is the emotional aspect of experience, always present, always giving a characteristic tone of liking or disliking or some mixture of the two, without which experience would be like lunar light, white and silvery but not warm and glowing.

But even from the intellectual standpoint used in the treatment, something essential is lacking. Man can think about what he does not know, may never know. His thoughts run where knowledge in any one of the proper senses of the word can not follow. He wonders about larger realities than he can know. Yet such thinking may be disciplined by the canons of self-consistency and consistency with the known. Such thinking, not being verifiable, is non-scientific. We refer, of course, to speculative or metaphysical thinking. To open wide one's intellectual prospect, this type of philosophy should be admitted as the fourth stage in the development of subject matter in the learner. It is not knowledge, but it is thought concerning the possibilities of existence, its nature, and its meaning. Without it, subject matter, though it embrace all knowledge and all scientific method, is lean and meagre.

And still further. When the appreciative aspect of experience is joined with the speculative, one result may be a spiritual interpretation of the universe, leading to a religious attitude on the part of the learner. Because this result is so frequent in historic and present experience, it too should form one phase of subject matter.

In sum, our treatment of subject matter should recognize the emotional as well as the intellectual, the philosophical as well as the scientific, and the religious as well as the social. These views may be graphically presented as follows:

Dr. Dewey on Subject Matter

Aspects	Intellectual:	1. Control 2. Experienced Information 3. Science
	Social	

Our View on Subject Matter

Aspects	Intellectual:	1. Control 2. Information 3. Science 4. Philosophy	Religion
	Social		
	Appreciative		

3. Subject Matter as Social

Exposition. We now pass from the intellectual to the social aspect of subject matter.

Subject matter in all its stages has been first worked out under social conditions and then transmitted by social means. It is social in origin and social in nature but this does not mean that all subject matter is equally valuable socially. Not all vital knowledge, motivated though it be by purposes and relevant to real problems, is equally broad and deep, for purposes differ in social scope and problems differ in social importance. Not all subject matter, social though it be, is equally valuable in forming the disposition of and supplying the equipment of the members of present society. In selecting subject matter education should use a criterion of social worth. The range of material to select from is wide and the criterion of social worth should be applied everywhere except in the most specialized fields. The questions to be raised in planning a curriculum are these: What are the needs of the existing community life? Which studies are adapted to these needs? Which studies will improve our common life, making the future better than the past? Which studies are essential, *i.e.*, having to do with the experiences shared by the widest groups? Which studies are secondary, *i.e.*, representing the needs of specialized groups and technical pursuits?

Education must first be human and then professional, as the saying runs. But we must understand what "human" means; it does not mean the interests of a highly specialized class of learned men who preserve the classic traditions of the past, it means the common interests of men as men. Subject matter, contrary to general opinion, is dehumanized when it belongs only to the classes; it is humanized when it belongs to the masses.

The influence of democracy in planning a course of study condemns both the "essentials" of an elementary education for the many and the "liberal studies" of an advanced education for the few, thus introducing and perpetuating social cleavage. Democracy can not flourish when the many are educated narrowly and the few are educated traditionally. The educational essentials in realizing democratic ideals are the problems of living together, the study of which develops social insight and interest. Reading, writing, figuring, spelling, and muscular skill are the "essentials" of an elementary education only in an undemocratic society in which most men and women "make a living" by doing things for others, things not significant, not freely chosen, not ennobling, serving ends unrecognized by those doing them, and all for a pecuniary reward. No more do traditions of a special cultivated class provide "liberal" education for the few; rather is such liberal education infected with illiberality; it is a somewhat parasitic cultivation bought at the expense of missing the enlightenment and discipline coming from concern with the deepest problems of our common humanity. Our "practical" elementary education is not democratic; our "liberal" advanced education is not democratic. Both elementary and advanced education can become democratic only by adopting a curriculum which acknowledges social responsibilities.

Comment. There is no doubt about Dr. Dewey's recognition of the rights of the individual, but they are social rights; or of his recognition of the rights of society, but they are the rights of common men and women. His real emphasis is upon the activities of the individual as a developing member of a social group. "Subject matter as social" lends no support to the "paidocentric" tendency.

Still, the activity element in his doctrine and the social element in his doctrine are not well unified. The activity element ties knowledge down to occupation with, and manipulation of, material things; the social element drops the materials and stresses social problems, responsibility, insight, and interest. A group of children building a toy town are learning through occupation how to work together practically but they are not facing real social issues. A group of settlement workers adjusting their program to the needs of their community are facing social issues but they are not manipulating materials. This disharmony would disappear in case the theory of knowledge as exclusively intelligent control of a material situation were surrendered.

CHAPTER XV

PLAY AND WORK IN THE CURRICULUM

1. The Place of Active Occupations in the Curriculum

Exposition. In the previous chapter we saw that the initial stages of knowing consist in learning how to do things and in becoming acquainted with things and processes in the doing. We pause a moment first to dwell upon this point. The ancient Greeks had this view in using the same word τέχνη (technē), for both art and science. (We have kept the same word to mean art in our "technology.") Thus Plato presented knowledge, or science, as something possessed by cobblers, carpenters, and musical performers; their art involved a purpose, the mastery of material, the control of tools, and a definite procedure; all this knowledge made the art or skill intelligent, and not mere routine.

Now if knowledge thus begins as a doing, the place of activities in education is evidently basic. And our curriculum is changing in accord with this principle. Forms of activity are being introduced into the school similar to those in which children and youth engage out of school. Thus we have plays and games, hand work and manual exercises. This is proper, in case they are used in the right way, as we shall see.

Three influences at least have contributed to this modification of the curriculum in the past generation. The first is the effort of educational reformers, like Froebel. The second is the increased interest in child-psychology; for the general ready-made faculties of the older theory a complex group of instinctive and impulsive tendencies has been substituted. The third is the direct experience of the school room; when children have a chance at physical activities which bring their natural impulses into play, learning is easier, going to school is a joy to pupils, and management is less of a burden to teachers. These three influences have enforced the lesson that education starts from and with the experiences and capacities of the learners.

It must not be thought, therefore, that the grounds for letting children play and do physical work in school are momentary agreeableness, and temporary expediency,—relief from the strain of "regular" school work. Something more fundamental is involved, even the acquisition of knowledge and the cultivation of a social disposition. Native tendencies to express joyous emotion, to explore, to manipulate tools and materials, to construct, and the like, have fundamental worth. When the regular school program includes exercises based on these impulses, the whole pupil is engaged, the artificial gap between life in and out of school is reduced, attention to a large variety of materials and processes distinctively educative in effect is motivated, and coöperative groups giving information a social setting are formed. Without such basic activities the normal estate of effective learning can not be secured, and the getting of knowledge becomes a school task instead of being an outgrowth of activities having their own end.

But do not children engage normally in play and active work out of school? Then should they not in school concern themselves with things radically different? Is not school time too precious to spend in doing over again what children are sure to do anyway? Let us see. Children do, of course, normally engage in play and work out of school. Under social conditions which make such occupation truly educative the school may very well devote itself to books. Such was the case in pioneer times. Then, outside occupations gave a definite and valuable intellectual, moral, and social training; on the other hand books and other printed matter were rare and difficult of access, and, when secured, they were the only means of outlet from a narrow and crude environment.

Now, however, in most communities, the situation is different. Especially in cities the opportunities for play are limited, and those for work are largely uneducative,—child labor is a menace whose prevention is a social duty; printed matter is cheap and plentiful; and opportunities for intellectual culture have been multiplied. Hence, there is less excuse for book work in school than formerly and more demand for the educational use of play and work. Modern urban life practically reverses the relation of the school to society that obtains under more primitive conditions. And what out-of-school society does not naturally supply to meet the needs of children, that the up-to-date school must provide.

Besides, it must not be forgotten that play and work out of school may miss their educational effect. Such play is affected by the surrounding adult life, reproducing and affirming its crudities as well as its excellencies. Such work often shares in the defects of existing industrial society,—defects nearly fatal to right development. Under such conditions the educative growth secured by play and work out of school is a by-product; incidental, not primary; and more or less accidental. So, even if children do engage in play and work out of school, all the more is it the business of the school by using rightly directed play and work to secure as a result the desirable kind of mental and moral growth. But having introduced games and hand work, everything depends upon the way they are employed.

Comment. The reference to Plato needs to be supplemented here by recalling that in addition to the practical knowledge that consists in the intelligent control of activities, he recognized also an absolute knowledge of the real nature of things, their essences, or "ideas." The world of practical activities he preferred to regard as the region of "opinion," whereas the world of the ideas yielded absolute knowledge. The former was full of change, being an admixture of real being and non-being; the latter was changeless, pure being. Plato's theory of knowledge was not pragmatic.

The argument in the text in behalf of the basic place of occupations in education, in so far as it rests upon psychology, is doubtless sound. In so far as it rests upon the contrast between pioneer and present social conditions, a few observations should be made. Pioneer schools, while making book work primary, did have much play and work too. There were charades and spelling-bees, water to bring and wood to cut, the floor to sweep and the blackboards to keep clean. The little ungraded school with a single teacher was, and still is, largely a self-dependent social unit. Almost half of our population is still in towns of less than five thousand and in the open country. Here the activities of the school children must be something different from the games and hand work used in city schools. The needs and interests of country life should be uppermost. Our rural schools have been too much urbanized. The aim is not to keep country children in the country, but to give them an intelligent appreciation of the meaning of life, both in the country and in the city. Such children need books to help introduce them to the life beyond their range, and local activities to help them participate fully in the life about them. In the same way children in city schools need books about the country, along with their games and manual exercises. The point is, books in school are not enough for pioneer and country children and active occupations in school are not enough for city children. This view is not opposed to that of the text but supplements it.

Again, the question arises whether all needed knowledge can be acquired through pursuit of active occupations, for example, the acquisition of a foreign language, or the history of ancient Rome. This is associated with the related question, whether the mind has a function transcending organic reactions. If not, all knowledge must come through active occupations; if so, some knowledge may come without any more organic reaction than the accommodation of the muscles of the eye and without any more active occupation than turning the pages of a book. If this be so, active occupations may very well give us our point of departure but not also our port of arrival. We might even then come to hold with Plato that some knowledge is valid without controlling, or needing to control, behavior.

2. Available Occupations

Exposition. In this section we will ask four questions, viz., (1) What occupations are available for educational uses in school? (2) What is the problem involved in the use of these occupations? (3) How is this problem to be solved? And (4) What mistakes are to be avoided in the solution?

(1) What occupations are available? These are numerous. It is a rich field. Already the list of activities used in the school program is long. Some of the materials used are paper, cardboard, wood, leather, cloth, yarns, clay, sand, and the metals. Some of the processes employed are folding, cutting, pricking, measuring, molding, modeling, pattern making, heating, cooling. Some of the tools used are the hammer, the saw, and the file. Some of the modes of occupation are outdoor excursions, gardening, cooking, scouting, printing, bookbinding, weaving, painting, drawing, singing, dramatization, story-telling, and a countless variety of plays and games. When even reading and writing are employed as active pursuits with social aims and not merely as exercises in acquiring skill for future use, they too belong in the list. So there is no dearth of available activities on which to base all learning.

(2) What is the problem involved in the educational use of such activities? It is this: how may pupils so engage in these activities as to achieve intellectual results and to form socialized dispositions? These are the primary objectives in the educational use of activities. Through action we are to come to knowledge and to character. At the same time certain sub-

ordinate results are not to be lost, such as, finding immediate satisfaction in the work, gaining manual skill and technical efficiency, and even preparing for later usefulness. The practical solving of the problem is as difficult as it is important.

(3) How then is the problem to be solved? The activities are to lead to intellectual and social results. Let us take gardening as an illustration. It should lead to knowledge of the place farming and horticulture have had in the history of the race, and do have in present social organization; the facts of growth; the chemistry of the soil; the rôle of light, air, and moisture; injurious and beneficial animal life; elementary botany, as a phase of life, correlated with the facts of soil, animal life, and human relations. The original direct interest in gardening may lead maturer students on to independent interests in such problems as germination, nutrition, reproduction. The initial active occupation may thus lead some students on to intellectual investigations and discovery. Gardening as a school subject has larger aims than passing time agreeably or preparing future gardeners.

And what is true of gardening is true of the other school occupations,—woodworking, cooking, and the like. Each occupation has its characteristic opportunities for learning and becoming. Yes, active occupations are opportunities for study, in both scientific subject matter and method.

Look at the question historically. In the history of the race the sciences have grown up out of the useful social occupations. So it was with physics, chemistry, and mathematics. The use of tools and machines led to physics. That branch of physics called "mechanics" testifies to its origin. In seeking means to accomplish practical ends, man discovered the lever, the wheel, and the inclined plane. These now familiar matters were among man's first great intellectual triumphs. The past generation was interested in using electricity in communication, transportation, lighting of cities and houses, and the economical production of goods; these practical interests led to the great advance in electrical science.

In like ways processes of dyeing, bleaching, and metal working led to the growth of chemistry, which has found in recent times innumerable new uses in industry. So earth-measuring led to geometry. Man's need to keep track of things and to measure things led to the invention of counting, which is even more needed today than when it arose. The history of any science shows the same practical origin. Such considerations do not mean that education should recapitulate the history of the race; or dwell long in the early rule-of-thumb stage, but that we, as never before, can use active occupations for scientific study.

Thus occupations stand in close connection with the subject matter of science. They also stand in equally close connection with the method of science. Occupation with things means experimentation; contempt for material things means logical reasonings and a resultant slow progress of science. Dropping acid on a stone to see what will happen is nearer the right way of knowledge than a syllogism isolated from experience. Men's interests in occupations, in controlling nature for human uses, began in the seventeenth and succeeding centuries. This same period saw the rise of the experimental method and its recognition as the authorized way of knowing. Now the active occupations, bringing appliances to bear upon physical things to effect useful changes, remain the most vital introduction to the experimental method of science. Thus the many occupations available for school work lead to intellectual results in both the subject matter and the method of science.

But occupations lead not only to intellectual but also to social results. They may be selected to typify social situations. The universal and fundamental concerns of man are food, clothing, shelter, household furnishings, and the appliances for the production, exchange, and distribution of goods. These concerns represent both the necessities and the adornments of life; so they tap the instinctive tendencies of man at a deep level; they are saturated with the social quality; they have social ends.

Because the active occupations are social in origin, operation, and results, they may be used in the social studies of the school, as well as in the scientific, as indicated above. Consider civics and economics; for beginning students the most direct road into the heart of these subjects is by way of the industries: what is their place and office in social life? For older students too the social sciences would be less abstract and formal if they dealt with the daily life of the social groups in which the student shares and less with formulated bodies of knowledge. Not only the present, but the past and the future collective life of humanity may be best understood and appreciated through the social sharing of occupations.

One may object to the use of the active occupations in school on the ground that they have merely a bread and butter value. This is to miss their point. The activities, like gardening, weaving, woodwork, metal work, cooking, and the like, really carry over into the resources of the school the fundamental concerns of man. They have scientific and social value; their economic value is subsidiary. If industrial occupations have evils, and they do, evils endured for life's sake, the fault is not in the occupations, but in the conditions under which they are carried on. Because of the growing importance of economic factors in contemporary life, it is the more important that the school should separate the industrial occupations from the notion of private gain by stressing their scientific content and their relation to public social interests. Occupations, such as the electrical industries, may indeed be deflected from their scientific and social ends to private uses,—a fact which puts upon the school the responsibility of emphasizing their scientific and social uses for the mind of the coming generation. In school, occupations are carried on not for pecuniary extrinsic gain but for their own intrinsic values. Freed from such extraneous associations as profits and the pressure of wage-earning, active occupations in school supply intrinsically valuable modes of experience; for this reason they are truly liberalizing.

(4) In case the use of activities in schools is to reach their proper intellectual and social results, certain mistakes are to be avoided. These are the following: activities must not be too definitely prescribed, the opportunity to make mistakes must not be denied; crude materials must not be excluded; exercises must not be isolated from purposes; and false notions concerning the simple and the complex must not appear in instruction. We will devote a brief exposition to each of these mistakes.

The exercises in both "manual training" and the traditional kindergarten have made the first mistake. They have followed definite prescription and dictation, they have exactly reproduced ready-made models. Such exercises may give muscular dexterity but they do not permit the perception of ends and the selection of means. (Really, ends and means are the same, but that is another story.)

What price initiative? The chance to make mistakes. Not that mistakes in themselves are ever desirable but that initiative and judgment are. If mistakes can not be made in selecting and using materials and appliances, initiative is restricted, judgment is minimized, and the power gained in such simplified situations is of little availability in the complicated situations of life. True enough, children exaggerate their powers and select too difficult and too complex projects. But one of the things to learn is the limitation of one's capacity, and, like other things, this too is learned by the experience of consequences. The danger is indeed great that, undertaking too complex projects, children will simply muddle and mess and acquire crude standards. (Producing crude results is a minor matter.) Here the teacher functions, in guiding the over-ambitious child in perceiving his inadequate performances and in attempting projects within his powers. Where accuracy and finish of detail in only portions of a complex project are within the pupil's capacity, they may be insisted upon. A creative and constructive attitude is more important than the external perfection that comes from too close regulation.

The teacher's orders may be too precise; likewise the materials used may be too finished. The intelligence embodied in finished material can be gained by the pupil only as he begins with crude material and subjects it to purposeful handling. We are not to be suspicious of the pupil's own experience. We are not to overdo external control. The fear of raw material and the demand for perfected material shows itself in the manual training shop, the Froebelian kindergarten, the Montessori house of childhood, and even in the laboratory. Perfected material will prevent errors but it will not develop intelligence. Also, it will exaggerate the formal mathematical qualities of the material without leading to a real knowledge of them; true, intellect finds the size, form, and proportion of physical things profitable, but it can know these properties of things only when it acts upon crude materials with a human purpose. A child may be given a wheel to play with and told that it is round but he knows what roundness means when he saws out a wheel for his cart, especially when by a split in the wood a section of his wheel is lost.

Active occupations should be concerned primarily with *wholes*. For purposes of education wholes are not physical, but intellectual, affairs; they are qualitative, dependent upon concern or interest; they are the completeness of appeal made by a situation. Acquiring skill by following exercises apart from purpose is not a whole. The kindergarten is an offender; vital purposes are absent; symbolism of the material is supposedly a compensation; the employments give information about cubes and spheres and form habits of manipulation without a human end in view. Manual training is another offender; it assigns the mastery of one tool after another; it secures a technical ability in various elements of construction, like the different joints; it is mistakenly argued that children must know how to use tools before attacking actual making; it is falsely assumed they can not learn how to do so in the process of making something desired, which would be a real whole. "Object lessons" also offend; they are intended to acquaint pupils with all the qualities of selected objects. Pestalozzi justly insisted on the active use of the senses instead of memorizing words, but it is a mistake to suppose the properties of objects must be known before the object can be intelligently used. The right way to observe properties is to use the object intelligently. Note the difference in a boy making a kite and having an object lesson on a piece of wood. In the former case the properties of wood are made to function in a real situation. And even in the laboratory of high school and college, exercises are divorced from purpose. Accurate measurements are made for the sake of accurate measurements without contact with the problems making the measurements important. Experimental apparatus is manipulated for the sake of facility in manipulation, apart from any discovery or testing which would make the manipulation significant. The properties of objects do not have to be known before they are intelligently used; it is by using we come to know. And the whole of which any activity is a part includes the purpose or end of the activity.

False notions concerning "the simple and the complex" have prevailed in instruction. They too are due to the failure to realize that for mind the functional development of a situation alone constitutes a whole. For the beginner his purpose is simple and the series of acts necessary to realize it is complex. This series of acts involves the complicated use of tools and materials in a technical process. The unity of purpose, involving concentration upon details, confers simplicity upon the elements of the activity, furnishing each with the *single* meaning of its service in the whole enterprise. *After* one has gone through the process and looks back upon it, its constituents are viewed as elements, each possessing a definite meaning of its own. At the beginning of the activity, the purpose of the learner is simple and the process is complex;

at the end of the activity, the phases of the process are viewed by an expert as its simple elements. The false notion indicated consists in taking the view of the expert for whom elements exist, in isolating them from purposeful action, and then presenting them to beginners as "simple." The true practice would be to let the beginner start with a purpose to do or to make something and to learn as he proceeds.

Thus we have seen in this section the long list of occupations available in school work; the problem of using them for intellectual and social results primarily; how this problem is to be solved by having occupations lead on to scientific knowledge, scientific method, and to socialized dispositions; and how a number of mistakes in using activities may be avoided.

Comment. This section shows us the beginning of the theory of "the project method." Even the very term appears more than once. (This text was written in 1915.) The essence of the method is that learning is a phase of purposeful activity. The method is bound up with the pragmatic theory of knowledge as a phase of action. That we learn much by doing is indisputable; that we learn much more without doing, without manipulating materials, is also probably true; that the project method is only one of many worth while methods would seem to be obvious.

A new notion of the historic term "liberal" also appears here. Historically a liberal education was intellectual, not manual, and was associated with leisure; here it is intellectual through being manual and is associated with physical production of some sort. The historic view eliminated the commercial motive; the new view only subordinates it. The strength of the new view is that it allows liberality to all workers, it is democratic. The weakness of the new view is that thought, if always tied down to action, is not truly free after all. Energy of contemplation, intellectual love, devotion to non-material pursuits, have a greater degree of liberality than manual occupations, though freed from the profit motive, can ever acquire. Since the worker does not have to be always at his work, this liberal road lies open to him also, according to his ability and training in following it.

The position that the properties of objects do not have to be known before the objects are intelligently used (p. 233) is dubious in some cases. Consider fire, fire-arms, explosives, poisons, live wires, razors, thin ice, the oncoming engine, and all such dangers. "Forewarned is forearmed." Only in a strictly experimental world of trial and error, where the results of the experience of others were not accumulated and transmitted, could the principle hold true. In dealing with tools in manual training and with chemicals in the laboratory it is necessary to know their properties before intelligent use can be made of them. This can be admitted without denying that we learn also by using and without allowing learning to go on independently of later using. We learn certain properties in preparation for succeeding intelligent use.

It may well be that scientific knowledge and scientific method arose in handling things for practical social purposes, and it may well be that general science may best be taught beginners by the occupational approach. But it would be a mistake to limit all scientific investigation to solving practical problems. The reason is we have many problems whose bearings are not obviously practical but whose solutions might at any time affect practice greatly; and if they did not, they still furnish intellectual stimulation and satisfaction to the pure scientist. Beginners may be held to practice, some experts may hold themselves to practice, but other experts will be devoted to the cause of truth for its own sake. It is even possible that such a disinterested search for truth is one of the main sources of scientific progress, and incidentally too of improvements in practice. Thus, Lord Kelvin and J. J. Thomson gave us wireless telegraphy as a fact before Marconi used it in saving lives at sea. Soaring intellects need not be held down to earth-bound practices. It is good to have men like Millikan, Eddington, Jeans, and Einstein, tell us what our cosmos may be like, though their speculations grow out of no practical human social problems and in turn solve none. There are mental as well as physical occupations. There are thinkers as well as doers. And if we learn by doing, we also learn by thinking.

3. Work and Play

Exposition. The active occupations described in the two preceding sections as belonging in the curriculum include both play and work. We are actively occupied in play and we are actively occupied in work. In this section we must seek to show both the likenesses and differences between play and work, and the effect upon each of them of our unfree and undesirable economic and social conditions. As a result we shall become more conscious of the need for changes in our present social order.

Play and work (industry) do not differ from each other in the fact that play has no end and work has an end. Play has an end too. In this respect they are rather alike than different. In fact, the antitheses commonly drawn sharply between play and work are themselves due to labor conditions that should not obtain. It is commonly supposed that play is for its own sake, but it too has an end. It is likewise commonly supposed that work is for the sake of the consequences; it is so too frequently, but it does not have to be so.

The distinction between play and work may be drawn either from the economic or from the psychological standpoint. Economically, play does not aim at earning a living and work does. Psychologically, the differences are these: in play the activity is likely to be shorter than in work and leads on to further activity enjoyed on its own account, while in work the activity is likely to be longer than in play and leads on not only to further activity but to some material tangible result or accomplishment. No play is work but all work should have the spirit of play, which makes work a form of art. Our economic conditions hinder this desirable result.

Play, like work, has conscious ends effected by the selection of suitable materials and processes, but the time-span connecting means with ends is shorter in play. In play the interest is more direct, the activity is for its own sake without being aimed at some ulterior result. But this does not mean the activity of play is momentary, without the look ahead, without pursuit. Hunting, a common form of adult play, has both foresight and direction.

In contrast with play activity having an end, there is a form of momentary activity, purely physical in character, and having no meaning. The motions are gone through blindly, perhaps imitatively, or else excitedly and exhaustingly. Some kindergarten games show these qualities, the idea of play being so highly symbolized as to be lost on the children. In these cases unless they read in some different idea of their own, they move about hypnotically, or else respond to a direct external stimulus.

In the case of the play activity, then, there is an anticipated result; it is a subsequent action. So play is free and plastic. One activity leads on to another, it is not necessary to look far ahead, and the activity may be altered easily and frequently. Thus, when a child is "playing boat," he may change the material and introduce new factors as fancy suggests, passing from chairs to blocks, to leaves, to chips, to anything that leads on.

The activity is different when the anticipated result is not another action but a specific change in things, a definite external outcome. Then the end has to be held to persistently. If the outcome is complex, requiring a long time-span, and many adaptations of means, still more persistence is necessary. Thus, if a child is not just "playing boat," but really making a toy boat, he must hold on to his single end and direct many acts by that one idea. His play becomes work.

From an early age the distinction between work and play is only one of emphasis and is not exclusive. Even young children desire and try to achieve definite external results. They have an eager interest in sharing the occupation of others. They want to "help," to engage in adult pursuits effecting external changes, such as, setting the table, washing dishes, helping care for animals, and the like. In their plays they like to construct their own toys and appliances, like airplanes, radios, and steering gear.

As children grow up there is more emphasis on tangible achievement and less on activity for its own sake. Children are serious when they play; they are seriously absorbed in things. When things cease to afford adequate stimulation, to continue playing with them becomes fooling, and habitual foolery is demoralizing. When maturing powers lead to the recognition of make-believe to be what it is, making objects in fancy alone and not really is too easy, not stimulating intense action. Only by observable results can persons get a sense of their own powers. Thus the initial play activity of the young passes gradually into the work activity of the older.

Work, then, is an activity having a foreseen, somewhat remote, and definite result, which enlists persistence in its accomplishment. Like play, work is purposeful and is subordinated to an external result, but, unlike play, the result involves a definite change in material, a longer course of activity to effect the change, more continuous attention, and more intelligence in selecting means. What was previously said under the captions of aim, interest, and thinking may be recalled here.

Why is it that so commonly and mistakenly play is held to be activity for its own sake and work is held to be activity for the sake of an ulterior result? Really, as we saw, play has an end in more activity, and work is purposeful activity which lasts longer because its end is more complex. The answer to the question is our unfree economic conditions which make work a species of drudgery. Industry offers little to engage the emotions and the imagination; it is a mechanical series of strains; only the reward of the work has hold enough upon the person to keep him going. The activity is not carried on because of its own significance, but because of external coërcion; it is not intrinsically satisfying, but a mere means of gaining some reward or avoiding some penalty; it may be even inherently repulsive, though endured to avert something worse or to secure an alien gain.

In contrast with work as drudgery, work should be art, the end should be intrinsic to the act, a part of the course of the act. In such work the stimulus to effort is real. The school has the rare opportunity of eliminating work as drudgery through the absence of economic pressure and introducing work as art. Occupations reproducing the industrial situations of mature life may be carried on for their own sake. The significance of the action may even be increased if it has also some pecuniary recognition as a secondary motive. It is for the schools to show that there can be work that is socially significant, artistic, and without drudgery.

He who works as a drudge is ill-restrained in play. Drudgery does not eliminate the demand for play but prevents play. No demand of human nature is more urgent or less to be escaped than that for recreation, or recuperation of energy. Drudgery fails to give adequate stimulus to emotion and imagination; so, in leisure time, there is an imperious demand for their stimulation; anything to pass the time agreeably; idle amusement; in more extreme cases, gambling, drinking, and the like. Drab work and exciting leisure go together. The well-to-do, freed from the urge to work, pay the same price for leisure as the coërced laborer.

Here again is the school's opportunity. Just as it can save work from drudgery, so it can save leisure from indulgence. The need for recuperation in leisure time can not be suppressed. The Puritanic tradition which disallowed this need has entailed an enormous crop of evils. Suppressed instincts find all sorts of illicit outlets, sometimes imaginative, sometimes overt. The school must afford opportunity for wholesome recreation and must train capacity for seeking and finding it. Education has no more serious responsibility than this, for the sake not only of immediate health but also of ultimate habits of mind. And how is the school to meet this demand? Again, art is the answer, for in art there is an activity intrinsically interesting yielding its own natural result, there is work permeated with the play attitude.

Comment. Can art eliminate drudgery? Art is work with the play spirit; drudgery is work without the play spirit. Can the play spirit motivate all work? It is a little difficult to see how work at a machine in one of our factories can be art, or in the mines, or in a lumber camp. But such work has to be done under any economic order. Drudgery as extrinsically motivated work seems a part, even if reduced to small proportions, of any world where living depends on effort. If one does not enjoy washing the dishes, the dishes must nevertheless be washed for health's sake. Extrinsic motivation seems to remain in many lives most of the time and in all lives some of the time.

There are several answers to the problem of eliminating drudgery. One is the historic answer of letting the slaves do it while the freemen enjoy leisure. Uncivilized societies still practice this solution. But it contradicts the principle of the inherent worth of every person.

Another is Dr. Dewey's answer of art. Let everybody work in engaging ways and everybody play in leisure time in wholesome ways. This sounds utopian in a machine age, where production is necessary and depends on effort. For the fortunate and the well-adjusted individuals this solution may be feasible.

Another is the use of robots and labor-saving machinery. This reduces drudgery but does not eliminate it. Some must tend the robot and the electric dishwasher.

Another is to let the morons do the dirty work. This suggestion emanates from high authority in cases. This seems another slavery and a surrender of eugenics.

Another is, to require work of everybody and so lessen it for everybody. This does not eliminate drudgery but lessens it by distribution. However, it may infringe upon the principle of division of labor and specialization.

Still another is to dignify necessary labor and to perform it in the spirit of social service. One may wash another's feet not because he finds it an expression of the spirit of play, but because it is a needful act performed in the spirit of service and so done willingly. Drudgery and menial work are not felt as such when done devotedly. This is a difficult, but hopeful way out. It does not contradict any of the other ways to the extent that they are practicable.

It should also be noted that some work undertaken under external compulsion may develop a sense of intrinsic value. Thus, what began as drudgery may end as art. This fact is important in both life and school. Useful studies, though uninteresting at the start, may, when well taught, be enjoyable at the finish. The recognition of this fact supplements the wishbone of the new education with the backbone of the old.

Dr. Dewey is clear as to the social and economic conditions he would reject but vague as to those he would accept. His views are socialistic but, so far as expressed, not radical. He does not advocate direct action and revolution, though he may justify these in the case of Russia. His educational theories have been accepted and adapted to Russian conditions but he himself is still to the Russians a bourgeois believer in democracy.[1] He rejects the motive of competition, and accepts the motive of coöperation, though the type of economic state his coöperative motive would fit into is not clearly depicted. He must approve the current tendencies toward coöperation in industry in our capitalistic society in so far as these are not a sop to quiet the discontent of labor. In the same way he is very much clearer in condemning the old individualism than in portraying the new.[2] The probability is that, dislik-

[1] Cf. Pinkevitch, A. P., *The New Education in the Soviet Republic*, New York, 1929.

[2] Cf. Dewey, John, *Individualism Old and New*, New York, 1930.

ing names and holding close to realities, he is willing for the socio-economic trends to work themselves out as they may while intelligence gives such immediate guidance as it can in taking the next step. This is a kind of guided experimentalism in social affairs without a set description of more remote social goals.

There is an increasing emphasis in our day on "social planning." This is due in part to the attention the world is giving to the "five-year plan" of the Russian Soviet. There is, of course, doubt about the success of the control of social change by intelligent direction; it is somewhat like "price-fixing"; but it is man's only way of taking an active part in shaping his own social future. Being such, social engineering is to be encouraged by both governmental and unofficial boards.

So, for what it may be worth, our own view is here set down as a remote future goal toward which inevitable social change should be intelligently directed:

1. World-mindedness, intelligent, sympathetic, practical, providing world-solutions for world-problems.
2. An internationalized world, with social unity, not uniformity, maintained by international law, international courts of justice, an international legislative body, and an international police.
3. Basic nationalisms, resting on the self-determination of peoples, in character just, understanding, sympathetic, coöperative, not provincial, not aggressive.
4. A warless world, based not on the fear of superior force, but on the love of peace as a condition of progress in the arts, and so a reduction of armament to police proportions.
5. Government in the interest of human welfare, including public employment agencies; the far-sighted planning of public works; preventive and remedial measures for periods of financial depression and unemployment; the

protection of childhood against excessive and improper employment; insurance for the sick, the invalid, the aged, and the unemployed; the free exchange of commodities; the extension of recreational and educational facilities; and an education for the increased leisure of a machine age.

6. A new economic order, involving a modified system of capitalism; a more just distribution of wealth and income; a shorter working day and week; a minimum income to all; an increased tax on inheritance, income, and excess profits; coöperation in industry; a maximum limit to private wealth; the increasing ownership and control by all of those things used by all; and provision for the inequality of ability with equivalence, not identity, of opportunity.

7. The whole fabric of human society is to be based on justice, respect for personality, the sense of the worth of the individual, freedom of individual initiative, and the recognition of the interdependence of all.

Utopian? Yes, but in process of accelerated realization through the joint improvement of physiological heredity (eugenics), of physical and social environment (euthenics), and of individual character. "Play and work in the curriculum," leading to art, as described in this chapter, will contribute to these ends. In addition, something we may call loyalty to duty and love of our fellows, leading us to undertake menial tasks for their sakes, is necessary. Life is really a great coöperative spiritual adventure. In these attitudes children are to be trained for the new day in the great society by all the arts of education in home, school, community, and church.

CHAPTER XVI

THE SIGNIFICANCE OF GEOGRAPHY AND HISTORY

1. Extension of Meaning of Primary Activities

Exposition. By "primary activities" here we mean the same as the active occupations of the preceding chapter. Active occupations in play and work are the direct instruments for the extension of meaning. This is their final educational importance. They are the magnets for gathering and retaining unlimited intellectual and social meanings; they are the vital centers for receiving and assimilating information. Information is informing when it enters into an activity pursued for its own sake; it may enter as a means to the end or as a widening of the end. Pupils who are doing things may be told things about what they are doing; then a fusion takes place between insight directly gained by themselves and what is told them by others. The experience of the individual in this way can assimilate the experience of his group, even the results of sufferings and trials over long stretches of time. The occupations used as media of assimilation have no fixed saturation point,—further absorption is always possible. In fact, the more taken in, the more can be taken in; the more absorbed, the greater the capacity for absorption. A new curiosity leads to a new receptiveness and information newly received leads to a new curiosity. Contrast this with information purveyed in chunks simply as information to be retained for its own sake: it does not enlarge vital experience, it stratifies over vital experience.

Consider an example of a primary activity without, and with, its meaning extended. A small boy and an astronomer look through the same telescope. It is the same tube, the same arrangement of glass and metal, the same little speck of light gazed at in the distance. But what a difference in the meaning of what is seen! To the small boy the speck of light is a speck of light; to the astronomer at a critical moment it might be the birth of a new world, signifying in its context all that is known about the starry heavens. Thus may primary activities have their meanings extended. Compare the difference between an activity as merely physical and the same activity rendered meaningful; nothing is more striking than that! Gurgles become speech and scratches become writing.

For another illustration consider the activities of the savage and of civilized man. As physical, the changes in activities from the one to the other are slight, both seek food, shelter, and a mate; even the effect of these activities on the surface of the globe is slight, imperceptible from the reaches even of the solar system. But as meaningful, the changes in activities from the one to the other are great, marking the difference between savagery and civilization.

There is really no limit to the meaning which an activity may come to possess. The amount of meaning all depends upon the context of the activity, its perceived connections. And the reach of the imagination in realizing connections is inexhaustible. Here is an infinity of possibilities.

We know that the education of man is more than the manufacture of a tool or the training of an animal. Why? Manufacturing a tool and training an animal are activities which increase efficiency; they are not activities which develop significance for the tool or for the animal. Man's activity can find and appropriate meanings; this is his advantage over tools and lower animals. Tools are made, animals are trained, man is educated. He is educated through the extension of meaning of his primary activities.

Every activity engaged in for its own sake reaches out beyond its immediate self for more meaning; this is its normal nature. It does not wait, it seeks. It does not passively receive information to increase its meaning, it finds. We speak of curiosity; it is a mistake to regard it as an isolated, accidental, possession; it is witness that experience, activity, is a moving, changing thing, involved in all kinds of connections with other things. Curiosity is the seeking to perceive these connections. Now there are environments which check curiosity and there are environments which give it free play. The one environment allows only a direct, tangible, isolated outcome of an activity; the other allows an enrichment of meaning, one activity leading on continuously to another. In the one environment one walks and walks and gets where his body arrives; in the other environment, in addition, one's step displaces the resisting earth, sending a thrill wherever there is matter; and within the body itself the structure of the limbs and of the nervous system and even the principles of mechanics are involved. The marvel of walking! In the one environment to cook is to cook and to secure edible food; in the other environment, to cook is to use chemistry, to utilize heat and moisture to change food materials, to make food assimilable and to make the body grow, metabolism, anabolism, katabolism! Such common activities as walking and cooking have more connections and consequences than all physics, physiology, and chemistry can exhibit, more than the most learned scientists can make perceptible.

The task of education is to supply this better sort of environment. The business of educators is to see to it that such activities as walking and cooking are performed in such ways and under such conditions as to render them meaningful, making their connections as perceptible as possible.

Let us state an obvious truism: the meanings with which activities become charged concern nature and man. Of course! But what is the educational equivalent of this truism? It is that the primary activities of man acquire meaning through geography and history. These subjects supply background, outlook, and intellectual perspective. Geography gives us the space connections, history gives us the time connections, together they make our doings significant. By them our ordinary daily experiences cease to be narrow personal actions or mere forms of technical skill, things of the moment; they gain enduring substance. We discover the scene in space of which we are denizens, as the astronomer helps us, and the endeavors in time of which we are heirs and continuers, as the historian helps us; and we realize that we are citizens of no mean city.

Thus, really to "learn geography" is to perceive the spatial, the natural, connections of an ordinary act; and to "learn history" is essentially to recognize its temporal, its human, connections. Learning geography and history is really a gain in power to perceive the spatial and the temporal, the natural and the human, connections of an act; these are its meanings. We live in the same natural medium as the geographer; our lives are continuous with the same human groups as the historians'. Formal geography is the body of facts and principles discovered in the experience of others about this natural medium. Formal history is the body of facts and principles about the experiences of these human groups. Those bodies of facts and principles explain and illuminate our particular acts, our customs, our institutions. They reveal the meanings of our primary activities.

Of course history and geography should not be taught as ready-made studies, occupying the learner for no other reason than that he is sent to school. If so done, the resulting evils are many and great. Many things remote and alien from everyday experience are formally learned. Activity, instead of being continuous, is divided, thus building up at two different times two separate worlds. The studied world is not animated, not made real, by entering into immediate activity and the direct interests of life. The world of ordinary experience is not enlarged in meaning, transmuted, by getting its connections; it is not even left the narrow but vital thing it was; its mobility, eagerness, and sensitiveness are partly gone; it is weighed down, it is pushed into a corner, by a load of unassimilated information from the other world of geography and history textbooks. With the disappearance of elasticity, mind itself becomes wooden. Children know there is a river flowing by their town, but they do not connect it with the Mississippi of their geography text. They know their mother can vote but what has this to do with the "Constitution" about which their history tells? This is the woeful price we pay for amassing mere information in school apart from life.

Comment. It is possible that the contrast between training an animal and educating a child is too sharply drawn, as shown earlier too. Of course education is more than training as meaning is more than skill. But education includes skill and the training of an animal may bring some meaning into his experience. Thus, dogs are trained to chase foxes, point partridges, and "tree" squirrels. Who can doubt that the preparation for the hunt means something to these trained dogs over and above their efficiency? The difference then between the extension of meaning of the activities of animals and of children would be one only of degree, based on differences in inherent capacities.

The argument takes it for granted that there are only two classes of meanings, the spatial of geography and the temporal of history. Of course, if there is a non-spatial and a non-temporal order in relation to which man stands, there might well be a third class of meanings. Such a transcendent world is suggested by Plato's doctrine of the ideas, by Aristotle's conception of God as the unmoved mover who thinks his own thoughts, by Spinoza's view of God or nature, by Bertrand Russell's account of relations that subsist between universals, like numbers, and by the religious conception of the Changeless One. Without a refutation of such a realm of transcendent meanings, and who can refute it? we should not calmly assume that space and time contain all meanings.

It might be worth while also to indicate that the two allowed classes of meanings might be reduced to one, the spatial, by regarding time as itself one of the dimensions of space. This is not a difficult conception. Viewed statically, space has its three Euclidean dimensions, right and left, back and forth, up and down. But this space continues to exist, it endures. Endurance then would be another dimension of space, its fourth dimension, and endurance is time. Thus all temporal meanings might be regarded as one phase of spatial meanings. In the interest of unity and continuity it is fruitful so to regard them. We should then have a space-time continuum.

The recognition of temporal meanings by our author as distinct from the spatial as usually conceived, the recognition, that is, of the historic and the human in addition to the geographical and the natural, saves this pragmatic philosophy from being behaviorism. Behavioristic it may be in associating all meanings with physical activities, but behaviorism it is not in allowing some responses to be purposive instead of mechanical.

It should be noted that the term geography as used by our author evidently covers all the physical and natural sciences, like physics, chemistry, astronomy, biology, physiology, and the like; while the term history likewise covers all the remaining types of learning, such as, the social, literary, and linguistic subjects. Here is an unusual, if not unwarranted, extension of the meanings of the terms geography and history. They are used as practical synonyms for the more usual division of meanings into the scientific and the humanistic.

An interesting study could be made of the influence of the Bible upon the vocabulary of Dr. Dewey. In fact, only one familiar with Biblical phraseology can understand the full implication of some of his modes of expression. In illustration, passages on the following pages may be cited: 46, 50, 150, 207, 244, 250, 253. Another interesting study could be made of the influence of Dickens on Dr. Dewey.

2. The Complementary Nature of History and Geography

Exposition. History makes human implications explicit, and geography makes natural connections explicit; still, these two subjects are just two phases of the same living whole of experience. The reason for this is that nature is not the accidental setting of man; it is the material and the medium for the development of man; in nature there goes on the associated life of men. This interdependence of man and nature is the justification for linking geography and history. It is the warrant for their complementary nature. The associated life of men takes place on the earth, not in the sky nor yet in a vacuum. On the earth man experiments, uses ways and means, fails and succeeds. A theatrical performance has its scenery; but nature is more than the scenery of man's deeds; it enters into their very make-up; it is the medium of the social occurrences that form history; it furnishes the original stimuli; it supplies obstacles and resources. Civilization itself is man's progressive mastery of nature's varied energies. Omit the interdependence, the complementary character, of history and geography, and the study of history either sinks into a listing of dates with an inventory of "important" events, or else it becomes a literary phantasy in which nature is only stage scenery.

History and geography are the main information subjects of the schools. The danger is great, in fact, nowhere greater, that these subjects will be taught and learned only because such is the custom. Then information is piled up in isolated heaps. Then the very mass and variety of the material discourages an analysis of its aim or of its use in widening the experience of pupils. The idea that these subjects can function in a worthy transformation of experience is regarded as a vain fancy, or else, as high-sounding warrant for what is already being done.

But the idea of a unifying and socializing direction in education is not a farcical pretense, and history and geography do aid in developing an intellectualized and a socialized experience. Historical and geographical facts and methods that do not serve in this way are to be sifted out. Geography emphasizes the physical side of man's life, history the social side; together they enrich and liberate the more direct and personal contacts of life by furnishing their context, background, and outlook.

Let us look carefully at geography as a study giving added significance to human experience. Geography is indeed "an account of the earth as the home of man." This classic definition expresses the educational reality. Geography connects natural facts with social events; in this consists its educative influence. It is some relation to man that justifies teaching geography; the residences, pursuits, successes, and failures of man are the reason for including specific geographic data among the materials of instruction. It is easier to define geography in this way than it is to teach it in this way. But not to teach it in this way, to break the ties between nature and man, is to turn geography into a hodgepodge of unrelated fragments, a veritable rag-bag of intellectual odds and ends: mountain heights, river courses, quantity of shingles, tonnage of shipping, county boundaries, state capitals, etc. Viewing the earth in this way as a miscellany of facts makes no appeal to the imagination.

But view the earth as the home of man and the study of geography becomes humanizing, unified, and full of appeal to the imagination. To hold nature and man together in teaching requires an informed and cultivated imagination. Geography appeals even to the romantic imagination, sharing as it does in the wonder and glory of adventure, travel, and exploration. There is infinite stimulation in the variety of peoples and environments it considers, in their contrast with familiar scenes and with the monotony of the customary.

The natural starting point is local or home geography. But it is the starting, not the stopping point; from it one moves out into the unknown. From fences of village proprietors to boundaries of great nations! Sunlight, wind, stream, inequalities of the earth's surface, commerce, civil officers, political relations come from near and lead thoughts afar, even to strange peoples and things. Following their course enlarges the mind, remakes the meaning of what was previously familiar matters of fact.

Home geography is not an end in itself, it is a basis for getting at the large world beyond. As object lessons summarizing familiar properties are deadly, so are geography lessons confined to the locality. No appeal is made to the imagination, only the familiar is catalogued, curious local facts are laboriously learned, the mind is stuffed with additional information.

There are many competing branches of geography,—mathematical, astronomical, physiographic, topographic, political, and commercial. How are their claims to be adjusted? Not by an external compromise that crowds in so much of each. By an internal coördination based on the human, the cultural, aspects of the subject; on their relation to the social experience of man. Does the material in question help one appreciate the significance of human activities? Then it is relevant; otherwise not. Civilizations differ in cold and in tropical regions; there are special inventions of peoples in temperate regions; these activities of man can not be understood without seeing the earth as a member of the solar system. This is astronomical geography. The economic activities of man reflect physical conditions; they also influence society and politics; this is commercial geography. And so with the other phases of geography. In all geography the educational center of gravity is man.

Geography, or earth study, includes "nature study." This seems a contradiction in words but it is not in idea. The two words, earth and nature, refer to one and the same reality; they should be equivalent terms; so should earth study and nature study. To make nature study a part of earth study would save it from its usual scrappiness, its dealing with isolated materials. Nature study has dealt with the flower's parts apart from the flower as an organ, it has dealt with the flower apart from the plant; it has dealt with the plant apart from the soil, air, and light in and through which it lives. These isolated parts of a whole are dead topics, feeding no imagination. The facts are torn to pieces by removal from their context; not belonging to the earth, they had no abiding place anywhere. The need for a human atmosphere was felt. What was done? "Let's revive animism!" This was seriously proposed. Natural facts and events were to be clothed with myths to attract and hold the mind. Silly personifications, artificial and sentimental associations, were actually resorted to in numberless cases. A poor remedy witnessed to a real need. But a real remedy is at hand. It is to make nature study a phase of earth study. Treat nature study as a study of nature, treat nature as a whole, treat the earth in its relations, and the phenomena of nature will appear in their proper relations of sympathy and association with human life. Thus geography, including nature study, as an information subject, will provide the significant account of the physical relations of the life of man, and so enlarge the meaning of the direct personal experiences of pupils.

Comment. The phrase, "the interdependence of man and nature," is used (p. 246) to suggest the basis of the complementary nature of history and geography. One can readily see the interdependence of these two studies, the course of man's history having been largely determined by coastal plains, mountain ranges, and river courses, and the content of geography having been modified by the conquests, wars, explorations, and engineering of man. But the interdependence of these two studies is not the same as "the interdependence of man and nature." Man is dependent on nature but nature is not dependent on man. Man must adjust himself to nature to survive and does so, and in a lesser way he adjusts nature to himself. His organs and his organism show his adaptation to nature; perhaps also his clothing. His tools are instruments for adapting nature to himself; his buildings and bridges and the other changes he has wrought in the face of nature are his adaptation of nature to himself. It might be said that nature in prehistoric time adjusted man to itself. But it can hardly be said that nature is dependent on man or adjusts itself to man. There is interdependence between geography and history for both are man-made, both involve man in different settings, the physical and the temporal. But there is no interdependence between nature and man, there is only a dependence of man on nature. There is, of course, an idealistic metaphysics [1] which regards nature as a self including the self of man, in which in a sense the self of nature is somewhat dependent on the self of man, but it can not be presumed that this is Dr. Dewey's view.

"Nature and the earth should be equivalent terms" (p. 250). This seems confusing. The position is being defended that geography should include "nature study." This may well be, but the reason assigned for it is dubious. Nature and earth equivalent terms? Hardly. Nature includes the earth but in no clear sense can the earth include nature. Nature includes human nature but in no clear sense does the earth include human nature. It would probably be better to continue to use the term earth to refer to our planet in the solar system and to use the term nature to refer to the whole realm of matter in space. It is possible the original statement means that "nature" and "the earth in all its physical relations" should be equivalent terms, to which there would be less cavil.

In rejecting the absurd suggestion of returning to animism to vivify "nature study," the author seems to reject also the use of fancy, personification, and the like, in favor of the realistic imagination which portrays actual, though absent, conditions. There is good ground, however, for using both kinds of imagination. The fancy of children in personifica-

[1] Cf. Royce, J.. *The World and the Individual,* Second Series, Lecture V. The Macmillan Company, New York, 1901.

tion and in dramatic action may well be used to bring home a realizing sense of the actual. Falling leaves, the winds of winter, the awakening spring, may all be dramatized effectively. Nature is appreciated thereby the more and the realistic causal explanations of such phenomena will later lose nothing of their significance therefor. Children do not think less of love because when younger they had Santa Claus. Fancy does not undermine either reason or a realistic imagination.

Of course these suggestions do not imply any criticism of the valuable fundamental viewpoint that geography and history are complementary subjects and that, though difficult to accomplish, they should be taught as such.

3. History and Present Social Life

Exposition. In this section we will deal in succession with the general principle relating history to social life and then with the different types of history,—biographical, primitive, industrial or economic, political, literary, and intellectual, ending with the ethical value of history.

Our general principle here is that the true starting point of history is always the present,—some present situation with its problems. The knowledge of the past is the key to understanding the present. It sounds paradoxical but it is true that the past with which history deals is the past of the present. To illustrate from American history. The social conditions of the United States to-day are too complex to be directly grasped; to study them in their process of formation opens them to comprehension. Thus, in studying the discovery of America, the early explorations, colonization, immigration, the pioneer movements westward, etc., we are studying under simpler conditions the country we now live in, we are understanding better the United States of to-day.

The way to get insight into any complex product is to trace the process of its making, to follow it through the successive stages of its growth. We understand what is by understanding how it came to be. This is the "genetic method" of study. It comes to us from evolutionary biology, and is perhaps the chief scientific achievement of the latter half of the nineteenth century. In history the use of this method means not only the one-sided truism that the present social state can not be separated from the past but also and equally that past events, to retain meaning, can not be separated from the living present.

Would you kill history? Divorce it from present concerns of social life. A segregated past is no longer our affair. If the past were wholly gone, done with, the only reasonable attitude toward it would be: "Let the dead bury their dead."

Let us now apply this principle that history begins with present social life to different types of history. And first, biographical history. The natural mode of approach to historical study is the biographical. This approach is both generally recommended and psychologically sound. The reason is that the lives of great men, of leaders, of heroes, make historic episodes into vivid pictures, concrete and vital. These episodes without the biography would be abstract, incomprehensible, a complicated and tangled series of events covering so much space and time that only a highly trained mind could follow and unravel them.

But there is a misuse of the biographical method. We have to remember that the study of history is a study of social life, a study of individuals in association. The biographical method is misused when the doings of a few individuals are thrown into exaggerated relief without reference to the social situations the great men represent, to the stimulating and arousing conditions to which their activities were a response. Such is not history but a sugar coating making it easier to swallow certain fragments of information.

Consider primitive history. It too is a good introduction to learning history. But here also there is a right and wrong way of conceiving its value. The right way is to simplify the complex present by recourse to the primitive. The present is hard to understand, conditions are complex, and they seem ready-made, hard and fast. There are almost insuperable obstacles to gaining an insight into the nature of the present. The primitive may furnish the fundamental and simple elements of the present, as the unraveling of a cloth of complex pattern reveals its coarser features. Being unable to simplify the complex present by deliberate experiment, we get the same sort of results by resorting to primitive life. Here social relationships and organized activities are reduced to their lowest terms. On the other hand, the wrong way of conceiving the value of primitive history is to overlook its significance in understanding the present, and to rehearse the the sensational and exciting features of savagery.

Consider industrial or economic history. Primitive history suggests it. How to procure subsistence, shelter, and protection are fundamental problems. Primitive history shows us how these problems were first solved. This gives us some conception of the long, long road from savagery to civilization, and the successive inventions standing at the turns of the road.

There are many disputes concerning "the economic interpretation of history"; we do not need to enter them here. Without doing so we can realize that industrial history is superior to all other types in giving us insight into two important phases of social life. One of these has just been mentioned,—inventions. By an invention science controls nature in the interest of man. Inventions have made social life secure and prosperous. They are the causes of social progress. The other is getting a living. It is necessary to live; every individual *must* do that; to do so he must make his contribution to the general well being. In turn society *must* justly reward him. The occupations, the values, connected with getting a living concern all men in common. Thus economic history is human, democratic, liberalizing, dealing, as it does, with the growth of the effective liberties of the common man, coming through control of nature. Another advantage of industrial history is its record of the advance and the results of knowledge. To this we will recur in dealing next with intellectual history.

Of all the types of history used in general education, the intellectual is perhaps the most neglected. The greatest heroes of the race are its scientific discoverers and inventors, and its artists and poets. These, not politicians, diplomatists, and generals, have advanced human destiny. We are only just beginning to realize this. It is the scientist who puts into man's hands the means for expanding and controlling his experience. It is the artist who celebrates man's struggles, defeats, and triumphs in meaningful expression accessible to all. Industrial history contributes to intellectual history; it shows how man's control of nature in his own behalf, his progress from savagery to civilization, is dependent upon improving his methods of knowing and of applying his acquired knowledge; it thus helps pupils to appreciate the true nature of intelligence. This result is not accomplished by the present conventional study of history; from it pupils get the notion that the human intellect is static, unaffected by the invention of better methods; or even that it is a negligible historic matter, save as a display of personal shrewdness in separate individuals. Intelligence and reason are eulogized only in general terms, and ineffectively. Most historical writings, so far from revealing intelligence as man's method of controlling nature in his own behalf, are taken up with side issues, or even with things which obstruct the progress of intelligence.

In comparison with the foregoing types, political, military, and literary history are of small account. Political history deals with the rise and fall of principalities and powers, forgetting the common man for whom principalities and powers exist. It is less human, less democratic, less liberalizing than industrial history. When reduced to the level of youthful comprehension, it easily runs into military history. When work is omitted, when the conditions of using the soil, forest and mine are left out of account, when no attention is paid to the domesticating and cultivating of grains and animals, to the manufacture and distribution of products, then history becomes merely literary,—a systematized romance of a mythical humanity living not upon the earth but upon itself.

Suppose history were studied in the better sort of ways, then an intelligent insight into present forms of associated life would result, then history would have ethical value. History is an organ for analyzing the warp and the woof of the present social fabric, for making known the forces which weave the pattern. The cultivating of a socialized intelligence is the moral significance of history. The sympathetic understanding of the present social situations in which individuals share is a permanent and constructive moral asset. In contrast, there is a misuse of history for ethical purposes. It consists in employing it as a reservoir of anecdotes to inculcate special moral lessons on this virtue or that vice. This is an effort to create moral impressions by means of more or less authentic material. At best, it yields a passing emotional glow; at worst, a callous indifference to moralizing.

Comment. The initial principle that history begins with the present is a challenge to the usual conception of culture as the love of knowledge for its own sake. There is a joy and an interest in knowing about the boy ruler of Egypt whose tomb escaped the despoilers for some fifty centuries, King Tut-Ankh-Ahmen, even if no present social problem is thereby enlightened. As Aristotle remarks, "it is neither fine nor noble always to be talking about what is useful." Man is not merely a solver of problems, a doer, and a thinker. He is also a lover, a lover of things beautiful, imaginative, and of "old unforgotten tales and battles long ago." History as a systematic record of the achievement of man on the earth may very well include much that does not aid in solving present social problems, the reading and enjoyment of which may only cultivate individual personality.

Can we say that all history is connected with the present, so that actually all study of the past would be a study of the present? Certainly not. There have been too many beginnings in too many different places leading to too many divergent lines of culture for any such position to be held. Taken all together, most peoples of the earth have known little of other peoples. Their culture has come down its own line of descent without having borrowed from all other cultures. In this sense history lacks the unity and the continuity that would actually connect all the past with all the present. Ethnologists hold that similarities of culture in different parts of the globe need not mean borrowings. If all history should be studied with the view to understanding the present better, it would have to be on the basis of analogy, not chronology. And to study only the past of our present would leave many large and interesting gaps.

And does making the present the starting point mean that history should be written backward? It can hardly be done. History flows downward with time. To write its record backward is to reverse the flow, to proceed from effects to causes. Historians have not essayed this task.

But at least should not history be studied backward? Trying to do so is an interesting experiment. One may read the last chapter in the book first, and so on back to the first chapter. The effect is somewhat confusing. At least each separate chapter must be read forward. Proceeding from the known to the unknown can hardly mean either reading or writing history backward. If one accepted the principle of the present as the true starting point of history, it could be followed only by using the present as the locus to which all studies of the past were constantly being referred by way of similarity or contrast.

The study of primitive life may well show us the skeletal framework of modern society. There is almost a fashion in our day to let the anthropologist solve our moral problems for us, to let our children learn as the primitive child learns, to let our youth behave as primitive youth or youth in arrested societies behave. This, of course, is fatuous. To allow it is to deny moral progress, to turn back the hands of the clock, to be retrogressive or atavistic. We must save the moral advances so painfully won by the race. Just because primitive life is simple, its solutions to moral questions can not be ours. Not, of course, that Dr. Dewey suggests this way of using primitive history.

He does refer to the economic interpretation of history and to industrial history as revealing "the successive causes of social progress." He does not refer to the spiritual interpretation of history. There can be none in a man-centered universe, or in a universe without a conscious center. Social progress is here traced to the inventive intelligence of man, not at all to "a power not ourselves that makes for righteousness." But man made most of his progress, if the theory of evolution is to be accepted, before he acquired an inventive intelligence. This suggests that inventive intelligence itself, so far from explaining social progress, requires to be explained. There seem to be non-human forces in our world making for advancement, certainly so if man is more than an amœba.

Concerning the ethical value of history the argument is left mainly in the region of an intelligence that understands, coupled with sympathy. It is not clear that an understanding intelligence would necessarily have sympathy. One may be coldly intellectual about social conditions. Whence comes the sympathy for man in understanding how he has come to be socially what he is? It may not come at all. It is not clear that a socialized intelligence in the sense defined would do anything to make the lot of mankind better. At this point Dr. Dewey, by implication, is on the Herbartian intellectual ground that ideas lead to feeling, and that ideas and feelings lead to action. It would be more consistent with his own position to say that moral feelings arise in shared social situations and that history provides ideas as to what should be done. History then would not have ethical value, it would serve ethical values when and where felt.

This brings us to observe that Dr. Dewey treats history as a science. He does not distinguish it on this count from geography. Both are sciences. This again fits in with the economic interpretation of history, which in a measure at least he accepts. But this view confuses the way of treating human events with their nature. There can be a scientific way of viewing and recording human events without there being any implied identification of the deeds of man with the phenomena of nature. In external nature we commonly suppose things happen because they have to; in human nature things happen because some one intends them. History is the scientific record of deeds that were intended. This means that history as a mode of treating events may be scientific, while the content of history is purposeful. One may have a causal account of a purposeful activity but this does not mean that science has the last word. It means that purpose has the last word. And it is even possible that what is true of human nature is also true of external nature. This would give us not only history as a science but also a whole world of purpose. This view is far removed from Dr. Dewey's form of pragmatism.

At this point it might be well to note the parallelism between the stages of "development of subject matter in the learner" (p. 216) and the account of geography and history. It can be graphically shown as follows:

SUBJECT MATTER IN THE LEARNER	GEOGRAPHY AND HISTORY
1. Intelligent Control	1. Activities
2. Information	2. Extension of Meaning
3. Science	3. Geography and History

Thus, the procedure of teaching is from activities through information to used knowledge and to science as rationalized knowledge. This naturally leads to the question of the place of science in the course of study, to be considered next.

CHAPTER XVII

SCIENCE IN THE COURSE OF STUDY

1. The Logical and the Psychological

Exposition. In this section we will deal with the so-called "logical" and "psychological" methods in teaching science. The successive phases of the discussion will be the nature of science, the "logical element in science," the objectionable "logical" method of teaching science, and the acceptable "psychological" method of teaching science.

The key to the discussion is that "the logical" is the mode of arranging what is learned and "the psychological" is the mode of learning itself. Each has its place, the former in advancing knowledge and the latter in teaching.

First, and once again, the nature of science. Really, science is two inseparable things; it is a growing body of logically arranged knowledge and it is a method of knowing. It is settled and assured, though not finished, subject matter; it involves the revising of current beliefs, weeding out the erroneous, increasing accuracy, and making obvious the mutual dependencies of various facts; this logical quality of the resulting knowledge is the controlling factor in the situation, as, through it, the next advance is made. The logical order of knowledge which is science, is thus the last stage in the perfecting of knowing. We shall see that educationally also this perfected type of knowing should come last. On the method side, scientific knowledge is the outcome of the deliberate adoption of observation, reflection, and testing; like all other forms of knowledge, such as, control of acts and information, it is an outcome of activity changing the environment; we have to do something to know anything. Thus, putting its two elements together, science is a logically arranged body of knowledge resulting from the dependable methods of knowing.

Though the matter is a little technical, let us develop at some length the logical character of scientific knowledge. This will help us to understand both the real nature of science and how it should not be taught. It is a familiar observation that from a few bones the competent zoölogist can reconstruct the animal; that from a fossil leaf the botanist can reconstruct the original plant. This is because their knowledge is comprehensive and logical. Similarly, from the form of a statement in mathematics or physics, the specialist in those branches can frame an idea of the system of truths in which it belongs. Remarkable, but true. This is because the scientific statement of subject matter exhibits to the expert both antecedent premises and consequent conclusions. This is the proper form taken by perfected knowledge. This is logical order, revealing the implications of what is known. Logical order is not a form imposed upon what is known, it is the form that knowledge derived from the control of experience properly takes.

In this logical form or scientific statement there is a symbolic element. All language, scientific or other, is symbolic; it refers to common sense things. But there is one outstanding difference between the language of science and the language of the vernacular. The language of the vernacular proceeds directly from symbol to the thing symbolized,—a "spade" is a spade; but the language of science proceeds from symbol to symbol,—a "molecule" leads to an "atom" and an "atom" to an "electron" and an "electron" to a "wave," and so on. Common sense is immediately practical; the organized common sense which is science is immediately theoretical and only ultimately practical. The language of science stands for things placed in a cognitive system, not for things as practically experienced; it thus has intellectual, not empirical, value; it is an instrument for carrying on scientific inquiry.

It sounds paradoxical, but it is true, that the more we know scientifically, the further we depart from reality. Even the circle and the square of geometry do not exist in nature. And the more mathematical our knowledge becomes, the less empirical it is. In mathematics, qualities that do not affect spatial relations are omitted; those that do are accentuated. Going still further in mathematics, even spatial relations may give way to the still more abstract number relations. Size, form, direction, may all be omitted from the highly abstract mathematical concepts of number relations. Are the latter then unreal mental inventions? Not at all. They are tools for organizing intellectual results, they are physical qualities transmuted beyond direct recognition; they are useful in advancing science.

How are such tools of physical, chemical, and mathematical research to be learned? Certainly not by pointing to any physical things, or even to the intellectual tools themselves, naming them, and repeating their names. They are to be learned only by using them in the system to which they belong, just as in the case of physical tools. Consider the knowledge one has of a machine; it is not enough to know its parts, their names, the material of which they are constructed; one must know the use of the machine and the function of each part. Just so, he who knows scientific formulæ, mathematical or other, is he who can use them in their proper system. Their meaning, their intellectual content, is the use to which they are put. The conclusion must be clear that science as a body of knowledge topically arranged to lead on to more knowledge is for the expert, not for the beginner.

But behold our mistake! We try to teach such logically arranged science to beginners! Almost incredible, but true! In the teaching of a science it is a frequent practice to start with the rudiments somewhat simplified, with texts which present the subject subdivided into topics according to the order of the specialist. Technical concepts and definitions are introduced at the outset. Then come laws, with slight indication of how they were derived. The method of the investigator dominates college teaching; the method of the college dominates the high school, and so on down the line. It being necessary to make the subject easier, omissions are resorted to. Thus we yield to the temptation to present subject matter in its perfected form. We falsely assume this is a royal road to learning. We naturally but wrongly suppose that the immature can be saved time, energy, and needless errors by beginning where experts end.

And what is the effect of this "logical" method of teaching science? To the non-expert, this perfected form of scientific knowledge is a stumbling block. Being stated so as to further knowledge as an end in itself, its connections with commonplace living are hidden. How could a layman see an animal in a few of its bones? The pupil learns the symbols without a key to their meaning; often he acquires simply a peculiar vocabulary. He learns "science," not the scientific way of treating the familiar material of ordinary experience. The "science" so learned remains a body of inert information, further from everyday experience than his literature.

In this connection the lesson of Herbert Spencer is instructive. He inquired in his famous essay what knowledge is of most worth. He concluded that from all points of view scientific knowledge is most valuable. But his mistake was in assuming that scientific knowledge could be communicated in ready-made form, passing over the method by which the material of our ordinary activities is transmuted into scientific form. Many scientists and educational leaders strove with him two generations ago, against great odds, to secure a place for science in education. The contrast between their expectations and the results is painful. Yet their claims were not unjustifiable. For our students have learned "science" as logical subject matter, not as a method of control of experience.

What then is the way to teach science? By learning to treat the familiar material of ordinary experience in a scientific way. Begin with the experience of the learner; develop from that the proper modes of scientific treatment; this is the chronological method; this is the "psychological" method of the learner in contrast with the "logical" method of the specialist.

The advantages of the psychological method for the beginner are many. True, there is an apparent loss of time, and there is not so much "ground covered," but the compensations are adequate. There is superior understanding, vital interest is secured, pupils are sure and intelligent as far as they go, independent power to deal with material within their range is gained, and confusion and distaste arising from learning symbols is avoided. After all, the mass of pupils will never become scientific specialists; what they need is scientific method; they need this far more than second hand copies of scientific results other men have won. And the few who do go on are better prepared. In fact, those who have gone on somehow managed by their own power to avoid the pitfalls of a traditional scholastic introduction to science. On all counts then the "psychological" wins over the "logical" method of teaching science.

In this connection a few words about laboratories. One might suppose that the use of a laboratory solved, of course, the problem of method. This is far from being the case. A laboratory is certainly an improvement upon a textbook arranged deductively, and laboratory exercises are an indispensable portion of scientific method. But the question is, are the laboratory exercises really connected with materials and processes used out of school? The physical materials of the laboratory and the ways of handling them and the problems themselves may be dissociated from the activities of life. The problem may be that of an initiate, not that of a novice. Attention may be devoted to acquiring technical skill without reference to real problem-solving. A heathen religion has its ritual; so may laboratory instruction. There is no magic in "going through the motions," or in stating material in correct scientific form. In contrast with the problems of the expert, there is value for the beginner in problems arising in the garden or in the shop. The laboratory is a resource for the better pursuit of these problems. The laboratory may not, but can, use the psychological method.

Comment. Attention may be drawn to the unusual meaning of the terms "logical" and "psychological" as used in the discussion. The "logical" here refers to a mode of arranging subject matter in scientific form and to a method of teaching subject matter so arranged; usually, and in a more general sense, the term refers to the science of correct thinking, "logic" being one of the branches of philosophy. Similarly, the term "psychological" is here used to refer to the mode of teaching science through utilizing the experiences of the learner. Usually, and in a more general sense again, it refers to the science of human behavior, "psychology" being now one of the biological sciences, having dropped its philosophical associations.

Again, attention may be called to the fact that the emphasis here on the psychological method is in line with the earlier discussion of "the development of subject matter in the learner" through the stages of control, information, and science (see p. 216 of *Democracy and Education*). The logical method would not lead to the learner's own development of subject matter. There is unity in the viewpoint presented.

Though the text is devoted to philosophy rather than to method, it would help to have a number of illustrations showing just how the psychological method does work when applied to different typical sciences. For example, to what extent do the courses in "General Science" meet the conditions of the psychological method?

Concerning laboratories it may be further remarked that, in addition to their failure to get the results desired, the expense of equipping and running them is far greater than in the social sciences, in consequence of which there is a tendency to return to the older method of class demonstration. Certainly a scientific laboratory using the psychological method does not require so much equipment as one intended for the research work of the specialist.

A last consideration, on the main issue. A little psychological learning will carry much logical learning. A little first hand experience of the matter in question will carry much vicarious experience. It is necessary that beginnings be experienced. But it is not necessary that by the use of the experimental method the pupil find out everything for himself and by reflection logically organize for himself all he has learned. The psychological method alone is too slow, the logical method alone is too abstract. And pupils do need to know much about our world that, for lack of time, they can not discover for themselves. Our pupils and we ourselves can not follow the processes of Compton, Millikan, Eddington, and Einstein. Yet we need to know the kind of world they say we live in. We could never get such knowledge by the psychological method alone. The logical method must supplement the psychological, in the case of the novice as well as the expert. Adults, particularly, must rely upon a much abridged logical method. Spencer, Huxley, Youmans, and Eliot were not altogether mistaken in advocating familiarity with the results of scientific investigation.

2. Science and Social Progress

Exposition. Our general question in this section is, what is the place of science in experience? The term science here refers to the perfected logical form of knowledge gained directly in occupations of social interest. This is the conception of science developed in the preceding section.

Our general answer is that science is the sole agency of conscious social progress. The meaning of this statement must be carefully shown as we consider the following points: the two phases of progress; the relation of science to each phase; the value in science of abstraction, generalization, and technical terms; and the educational use of science.

There are two phases of progress, a minor and a major. The minor phase of progress consists in the improvement of means in reaching given ends. This is an advance in technique. It helps us to arrive sooner at an end already desired. Such progress consists in providing more efficient means for satisfying preëxistent desires.

Now science is the chief means for securing this minor form of progress. It perfects our control of the means for reaching ends. Science has intellectual command of the secrets of nature. From such knowledge come inventions. Inventions transform our social life in both its smaller details and its larger aspects. We witness the applications of science to living in the railways, steamboats, electric motors, telephone, telegraph, autos, airplanes, dirigibles and the radio. The "industrial revolution" itself, wonderfully transforming the production and distribution of goods, is the fruit of experimental science. Thousands of less sensational inventions show how science is tributary to our daily life.

The major form of progress consists in the improvement, not of means to reach ends, but of the ends themselves, enriching prior purposes, and forming new purposes. Progress is increase not only in the amount of satisfaction but in the quality of the satisfaction.

Be it said that our progress since the advent of experimental science has been mainly of the minor instead of the major sort. We have learned better how to satisfy our desires than how to improve them. We have improved our technology more than our teleology. Surprising as it may sound, no modern civilization, with all its science, has equalled in all respects that of the Greeks. Our ends remain too largely what they were prior to the scientific enlightenment. Science is too recent to have become absorbed yet into the imaginative and emotional disposition of man. The educational problem growing out of this situation will be indicated presently.

Yet, even here, just as in the case of minor progress, so in the case of major progress, science is our sole reliance. It marks the emancipation of mind from devotion to customary purposes; it makes possible the systematic pursuit of new ends. A new mastery of nature, increased culture, lead to the intelligent perception of new possibilities of action, which in turn lead to new desires, to demands for new qualities of satisfaction. Thus from science comes both the new end and the new means, the major and the minor forms of progress.

There is evidence that science, though young, is already transforming human desires, modifying men's thoughts of the purposes and goods of life. By science physical barriers formerly separating men have been broken down; the area of human intercourse has been immensely widened; the interdependence of human interests on an enormous scale has been brought about; the conviction that nature can be controlled in the interest of man has been established; men have been led to look to the future for the golden age instead of the past; progress itself has become an ideal; the belief that intelligence properly used can abolish "inevitable" evils has become fixed; the subjugation of devastating disease is no longer a dream; the abolition of poverty is no longer utopian; the idea of the gradual amelioration of the estate of our common humanity has become familiar. Such are the omens and the tokens of the new humanity science is giving us.

Not the least of the significant services of science is the new philosophy it is giving us. The function of reason is to be found not beyond experience but within experience. Reason is not remote, aloof, concerned with a sublime region beyond life, speculative theorizing; it is present, indigenous, concerned with purifying past experiences and rendering them useful in new discoveries and advancement. Idle theory is antithetical to practice, in permament dislocation from practice; the abstractness and generalities and technicalities of science lead to a wider, freer, application in later concrete action. Genuine scientific theory falls within practice as the agency of its expansion and its direction to new possibilities. The new philosophy has ceased to be "classical," transcendent of experience, and has become pragmatic, immanent in experience.

In order to show just how science is the sole instrumentality of conscious, as distinct from accidental, progress, and just how it functions within experience, we must go somewhat carefully into the nature and uses of "abstraction," "generalization," and technical terms.

And first, abstraction. We must distinguish between the popular and the scientific meaning of this term. It is as important in scientific thought as it is objectionable in popular thought. Popularly, to be "abstract" is to be both abstruse, hard to understand, and remote from life. Scientifically, abstraction is selecting from old experiences things useful in dealing with the new. The selection is done deliberately. So abstraction is the conscious transfer of meaning from old to new experiences. By it the earlier experience guides the later. It is thus the very artery of intelligence, an indispensable trait in the reflective direction of activities. It is indispensable because situations do not literally repeat themselves. If they did, habits would be adequate in dealing with recurring situations without the aid of abstraction; habits neglect the novel element. But when the new element requires especial attention, the choice is either costly random reaction or abstraction.

Now how does science use abstraction? Successive experiences have two elements in them: the personal, the immediate, the peculiar, the unreduplicable and the common, the general. Science treats the former as accidental and the latter as essential. The former may be precious to the individual but the latter alone is available for further use. What is common in experiences is abstracted, fixed by a suitable symbol, and so preserved for further use. No one can foresee in detail when or how the abstraction may be of further use. The manufacturer of tools does not know who will use them or when; so is the scientist in developing his abstractions. They are an indispensable factor in all progress.

Science works over prior experience into usable abstractions on a large scale.

Then comes generalization. From the concrete to the abstract, and from the abstract to its application. Generalization is the application of the abstraction to the new concrete situation. It is thus the counterpart of abstraction. While abstraction distills the essence of the old, generalization uses this essence in clarifying and directing the new. Without generalization, abstraction would end in a fruitless, barren formalism. It is because of their abstractness that scientific concepts are widely applicable. Thus, numbers are abstract and everything can be counted by their aid.

Because abstraction and generalization stress the essentials in dealing with novelties, they take the point of view of any man at any place at any time. As Aristotle remarked, "fire also burns in Persia." Thus science has a wide and free range. It widens interests beyond the concerns of a narrow group, living in a contracted space, for a short time, and limited to its own established customs as a measure of all values. The "rustic murmur of one's burg" is not taken for the "sound heard round the world." Thus generalization is essentially a social device for widening one's outlook on life.

And now the use of technical terms and formulæ. For abstraction to function as a generalization in a new situation, it must be transferable. To be transferable, it must have a local habitation and a name. Technical terms record, fix, and make conveyable what is abstracted. Abstract meanings detached from concrete experiences can not remain hanging in the air; through being named they acquire a physical locus and a body. Technical formulations are not after-thoughts or by-products; they are essential to the completion of the work of thought. So we have laws of gravitation, motion, expansion of gases, and the like; so we have chemical symbols and mathematical equations.

There may be knowledge without the ability to express it, and there may be knowledge with the ability to express it in different ways, such as the literary and the scientific. Untransferable knowledge is practical, direct, personal, usable by the individual having it, and, as it were, instinctive. All of us have some knowledge of this kind. How do you manage to walk, to paint, to run your business? Artists and executives often have this kind of knowledge. For knowledge to be communicable and understandable, common elements between the experiences of others and oneself must be found. Literary expression is the supreme instance of success in so stating experiences that they are vitally significant for others; it reveals and enhances the experiences one already has; and it is for all. A scientific vocabulary is designed to express the meaning of experienced things in symbols and tools intelligible to the expert; by these, new experiences with transformed meanings may be constructed; such a mode of expression is for the few.

Thus, through abstraction, generalization, and technical modes of expression, science is enabled to master the forces of nature and so to minister to the progress of man.

Now, then, our last question in this section: what are the educational uses of science? These are three, all interrelated, and they are tremendous. The educational uses of science are, first, to modify the habitual attitude of imagination and feeling; second, to create an intelligence with belief in its own ability to direct human affairs by itself; and, third, to change men's idea of the nature and possibilities of human experience. To modify an attitude, to instill a belief, and to change an idea,—these three great things. Of course they are interdependent. By modifying our attitude, science is to improve the quality of human progress; it is not to be merely an extension of our arms and legs. By instilling a belief in human intelligence as capable of directing human affairs, science is to substitute experimentalism for empiricism, thus making experience itself intelligent and reasonable. By changing men's idea of the nature and possibility of experience, a static social order is to be replaced by a growing dynamic one in which science is not used for the exploitation of man.

The central educational use of science is the second one, to generate self-confidence in human intelligence by substituting the experimental for the empirical method. "Empirical" ought to mean "connected with experiment"; it does mean ordinarily the crude, the unrational. Even the ruling philosophies of the past, originating prior to experimentalism, have opposed experience to reason, to the truly rational. "Empirical" knowledge was held to be based on many particular instances without intelligent insight into principles. Medicine was "empirical," not scientific, because it was based on observations of diseases and random remedies; its practice was happy-go-lucky; its success depended on chance; it lent itself to deception and quackery. Likewise "empirically" controlled industry depends on the slavish imitation of old past models, not the constructive application of intelligence. Now dawns experimentalism; it dignifies experience; it renovates empiricism; it emancipates from rule of thumb, from routine; it uses past experience as the servant, not the master, of the mind; it means that reason operates within, not beyond, experience. By education the method of experimental science is to be engrained as a habit in human nature. Then man himself will control his own experience in ways directed by himself. Then comes democracy.

Comment. What shall we say of these things? Has the encomium here pronounced on science and the experimental method overreached itself? In considering this question, a number of points will be noted.

(1) Beginning with something simple and familiar, here again we have illustrations of how Dr. Dewey uses familiar terms with somewhat unfamiliar meanings. The term "abstraction" is here used to designate the process of reaching a concept or a principle drawn from many similar preceding experiences; this process is more commonly known as "gen-

eralization," or even "induction," indeed involving abstraction from the concrete.

Another illustration of the same. The term "generalization" is used in the text to describe the process whereby the "abstraction" functions in new situations. This process is more commonly called "application," or even "deduction." The names used, however, need not confuse us in recognizing that thinking does move first from the particular to other particulars and then to the general, and then from the general back to new particulars.

(2) Dr. Dewey here uses the term "habit" in its customary meaning of stereotyped response to a familiar situation, thus not being able to take care properly of novel situations. This use of the term is not consistent, however, with the doctrine of "active habits" developed on page 54 and following of the text. There habits may be either physical and passive or mental and active. Here they are only the former, and what is there described as "active habits" is here described as "abstraction," etc. There is no contradiction in viewpoint, only in nomenclature.

(3) In such a closely reasoned and abstruse discussion as that in the text, more illustrations would help clarify the exposition. We have taken the liberty of inserting a few. Dr. Dewey's philosophy emphasizes the concrete, action, and closeness to empirical experience, but its exposition moves mostly in the region of the highly intellectual and the abstruse.

(4) There seems to be both a contradiction and a *tour de force* in the presentation of "generalization." It is held to be an instrument of the few experts; at the same time it is held to be "essentially a social device" and so an instrument for the many. There seems to be some forcing of the social emphasis in holding that a strictly logical process like generalization (= deduction) is essentially social. The matter might be somewhat cleared up if it were recognized that "generalization" is a mode of thinking common to all men, that it is used with varying degrees of success by different

men according to their ability and training, that it is used best by the expert few, and that, as civilization advances, wider social experiences occur which are the basis for wider generalizations about society and the races of mankind. The process of generalization remains logical, it is not essentially social, though society as well as nature may be a sphere for its operation.

(5) In this section Dr. Dewey repeats his familiar view that speculative theorizing is in "permanent dislocation from practice." This is again the conflict between the pragmatic and any form of transcendental philosophy. But the pragmatic position can not maintain itself here, for nothing in history has more moved the course of human affairs than man's thought of the transcendent. It would be truer to fact to say that man's speculations have been in permanent articulation with practice. The argument might be pointed by reference to primitive animism, and the various historic philosophies and religions of the East and the West. Dissident philosophers have largely arisen and thriven on their negations of the transcendent.

Further, if speculation and practice are really permanently dislocated, then practice is unaffected by speculation, then speculation is harmless, then why attack it so? But no, the real objection to speculation must be not that it is dislocated from practice but that it affects practice in unwholesome ways. And there the issue is at least clearly joined. It is, do we live in a universe of transcendent value or not?

And still further. Speculative theorizing exists. If it is improper, undesirable, obstructive, but yet man has always engaged in it, and the best minds at that, then here is the problem of evil in a new form breaking out within the pragmatic philosophy. It has a human nature to deal with which it must regard in this respect as bad.

Perhaps a better view is that man is a microcosm whose nature reflects the macrocosm, that man's experience with things and associations with his fellows are set in a wider context of reality, that it is both natural and good to think about what man has not yet fully experienced, and that he may do so profitably in case his thinking lays hold on realities unknown to his sense-perceptions. As an American scholar has written: ". . . all that has in spirit, idea, or organization, expressed any aspect of the fundamental search for the good that, to the vision of faith, lies beyond experience, expresses in some degree one broad characteristic of our western culture since the Renaissance. . . . Out of this welter of contending and incongruous values, the idealist hopes for the progressive emergence of righteousness and justice; the pragmatist often surrenders to the relativity of interest and opportunity."[1]

(6) Does Dr. Dewey expect too much from science? Can it, unaided, transform the attitudes, beliefs, and ideas of men as he suggests? Is science the sole agency of conscious social progress? In our judgment the case for science is decidedly overstated. We can give science all the freedom it requires for its best work and yet not assign it such an extravagant rôle as is here done. After all, science is a method of experimental inquiry and a resulting, changing, body of knowledge. And this is all it is. It is not beauty, it is not morality, it is not sociality, it is not living itself, it is not loving, it is not appreciation of value. It is an intellectual method and an intellectual result. All these other things may be studied scientifically but the scientific study is no substitute for the realities studied. There may be a science of value but the value itself as a felt experience or as a transcendent object is not science. Real is the life we live; science is one way of studying this life. The very desire to master nature and so to aid man is a motive for scientific study but it is not science. Henry Adams was so engaged in studying the game of life that he never played it.

Science is indeed an instrument to assist us in realizing our ends, but it can not determine our ends; that is, it is a

[1] Bouton, Archibald L., *The Greek Element in Modern Life*, pp. 5, 6. American Classical League Publication, No. 38.

means of minor, but not of major, progress. It is just as scientific to use dynamite to blow a man to pieces as to blast rock. Our ends are expressions of our choice between possible satisfactions. Our choices may utilize scientific data. But they are influenced also by our training and our attitudes as well as by our scientific knowledge.

It can not be maintained that science is the sole agency of conscious social progress. Social progress is partly due to great individuals. There have been great individuals who were not primarily scientists or primarily motivated by scientific data, such as, Rousseau, Washington, Lincoln, and Wilson. Furthermore, there have been movements that worked in the interest of conscious social progress which were not motivated primarily scientifically, such as Hebrew prophetism, Christianity, the Renaissance, the Reformation, and the French Revolution. All this, once again, is not to deny the large and legitimate place of science in education and in life; it is only to maintain that there are real limits to what science, unassociated with beauty and reverence, can do to improve mankind. It is not due to the recency of science but to the nature of science, and to many other causes, that scientific advance has not been followed by more moral progress.

(7) It should also be pointed out that the pragmatic philosophy aims at this point to teach man to rely upon himself, and only on himself. And science, it is held, should be used by education to secure this result. It has often done so! "The problem of an educational use of science is then to create an intelligence pregnant with belief in the possibility of the direction of human affairs by itself" (p. 263). This is not historic religion in any of its forms except that advocated by Auguste Comte; it is the religion of the new humanism. In this religion man becomes the centre of the universe, there is no occasion for praise, prayer, or worship of any Being, though the possibilities of existence within man's power as he uses appropriate means to realize his ends may properly inspire within him a pious attitude toward the

materials of life. Faith would not be centred in an Object but would be the vision of possibilities and the will to realize them.

This view has some strength in it, just the strength of social man using science. It lacks the strength that comes from the sense of man's kinship to any spiritual reality in the universe as a source of comfort and power. In the face of the overwhelming calamities of life which man's science can not control, it has the Stoic attitude of endurance and fortitude. It lacks the view that man's science is a re-thinking of Divine thoughts and that man's power over nature is a form of co-operation between the Giver and the user. Science may be used educationally to create an intelligence pregnant with the belief in itself as a pale though effective reflection of a rationality embodied in the universe. This, however, would add philosophy to science.

3. Naturalism and Humanism in Education

Exposition. We will recur to this topic in Chapter XXI below but, in connection with the preceding section, it is appropriate to introduce it here also. The term "naturalism" has many meanings; here it is used to refer to all those studies in the curriculum that have to do with the sciences. And "humanism," too, has many meanings but here it will be used to refer to all those studies in the curriculum that have to do with man. Thus biology is an illustration of naturalism and history is an illustration of humanism.

Now the main point of our argument here is that naturalism, when rightly understood, is humanistic, and so its interests are not antagonistic to those of humanism. Of course this harmony is not historic. There is an educational tradition which opposes science to literature and history in the curriculum. The quarrel between the representatives of the two interests dates from the Renaissance and is easily explicable historically. Literature, language, and an educational philosophy favorable to literature were entrenched in all the higher institutions of learning before experimental science was born. The latter had to fight for survival and recognition. The sciences had to win their way by struggle, against the humanities, just as earlier the humanities had to win their way by even a greater struggle against the Seven Liberal Arts and Divinity of the Middle Ages. No fortified, protected interest readily surrenders any monopoly it may possess.

The conflict between humanism and naturalism was a reflection of aristocratic social conditions. The leisure classes studied the humanities; slaves and serfs performed all useful work. Even industry was controlled by customary models rather than by intelligence. So the notions grew up that "pure" knowledge was more worthy than "applied," and that "pure" knowledge was identical with pure theorizing, and that such "pure" knowledge alone deserved the name of science, and that all useful knowledge suffered the same stigma as the useful social classes.

These false notions survived after science dropped its Greek meaning of pure theory and identified itself with the methods of control used by the practical arts; they survived even after the rise of democracy. Even the educational advocates of science adopted them, and thus put themselves at a strategic disadvantage in their worthy fight. Having mistakenly separated man from the physical world, they naturally attached more significance to the humanities than to the sciences.

The true position is that the study of the sciences, when properly done, is humanizing, and the study of the humanities, when improperly done, without the sciences, is dehumanizing. The practical scientific studies, conducted in relation to man, are liberal and the non-practical humanistic studies, conducted out of relation to the sciences and the needs of the masses of men, are illiberal.

Consider first the humanistic quality of the sciences. Man and nature are one. Human life does not occur in a vacuum, and nature is not merely stage scenery for the drama of human life. Man's life, his success, his defeat, are bound up with the processes of nature. Man controls his own affairs deliberately by directing the energies of nature; and he directs the energies of nature through insight into nature's processes. The sharp separation of the sciences from the humanities depends upon this false separation of the physical world from man.

For the scientific specialist indeed, the realm of nature may be studied apart from man. But for educational purposes natural science gives the knowledge of the conditions of human action; makes one aware of the medium in which social intercourse goes on, and of the means and obstacles to its progressive development. Is not such knowledge thoroughly humanistic in quality? And the history of science. One who is ignorant of it has missed the struggles by which mankind has passed from routine and caprice, from superstition and magic, to intellectual self-possession.

It is indeed true that the study of science in schools may be separated from man. It may be taught as a set of formal and technical exercises, making information about the world an end in itself. Such instruction, of course, produces no culture. It exhibits a wrong educational attitude. It is no evidence that the knowledge of nature is antithetic to the course of man.

It is also true that the study of the humanities in school may be separated from the needs of man and from the study of nature. Then they too are hampered. They are reduced to the exclusively literary and linguistic studies, even to languages no longer spoken, to "the classics." Even the modern languages, being useful, fall under the ban. Some educational practices have identified the "humanities" exclusively with a knowledge of Greek and Latin. Such irony! Such neglect of subject matter accessible to the masses! The result is the cultivation of narrow snobbery in a learned leisure class. Natural science is more humanistic than such alleged humanism, more appropriate in its experimental method to the movements of an industrial and democratic society. Of course, be it said, Greek and Roman art and institutions, in distinction from the Greek and Latin languages, made important contributions to our civilization, so important in fact that there should always be the amplest opportunity for making their acquaintance.

In sum, then, on this question, language and literature are not exclusively humanistic in quality, science is not exclusively physical in import. The "humanities" may be illiberal, and the sciences may be liberal. Whether knowledge is humanistic or not does not depend on what it is *about* but upon what it *does*. It is humanistic if it liberates human intelligence and human sympathy, be it about literature or science; and if it does not do this, it is not only not humanistic, but not even educational.

Comment. This short section seems to have been an afterthought. No summary of it appears on p. 270. Possibly it was inserted after the summary was written. The subject itself is treated again later (Chap. XXI). The purpose is obviously to enhance regard for the sciences in the course of study. It is a piece of polemic and defensive writing. No adequate presentation is made of the claims of the humanities in the course of study. It is shown that the sciences may be humanistic or not, and that the humanities may not be humanistic. It is not stressed that the humanities may be humanistic. And it is not shown at all that the study of the humanities may use the scientific method. Such, however, is the case. President Hadley of Yale claimed that his father, the author of a Greek grammar, was the first user of the scientific method in any field in this country, since he employed the inductive method. Mathematics, historically associated with "the classics" in the college curriculum, is strictly scientific, and the very tool of science. History, one of the humanities, is amenable to the strictest canons of scientific investigation, allowing all the steps of reflective thinking: interest, problem, data, hypotheses, testing. And as there is a science of history, so there is a science of language. And literature and even religion admit of being studied scientifically. Of course, it is one thing to apply the scientific method to the study of the humanities and another thing thereby to exhaust their significance. There may be a science of everything, but anything is more than the science of it.

PART III

OUR EDUCATIONAL LIMITATIONS

CHAPTER XVIII

EDUCATIONAL VALUES

A value is an interest. That is our key thought. Interest coincides with aim. What we are interested in, we aim at. Educators have been interested in utility, information, preparation, mental discipline, mental power, culture, social efficiency, etc., and so they have aimed at these things. So, in previously discussing interest and aims, we have already covered the general field of value.

But there is a new specific angle to the discussion which we have not covered. Values have usually, and incorrectly, been treated in connection with specific subjects in the curriculum; such treatments have vainly sought to justify certain subjects by pointing out the significant results of studying them. We shall see that such segregation of studies from each other is unjustifiable.

We turn then to an explicit discussion of educational values, thus reviewing our previous findings on interest and aims, while connecting them with the specific studies in the curriculum.

We value a thing when we prize it intrinsically, or appreciate it; so we must consider the nature of appreciation of subject matter. But we also in a second sense value a thing when we set a value upon it, or value it with reference to something else; so we must also consider the valuation of studies. This seems to suggest two groups of studies, those having intrinsic and those having instrumental values; but such a division of studies should not be made, for every instrumental subject should also have for the student of it an intrinsic, æsthetic, value somewhere. So we also have to consider that studies should not be segregated from each other, but should be organized with each other; just as society should not be composed of isolated social groups but of one democratic social group. We turn now to these successive considerations in detail.

1. The Nature of Realization or Appreciation

Exposition. We realize or appreciate a thing when we really experience that thing and its meaning. "He jests at scars who never felt a wound"; he realizes war who has shared its dangers and hardships. A realizing experience is direct, immediate, first hand, vital. In a direct experience there is urgency, warmth, intimacy. One really sees the picture for himself, is perhaps moved by it; or one is carried away by some peculiarly glorious illumination of a misty landscape. Thus one acquires the realizing sense of a thing, mentally realizes it, appreciates it, genuinely appreciates it, really takes it in, finds it coming home to him. There is no realization, no appreciation, of a thing without such first hand experience of it and its meaning.

But much, even most, of our experience is indirect, dependent on signs intervening between ourselves and the things, signs standing for or representing the things. One does not engage in war, but one hears or reads about it. One does not see the picture but reads a description of it. One is not carried away by an illuminated landscape, but learns mathematical equations about light. All language, all symbols are such implements of an indirect experience; such indirect experience, procured by means of intermediaries, is said to be "mediated"; it is not immediate. A representative experience, in contrast with a direct or presentative experience, seems remote, pallid, coldly detached.

Thus, some experiences are direct and are the basis of all appreciation, while other experiences are indirect and can be had only by symbols. Without adequate direct experience first, symbols are meaningless. But without the symbols, no civilization. The scope of personal, direct experience is very limited, like that of the brutes. Symbols represent the absent and the distant; thus man does not remain near the level of the brutes; he passes from savagery to civilization by the aid of symbols; they widen the range of his experience from the immediate to the remote; they deepen the meaning of his immediate experience by connecting it with the things symbolized, lifting him out of the limits of the here and the now. Letters are symbols; they effectively give us indirect experience; this is doubtless why the unlettered are identified with the uncultivated.

Thus we go from direct experience by means of symbols to indirect experience. There is a danger lurking in this situation. It is, as previously repeatedly noticed, that symbols will fail to symbolize, will fail to call up the absent and the remote, and, so failing, will become ends in themselves. Then come words for their own sake. From immediacy of experience to literacy, and from literacy to formal, bookish, academic education. How easily technique encroaches upon appreciation! So Plato could lament the invention of writing and Pestalozzi the invention of printing.

One danger leads to another. Too readily do teachers incorrectly assume that pupils already have direct experience. Formal school studies thus build an airy superstructure of symbols upon a non-existent foundation. Instead, direct experience must first be had, sufficient in both bulk and quality to connect readily and fruitfully with symbolic instruction. Let the school educate by direct experience before it teaches by symbols of indirect experience. Situations before signs! Personal experience of problems before their symbolic solution! Such first-hand, direct experiences are felt as worth while on their own account to the pupils; from the teachers' standpoint, they make symbolic instruction, when it comes, intelligible, welcome and a matter of interesting concern.

How shall subject matter be made educative? Our own solution was, it will be recalled, by means of play and active occupations embodying typical situations. Thus a background of realization is provided. That discussion of ours dealt specifically with the subject matter of primary education. Here the demand for an available background is most obvious. It is easy to misunderstand the fundamental intent of these primary school activities. Let all take notice! The intent is not to amuse; it is not to convey information with a minimum of vexation; it is not to acquire skill. All these results may indeed accrue as by-products. No, the fundamental intent is to develop the scope of experience, to enrich the quality of experience, and to keep alert the interest in intellectual progress. Upon such foundations a solid superstructure of even symbolic instruction may be built.

But something more. This fundamental principle of primary education applies equally to the primary or elemental phase of every subject in the course of study. Appreciation comes first. Take, for example, laboratory work in a new field in high school or college. Its first or basic function should be to give the student a "feeling" for his new enterprise, to familiarize him at first hand with a certain range of new facts and problems, to provide him basic realizing experiences. At the beginning such things as getting command of technique, learning how to generalize and to test generalizations are secondary, however important they may be later.

Thus we see that appreciation is a matter of direct experience, after which further enrichment may come indirectly through the use of man's greatest invention,—the symbol.

While the significant subject of appreciation is before us, we may appropriately bring out three further principles, viz., that standards of value depend on appreciative experiences of value; that all appreciation depends on imagination; and that the function of the fine arts in the course of study is to intensify appreciation. To each of these principles we will give separate attention.

(1) The nature of standards of valuation. Standards of value are either real or nominal. Real standards of value

depend on personal appreciative experiences; nominal standards of value depend on symbolic, indirect experiences. The real standards of adults are only nominal standards to the young. The direct experiences of an older generation when formulated and transmitted to the younger generation are symbolic, conventional, unreal.

Every adult has acquired certain important standards of value. These have come from his prior experiences and education. For example, in the field of morality, he has learned to look with favor upon such qualities as honesty, amiability, perseverance, and loyalty; he has also learned "the golden rule" for securing these values. Likewise, in the field of art he has learned to appreciate the classics of literature, painting, and music; he has also learned that the way to secure æsthetic values is through harmony, balance, proportionate distribution, etc. So in the field of intellectual accomplishment he has learned the value of definition, clarity, and system.

Should such principles be taught directly to the young? They are so important that parents and teachers are always inclined to do so. But there is the same old danger here that standards of value so taught will be *merely* symbolic. In matters of morals, art, and logic, as elsewhere, real working standards depend upon the individual's own experience, upon what, in concrete situations, he himself has specifically appreciated as deeply significant.

Take music. Suppose an individual has given his time to jazz, has most enjoyed jazz, loves jazz. But he has been taught that jazz is not classical music, that there is no syncopation in classical music, that there is less accentuation of physical rhythm in classical music, etc. He may be able to converse correctly about classical music, he may even honestly believe that the classical standards are his chosen own. His nominal standard of music is classical, his real standard is jazz. What he has been told is one thing, what he has himself felt is a more real thing.

The same is no less true in standards of moral worth. Without the pupil's experience of the worth of unselfishness, the teaching of unselfishness is symbolic. His knowledge is second-hand; he knows others prize unselfishness, and esteem him when he exhibits it. Practicing one standard, he professes another; his inclinations lead one way, his opinions another; a split grows up of which he is unaware; he suffers from the conflict between doing what he loves and professing what others love; an unconscious hypocrisy, an unstable disposition result. The teaching of the virtues must impinge upon the prior experience of their worth.

The same principle holds in standards of thinking. He appreciates clarity and definition who has fought his way out of the intellectual fog. Thereafter, clarity and definition are real standards of thinking for him. Without this basic experience, he may be trained externally to analyze and divide subject matter, and acquire information about how to do it, but logical norms mean as little to him really as the rivers in China. His glib recitations are mechanical rehearsals.

So, everywhere, in art, morals, and thinking, as Kant said, concepts without percepts are empty; symbols not based on first-hand experience are meaningless. The place of appreciation in all education is basic. Habits based on appreciation are also *tastes,*—modes of preference and esteem, an effective sense of excellence; not so based, habits are mechanical things. Schools do not give adequate attention to life situations in which the meaning of facts, ideas, principles, and problems is vitally brought home; if they did do so, they would not need to put such a premium on "discipline," marks, rewards, promotions, and keeping pupils back. Lacking real incentives, pupils must be stimulated artificially.

(2) The place of imagination in appreciation. All appreciation depends on imagination. It is by imagination that *meaning* is sensed. Even pure "facts" can be realized only by the understanding, involving imagination. Not in one field only but in every field the imagination is the medium of

appreciation. The warm and intimate taking in of the full scope of a situation is imaginative. Cultivate then imaginative vision, the sense of meaning, full realization, the perception of connections, in every type of direct experience.

There are both failures and misuses of imagination in current educational practice. A direct experience, as we have seen, is to be distinguished from an indirect, symbolic, representative experience. Unless direct experiences are realized imaginatively, indirect experiences must remain symbolic. Imagination is the road from presentative knowledge to representative knowledge; it translates symbols into direct meanings; it integrates symbols with a narrow activity, thereby expanding and enriching the activity. When the creative imagination is cut off from activities and made merely literary and mythological, symbols may be mouthed but are not understood. Present activities imaginatively understood are the basis for the imaginative understanding of absent and remote experiences.

Without the engagement of the imagination any activity is only mechanical. This is as true of teaching as of other activities. The mechanical teacher is unimaginative, the imaginative teacher is not mechanical.

This book has emphasized activity. This emphasis is in accord with many tendencies in contemporary education. Manual activities, laboratory exercises, and play have all been stressed. But be it distinctly understood that the imagination is as much a normal, integral, part of human activity as is muscular movement. Once again, without imagination, a physical response is only mechanical; even the resulting skill, when isolated from appreciation, is unimportant. The educative value of all activities depends on their imaginative element; it is this which brings about a sense of the meaning of what is going on. All activities that are educative are in effect dramatizations.

Let us consider play in detail from this standpoint. Play-activity is an imaginative enterprise; theory so recognizes it;

even practice to some extent does the same. But the mistake is made of regarding play as childish, as something not for adults, and likewise of regarding serious employment as for adults, not for children. Both children and adults should both play and work with imagination. The difference between play and work is not that play has it and work does not; both have it, or should have it; the difference is in the materials with which imagination is occupied. In play the imagination is occupied with the meaning of the activity itself; in work with the significant results of the activity. In this way the main effect of education,—the achieving of a life of rich significance, can be secured. The results of the mistake of associating imagination only with play are deplorable; the phantastic and "unreal" phases of childish play are unwholesomely exaggerated; serious occupations are reduced in deadly fashion to an efficient routine, prized simply for its external results; achievement comes to mean what a robot can do well and a man can do poorly; significant living drops by the wayside; mind-wandering and wayward fancy are the price paid for cutting loose the insuppressible imagination from one's serious work.

Another mistake is to identify the imaginative with the imaginary. The imaginative takes in the full meaning of a situation; the imaginary is concerned with the non-existent. The evil results are two. First, there is an exaggerated estimate of certain agencies for developing imaginative appreciation, such as, fairy tales, myths, fanciful symbols, verse, and something labeled "Fine Art"; such things are rather imaginary than imaginative. Second, imaginative vision is neglected in everyday affairs, and instruction is often reduced to an unimaginative acquiring of specialized skill and to an equally unimaginative amassing of a load of information. It is imagination, rightly understood and used, that saves education and life from being humdrum and that makes them richly significant.

(3) The place of the fine arts in the course of study. In our previous accounts of the course of study it may have been noted that nothing was said explicitly about the place of literature and the fine arts. The omission, then made intentionally, will now be supplied in its appropriate setting.

The arts of primitive man, like the arts of children, are not to be distinguished into the useful and the fine. The same is true of the list of active occupations given in Chapter XV. The distinction grows up within the activities themselves. Certain factors in these activities develop into the useful arts; other factors develop into the fine arts. Emphasis on the product of the activity and on its socially serviceable value leads to the useful or industrial arts, like the manufacture of soap. Emphasis on the immediate qualities of the product, and on their appeal to taste leads to the fine arts, like the carving, even of soap, into attractive forms. The occupations of primitive man and of children engage the emotions and the imaginations; in this respect they have the qualities of fine art. They also demand method and skill in adapting tools to materials; in this respect they have the technique indispensable in any art. The products of such early activities are naturally defective in æsthetic quality though even here the embodiment of genuine appreciation may often lend a rudimentary charm. The experiences themselves of these active occupations have then the traits of both the useful and the fine arts. The path of activity leads both to industry and to beauty.

Appreciation usually means prizing. In one of its meanings, however, it is opposed to depreciation. Depreciation is a lowered, a degraded, prizing. Appreciation, as its opposite, is a lifted, an *intensified* prizing. Now the prime function of the arts in education is to secure this intensified appreciation. We refer to literature, music, drawing, painting, and the like. They enhance the qualities which make any experience appealing, capable of full assimilation, and enjoyable. They are not the exclusive agencies of general appreciation; they are the chief agencies of intensified appreciation.

Literature and the fine arts, through enhancing appreciation, serve a double purpose. First, they are intrinsically and directly enjoyable. They reveal a depth and range of meaning in experiences otherwise mediocre and trivial. Scattered and incomplete elements of good they concentrate and consummate. They select and focus the directly enjoyable elements of any experience. The landscape artist, Turner, overheard a critic of one of his paintings say, "I never saw a sunset like that"; to which he replied: "But don't you wish you could!"

Second, literature and the fine arts serve a purpose beyond themselves; they supply organs of vision; they form standards of worth; they fix taste; they arouse discontent with ugly conditions; they create a demand for æsthetic surroundings. For these reasons they are not to be regarded, as by Herbert Spencer, as the luxuries of education; they are emphatic expressions of the necessities of any worthwhile education.

Comment. The first is a caution. In his statement here concerning value Dr. Dewey may be easily misunderstood. He writes: ". . . There is no difference between speaking of art as an interest or concern and referring to it as a value" (p. 271). This reads like interest equals value; that to be interested in something, to desire something, is to value it; that likings are values. This, however, is a misinterpretation. To Dr. Dewey likings become values only when they are intelligent. When what we like is seen to have desirable connections and consequences, it is a value. It is not likings that are values but intelligent likings. A thing has value when it is both felt as a value and seen to be valuable.[1]

Even so it should be noted that the values of life are held by Dr. Dewey to inhere in certain forms of human experience. A natural process apart from man lacks value, as it lacks reason. It is amenable to man's production of value but it

[1] Consult *The Quest for Certainty*, pp. 265–270.

has no value in itself. Thus values are humanly, socially, subjective; they do not inhere in nature beyond man.

This view may well be questioned. It involves the contradiction that man as a child of nature has value but that nature as the mother of man lacks value. One might well defend the position that, unless value existed in the whole, it could not arise in the part. Otherwise, adequate explanation of the appearance of value at all is lacking.

And for a second reason the position may well be questioned. It introduces an unwelcome dualism between nature and man. If man has value, and nature has none, then there is discontinuity between the two. In view of man's many affinities with nature, such discontinuity is repugnant to reason. Furthermore, it is inconsistent with the main emphasis on continuity maintained in Dr. Dewey's total argument.

Instead of making value man-centered, it might well be made reality-centered. In this case the intelligent liking of man does not create value so much as discover preëxistent value. So man's education would be a process of realizing values already inherent in the universe of reality. Man does not create logical truth, emotional beauty, and ethical worth; he discovers them, and re-creates them in individual thought, feeling, and conduct. Man not only makes value, he discovers and uses it. This view enriches not only human experience but the universe itself. And it solves the intellectual difficulties inherent in the theory of socially subjective values.

A second matter is less metaphysical and more practical. It concerns the theory that we can not appreciate what we have not experienced directly, that we must learn by doing, that without a basic direct experience we lack the organs for appreciating indirect experiences. Plato long ago taught that it might help a physician to have had the diseases he treats, but that it would not help a judge to have had the vices he must condemn, for, to have been vicious may leave the judgment blind.

The issue is, shall the teaching concerning vice depend upon the prior experience of its lack of worth? The theory advocated would seem to answer in the affirmative; or else, the realm of vice is not to be referred to at all. The issue puts the theory under a strain. The vices would be learned by initial experience, or else not learned at all. But it is objectionable that children should experience the wrong before being warned against it. It is also objectionable that they should not be warned at all.

The dilemma vanishes if the theory that all teaching depends on actual experience is dropped. The Roman poet, Horace, describes how his father taught him the virtues by taking him by the hand through the streets of Rome and warning him against the vices they saw. Here is observation but not participation. It is indirect experience. The vice begins and remains in the symbolic, though near-experience, stage. Some things may well be learned from the experiences of others. Some things are not worth learning, for example, how it feels to commit crime. It is better to learn not to do some things. It is true the burnt child dreads the fire, but this does not warrant the burning.

The rejection of the principle of learning the vices by direct experience does not mean that children will never fall into error and wrong-doing; but it means they will be prevented from doing so as much as possible, and, when they do so, the fact of such an unfortunate experience is to be properly utilized for instructional purposes. The theory works, not in providing the direct experience of wrong, but in using the unwelcome instances of it.

Another matter. As it is possible to respond to what one sees as well as does, so also is it possible to respond to what one imagines. Thus an ideal, or an ideal person, never seen, may yet be held imaginatively before the mind, and thus invoke responses. The imagined ideal has never been experienced, though features of it may have been experienced in part. One may never have met his ideal, and yet be influenced by it. This principle of response to the ideal likewise modifies the theory of basing all learning on direct experience. That is, we may have effective symbols of what has never been experienced, as in geometry we have ideal triangles and squares which do not exist in space.

A matter of interest but not of importance. Dr. Dewey, like most psychologists since Herbart, rejects, of course, the theory of mental faculties. But the terms he uses in this section, "the intellect," "the understanding," "the imagination," sound like "the faculties." And it is not easy to avoid using such terms. Changes in language do not keep pace with changes in thought.

As in other places in this text, a bias is shown in favor of the sciences in contrast with the fine arts. Science in the course of study receives the attention of a whole chapter (XVII); the fine arts receive the attention of a fraction of one section of a chapter (pp. 278–279). As in the case of Darwin, whose influence on philosophy he so values, Dr. Dewey's mind is loaded on the scientific rather than the æsthetic side. It should be said, however, absolutely, if not relatively, there is real appreciation of the place of fine arts in education.

2. The Valuation of Studies

Exposition. We begin with a distinction already made in the preceding section. It concerns the difference between value and evaluation. To value means to prize, to esteem, to feel the inherent worth of something, to realize the worthwhile meaning of something, to appreciate, to cherish, to hold dear. To evaluate means to set a value upon, to estimate, to judge the amount of something in comparison with something else.

The distinction coincides with that between intrinsic and instrumental values. A thing has intrinsic value on its own account; it has instrumental value on account of something else of value to which it leads. Intrinsic values are prized for themselves; instrumental values are prized for ends beyond themselves.

Now as intrinsic, values are incomparable. They are invaluable, not objects of judgment, not greater or less, not better or worse, not more or less than any other invaluable. But as extrinsic, or instrumental, values are comparable. Occasions present themselves when one must choose between invaluables, when it is necessary as a practical matter to let one invaluable go in order to take another. Such a necessary choice involves a judgment concerning greater and less, better and worse, and establishes an order of preference. Things so passed upon are estimated in relation to some third thing, some further end, held also to have value in itself. With respect to this third thing the value chosen to reach it is instrumental.

It is evident at once that one and the same value is both intrinsic and instrumental. It is intrinsic in itself; it is instrumental in leading to something else. Not unduly to cloud the issue, it can be said that the instrumental value, too, has intrinsic value as an instrument. This would seem to wipe out the distinction between intrinsic and instrumental values, but it does not. One and the same value is indeed both, but not in the same sense; it is a matter of viewpoint; viewed as value in itself, it is intrinsic; viewed as value leading to another value, it is instrumental.

Another related distinction. It is easy to see that what we have called intrinsic values are values viewed as ends in themselves, and what we have called instrumental values are values as means to other ends. Ends have intrinsic values, means have instrumental values.

To continue the same line of thought about means and ends as was developed above about instrumental and intrinsic values, it must be said that ends, when they become means to other ends, have instrumental as well as intrinsic value; and that means to ends have intrinsic as well as instrumental value. Again, the difference is in the viewpoint. Both ends and means have both intrinsic and instrumental values, but not in the same sense. Ends in themselves have intrinsic values; when viewed as means to other ends, they have also instrumental values. Means to ends have instrumental values; when viewed as a tool or instrument they also have intrinsic value. The process of living is continuous with itself, which, as it passes, has felt intrinsic values, which in turn become instrumental in leading on to other values. Thus means and ends are inseparable, though distinguishable.

After so much abstract discussion some illustrations will be welcome, after which the paragraphs above should be re-read. Among the possible intrinsic values of life are conversing with friends, hearing a symphony, eating, reading, earning, and so on. Each occupies a particular place in life, each serves its own end, each allows no substitute, each is invaluable, incomparable, and imperative, each is a specific good, each in its own place is not merely a means to anything beyond itself.

But situations arise in which these intrinsic values compete and conflict. One can not have all at once. A choice has to be made. Comparison comes in. It is the specific situation that causes the conflict and demands a choice. One can not at the same time enjoy his meal and attend the symphony. Intrinsic, specific goods must now be viewed instrumentally. If one is well fed, he may prefer the symphony; if he is hungry and music is no rarity, he will naturally judge the food to have the greater worth. Let it be carefully noted that in the abstract or at large there is no such thing as instrumental values, or degrees of value, or order of value. Instrumental values always inhere in concrete specific situations where choices between values intrinsic in themselves have to be made. Instrumental values grow out of the conflict of intrinsic values with each other in definite situations.

Having thus seen the nature of valuing, of intrinsic values, of values as ends in themselves, and also of evaluating, of instrumental values, of values as means to ends, we turn now to the specific question of the valuation of studies. This evidently refers to the instrumental values of studies primarily, though their intrinsic values will not be omitted. In our previous section we saw that appreciations fix the standard of later valuations. We now have to see what these valuations are. This, too, is a part of the general theory of educational values.

From the preceding discussion of values in general, certain conclusions follow for educational values. These will be enumerated in order.

1. We can not establish a hierarchy of values among studies. By such a hierarchy is meant the location of each study on a scale of values. It is not possible to say in general that one study is more valuable than another. It is futile to attempt to arrange studies in an order ranging from least worth to most worth. A study of least worth in one specific situation may be one of most worth in another specific situation, like the choice between food and music. Specific situations can not be so generalized that one can say that one study "on the whole" is more valuable than another. So there is no hierarchy of the instrumental values of studies. And since the intrinsic values of studies are incomparable, there of course could be no hierarchy of these. Each intrinsic value of a study is unique, irreplaceable, marking a characteristic enrichment of life. Education is not a means to living; it is living fruitfully and significantly. So the only ultimate value which can be set up is just the process of living itself. Living is its own end; each of life's values is intrinsic; no hierarchy of values is possible. Studies and activities are not the subordinate means to life as an end; they are the ingredients of life as a whole.

2. Every study in one of its aspects ought to have intrinsic value, *i.e.*, ultimate significance. It is easy to see that poetry is at some place and time a good to be appreciated on its own account, really an enjoyable experience. But this

is just as true of arithmetic, or of any other subject. If studies lack intrinsic values, they will be handicapped as instrumental values. A study unrealized in itself is thereby partly unrealized as a resource. Enjoyment enhances utility.

3. Specific situations determine what instrumental values studies have. To realize the instrumental value of a subject, one must be placed in a specific situation requiring its use. A pupil does not see the use of arithmetic? Let him discover that success in something he is interested in doing depends upon ability to use numbers. It would be a mistake to lecture such a student on the benefits arithmetic will be to him in some remote and uncertain future. Subjects are to be both enjoyed and used. They thus have both intrinsic and instrumental values.

4. Different studies do not have distinct sorts of instrumental values. The attempt to make such distribution is misguided, notwithstanding the amount of time recently devoted to the undertaking. First, take the example of science. Among the possible instrumental values it may have are these: (1) military, as an instrument strengthening the means of offense and defense; (2) technological, as an instrument of engineering of all kinds; (3) commercial, as an aid in the conduct of business; (4) philanthropic, rendering service in relieving human suffering; (5) conventional, helping to establish one's social status as an "educated" person. As a matter of fact, science does serve all these purposes. It may in fact have *any* kind of instrumental value, depending upon the specific situation. It would be arbitrary to fix upon one of these values as the "real" end of science. But, turning from instrumental to intrinsic values, we can be sure educationally that science should be so taught as to have intrinsic value, as to be an end in itself in the lives of students, making its own unique contribution to the experience of life, having "appreciation value," and this is all we can be sure of educationally.

The same thing is true of poetry, though it seems to be at the opposite pole from science. Some of its possible assignable instrumental values are: (1) the enjoyment of leisure; (2) moral and religious, serving to penetrate the mysterious depth of things; (3) patriotic, as Homer to the Greeks; and even (4) as a resource in the business of life. Poetry may serve any or all of these ends. It is impossible to say which is its true instrumental value. The one thing sure is that poetry should be enjoyed on its own account, that is, have intrinsic value. In this connection let us remark that at the present time the chief instrumental value of poetry seems to be the enjoyment of leisure; this however may represent a degenerate condition of human society, not anything necessary; any poetry not artificial is a resource in the business of life as well as in its leisure, and the education which does not succeed in making it so has something the matter with it.

5. How are the values of a study related to the motives for studying it? This important question we will consider at some length. It is important to consider it because the fact that a study appears in the curriculum and that children have to study it is no guarantee that it has value. Such a study may be only inherited, traditional matter; it may represent only the energy of some person or group of persons in behalf of a cause dear to them; it may represent, and probably does, the values of adults instead of those of children and youth; or it may represent the values of children of a generation ago. For these reasons the curriculum requires constant inspection, criticism, and revision; only so can we be sure it is accomplishing its purpose.

The answer to our question is that studies should have both intrinsic and extrinsic values. Those who plan courses of study and those who teach them should have good grounds for thinking that thereby pupils are both enriching their present lives and gathering useful materials for other directly interesting concerns. Every subject should have both intrinsic and instrumental value to the pupil; but be it noted that this does not mean that the pupil is able to tell about the values of his studies. He can feel an interest without being aware of it as a value. Our pupils are not educational theorists.

We will consider in turn the intrinsic and the instrumental values of subjects. Any topic making an immediate appeal has intrinsic value. "Some goods are not good *for* anything; they are just goods." We can have instrumental goods only because there are intrinsic goods. The intrinsic good is the aim of the instrumental good. To a hungry, healthy child, food is an intrinsic good of the situation; it is a motive. To a mentally eager pupil, the subject is likewise an intrinsic good of the situation; the response of the pupil is the proof of the good; "his response *is* use"; it shows the subject functions in his life. Take Latin as a test case; if pupils are genuinely concerned in learning it, that is proof enough of its value.

Let us turn now to the inseparable question of the instrumental values of studies. This is the question of what they are *good for*. It is like the case of a sick child without appetite who needs to know that eating food is good for him in order to supply a motive for eating. So a child with a perverted appetite for candy instead of spinach needs to know about the results. There is no occasion for using instrumental values as motives so long as the intrinsic values are effective; furthermore, instrumental values, as we have seen, can not be foretold with exactness. Who knows in a given case the purpose to which learning is to be put in the future? Still, at times it is proper even under normal conditions to use instrumental motivation. Such is the case when the pupil does not grasp just how the doing of this uninteresting thing will secure for him that interesting result. Take the case of Latin again. If it elicits the interested response of pupils, it has intrinsic value. If it leads to some desirable end beyond itself, it has instrumental value; however, in this latter case, a definite future use can not be assigned by either teacher or pupil. If it is claimed that Latin should be taught because it has value in the abstract, without reference to present interest or future use, the position is unsound. But it is proper to ask concerning Latin, even when it has intrinsic value, whether, in view of the shortness of time, there are not other things of intrinsic value which in addition have greater instrumental value.

In general, then, on this point, every subject should be so presented as to have either an immediate value, and so require no further justification, or else a perceived instrumental value, and so be justified as a means of securing an immediate value.

6. Before leaving this section on the valuation of studies, two general comments may be made concerning some of the present pedagogic interest in this subject. At times it is excessive; it makes a labored effort to defend studies which ought to go,—studies which no longer operate to any purpose, either direct or indirect in the lives of pupils. If certain studies are neither interesting nor useful to pupils, why defend them? At other times, it is too narrow, the reaction against the useless goes to the extreme of omitting the joy of the present and demanding that some definite future utility of the subject to be taught be pointed out by the curriculum-maker or the pupil himself. But life is its own excuse for being, and any definite utility must itself be justified by its contribution to the experienced content, the immediate value, of life itself. By enjoyments shall utilities be justified!

Comment. 1. Our Homer has nodded in this section. He is an instrumentalist indeed in his pragmatic theory of ideas, but an immediatist in his theory of values. An idea has truth only if it is a good instrument in controlling a situation. But an experience has value in itself or because it leads to an experience having value in itself. What is praised in an idea is that it successfully leads on; what is praised in a value is that it successfully stops. What is condemned in an idea is that it does not work; what is condemned in a value is that it only works. Here is a dualism in viewpoint in the very nature of the process of experience itself. A harmony could be effected in one of two ways, that is, by adopting either another theory of ideas or another theory of value. For example, it is said that, when Anaxagoras was asked for what man was born, he replied: "For the contemplation of nature." Such a theory of ideas would harmonize with the proposed theory of value. Or, if values were identified with the problem-solving attitude, with the sense of satisfaction in intellectual inquiry, then the theory of value would harmonize with the pragmatic theory of ideas.

2. Not only is the theory of value as ultimately intrinsic inconsistent with the basic pragmatic doctrine of ideas, but it is also inconsistent with the recognition of the universality of instrumental values. In fact, while intrinsic values do not merge into instrumental values, instrumental values do merge into intrinsic values. "Some goods are not good *for* anything" (p. 283). This view makes intrinsic values self-contained. The doctrine that the inherently valued "response *is* use" absorbs the instrumental in the intrinsic. "An instrumental value then has the intrinsic value of being a means to an end" (p. 284). This view merges the instrumental in the intrinsic. It is evident the instrumental values tend to fade into the intrinsic. But this wipes out the distinction between the two kinds of value, and the instrumental values cease to be a universal aspect of the experience of value.

3. But such a recognition of the primacy and supremacy of intrinsic value provide a conception of culture inconsistent with that previously presented (p. 142) and more in harmony with the traditional view. There it was held that acceptable culture must be a socially efficient force; here it is implied that it may be a self-contained enjoyment. There instrumental values were made primary; here intrinsic values are made primary. There culture appeared as the halo of vocation; here it appears as a rainbow beautifying the landscape, and solving no social problem. There use appeared as utility;

here it appears as enjoyment. In view of the narrowness of action and the breadth of thought and feeling, the later view appears preferable to the earlier. It could be used to justify the continuance of the liberal, in distinction from the vocational, college, in case such liberal education were enjoyable, and felt as inherently worth while.

4. The limited acceptance accorded instrumental values and the outright rejection of a hierarchy of values is likewise an inconsistency. If studies have instrumental values, as claimed, a hierarchy of instrumental studies is theoretically, if not practically, possible. The very reference to "greater instrumental value" (p. 284) suggests a scale of such values. It is clearly implied that instrumental values are more or less. The rejection of a hierarchy of values seems to be due to two other considerations, viz., that intrinsic values are incomparable, and that instrumental values can not be correctly foretold. It is a decided limitation on the concept of education as a science to be told that one can not say that any subject is more valuable than any other. This amounts to saying that one subject is, so far as we can tell, as valuable as any other. This is repugnant to common sense. It is an expression of the individualistic and goalless pragmatic philosophy of education. If education has a goal, then all studies can be evaluated, at least theoretically, according to their contribution to the attainment of this goal.

5. If the two views be accepted that intrinsic values are primary and that instrumental values can not be foretold, it would put an end to curriculum-making by "job-analysis." The theory behind such a "scientific determination of the curriculum" is that the school work of to-day should stress the "knowledges," attitudes, and skills required by the jobs of to-morrow. This is a sociological approach to the problem of curriculum construction. At this point the view of Dr. Dewey stresses the enjoyments of the individual more than the requirements of society, and, as before, an enriched present more than a prepared-for future.

3. The Segregation and Organization of Values

Exposition. Our main view here is that the values of education and life, like the classes of society, should not be segregated but should be organized. In presenting this view the following matters will engage our attention: (1) the various valuable phases of life, (2) the proper uses of such a classification, (3) the segregation of educational values, (4) the effects on education of such segregation, (5) the historic background of such segregation, (6) its reflection of our social conditions, and, finally, (7) the proper organization of the values of life.

(1) We begin with the classification of the valuable phases of life. It must be understood at the outset that such a classification can have only a provisional validity. And yet, it is to these phases of life that the work of the schools should contribute. There are five of these classes, which may be designated the executive, the social, the æsthetic, the intellectual, and the ethical. Executive competency means efficiency in the management of resources and in overcoming obstacles. Sociability means interest in the direct companionship of others. Æsthetic taste is the capacity to appreciate artistic excellence in at least some of its classic forms. A trained intellectual method involves interest in some form of scientific achievement. And conscientiousness is sensitiveness to the rights and claims of others. These, tentatively stated, are the five valuable phases of life.

(2) What is the use of such a set of abstract terms? They are criteria for the survey, criticism, and organization of existing methods and subject matter. They are points of view elevated above the details of life from whence to survey the field. They thus help to give breadth and flexibility to the enterprise of education.

But let no one suppose they are standards of value. They are not ultimate ends to which the concrete satisfactions of experience are subordinate. They are nothing but more or less adequate generalizations from concrete goods. Abstract terms sum up a multitude of particulars; the abstract is derived from particulars. Such abstractions are illustrated by such things as health, wealth, efficiency, sociability, utility, culture, and even happiness itself. To turn such abstractions into standards of valuation for the concrete topics and processes of education is to subordinate the particular as source to the general as derivative. So, if we are looking for standards of value, they must not be found in generalizations but, as previously seen, in the *specific realizations* which form preferred tastes and habits, that is, in present direct appreciation.

The proposed tentative classification of the five valuable phases of life is needed to condemn the isolation of the various pursuits of life from each other. We incorrectly conceive life as a patchwork of independent interests existing side by side and limiting each other. It is like the "check and balance" theory of the powers of government familiar to students of politics: the legislative, executive, judicial, and administrative functions of government are supposed to be separate and independent, each checking all the others, and thus creating an ideal balance. Just so there is a false check and balance philosophy of life. It holds that life presents a diversity of interests, tending to encroach on one another if left to themselves. This situation requires that a special territory be assigned to each till the whole ground of experience is covered and that each interest remain within its own boundaries. Such competing interests are politics, business, recreation, art, science, the professions, polite intercourse, and leisure. Further, each of these has its own ramifications; thus, business leads off into manual occupations, executive positions, bookkeeping, railroading, banking, agriculture, commerce, etc., and so with each of the other competing interests. This false view of life leads to the equally false view of an ideal education as supplying the means of meeting these separate and pigeonholed interests. This false view of education we will next examine more in detail.

(3) Corresponding to the isolation from each other of the various pursuits of life is the segregation of educational values from each other. Different studies are falsely held to represent separate kinds of values. A curriculum is then constituted by gathering together various studies representing a sufficient variety of independent values. Special values are parceled out to segregated studies.

This idea is so prevalent in contemporary educational philosophy that we will cite and analyze a specific illustration. "Memory is trained by most studies, but best by languages and history; taste is trained by the more advanced study of languages, and still better by English literature; imagination by all higher language teaching, but chiefly by Greek and Latin poetry; observation by science work in the laboratory, though some training is to be got from the earlier stages of Latin and Greek; for expression, Greek and Latin composition come first and English composition next; for abstract reasoning, mathematics stands almost alone; for concrete reasoning, science comes first, then geometry; for social reasoning, the Greek and Roman historians and orators come first, and general history next. Hence the narrowest education which can claim to be at all complete includes Latin, one modern language, some history, some English literature, and one science."

Here is the fundamental notion of assigning special values to special subjects, along with several matters irrelevant to our main point, such as, the assumption of "faculties" to be trained, a dominant interest in the ancient languages, and a comparative disregard of the earth on which men happen to live and the habits they happen to carry around with them.

The segregation of educational values is a species of educational disintegration. Even when some unifying end like "social efficiency" or "culture" is set up as a standard of value, it is often only a verbal heading comprising a variety of disconnected factors.

Such schemes of values of studies as the quotation illustrates are, as a matter of fact, largely just rationalizing, just unconscious justifications of the existent familiar curriculum. Take mathematics as an example. It is said to have (1) disciplinary value in habituating the pupil to accuracy of statement and closeness of reasoning; (2) utilitarian value in giving command of arts of calculation necessary for trade; (3) cultural value in enlarging the imagination as it deals with the most general relations of things; even (4) religious value in its concept of the infinite. Lackaday! It has these values if and when it accomplishes these results, and not otherwise. Such a statement of values may serve to challenge the teacher to realize them. Mathematics does not accomplish such results because of any miraculous endowment of potencies called values. The evil is that such statements are used to give the subject a rigid justification. And if the subject does not yield the results, the blame is put not on the method of the teacher where it belongs, but on the indifference and recalcitrancy of the pupils!

(4) Isolated pursuits in life, segregated educational values, and a patchwork course of study! Viewing life mistakenly as a series of competing interests, the schools task themselves to meet its demands. The course of study parallels the supposedly fixed interests of life. So it includes some civics and history for political and patriotic reasons; some utilitarian studies; some science; some art (mainly literature of course); some recreational provision; some moral education; and so on and on. Current school controversies concern largely the recognition due in the course of study to each of these competing interests in life. A "reform" introduces a new study in the curriculum. And if it can not be done in the existing system, then, start a new school to do it! Thus in the multitude of educators, education is forgotten.

The outcomes? A congested course of study, over-pressure and distraction of pupils, superficiality, and a narrow specialization fatal to true education as a full life experience. Some observers, seeing the evils, can apply only a quantitative criterion, cutting off the fads and frills, returning to the "three R's" in elementary education, and the classics and mathematics in higher education. All such expedients are futile. Let the evils be laid where they belong,—at the door of the isolation of the existing subjects and the narrowness of their teaching. Let the real remedy be applied,—the re-organization of the system itself.

(5) This conglomerate situation has, of course, its historic explanation. Our schools are the result of a series of past social upheavals and deposits, as the surface of our earth is a set of geologic strata. Distinct studies, distinct courses of study, distinct types of schools, are deposits of past social struggles. The nineteenth century witnessed rapid changes in political, scientific, and economic interests. The schools had to make provision for new values. The older courses first resisted, then surrendered their monopoly. They have been reduced in amount, but they have not re-organized their content and aim. And the new studies were added on to the old; they have not been used to transform the method and aim of all instruction. Thus our curriculum is a conglomerate, whose only cement is the mechanics of the school time table. Thus have arisen those objectionable schemes of value and standards of valuation.

(6) Such is our reprehensible situation in education. But our education only represents our social life. It too is full of divisions and separations. The variety of social interests have not been organized into a rich and balanced experience, they have been segregated, torn asunder, and deposited in separate institutions, with diverse purposes, and with independent methods. Thus we practice that business is business, science is science, art is art, politics are politics, social intercourse is social intercourse, morals are morals, and recreation is recreation. Each, possessing a separate and independent province, contributes to the others only externally and accidentally. The opposition and addition of all of them together make up the whole of life. Thus we practice the mistaken check and balance philosophy of life.

Consider business, for example. What does one expect from it? That it should furnish money, to make more money, to support self and family, to buy books and pictures and tickets to cultural concerts, to pay taxes, to support charity, and the like. It is business for profit and the things profit leads to, and "business is business." How unreasonable to us it appears that the pursuit of business should be itself a culture of the imagination in breadth and refinement; that it should be animated directly by the principle of social service, and not merely indirectly through the money it supplies; and that as an enterprise it should be conducted in behalf of social organization! And so equally with the pursuit of art, or science, or politics, or religion. Our social life is divided, and so unconsciously our courses of study and our theories of educational values are divided.

(7) The point at issue is the unity, the integrity, of human experience. It is the moral question of the organization of the interests of life. Educationally it is the question of that organization of schools, materials, and methods which will achieve breadth and richness of experience.

How shall human experience be full and varied without losing unity of spirit?

How shall it be a unity without narrowness and without monotony?

How shall we be broad in outlook and still efficient in education?

How shall we have diversity without isolation of interests?

How shall the individual be executive with his intelligence and not at the cost of it?

How shall art, science, and politics reënforce one another in an enriched temper of mind instead of competing?

And finally, how can the interests of life and their study unite men in a common enriched experience instead of dividing men from each other?

Our coming chapters will be concerned with these fundamental questions of reorganization of school and society.

Comment. In reviewing the five-fold classification of the valuable phases of life it will be noted that the physical and the spiritual are not specified. It is likely the omission of the physical, covering health and related matters, was an oversight, the classification being tentative and suggestive rather than exhaustive. It is also likely that Dr. Dewey would identify the spiritual with the social and the ethical, as in his philosophy all values are human and socially subjective, the universe itself not being interpreted in personal terms. Some might think the vocational was omitted too. This, however, would be a mistake. In the broad sense of the term vocation, all the interests specified would be vocational; in the narrow sense of the term vocation, the executive phase of life would probably cover it (cf. Chapter XXIII).

In this connection Dr. Dewey's analysis of the valuable phases of human experience might profitably be compared with similar lists made by others, as follows:

THE VALUABLE PHASES OF LIFE

DEWEY	HERBART[1]	SPENCER[2]	CABOT[3]	SOARES[4]	HORNE[5]
1. Executive	1. Social	1. Direct Self-Preservation	1. Work	1. Work	1. Health
2. Social	2. Æsthetic	2. Indirect Self-Preservation	2. Love	2. Money	2. Vocation
3. Æsthetic	3. Scientific	3. Family	3. Play	3. Play	3. Justice
4. Intellectual	4. Ethical	4. State	4. Worship	4. Art	4. Art
5. Ethical	5. Philosophy	5. Leisure		5. Knowledge	5. Truth
	6. Religion			6. Worship	6. Goodness
					7. God

[1] Herbart, *Outlines of Educational Doctrine,* Lange and De Garmo, New York, 1909, Chap. V.

[2] Spencer, "What Knowledge Is of Most Worth," in his *Education.*

[3] Cabot, *What Men Live By,* Boston, 1914.

[4] Soares, *Religious Education,* Chicago, 1928, pp. 98–120.

[5] Horne, *Essentials of Leadership,* Nashville, 1931, Chap. IV.

In comparing these lists it will be noted that Spencer alone arranges his values in a hierarchy (decreasing); that Spencer and the writer alone recognize the physical as a major factor in experience; that Dewey, Spencer, Soares, and the writer recognize the vocational interest; that all but Soares recognize the social interest, though he would associate this with worship; that art alone is recognized by all; that Spencer associates science with each of his five; that Cabot alone omits science; that Spencer associates the ethical with the social life; that Herbart alone separates philosophy from science as phases of the intellectual; and that Dewey and Spencer alone omit specific reference to the spiritual. What analysis of complete living would the reader propose?

Though Dr. Dewey regards his classification as only tentative, he does make the classification, and in so doing runs the risk of segregating values from each other that he holds should be organized. He does indicate how business interests might include other interests, but it is not clear how the æsthetic could do so.

In the light of the present section and what it suggests concerning the discussions to come, this is the place to remark that the continuity of human experience is one of Dr. Dewey's main emphases. He seeks the organization of human interests, the integration of human experience, excluding, as we said, only man's sense of relationship to the ideal beyond the natural and the human. He rejects all dualisms; they are offensive to his emotional nature.

In this connection a passage in his brief autobiographical sketch[1] should be noted: ". . . the sense of divisions and separations that were, I suppose, borne in upon me as a consequence of a heritage of New England culture, divisions by way of isolation of self from the world, of soul from body, of nature from God, brought a painful oppression—or, rather,

[1] *Contemporary American Philosophy,* Adams and Montague, New York, 1930, Vol. II, p. 19.

they were an inward laceration.'' It was Hegel's philosophy that brought him ''an immense release, a liberation.''

So here he rejects the segregation of values and announces a program for the organization of human interests. And in succeeding chapters a series of syntheses, in real Hegelian fashion (note the Dedication of this book), will be effected. Among these dualisms to be overcome are labor and leisure, intellectual and practical studies, physical and social studies, the individual and the world, the knower and the known, and the inner and the outer elements in morality.

What shall we say to this program of the unification of life? Two things. First, as each separate dualism is ''overcome,'' the merit of the continuity proposed will be considered. This is ahead of us. Second, the program at one point is foredoomed to failure. There is one dualism not overcome. It is a dualism inherent in all positivism and humanism. It is the dualism between the realm of sensuous experience on the one hand and the realm of supersensuous experience on the other hand. It is a dualism overcome not by humanistic experimentalism but by either mysticism as an emotional experience or by absolutism as a system of thought.

The following quotation, interpreted as an expression of theistic monism, which possibly the writer did not intend, illustrates a unification of human interests without a remaining dualism: ''Life may be conceived as the great human experiment. History is the story of how the experiment has been carried on; geography is the habitat of the experiment; mathematics is the number relations of the experiment; natural science is the physical conditions of the experiment; art is the ideal interpretation of the experiment; literature is what gifted souls have thought and felt about the experiment; philosophy is contemplation of the meaning of the experiment; religion is appreciation of the divine quality of the experiment.''[1]

1 Soares, T. G., *Religious Education,* Chicago, 1930, pp. 132–133.

CHAPTER XIX

LABOR AND LEISURE

1. The Origin of the Opposition

Exposition. Labor and leisure were two things in Greece, they still are two things in modern society, but they should be one. The origin of the opposition was in Grecian society composed of the free and the slave.

Of all the antitheses in education and in life, probably the most deep-seated is that between labor and leisure. So we have one education for utility and another education for culture. The values of utility and culture, being first isolated from each other, end by becoming opposed to each other. The initial isolation of values from each other and the final opposition of values to each other reflect, as we saw, a division within social life itself. The very terms, "useful labor," and "leisure," show this. Just suppose the different members of a community equally labored for a livelihood and equally enjoyed a cultivated leisure! There would not be two educations,—one for utility and one for culture; one professional and industrial, the other liberal. There would be only one education contributing to both ends. The only question would concern how effectively it could be done. Some instructional materials might indeed contribute chiefly to utility, and others to culture, but care would be exercised to secure the maximum of overlapping: the cultural education would contribute also to the efficiency and enjoyment of work, and the useful education would produce emotional and intellectual habits procuring a worthy cultivation of leisure.

Labor is a necessity. It supplies the resources of living. There is nothing about it that should lead to the neglect or contempt of the kind of education preparing for it. Such neglect is due to a division of social classes which should not exist. It may be claimed that getting a living is material and that enjoying leisure is higher; it may also be claimed that material interests are engrossing, insubordinate, striving to usurp the place of higher ideal interests. Let the claims be admitted! Still, the solution would not be to neglect useful education, leading to evil results flourishing in obscurity. It would be to exercise scrupulous care to train for the useful pursuits, while keeping them in their place. But let useful education be identified with the interests of an inferior social class, then it suffers from both neglect and contempt. It is society, not necessity, that rigidly identifies work with material interests and leisure with ideal interests.

There is nothing inevitable about such a division of education into two kinds as we have. How it grew up in Greek life as a social distinction and was thence wrought into educational philosophy can be traced. Greek society was divided into two classes; the one had to labor for a living, the other did not. The one class was slave, the other was free. The slave labored both for himself and for the superior class. The time of the slaves was occupied practically, that of the free was spent intellectually. The social status of the slaves made their training servile, that of the free made their education liberal and intrinsically higher.

The educational formulations made over two thousand years ago to meet social situations have been influential. They deserve special notice. Aristotle's psychology and politics will reveal their nature, and so will be briefly sketched.

In the scale of animate existence, man occupies the highest place. In part he is like the plants and animals, and in part not. He is like the plants in having a nutritive and reproductive soul, and like the animals in having a nutritive, reproductive, and motor soul. He is unlike the plants and animals, and so distinctively human, in having a rational soul, existing to behold the spectacle of the universe. The true end of man is the fullest possible realization of this distinctive human prerogative. The proper life of man is observation, meditation, speculation, pursued as an end in itself. Furthermore, the vegetative and animal soul of man is controlled by his rational soul; the lower elements of his nature, the appetites and the motor impulses, are in themselves greedy, insubordinate, lovers of excess, aiming at their own satiety; they observe moderation, obey the law of the golden mean, and serve desirable ends only as they are subjected to the rule of reason.

Even among those living a life of reason there is a distinction of inferior and superior. The free citizen is inferior to the pure thinker. The free citizen leads a life accompanied by reason as he devotes himself to the public life of his community, sharing in the management of its affairs, and winning personal honor and distinction. His activity in his civic relations retains some of the taint of practice, of external instrumental doing. Civic activity and excellence need the help of others; one can not engage in public life by himself. But this need for others betrays the infection of the material things of life. All needs and desires imply lack, privation, and dependence on something else for completion. The pure thinker is not so. He devotes himself to scientific inquiry and philosophical speculation. His life makes reason its own medium; he works *in* reason, not simply *by* it. Such a purely intellectual life one carries on by himself, in himself. Such intellectual assistance as others afford is accidental rather than intrinsic. In the life of theory, in *knowing,* in knowing for the sake of knowing, irrespective of any application. reason finds its own full manifestation, is independent and self-sufficing. Such is Aristotle's theoretical psychology.

Turning now to his practical politics, what do we find? The same views are reflected in the classes of men and in the organization of human society. The function of reason as the law of life can operate in a comparatively few. Vegetative and animal functions dominate the masses; bodily appetite and passion overpower their feeble and inconstant intelligence. Lacking reason, which alone constitutes a final end, such persons are not truly ends in themselves. Like physical tools and plants and animals, they are means for attaining ends beyond themselves, though, unlike them, they have enough intelligence to execute with discretion the tasks committed to them. Thus some men are slaves by nature, means for the ends of others. These are the class of natural slaves, not made so by social convention, and not necessarily coincident, of course, with the class of actual slaves.

In such a divided society the great body of free artisans are worse off in one important respect than even the slaves. Like slaves, they are given up to the service of ends external to themselves, but, unlike domestic slaves, they do not enjoy intimate association with the free superior class.

Women, moreover, are classed with slaves and craftsmen. They, too, are animate instrumentalities of reproduction, and of production of the means for a free rational life. Slaves, artisans, and women labor for the means of subsistence for themselves and for their superiors. Thus the latter, being adequately equipped with intelligence, may live the worthy life of leisurely concern with things intrinsically worth while. And so, means become menial, and service becomes servile. The worthy life of the few is conditioned by the unworthy life of the many. Making a living unfits for true living, has no inherent rational meaning, and detracts from the time and energy available for ideal interests.

Turning from Aristotle's psychology and politics with their divisions to his theory of education, what do we find? Exact correspondence. As there are two kinds of occupation, or "arts," the servile and the free, so there are two kinds of education, the base or mechanical, and the liberal or intellectual. The base education consists in training persons to do things, to use tools. Thus personal service is rendered and physical commodities are turned out. Such training is a matter of habituation and technical skill; it is acquired through repetition and assiduity in practice, not through the awakening and nurturing of thought.

But a liberal education aims to train intelligence for its proper office: to know. The less education is concerned with the practical affairs of making and producing, the more it engages intelligence. The less activity has to do with physical things or with the body, the more mental it is. The more mental it is, the higher, the more independent, the more self-sufficing it is. Hence, the only truly liberal or free education is that which makes for power to know as an end in itself, without reference to the practice of even civic duties.

An instructive instance of Aristotle's sharp distinction between menial and liberal education is in his treatment of what we call the "fine" arts,—music, painting, sculpture. The practice, but not the enjoyment, of these he classifies with the menial arts. They all involve physical agencies, constant practice, and external results. Take music, for example. How far should the young be practiced in the playing of instruments? His answer is, enough to appreciate music, but not to produce it professionally. When professional production is the aim, music sinks from the liberal level. "One might then as well teach cooking," says Aristotle. Thus even the freeman's enjoyment of fine art depends upon the hireling who has subordinated the development of his own personality to attaining skill in mechanical execution.

Comment. It would perhaps have capped the climax of Dr. Dewey's argument had he gone on to give Aristotle's conception of God as pure form without any material element at all, pure realization without any remaining potentiality, the thinker not of the material existence but of his own thoughts, not knowing the world and by the world unknown, yet attracting all things toward himself as end even as the beloved attracts the lover.

One may question at this point Dr. Dewey's genetic mode of refuting a position and his social explanation of psychological and philosophical views. It is suggested that Aristotle held the views he did because he was rationalizing the kind of society in which he lived and believed. It is also suggested that views which were the effect of one kind of society are no longer tenable when the social pattern changes. Both of these positions are open to question. A psychologist and a philosopher may hold views independent of the economic and social conditions of which he is a part. Else how would progress through social planning be possible? Else how could the process of thought be free? Else how could a man be ahead of his times? This is not to suggest that a man's thinking is wholly independent of the times in which he lives, far from it; it is only to suggest that a man's thinking is not wholly dependent upon the times in which he lives. Some thinking is rationalizing, conformative; some thinking is creative, reformative. Suppose Lincoln, facing modern slavery, had been a rationalizer!

Now thinking that arises under one set of social conditions may be true as representing ideals, and so may carry over to other social conditions unlike themselves. Euclid's geometry has not been proven false by Riemann and Lobatchevski; it has only been supplemented by new conceptions concerning the nature of space; the changing social conditions have had little to do with it; the changing intellectual conditions have had much to do with it. Ideas arising under conditions of slavery may have truth under conditions of freedom. Aristotle's conception of the soul may have validity under modern democratic conditions; many opponents of slavery think that it has. It is no refutation of his psychology to say we no longer believe in slavery.

And similarly concerning liberal and technical education. The distinction between them is not wiped out by the extinction of Greek slavery. A liberal education is no longer that intended for freemen; it is still that which makes men free. A technical education is no longer that intended for slaves; it is still that which enables men to earn a better living. Whether liberal, and technical, education should be two things or one thing can not be settled by the lapse of Greek slavery. Very likely each man's education should be liberal at the base and technical at the apex, but the conclusion does not follow automatically from the change from Greek aristocratic to modern democratic conditions. Modern conditions themselves may and do need changing!

In this connection it may be recalled that the Greek Sophists were the first Western pragmatists in education. They were "humanists"; they made man the measure of all things; they taught the practical arts of public speaking, domestic economy, how to think and how to act, to the noble youth of Greece. They rejected ideal changeless truths and standards of conduct. Their theory was a form of practice. And they arose under social and economic conditions similar to those of Socrates, Plato, and Aristotle. And their views too survive and have their modern adherents. Here the original argument, if accepted, would tend to undermine pragmatism itself!

The views here presented are in line with those of both a classical scholar and of a contemporary philosopher. One writes: "The most important part of the material with which he [Plato] had to deal in his metaphysical or logical investigations does not vary from age to age or from one country to another. The fundamental characteristics of the processes of rational thinking are the same always and everywhere. So are the processes of sense-perception. So are the physical processes of the material world; 'fire burns both here and in Persia,' as Aristotle says. So is the nature of numbers and figures, which the science of mathematics investigates. Much more, of course, is known about these things in some periods than in others. But the material from which the investigation starts is the same at all times."[1] The same is not so true, as Field points out, for moral and political speculation. Aristotle's speculations, of course, embrace both the meta-

[1] Field, G. C., *Plato and His Contemporaries*, New York, 1930, p. 77.

physical and the political. They partly are and partly are not due to the social conditions of his period.

Likewise, Morris Cohen defends the view that values and historical existence are in a sense independent of each other.[1]

2. The Present Situation

Exposition. The simple fact is that the present situation in both life and education is a continuation of the Greek situation, despite certain social changes. Let us see.

Aristotle simply described without confusion and with sincerity the life before him. But for this his conception would be just personal, a more or less interesting historical curiosity, an illustration of the lack of sympathy or the amount of pedantry co-existent at times with extraordinary intellectual gifts, and could be dismissed as such. The actual social situation has greatly changed since his day: legal serfdom has been abolished; democracy has spread; and science and general education have been extended, not only through schools but also through books, newspapers, travel, and general intercourse. Despite these changes, however, our situation is enough like his situation to merit criticism. His point of view helps us to see ourselves as we are. We too have an educational cleavage dependent on a social cleavage. We too distinguish between culture and utility in education because our society has a learned and an unlearned class, a leisure and a laboring class, a class concerned with intellectual things and controlling others and a class concerned with practical pursuits, without æsthetic appreciation, with a minimum of self-directive thought, being controlled by others.

Be it said there is a right and a wrong in Aristotle. He was certainly permanently right in holding that whatever activity deprives free persons of excellence is mechanical, or, in his words: "any occupation or art or study deserves to be called mechanical if it renders the body or soul or intellect of

[1] Cf. his *Reason and Nature*, New York, 1931, p. 385.

free persons unfit for the exercise and practice of excellence." How much more this statement means if all persons are free! If most men and all women are unfree by nature, a mechanical training for them involved for the Greeks neither intellectual confusion nor moral hypocrisy. But we say all are free by nature, and then provide a mechanical training for the many, depriving them of sharing a worthy life. Our mental confusion and moral hypocrisy remain!

In another respect Aristotle was conditionally right. He held that mercenary and physically injurious pursuits were mechanical, or, in his words: "All mercenary pursuits as well as those which degrade the condition of the body are mechanical, since they deprive the intellect of leisure and dignity." He mistakenly held here that all mercenary pursuits are mechanical; they were in his day; they usually are in our day; but they do not have to be so. His mistake was in taking a social custom for a natural necessity. If gainful pursuits do as a matter of fact deprive the intellect of its exercise and dignity, then indeed are they mechanical, as he said. It profits us nothing to improve on Aristotle's theory and continue the Greek practice of enslaving the intellects of the many. We say we have a better conception than his of the relations of mind and matter, mind and body, intelligence and social service; we say, contrary to his view, that the realms of matter, body, and society, are the proper fields for intellectual self-expression; but our theory is no better than his if our practice remains the same as his; it is better only if the intellects of free persons are freed by their occupations in education and in life.

What was Aristotle's error? It lay in assuming a necessary separation between the free and the slave, understanding and skill, culture and utility, productivity and self-direction, knowledge and practice. We hardly better matters by correcting his theory while tolerating a social state of affairs which generated and sanctioned his theory. Nay, rather, we lose instead of gain by changing from serfdom to citizenship, if our main prize thereby is the increased efficiency of human tools. What boots it to think of intelligence, not with Aristotle, as the organ of pure knowledge, but as the organ of control of nature through action, if we remain content that workers be ignorant and enslaved while remote scientists and captains of industry alone exercise intelligent control? Train the many for skill in production and the few for ornamental knowledge,—this is what we do. If responsible for this practice, we can not honestly criticize the division of life into separate functions and of society into separate classes. We may think with the moderns but we act with the Greeks.

To transcend the Greek philosophy of education and of life, three things are necessary, the first two of which we have to some extent. One is to change the meaning of the theoretical symbols, "free," "rational," "worthy." Another is to change our emotional attitudes toward "labor" and "service," esteeming them worthy and dignified. But the most important is to develop a truly democratic society, in which all share in useful labor and all enjoy a worthy leisure. For this last an educational revolution is needed. It is here already but it is not complete. The "masses" have been somewhat emancipated, politically and economically; this emancipation has shown itself in the development of a public, free, common school system. The idea that learning is properly a monopoly of those few predestined to govern social affairs has been destroyed. But the aristocratic idea still prevails that a truly cultural education for the few has nothing directly in common with industrial affairs, and that a useful education for the many has nothing directly in common with the nurture of appreciation and the liberation of thought. Let this solid remainder of Greek practice be destroyed!

What an inconsistent mixture our actual educational system is! It is a consequence of the alleged opposition of labor and leisure, of utility and culture. Some examples: Certain studies are retained in college and in college preparatory courses because "liberal," *i.e.* useless for practical ends; and this view has filtered into and infected elementary education. On the other hand, certain "utilitarian" concessions have been made to modern economic activities and to the masses engaged in earning a living; so we have special schools for the professions, for engineering, for manual training, for commerce, and we have vocational and pre-vocational courses. Even the "three R's" in elementary education are taught in the same spirit. The result? An inorganic composite of "cultural" and "utilitarian" subjects, in which the former are not dominated by the purpose to be socially serviceable and the latter do not liberate imagination and the power to think.

Worse confusion remains behind. Subjects labelled "practical" we teach in a useless way as though they were liberal, and subjects labelled "liberal" we teach in a technical way as though they were practical. All this is due to the fact that ours is an inherited situation. The outcome would probably be better if either of the two principles in the mixture were consistently followed. It would be hard to find a subject in the curriculum without the evil results of the compromise between liberality and utility. To illustrate, natural science is both recommended by some and opposed by some because of its practical utility, but it is taught as a special accomplishment without applications. On the other hand, music and literature are recommended for cultural reasons and are then taught as though they were practical with chief emphasis on the acquisition of technical skill. A specially instructive case is the elementary studies of the first few years of schooling,—reading, spelling, writing, and arithmetic. They are popularly supposed to be taught because they are useful; they are instruments for more schooling or for life, so there is much drill to secure automatic skill. But even so the idea of utility is not thoroughly adopted; in that case they would be tied up with situations in which they are directly needed and immediately helpful; instead they are treated as preparatory to remote situations; they are reduced to symbolic devices, they are isolated from practical application. Here is a survival of the idea of liberal training divorced from utility, though in an anemic form. For its ancestor, turn to the Greek schools. There from the earliest years the acquisition of skill was subordinated to the acquisition of literary and musical content having æsthetic and moral significance. We are neither so liberal as the Greek education of freemen nor so practical as the Greek training of slaves; our compromises result in confusion.

What is the educational solution of the problem of culture and utility? A course of study both liberal and useful at the same time. To believe that culture and utility are hostile is only superstition. A useful subject is not illiberal; a liberal subject is not useless. There is a narrow utility which is illiberal, but there is a broad utility which is liberal. Aim at utility and sacrifice breadth, and you get limited utility. Aim at utility and include breadth, include, that is, the development of imagination, the refining of taste, and the deepening of insight, and you get broad utility, really a cultivated utility. Narrow utility is restricted to routine activities under the supervision of others; broad utility is applicable to new situations under one's own personal control. A culture that is useless and a utility that is uncultivated we reject in a democratic society as survivals of aristocratic Greece.

The same activities that to the Greeks lacked culture may to the moderns have culture. The reason is that these activities themselves through applied science have acquired intellectual, personal, and social meanings. The Greeks regarded farming and trading as illiberal not merely because they were useful but because they were rule-of-thumb occupations, pursued for external results, not requiring a trained intelligence, not yielding a personal appreciation of their meaning. Plato deprecated the learning of arithmetic and geometry for practical ends; it was natural for him to do so, for, in his day, the practical uses to which they were put were few in number, lacking in content, and mercenary in quality. But now their social uses have increased, and in so doing their liberalizing and their practical value approach each other. And so generally; the most important occupations of to-day depend on applied mathematics, physics, and chemistry. Science in industry is replacing custom and routine. The understanding of economic production and consumption in moderr society involve universal geography and world-wide politics. In our day the cultivated vocationalist is liberally educated.

Why do we not fully recognize this truth? Because of the conditions under which so much work is still carried on. We train, we do not educate, our workers. We train them to tend our machines skillfully, automatically, mechanically. We do not furnish their minds for the enjoyment of the leisure our machines allow both on and off duty. Their preliminary years in schools are spent in acquiring rudimentary symbols of learning, not in the study of science, literature, and history. Worse yet, they do not work for themselves, they work for their employers for wages; they are means, not ends; they lack insight into the social aims of their pursuits; they lack personal interest in what they do; they do not act freely and intelligently; they are our modern industrial slaves. Their activities are illiberal, not because of the inherent character of the activities but because of the limited character of the education they have received. Such education, aiming simply at skill in performance, is not only illiberal, it is immoral.

The solution? Democracy in education and in industry as well as in politics. Democracy will give us at one stroke both a better education and a better economic order. Education in a democratic society will reconcile liberal nurture with social serviceableness; all will share efficiently and happily in productive occupations; men will have a vital concern in the ends controlling their activity; they may thus continue to do the same work, but now as free men. Democracy provides for direct participation in control; we have democracy in politics; we lack it in industry; in industry control remains external and autocratic; whence comes the split between inner mental action and outer physical action, of which the traditional distinction between a liberal education and a utilitarian education is the reflex. Let education unify the disposition of the members of society; in so doing it will help unify society itself. The problem of education in a democratic society is to heal the dualism between the inner and the outer man, between thinking and doing, by constructing a course of studies which makes thinking a guide of free practice for all. Leisure should be a reward of labor, not exemption from it.

Comment. There are several things to note here. The first is that Dr. Dewey is revolutionary in his aim but not in his method. He aims at an industrial democracy but his method is that of educational reform. He is a pedagogic Fabian. We are in the thick of these economic problems to-day. An education that could give us an industrial democracy might mean either a modified capitalism or the overthrow of capitalism. With industrial democracy as an aim there is no need to quarrel; something of the kind is already here and growing; profits are being shared, workers are participating in control increasingly, workers are becoming joint owners of the business; the personal relations in industry are being established and emphasized.

Going as far as he does toward the economic reorganization of society, one can understand how Dr. Dewey is criticized by the economic radicals for not going further and by the economic conservatives for going so far. For the economic radical it may be said that the logic of Dr. Dewey's position seems to demand that he go further. Historically he holds that society has made our schools; but he recommends for the future that our schools make our society. What hope is there that they can or will? The schools work with the young generation; they are supported by adult society; they reflect the adult society that supports them. How then can they do other than continue the type of society in which adults believe? The adults live where the economic problems are, where the changes are going on. Is not the expectation that the school will change society the use of education as "preparation" after all? Should not an adult society reform itself instead of expecting the school to do it? If it is a problem of education at all, is it not a problem of adult education? So might a radical reformer turn the argument.

Two things are to be said there. One is, that the ideals acquired in progressive schools and colleges are sometimes actually lost in the mælstrom of our competitive economic order, and in this respect Dr. Dewey's prescription for a reformed society is faulty. The other is just the opposite, that one in life stands by the reforming ideals of his youth and becomes a conscious centre for social improvement, and in this respect Dr. Dewey's prescription is valid. Which is the more frequent outcome is hard to say. Just to what extent the schools can become an agency of social reform is consequently uncertain. But it is certain that the proposed remedy would operate slowly and without social cataclysm. The objectives of Dr. Dewey are similar to those of Soviet Russia; his "ideology" and methodology are different. While the reformed schools he proposes might slowly reform society, a transformed society in Russia has quickly transformed the schools. If America ever chooses at all between Dr. Dewey and Russia, it will probably choose Dr. Dewey. And the reason will be the economic one that the American working man has a high standard of living.

Turning from the social and economic to the educational aspects of the problem of labor and leisure, what shall we say of Dr. Dewey's proposed union of culture and utility? This, it is a one-way union. Much culture may be attached to any utility but utility simply can not be attached to all culture. By utility is here meant what Dr. Dewey means,—earning a livelihood and social serviceableness. Every occupation of man may and should have its meaning culturally extended through social, geographical, and historical associations. But the culture to which utility can not be attached is the set of personal interests an individual may have over and above his useful occupation or occupations. Such interests are his avocation, perhaps his hobby. He may collect stamps or coins, do cabinet work in wood, read Latin epigraphy, compose poetry nobody sees, commit classic selections to memory, study the Chinese ideographs, read ancient Egyptian history, sight the stars with his own telescope, dig into Einstein, and so on. Utility in the sense defined? No. Useful only in the sense that thereby is a personal interest gratified and leisure time enjoyed. That such interests make one a larger personality, more interesting, more intellectual, perhaps more æsthetic in taste, is undeniable. But this is culture. All utility may acquire some culture; not all culture can acquire utility. Some branches of mathematics are liberalizing without being socially useful. Life is for enjoyment as well as for service. If one still insists that enjoyment is use, then the reply is that "use" has ceased to have a useful meaning. A useful activity sends one beyond itself for its significance; an enjoyable activity is its own excuse for being. Dr. Dewey's proposal can succeed in making all utilitarian education more liberal; it can not succeed in making all liberal education utilitarian. This defect is inherent in the pragmatic philosophy itself which holds all ideas are only tools, allowing no knowledge to exist for its own sake, and maintaining that the human intelligence, responsible as it is for all theories of education and of life, is only "an organ for the control of nature through action."

CHAPTER XX

INTELLECTUAL AND PRACTICAL STUDIES

1. The Opposition of Experience and True Knowledge

Exposition. On way of regarding experience and knowledge is to oppose them to each other. In this case experience is regarded as changing and knowledge is regarded as changeless. This is the Greek way of regarding the two. It accounts for the corresponding opposition between the practical and intellectual studies. The practical studies were based on experience and the intellectual on knowledge. But in truth this Greek way of opposing experience and knowledge is mistaken, the notion that true knowledge is changeless should be given up, and the practical and intellectual studies should not be two but one. We will go somewhat more in detail into these views. Just as we saw labor and leisure were mistakenly opposed to each other, so also are practice and theory, execution and intelligence, activity and knowledge. The same Greek social conditions are the fountain of these false oppositions. The alleged separation of doing and knowing is connected so directly with certain educational problems that we must discuss it explicitly.

The notion is that knowledge is derived from a higher source than practical activity, and so possesses a more spiritual worth. The notion is false, but it has a long history. Plato and Aristotle first consciously opposed experience and reason. Though differing in many respects, these thinkers agreed in identifying experience with practical concerns, whose purpose was material, and whose organ was the body; experience always involved lack, need, desire, and was never self-sufficing; it was a perpetual flux. But knowledge was free from practical reference; it existed for its own sake; its source and organ were an immaterial mind; it dealt with spiritual or ideal interests; it was complete in itself; it was concerned with eternal truth. What a contrast!

Plato said that philosophers should be kings in the ideal state. This is a social statement. It means that rational intelligence should regulate human affairs, securing unity, order, and law. Negatively it means that human affairs should not be regulated by habit, appetite, impulse, and emotion, signifying multiplicity, discord, and irrational fluctuations from one estate to another.

Experience at its best to these thinkers is represented in the various handicrafts,—the arts of peace and war. The discipline of experience leads to skill. So with the cobbler, the flute player, the soldier. The senses, and the other bodily organs, have had repeated contact with things, whose results have been preserved and consolidated as ability to foresee and to practice. Such knowledge and skill were "empirical"; they were not based on insight into rational and universal principles; they were the result of a large number of separate trials,—what we call the "method of trial and error," with special emphasis on the accidental character of the trials. The ability to control was a matter of routine, a rule-of-thumb procedure; if the new situation was like the old, it might work well enough; otherwise, failure was likely. The common craftsmen of Athens mistakenly assumed that, because they could do the specific things of their trades, they could manage household affairs, education, and politics.

Experience thus has a definitely material character; it deals with physical things in relation to the body; it is an affair of the senses; the senses are connected with the appetites, wants, and desires; they lay hold on things which give pleasure by satisfying the wants of the body; the body itself is but the substratum of a higher life; the senses do not lay hold on the reality of things. Moreover, there is something morally dangerous about experience, suggested by such words as sensual, carnal, material, and worldly. Further, experience is ineradicably connected with the changing, the shifting, the manifold, the desires, the variable, the untrustworthy, the unstable, the anarchic, the "many." Experience is not dependable, changing as it does from person to person, from day to day, from country to country. From experience come warrings, conflicts, both within the individual, and between individuals. Local customs vary, so no standard of belief can issue from them. The logical outcome was drawn by the Sophists: that is good and true which to each individual at each time and place seems good and true.

In contrast, true knowledge, reason, "science," are not so. They lay hold of the immaterial, the ideal, the spiritual, the morally praiseworthy, the single, the uniform. They assure coherence and harmony.

All this opposition between experience and true knowledge comes to a head in the contrast between doing and knowing. Practice falls within experience. Doing proceeds from needs and aims at change. To produce and consume are to alter. All the obnoxious characters of change attach to doing. Knowing, on the other hand, having a permanent object, is itself permanent; it grasps a thing intellectually, theoretically; it is out of the region of chance and change; its object, truth, has no lack, it is calm and untouched by the perturbations of sense; it is universal and eternal. Only the law of reason can properly subject the world of experience, giving it control, steadiness, and order.

Whence came this sharp antithesis? In part from the fact that philosophy in Athens began as a criticism of custom. Tradition and custom as providing standards of knowledge and conduct proved unsatisfactory. They held men in bondage. What should replace them? Athenian philosophy hit upon reason as the answer. It was to be the only adequate guide of belief and activity. But custom and tradition were identified with experience. So reason, the new authority, and experience, the old authority, declared war on each other.

Reason held itself superior to experience as unstable and inadequate; experience in turn refused to acknowledge the authority of reason. So what began in the historical criticism of custom ended in the philosophical opposition of experience and reason.

But why identify experience with custom? The grounds for the identification are not far to seek. The condition of things was unsatisfactory. But this state of affairs was itself due to custom. The customs and beliefs of different communities were found to be different. Increasing trade, travel, colonizations, migrations, wars, broadened the intellectual horizon, bringing the knowledge of different communities. Civil disturbances had become one of the customs in Athens; the fortunes of the city fluctuated with factional strife. The increase of leisure accompanying the broadening horizon brought new knowledge of nature, with new curiosity and speculation. The questions arose, What is constant in Nature? What is universal in Society? And the answer came: the universal principle and the constant essence are apprehended by reason; the changing and the unstable are perceived by the senses. The work of the senses was preserved in memory and imagination, in habit and in skill,—and this was the world of experience. Thus, because customs were matters of experience and were unsatisfactory, experience came to be debased and reason exalted.

Not that all the sharp distinctions thus portrayed persisted in their fullness. Nevertheless they did profoundly influence men's subsequent thinking, especially about education. Here are some examples: the contempt for the senses, for sense observation, for physical science; the contrasting high regard for mathematical and logical science; the disesteem of knowledge of the concrete; the contrasting feeling that the knowledge which deals with ideal symbols is high and worthy; the scorn of all particulars not deductively subsumed under a universal; the disregard of the body; and the depreciation of arts and crafts as instruments utilizing intellectuality. All these things found sanction in the opposition of experience and reason, the practical and the intellectual.

Mediæval philosophy accepted, continued, and reënforced the same tradition. To it experience dealt with mundane, profane, and secular affairs; these were indeed practically necessary but relatively unimportant when compared with supernatural objects of knowledge. All action was subordinate to the knowledge of supreme reality, whose contemplation was the ultimate end of man. Such knowledge meant relationship to God, and the enjoyment of the eternal bliss of that relation. It was the beatific vision.

Take an illustration from medicine in our own day. If a physician is called an empiric, it is discreditable; it implies he lacks scientific training; that he has learned only from practice; that there is no reason in what he does; he does not know where his knowledge begins or ends; in new situations he must pretend; he makes claims without justification; he trusts to luck; he imposes on others; he "bluffs"; he degenerates into the quack. Thus we still discredit experience and practice,—the real source of all our true knowledge.

All told, take the Greek philosophic tradition, add the literary character of Roman education, add again mediæval otherworldliness, add still again the aristocratic social preference for the alleged higher studies, and you have four great forces tending to subordinate the practical to the intellectual. Small wonder that the higher schools and educational philosophies were drawn into their train.

Comment. Again, let it be noted that Dr. Dewey is utilizing the genetic mode of refutation. The practical and the intellectual should not be opposed to each other because the social conditions under which the opposition arose have changed. Thus he holds that problems are not solved, they are outgrown; philosophies are not refuted, they are shelved. The river of time carries all its sons away.

But this mode of refutation is emotionally unsatisfactory and intellectually unconvincing. What we want to know is whether there really is a world of reality, changeless in character, which is grasped by the intellect, which remains despite man's denial and social change, which is implied even by the process of change itself.

Now thought does possess just such a world, and it can be shown to do so. In general, it is the realm of concepts, essences, universals. The very notion of change implies the changeless. Without the permanent there is no impermanent. The only constant may be change, yet there is a constant. If there were only change, we might not be conscious of it, as we are not conscious of the weight of the air which is always present but never sensed. Certain characteristics even of changing phenomena do not change, for example, all phenomena have both form and content, both figure and stuff. Here is a formal changeless truth about our changing world. There may be many changing shades of blue, but the truth of the proposition that all sensory blues have some extension does not change. There are many pairs of twos but the truth that two pairs of twos is four does not change. The illustrations are many of the fact that there is a changeless realm of truths, grasped by thought. The changeless conceptual order is one thing, the changing perceptual order is a different thing. And the changeless conceptual order permeates the changing perceptual order as changeless space permeates changing matter. These views remain in any actual or conceivable form of human society. Educationally, they mean that there is an intellectual which is concerned, as the pragmatic philosophy says, with the changing practical; and also that there is an intellectual, denied by the pragmatic philosophy, which is concerned with the changeless order of things. Our education should adjust us to the changeless as well as the changing. That is the kind of world we live in.

Two quotations will be in order at this point, one from a psychologist, and one from a mathematician. Says the psychologist: "Each conception thus eternally remains what it is, and never can become another. . . . The paper, a moment ago white, I may now see to be scorched black. But my *conception* 'white' does not change into my *conception* 'black.' . . . Thus, amid the flux of opinions and of physical things, the world of conceptions, or the things intended to be thought about, stands stiff and immutable, like Plato's Realm of Ideas."[1]

The other quotation: "Transcending the flux of the sensuous universe, there exists a stable world of pure thought, a divinely ordered world of ideas, accessible to man, free from the mad dance of time, infinite and eternal."[2]

Our conclusion here must be that the opposition between changing experience and changeless reason can not be entirely rejected. Many things change in our practical world; with these man's intellect may be concerned. Some things do not change in our conceptual world; with these man's intellect may also be concerned. Our debt to Plato remains.

2. The Modern Theory of Experience and Knowledge

Exposition. By "modern" is not here meant "contemporary"; the term is used to refer to the post-Renaissance theories of the seventeenth and eighteenth centuries. In brief, this theory is somewhat like the Greek, just considered, in identifying experience with sensation, but it is unlike the Greek in making knowledge dependent on sensation. These views too, as we shall now see, provide an unsatisfactory basis for a philosophy of education. They make experience entirely too passive.

These modern reformers, like Bacon, Locke, and Helvétius, held views concerning reason very different from those of Plato, and much less appreciative. To Plato, as we saw, reason meant the principle of reform, of progress, of control, devotion to whose cause meant breaking through the limitations of custom, and getting at things as they really are. To these

[1] James, W., *Psychology*, pp. 239–240.

[2] Keyser, C. J., *The Human Worth of Rigorous Thinking*, Columbia University Press, New York, 1925, p. 57.

modern reformers reason meant either blank mental forms or prejudices. In the one case reason was not self-sufficient, and in the other case it was evil. Reason as blank forms, *a priori* notions, universal principles, had to be filled in by experience, by sensation, to become significant and valid. Reason as prejudices were dogmas imposed by authority, masquerading and finding protection under august names. The need, as Bacon felt it, was to break with reason and resort to experience. Conceptions which "anticipated nature" and imposed human opinions upon her were bonds to be broken. Experience would tell us what nature is like. This Baconian appeal to experience meant a break with authority; openness to new impressions; eagerness to discover and invent; the irruption into the mind of things as they really are, free from the veil of preconceived ideas. Men's minds were no longer absorbed as in the mediæval days of tabulating and systematizing received ideas and "proving" them by means of their own mutual relations.

The effect of the change from the Greek to these modern views was two-fold, both lamentable. Experience ceased to be practical and became cognitive, and the mind ceased to be regarded as active and became passive. (1) Experience ceased to mean ways of doing and being done to; it came to mean apprehending material to balance and check reasoning; a way of knowing. How good a way is it? That was the only question. If "intellectualism" designates an emphatic interest in knowing isolated from doing, here is intellectualism beyond even that of the Greeks. Practice was indeed subordinated to knowledge by the Greeks but it was not treated as a kind of tag-end, or aftermath, of knowledge as by these modern philosophic empiricists. (2) As "experience" now was a means of basing truth upon objects, upon nature, the mind was looked at as purely receptive. Objects can truly impress themselves only upon a passive mind; for the mind to be active in knowing would vitiate the process, would defeat its own purpose. The ideal for the mind of man was a maximum of receptivity!

The most influential of the empiricists was John Locke (d. 1704). The empiricists derive all knowledge from impressions made upon the mind by objects. Locke allowed two sources of knowledge, viz., sensation and reflection. The sensation came from the object; the reflection from the mind. At birth the mind, he held, is like a blank sheet of white paper, or like a wax tablet without any engraving on it (*tabula rasa*). Still, the mind, though blank and empty at birth, has powers it exercises on the material received. Such powers, or faculties, are discrimination, comparison, abstraction, generalization, etc. These faculties work up the sense-material into definite and organized forms. They even evolve new ideas on their own account, such as the fundamental conceptions of morality and mathematics.

In crossing the channel, British empiricism became French sensationalism (cf. the writings of Baron Holbach, Lamettrie, Condillac, and Helvétius). The impressions made upon the mind by objects were generally termed "sensations," whence the name, "sensationalism" which, of course, has other distinct meanings. The doctrine of sensationalism identifies knowledge with the reception and association of sensory impressions. It belongs to the latter part of the eighteenth century. What if the faculties allowed the mind by Locke were themselves only sensations? Peculiar sensations, indeed, made in us by the conjoint presence of other sensations. Thus even discernment and judgment became effects in us of prior sensations. The French successors of Locke razed away the faculties from the mind, deriving even these from the sensations received. Thus the doctrine of mind as passive and sensational experience as cognitive reaches its limit.

What were the educational effects of the view that experience is a matter of sensation upon which knowledge depends? These were several, viz., (1) greatly to increase faith in what education could accomplish; (2) the rejection of bookishness;

(3) the rejection of tradition; (4) the introduction into schools of real things, "object-lessons"; and (5) the exclusion of active pursuits from the school. The second alone of these was an unmitigated good.

(1) It was a time when education was fostered as a method of social reform. The "sensationalists," who advocated a first-hand contact with things, found the harmony in nature which was lacking in society. The emptier the mind at the beginning, the more it can be made into anything through its educational environment. Helvétius was perhaps the most extreme and consistent sensationalist. He proclaimed the omnipotence of education.

(2) Empiricism protested against mere book learning in school. This was its directly beneficial office. Without objects to impress the mind, no knowledge. Things before words! Without prior objects, words are symbols. Words without objects give a knowledge of the symbols themselves, not of the realities symbolized. The knowledge of symbols is not instructive.

(3) Sensationalism combatted mere tradition. Doctrines resting merely on authoritative opinion it repudiated. It set up its own test of knowledge: What are the real objects of sense from which these ideas, beliefs, opinions, and doctrines are derived? If these basic objects could not be produced, the ideas in question were pronounced untrue; they were the result of false associations and combinations of sensation. Such crude psychology!

(4) With the rejection of bookishness went the demand for instruction by means of objects. The object must make its own impression upon each individual. Empiricism demanded a first-hand contact with things. The impression must be made upon *my* own mind. The object itself is the direct first-hand source of knowledge. The further we get from the object, the vaguer the ideas and the more the error.

(5) Practice, which we have taken as the source of knowledge, was excluded from the school. Active pursuits had no

place in the schools. If allowed at all, they were brought in for purely utilitarian ends,—to acquire habits by drill.

What shall we say of these effects of sensationalism on education? They were better on the negative than on the positive side; better in the elimination of bookishness and unsupported opinion than in the substitution of object-lessons. The full use of a good thing was here vitiated by a false theory. It was good to have first-hand acquaintance with natural objects in the schoolroom. The theory did not allow anything to be done with the object; it allowed only an impression to be made by it on the mind. The object was isolated, its sensory quality was isolated, so that the sense-impression as a unit of knowledge might be the more distinct. Sense-activity became an isolated end in itself. Instruction was reduced to the physical gymnastics of the sense-organs, thinking was neglected. Strictly speaking, the theory did not allow thinking in connection with sense observation; thinking came after the impressions had been made in properly sorting and combining them.

Because of the bad theory of sensationalism, it has never been widely put into practice educationally, except in early infancy. Instead, it has been modestly used to lend greater "interest" to barren symbols, and to give point by illustrations to "rationalistic" knowledge, such as, definitions, rules, classifications, and the use of symbols. It did inject the new factor of natural objects into the older curriculum; it brought about a greater regard for pictures and graphic descriptions; it reduced the importance attached to verbal symbols; thus it incidentally modified older studies and methods. But it required supplementation; its scope was too limited; the resources of direct sense-perception are too meagre; and there are important matters which do appeal more directly to thought. Because of its inadequacy, sensationalism left practically unimpaired the reign in the curriculum of informationism, abstractionism, and the "rationalistic" studies.

We may sum up under three heads our objections to sensationalistic empiricism as an educational philosophy of knowing. In doing so, our own views will become clearer. (*a*) The work of education is constructive, not critical. Education needs to build up new experiences into intellectual habits. Everything should be as correct as possible from the start. Mind denotes responsiveness to meaning. Meaning exists only in a context. In contrast, sensationalism was critical; it destroyed hard and fast dogmas; it presupposes the existence of old beliefs needing to be revised or eliminated; the historical value of the theory is in its negative attitude; it is unfitted for the constructive task of education. It falsely regarded mind as response to direct physical stimuli; it falsely identified knowledge with a combination of sense-impressions. The theory led in the schoolroom to extolling physical excitations, or else to heaping up isolated objects and qualities.

(*b*) Direct impressions, though having the advantage of being first-hand, have the disadvantage of being limited in range. Some illustrations will make the point clear. Home-geography is all right as far as it goes, but it does not go far enough. Children should be directly acquainted with the natural surroundings of their homes; thereby ideas about portions of the earth beyond perception are made real; and thereby intellectual curiosity is aroused. But geographical knowledge can not be limited to the home environments; that would be a fatal restriction. Again, in realizing number relations, it may be helpful to utilize such things as beans, shoe pegs, and counters. But they should not arrest growth on the low plane of specific physical objects, thus becoming an obstacle to arithmetical understanding; they should aid in the apprehension of meaning. In the historic growth of our number system, the use of the fingers as numerical symbols got in the way; so especial symbols were developed as tools of mathematical calculation. Just so, the individual must develop from concrete to abstract symbols whose meaning involves conceptual thinking. This desirable development is hampered by unique absorption at the outset in the physical object of sense.

(*c*) Sensationalistic empiricism has a false psychology of mental development. Children grow not by being impressed by physical objects but by trying to use them. Experience is not passive reception; it is active initiation; it is instinctive and impulsive activities; it is interaction with things. The experience of an infant consists of what he does to things and what things in turn do to him. He handles, throws, pounds, tears, an object; what happens to the object directs his subsequent activities. The traditional empirical philosophy neglects the deep-seated motor factors of experience; it is a fatal defect. A scheme of object lessons leading to passively received sensory qualities is as uninteresting as it is mechanical. On this point the Greeks knew better; their notion of experience as a practical matter is closer to fact than the post-renaissance notion of it as a mode of knowing by means of sensations. Because of these three defects, sensationalistic empiricism can not furnish a satisfactory philosophy of the learning process.

Comment. Undoubtedly the school of sensationalism provides an inadequate philosophy of knowing and experience. It is too bare, too mechanical, too deterministic, too naturalistic. Still, the discussion of it in the text leads us to make three suggestions. The first concerns the real importance of sensations. They may not be important enough to provide an adequate basis for a philosophy of knowing, but no philosophy of knowing can dispense with them. The sensory qualities of experiences can be directly known to us only through sensations, of course. All the colors, all the sounds, all felt physical contacts, all odors, all tastes, all muscular and joint movements and strains, are first of all sensations. Without them to awaken the mind into activity, we should not only lack knowledge of the sensory qualities of the world, we should probably be without knowledge altogether.

This leads, second, to the recognition of the importance of passivity; not that passivity is an adequate foundation for an educational philosophy, but that it is indispensable. It is one phase of our experience. We are active when we do things to our environment; we are passsive when our environment does things to us. What is done to us is probably as significant as what we do. Sensations themselves are received passively as stimuli; they are not actively created without stimulation. The nervous system may be tensely set for their reception as a tiger stalks its prey; still one must wait for the stimulus to arrive from without The educational uses of quiet and silence have not been adequately recognized.

Third, we may note the importance of sensory activity for its own sake, apart from the use to which the things sensed are put. One may lie on his back on the ground and enjoy looking at the blue sky overhead. He is not trying to do anything with the sky, he is seeing it with pleasure on its own account. So with harmonious sounds, sweet tastes, pleasant perfumes, smooth surfaces, and the like. When a sensory experience develops pleasure in itself, apart from the uses of the object sensed, we have one form of æsthetic enjoyment. Such sensory experiences do not lead on to further activity in any practical way; they tend to continue themselves, they are worth while on their own account. Thus, while agreeing in rejecting sensationalism, we would emphasize the importance of sensation, of passivity, and of certain sensory experiences on their own account.

3. Experience as Experimentation

Exposition. Experience is experimentation. This is our own view in contrast with the rationalism of the Greeks, which put reason above experience, and with the sensationalism of the early moderns, who put experience as sensation above reason. Our view will put reason in experience.

This view of experience as experimentation will stand out more distinctly if the reasons for rejecting sensationalism are held clearly in mind. These are two, viz., (1) it is contradicted by modern psychology, and (2) it is contradicted by modern scientific method. To each of these we will devote some consideration.

(1) As already intimated, sensational empiricism omits the primary position in experience of active response. Children learn about things not by being passively impressed by them but by putting them to use. Five minutes of unprejudiced observation in a nursery is enough to refute sensationalism. The infant does not passively receive impressions of such qualities as sound, color, and hardness; he makes motor responses to sensory stimulation, he reaches and handles, he learns from the results of such responses. He does not learn isolated, ready-made, sensory qualities of things; he learns the changes in the behavior of things and persons including himself, produced by his activity; in brief, he learns connections between acts and consequences. Even sensory qualities, like red color, high pitch, hard and soft, are learned through the activities they stimulate and the consequences of these activities. Children learn about persons in the same way; they respond to persons, and persons respond to them. What things and persons do to us and what we in turn do to them is experience; they further and check our action, we produce changes in them; it is all a process of experimentation. Sensory qualities are not impressed on a passive mind; experience is had by an active organism responding to stimulation.

(2) The methods of science teach the same lesson. These methods have to their credit the revolutionizing of our knowledge of the world since the seventeenth century; they are the refinement of the methods of learning in the nursery; they are only experimentation under deliberately controlled conditions. The infant with his ball; the cobbler with his leather, awl, needle, thread, and wax; the scientist with his acid and metal; these all are learning in the same way; they are all

experimenting; they all are using the only method to acquire an adequate knowledge of the world. Of course the purpose of the cobbler is trade, not knowledge. Science is the extension of the child's method of learning; more sense data are had, by the aid of microscope, telescope, and other experimental apparatus; the data arouse new ideas, hypotheses, theories; general ideas as tools, like those of mathematics, are required; such tools aid in conducting experimental inquiries and in formulating their results.

This scientific procedure was a stumbling block to the Greeks and foolishness to the early moderns. The Greeks looked for true knowledge to reason above experience, not to a cobbler punching holes. The early moderns, like Francis Bacon, looked for true knowledge to sense perceptions, supposed to contain within themselves some universal "form" or "species" in a disguising mask which reason could strip off. In contrast the scientific method neither puts reason above experience, nor experience above reason, but puts reason in experience,—defining problems, collecting data, forming hypotheses, drawing and testing conclusions. This is scientific experience, and this is experimentation.

There results in our day a new philosophy of knowledge and of experience. Rational knowledge and experience are no longer opposed to each other as with the Greeks. Experience is no longer a mere summarizing of the more or less chance results of the past, as with the early moderns. Experience ceases to be a matter of chance, impulse, and custom. Experience becomes experimenting, inspired by a purpose, guided by an aim, conducted by method, leading to consequences. Such experience is reasonable, rational, significant, enlightening, instructive. When experience thus becomes rational and reason becomes functional in experience, what happens to the old antithesis between empiricism and rationalism? It vanishes, like the human situation of master and slave which once lent it meaning and relative justification. A new science gives us a new epistemology to match a new society.

Returning now to our main topic of the intellectual and practical studies. What happens to their opposition? It may and should vanish too, it is not intrinsic and necessary, it is dependent upon modifiable conditions. Practical activities and studies *may* be intellectually narrow and trivial, a matter of routine, pursued under authority, aiming at some external result. But they do not *have* to be so. Childhood and youth,—the period of schooling, allow practical activities to be carried on in a different and more liberal spirit. Our discussion of thinking showed it deals effectively only with practical situations. Our discussion of subject matter showed it develops finally into logical form out of childlike work and play. Our previous chapter shows leisure as the true spirit of labor. Our present chapter shows the intellectual is a function of the practical. These conclusions all indicate the continuity of all the valuable phases of education and of life.

We will here for convenience sum up our now familiar results concerning experience and the school in three propositions.

(i) Experience primarily consists of the *active* relations between a human being and his natural and social surroundings. These relations are reciprocal. Either the individual or the environment may initiate the activity. When the environment initiates, the individual undergoes stimulation, checking, or deflection of activity. When the individual initiates, the environment causes him to succeed or fail; he undergoes the consequences of his own efforts. Through connecting these initial acts with their consequences, both his own deeds and things and men acquire meanings. He and his world become intelligible and meaningful.

What then is the business of schooling? The purposeful providing of an environment, interaction with which involves acquiring important meanings. Such meanings become in turn instruments of further learning, as we saw when discussing the rôle of reflection in experience.

But are not children out of school in most active relations with their environment? Yes, and the results are vital and genuine as far as they go. But, as we have repeatedly seen, such activities are limited in many ways. The environment is not deliberately planned; it is not always adapted to promote understanding; some powers are left undeveloped, being undirected; others are stimulated only occasionally or whimsically; others grow into habits of routine skill at the expense of resourcefulness and inventiveness; the chance activities so stimulated bear an accidental relation to insight and thinking.

No, the business of the school is not to transport youth from an active to a passive environment, requiring a cramped study of the records of the learning of others. Rather is it to transport from an environment of unregulated to regulated activities, regulated to guide learning. *"Intellectual" studies are not opposed to practical pursuits, they intellectualize them.* The progressive schools have laid hold of this principle, more or less consciously; it remains to grasp it more firmly and to practice it more widely.

(ii) The practical pursuits of modern man are of a kind to allow intellectualizing. Play and work in the modern school, reflecting the content of modern social life, may be intellectualized. Modern occupations,—domestic, agricultural, manufacturing, transportation, communication, are instinct with applied science. It has not always been so. Practical activities in the Greek and mediæval periods were mostly matters of routine, external, even servile; this was due to the social environment of master and slave or the noble and the peasant. Small wonder that educators rejected such practical pursuits as unfitted to cultivate intelligence. True enough it is that many modern workers are unaware of the intellectual content of the activities in which they engage. This, however, is only another reason why the schools should utilize these pursuits, thus allowing the coming generation to acquire what the present generation lacks, and to carry on labor not blindly but intelligently.

(iii) The progress of experimental science has given the most direct blow at the traditional prestige of purely "intellectual" studies, at the traditional separation of knowing from doing. This progress has demonstrated many things, among them the fact that all genuine knowledge, all fruitful understanding, is the offspring of *doing.* When men wish to find out something about things, they have to do something to things, they have to alter conditions. The growth of knowledge, of the power of explanation, of right classification, involve the analysis and rearrangement of facts which can not be done purely mentally, just inside the head. This is the lesson of the laboratory method. All education has to learn it. Etymology suggests that in the laboratory one discovers *labor:* the conditions under which it is not merely externally productive but intellectually fruitful. In too many cases at present even the use of the laboratory results only in acquiring an additional mode of technical skill. For this evil result there are several reasons, viz., the laboratory still remains too largely an isolated resource; it is not resorted to until pupils are too old to derive full benefit from it; it is still surrounded by other studies where traditional methods isolate intellect from activity.

The Greeks were right: experience is primarily practical, a matter of doing and undergoing the consequences. The sensationalists were wrong: experience is not primarily cognitive. But the Greeks were wrong too in separating knowing from doing. Doing should be so directed as to take up into its context all fruitful ideas and so to result in securely tested knowledge. In this way experience ceases to be empirical and becomes experimental, and reason ceases to be a remote, ideal faculty and becomes all the resources of fruitful, meaningful, activity. Educationally, this change denotes the plans of studies and methods developed in the preceding discussions.

Comment. Dr. Dewey has dropped the liberal New England theology of his upbringing, and all Puritan social conventions, but he has retained his New England conscience concerning work. Every thought must be harnessed to labor. There is to be no intellectual interest which does not guide a practical activity. Following Kant's famous phrase, we may say that in Dr. Dewey's system action without thought is blind, while thought without action is empty. There is to be no occasional daydreaming, no intellectual idling, no playing with concepts, no mental fooling around, no joy of thinking for its own sake, no revelling in bare intellectuality, no sheer speculation, no probing beyond the practical, no vacation for mentality, no philosophizing in the region of the unprovable guess, no thinking where there is no experimental testing. Life a laboratory! Shades of an intellectual prison house! Here is indeed a drab intellectual Puritanism.

There are two propositions involved here. One is, all practical pursuits should be intellectualized. The other is, all intellectual pursuits should be practicalized. Both are involved in the proposed functional unity of the intellectual and the practical, of knowing and doing. The first of these propositions is unexceptionable, bearing in mind that some practical pursuits, like steel-riveting, have less intellectual content than others, like designing a skyscraper. The second proposition is objectionable. It keeps the intellect of man in working clothes.

Educationally, the school should have a laboratory, true enough; but it should not be only a laboratory. There are problems for the laboratory, but there is a place for the thought-provoking classroom, for the stirring auditorium, for the quiet library, and for the noisy playground, in which one may enjoy beauty, read for pleasure, listen to a good story, see a good movie, hear good music, play for fun, and even formulate unprovable hypotheses. There is an intellectual element in each of these, but it is not tied down to practical pursuits.

Dr. Dewey's doctrine of learning by doing, found also in Rousseau, Pestalozzi, and Froebel, is a good one for elementary education, but it has never fully grown up. Adolescent and adult education involve also learning to think by thinking. Some problems worth thinking about are not matters of practical pursuits. It is well enough to liberalize with thought our professional schools; it is highly objectionable to professionalize our liberal schools. If the educators surrender the cause of liberal education, the professions will take it up. In the broader sense of practicality,—perspective, range of knowledge, joy in knowing, cultivation of a refined personality, a liberal education is the most practical. "Image the whole,"—that's liberality; "then execute the part,"—that's practicality.

The conception of experience as experimentation is inadequate. Experimentation is indeed one phase of experience, but experience is much more than experimentation. Experimentation is trying out an hypothesis under controlled conditions. It is strictly intellectual and practical. But there are emotional factors of experience over and above experimentation; we do not experiment with the love of family and friends. Münsterberg said we should not take the experimental attitude toward our pupils. Besides, in experience, there are the elements of intellectual curiosity on its own account, of custom, of impulse. No one of these is primarily experimental. The dentist may engage in experimentation, while the patient gets the experience.

Difficult as are the distinctions between pure and applied research, they nevertheless exist. The difference is not so much in the field studied as in the attitude of the student. One engaged in pure research is trying to find out the truth for its own sake; it satisfies his desire to know; it may or may not lead to practical use; he is not concerned with that aspect of the question. One engaged in applied research is trying to find out the truth for the sake of the use he can make of it. The World War greatly stimulated applied research. Most of our industrial research to-day is applied, some of it is pure. Most of our graduate school research to-day is pure, some of it is applied.

It would hamstring research all along the line to limit it to application. Pure research is basic to all applied research, as Clerk Maxwell and J. J. Thomson preceded Marconi in the field of wireless telegraphy. Those who want to know have regularly provided the materials for those who want to do. Those who want to do have often "drawn the circle premature." It is not yet clear whether the theories of cosmic rays of Millikan are true or not; or, if true, what the practical effect will be on living. But who would say to Millikan that his intellectual studies should confine themselves to practical pursuits? It is not yet proven and may never be proven experimentally that gravitation is electro-magnetism, as Einstein says; the equations seem not to fit the facts exactly as yet (1931). Neither is it clear what practical use could be made of this theorem if it were experimentally proven. But who would limit Einstein's intellect to practical pursuits? It is not yet experimentally proven and may never be so whether Millikan is right in saying the universe is winding up or Eddington and Jeans are right in saying it is running down; or what practical pursuit would be different if it were. But who would say to these astro-physicists that their intellectuality should be limited to practicality? If one replies that what these men are doing is practical and so justified, then do Plato and Aristotle come among us again as real teachers, though they did separate some intellectual knowing from some practical doing. If all intellectuality is practical, then there is no issue. The intellect of man is broader than doing, while including the directing of doing, and always will be so. Our philosophy of education must not clip the wings of intellect; it need not keep it always on solid ground; it needs only to assure it a safe landing.

CHAPTER XXI

PHYSICAL AND SOCIAL STUDIES: NATURALISM AND HUMANISM

Physical studies deal with nature; social studies deal with man. There has been conflict between these two groups of studies for a place in the curriculum. It is the conflict between naturalism and humanism. The solution of the conflict hitherto has been only a mechanical compromise: the curriculum was divided between the two. This is only another instance of the external adjustment of educational values, another dualism to be overcome. Are nature and man two things or one? How is nature really connected with human affairs? The compromise between the physical and social studies suggests that nature and man are two; that the world and mind are two independent realms, though having certain points of contact with each other; that each realm has its own separate group of studies. With such an objectionable division between nature and man, it is natural that the growth of the physical, scientific, studies of nature should be suspected of marking a materialistic encroachment upon the domain of the spirit. If our education is to be unified, then nature and man must somehow be unified.

We will study the problem from three angles, viz., the historic background of humanism before the great renaissance, the post-renaissance scientific interest in nature, and the resulting present educational problem.

1. The Historic Background of Humanistic Study

Exposition. The Greeks are not the ones responsible this time for a dualism. The isolation of man from nature took place in the Roman days and continued in the mediæval period. Plato and Aristotle did not follow their leader, Socrates, in neglecting the study of nature and centering on the study of man. Socrates seems to have thought that the knowledge of nature was not attainable, and not very important, while the knowledge of the nature and end of man was the chief thing, for upon this knowledge hang all moral and social achievements. Cicero praised Socrates for bringing philosophy down from heaven to earth, that is, for shifting attention from astronomy to ethics.

Plato made the study of nature indispensable for the study of man. He connects the good of man with the good of nature. The knowledge of nature is not an end in itself but is a necessary means of bringing man to a knowledge of himself. Through studying nature man comes to realize that his law is one with the purpose of all existence. Thus, his chief work, the *Republic,* deals both with morals and metaphysics. He agrees with Socrates that right action depends on knowledge, but he disagrees with Socrates that all we know is our own ignorance. The end of man can not be determined apart from the knowledge of the end of nature, whence come law and unity. He consistently subordinates the studies of man (called "music") to the studies of nature,—mathematics, logic, physics, and metaphysics. He found the study of nature indispensable to the interests of man. There was no conflict in Plato between naturalism and humanism.

Plato's greatest pupil, Aristotle, goes even further, if possible, in recognizing the study of nature. Unlike Socrates, to Aristotle the proper study of mankind is not man but nature. The things of man are transient but the things of nature are permanent, universal, necessary. As we saw before, Aristotle subordinates citizenship to philosophizing. The highest end of man is not social but cognitive, not human but divine, not being a citizen but being a thinker. Pure thinking, said he, is the essence of divinity. So Aristotle too felt no conflict between the literary studies of man and the scientific studies of nature. Plato and Aristotle were interested in the free inquiry into natural fact, they enjoyed nature æsthetically; and they were conscious that human society was rooted in natural law. These things kept them from bringing man and nature into conflict with each other.

But a change came in the Alexandrian and Roman days. The literary studies, those dealing with man, got the upper hand. The reason is two-fold: culture became increasingly reminiscent and borrowed, and the bent of Roman life was not scientific, but political and rhetorical.

Athens achieved civilization and culture for itself; it looked out directly upon nature and society. Alexandria and Rome inherited their civilization from alien sources. Instead of looking out, they looked back. They took the short road to culture. The administrative talent, the practical genius, of the Romans was directed to the conquest and control not of nature but of men. The educational effect was the study of literature, not the study of nature. The study [1] by Hatch has well shown this result. He holds (taking much succeeding history for granted) that it is the influence of the later Greeks which causes us still to study literature rather than nature. And the later Greeks did so because, though having lost their state, they kept their literature, and devoted themselves to it, and so paid attention to cultivated speech; and the Romans employed Greek teachers to educate their sons.

Mediæval Europe was literary too rather than scientific. As Rome was taught of Greece, so the barbarians were taught of Greco-Roman civilization. They too borrowed their culture, they did not evolve it; they borrowed their general ideas; they borrowed the artistic mode of presenting these ideas; they borrowed even their laws. They relied on the records of alien peoples; they depended on tradition. Furthermore, the dominant theological interests of the period increased the dependence on tradition; the authorities appealed to by the Church were literatures in foreign tongues. Learning became

[1] Cf. *The Influence of Greek Ideas and Usages upon the Christian Church,* pp. 43–44.

identified with linguistic training and the speech of the learned was not the mother tongue but an alien literary language.

What was the effect on education of such subject matter? It compelled recourse to the *dialectical* method of scholasticism. By scholasticism is meant simply the method of The Schools or the School Men. Their method was appropriate to their problem. Their problem was to transmit an authoritative body of truths. Contemporary society and nature were not studied; the literature of the past was studied. Inquiry, discovery, and invention were not required; defining, expounding, interpreting were required. Scholasticism developed as the method of transmitting, not discovering, truth. Since the close of the middle ages and the revival of learning, it has been used as a term of reproach, and justly so. The mistake has been in not recognizing that this mediæval method is still used to-day, and not used so well. The body of authoritatively received literature has indeed been increased by the addition of geography, history, botany, astronomy, etc., but schools still generally teach from textbooks and rely upon the principle of authority. Pupils are led not to inquire but to acquire. This is Scholasticism continued, minus mediæval accuracy and plus modern laxity.

So the Greek tradition of humanism was lost; the knowledge of nature was not made basic to the progress of man; life became interested in authority; the very study of nature was suspect: it drew men away from the documents already containing the rules of living. Moreover, nature could be studied only by means of the senses which were material and hence opposed to the immaterial interests of the spirit. Furthermore, the knowledge of nature was utilitarian, physical, secular, temporal; but the knowledge of the authoritative, traditional literature led to man's spiritual and eternal wellbeing. So the Greek unity of man and nature gave way to their mediæval disunity. Thus the matter stood at the time of the Revival of Learning.

Comment. How is it that the Greeks are now dualists and now monists? They gave us the dualism of labor and leisure, and the dualism of experience and true knowledge, but now they give us the unity of man and nature? The answer is that Dr. Dewey has here probably overdrawn the doctrine of unity between man and nature in the Greek thinkers. Socrates is admittedly an exception, depreciating the knowledge of nature and appreciating the knowledge of man. Plato made up his curriculum from the study of man rather than the study of nature; it was composed of gymnastics and music till twenty, mathematics as a discipline till thirty, and philosophy till thirty-five, after which the philosopher ruled the state with his eye on the eternal pattern of justice until fifty, when he was released again for the study of philosophy until his soul at death rejoined its kindred heavenly essences whence it had once come. Plato allowed the study of mathematics as a discipline in thinking the abstract; he allowed the study of nature, for example, astronomy, as embodying the idea of harmony. Man was not in his essence a child of nature at all but of heaven; "man is a creature not of earthly but of heavenly growth." Plato regarded nature as a mixture of being and non-being; he did not despise it; but he allowed man to transcend it. He was a quantitative dualist but a qualitative idealist, that is to say, ideas and matter both exist, but ideas are the reality; in no sense was he a naturalist, unifying man and nature. Like Socrates, he can hardly be cited as a precedent for unifying humanism and naturalism.

Neither can Aristotle. The dualism remains between form and matter, between entelechy and *energia.* So far from the soul of man being one with nature, it gives form to the body; it is an active principle. It has in it a rational element which is immortal, at one with the pure thinking of thought which is God. True enough, Aristotle is the father of most of our sciences. And doubtless the lost portions of his educational theory included the biological sciences as a part of his curriculum, supplementing the gymnastic and musical training he describes. But the characteristic excellence of man, his rational soul, Aristotle did not find in the realm of nature, in plants and animals. The forms and essences that were in nature were also in man but man had an additional trait that other natural types lacked. Aristotle too is a dualist, not a humanistic naturalist. There is warrant for citing him as a precedent for studying nature but not as a precedent for man's continuity with nature. The Greek thinkers were dualists with emphasis on the intellectual as the more real, to whom no scientific study of nature was equal in educational value to philosophy.

One additional point. One might conclude from the text that the dialectical method, to which exception is taken, first arose among the mediæval schoolmen. They took it from Plato. It is the method of the rational analysis of concepts with a view to securing logical consistency. It is not yet outworn as one phase of method; the other phase is the admission of new data not found in the initial concepts. Plato admitted new data, thus widening concepts; the schoolmen did not.

2. The Modern Scientific Interest in Nature

Exposition. Following the great Renaissance the scientific interest in nature widened the breach between man and nature, and thus widened also the breach between the humanistic and the physical studies. From the Renaissance till now we have had centuries of dualism between man and nature, between the humanities and the sciences. Such dualism is as regrettable as unnecessary. How it came about we are now to see.

The period of the revival of learning and the great Renaissance ushered in modern timess. The trouble began not during the Renaissance but following it. During the Renaissance the science of nature was a daughter of humanism, as Windelband has said. The scholars of the Renaissance were interested in man's present life, and so in his relations to nature; they were not interested in mediæval supernaturalism; they turned from divinity to humanity; they are called "humanists." This change in the centre of man's interest was due to the contemporary conditions,—new inventions, new geographical discoveries. It was not so much the revival of interest in Greek literature sending men to observe nature as it was a revival of interest in nature sending men back to Greek literature for congenial sustenance and reënforcement. They were seeking not so much the Greek literature as the Greek spirit, the spirit of mental freedom, the spirit of joy in the order and beauty of nature, the spirit of untrammeled observation. The content of Greek literature inspired the dawning physical sciences of the sixteenth century. They sought in nature the macrocosm of which man was the microcosm; the big world of nature and the little world of man were one.

How then did man and nature come to be divorced? Whence the sharp division between the humanities and the sciences? There were four causes of this result.

(*a*) The institutional cause. The old authoritative tradition was firmly intrenched in the educational institutions of the day. Politics, law, diplomacy, and history were still rooted in bodies of authoritative literature. Effective methods of language teaching were already developed and possessed the field; these profited by the inertia of academic custom. Greek itself had to fight its way into the scholastic universities; it was the "Greeks against the Trojans" over again; the Greeks finally won, but having won, they joined the forces of their erstwhile foes against the newcomer: experimental science. The teachers rarely knew science; the scientists rarely taught, but worked in private laboratories and held membership in scientific academies. And the mighty aristocratic tradition still looked down upon material things, the senses, and the hands.

(*b*) The revolt of Protestantism. North of the Alps the Renaissance affected religion. The Protestant Reformation resulted. The interests of men centered in theological controversy. The appeal of the disputants was to authoritative literature. Men were trained to study and expound the literary records; the respective faiths must be defended and propagandized. By 1650 the gymnasia and universities were tools of linguistic training, religious education, and ecclesiastical controversy. The prestige of Latin, Greek, and Hebrew in education to-day is due only indirectly to the revival of learning and directly to the theological controversies of the Reformation period.

(*c*) The misconceptions of natural science itself. Men did not follow Francis Bacon; he taught the progress of science in the service of man. We do not follow him yet; we practice the progress of science in the exploitation of man. Thus science has been misused to war on the interests of man. And so the physical and social studies are not unified.

Francis Bacon ideally unified naturalistic and humanistic interests. He rejected the mediæval learning and logic as controversial and argumentative; it did not discover the unknown. Men should cease the futile effort to dominate each other and should join in the coöperative task of dominating nature in the interest of man. Scientists should give up "anticipating" nature by imposing their own preconceived notions upon her and seek instead humbly to interpret her. Intellectual obedience would lead to practical command: "knowledge is power." The old logic of deduction should yield place to his new logic of induction, whence would come expansive discoveries and fruitful inventions. Bacon was a prophet of a new scientific knowledge and a new social order. The former has come, the latter not yet.

The new science has regrettably, not necessarily, been worked in the interest of the old order of human exploitation. It has given man not new ends but new means to old ends. The revolution in science has been followed by the revolution in industry; the revolution in industry has not been followed by the revolution in society. It is taking the scientific revolution many centuries to produce the new mind. It doomed feudalism to transfer power from the landed noble to the urban manufacturer, but it has led to unsocial capitalism instead of to social humanism. Capitalism in self-interest uses science in the economic production and distribution of goods; it misses the moral lesson of the new science, which is that man has human interests beyond making, saving, and spending money. This untoward and unwelcome situation played into the hands of the professed humanists; they claimed that science was materialistic, and that languages and literature represented the moral and ideal interests of humanity. So the gap was further widened between man and nature.

(*d*) A mistaken philosophy. This post-Renaissance philosophy purported to be based on science. In form it was either dualistic or mechanical. In either case the breach between nature and man was widened. Dualistic philosophy made a sharp division between mind and matter. It was represented by Descartes. Mind was *res cogitans;* matter was *res extensa.* Man had mind; nature had no mind. Men would of course regard human affairs as of chief importance. The effect on the curriculum was to exalt the humanities and to debase the sciences.

Mechanical philosophy (Lamettrie, Baron d'Holbach) had the same net effect. It reduced the signal features of human life to illusion. It thus threw suspicion on physical science, giving occasion to treat it as an enemy to man's higher interests. Some explanation is desirable here.

The mechanical philosophy gave a new slant to the new science, treating nature as having only quantity and lacking in quality. This was contrary to both Greek and mediæval views, which accepted the world in its qualitative variety and regarded the processes of nature as purposeful, teleological. Not so to the mechanical philosophy. Sounds, colors, purposes, good, bad, were regarded not as objective but as subjective, as mere impressions on the mind. All qualities being thus withdrawn from objective existence, only quantitative aspects remained. Objective existence was mass in motion. The only differences left in nature were that in some places there were larger masses and faster motions than in others. Lacking qualities, nature lacked significant variety. Uniformities, not diversities, were emphasized. The grandiose scientific ideal was thought to be the discovery of a simple mathematical formula explaining all the variety of the universe. Though Einstein is not a philosophical mechanist, his mathematical formula seeking to unify gravitation and magnetism illustrates this ideal. The effect of the mechanical philosophy was, of course, to separate the physical and social studies from each other.

We pause to indicate that a mechanical philosophy misses the genuine purport of science. It is true that science is mechanical and quantitative, that it ignores the qualities of events, that it confines itself to the prediction and control of events. But in leaving qualities and ends out of account, it does not exclude them from reality; neither does it relegate them to an ineffective mental region; *it furnishes the means for realizing ends.* A mechanical philosophy takes the technique, the apparatus, the terminology, for the reality; it substitutes the method for the subject matter; it thus reduces the rich world of possibilities to a barren and monotonous redistribution of moving matter in enveloping space. The new science in fact increases man's power over nature, enables him to realize his legitimate cherished ends, and allows him to diversify his activities almost at will.

Looking back at the modern scientific interest in nature we see how various reasons have combined to separate man from nature, destroying the unity he once had with it in the Greek days, and splitting the curriculum of his studies into two contending parts, the physical and the social. This leads us to consider the resulting educational problem.

Comment. The title of this section refers to only one of the points made in the argument. A more descriptive title might be: The Post-Renaissance Separation of Nature and Man.

Francis Bacon is shown to have been mistaken in supposing a scientific revolution would usher in a new social order. Science did not have in it the motivation Bacon supposed it to have. Three centuries have made this clear. Yet Dr. Dewey is still trusting science to give us a new social mind. This seems fatuous.

One might gather from the discussion that all modern philosophies of science have been either dualistic or mechanistic, and that all modern educators have opposed the sciences to the humanities. No monistic philosophy of science is mentioned and no educator advocating science is named. However, these two conclusions would both be mistaken. Among such philosophers should be mentioned Spinoza, Leibniz, Kant (?), Hegel, Fichte, Schelling, and Schopenhauer. Among such educators should be mentioned such early sense realists as Ratke and Comenius. These philosophers all found man and nature at one with each other either directly or through some deeper synthesis. And these educators, while espousing the cause of Latin, Greek, and Hebrew, also found a place for the science of their day, and urged its place in the curriculum on the grounds both of utility and training. It would take us too far afield to show the validity of these statements in detail but reference may be had to the histories of philosophy and to the histories of education, or better, to the sources.

Not of course that these statements contradict the views of the text, but that they are needed to supplement the position in the text. It is true that the sciences have had to wage a mighty war against the classics for a place in the curriculum, but we are not to think that they have not had their proponents among some of the educators and we are not to think that all philosophy of science has been either dualistic or mechanistic.

There is another reason that might be added to the list to explain the long conflict between the languages and the sciences. It is that the languages were old and perfected and the sciences were new and perfecting. For this reason the languages were better taught than the sciences,—they probably still are. The study of the languages develops powers of expression; the teachers of the languages express themselves well; they have a developed feeling for speech. Thus the humanities, being older, being taught better, being in possession of the educational field, naturally resented sharing the field with the somewhat rude and obstreperous youngster.

3. The Present Educational Problem

Exposition. That is, as regards the physical and social studies. The present problem is to unite them. This can be done, as we shall now see, by making proper educational use of industries. In following through this argument, the following points will be noted: (1) the real unity of nature and man, (2) the proper way to teach the sciences, (3) the limitations in Greek humanism, and (4) the educational use of industries.

(1) Our experience shows us no division between a human non-mechanical world on the one hand and a physical mechanical world on the other. Man's home is nature. All human purposes depend for execution upon natural conditions. Separated from nature, the purposes of man are empty dreams and idle fancy. Any justly made distinction between man and nature rests on the difference between purposes and the means for their realization; the purposes are man's, the means are nature's. This distinction is a matter of experience. Educational endeavor should recognize it, but allow no dualism between human concerns and a mechanical world.

This philosophy of the unity of nature and man is vouched for by two things, viz., biology, and the experimental method of science. Biology teaches us in its doctrine of development that man is continuous with nature, that he is a higher animal, that he is not a transcendent alien entering the processes of nature from without. And the experimental method of science shows that knowledge results from directing physical energies toward social uses. Man derives his knowledge from a naturalistic source. This experimental method of inquiry, as now repeatedly indicated, consists in defining a problem arising within experience, collecting data upon it, formulating an hypothesis about it, and then testing out the hypothesis. This process of manipulating material is the source of man's knowledge. This is the method of knowing, and the only method. It arose with the natural sciences.

And progress in the social sciences depends on using both the method and the results of the natural sciences. These social sciences include history, economics, politics, and sociology. Social welfare is intelligently promoted only as the scientific method is used in handling social questions and only as the technical knowledge ascertained by physics and chemistry is utilized. Among such perplexing social problems the following may be mentioned: the conservation of natural resources, insanity, intemperance, poverty, public sanitation, city planning, and the use of government for the public welfare without weakening personal initiative. So, man's organism is one with nature, man's knowledge is one with nature, man's progress is dependent on his using the means provided by nature. Hence we conclude man is one with nature; his whole being is naturalistic.

Such being the case, the humanistic and naturalistic studies are really interdependent. Let education take notice! Science should not be kept apart from literature; the study of nature should not be isolated from the interests of man. The sciences are more than technical forms of manipulation and technical bodies of information; they are the condition of man's progress, from which the humanistic studies should not be isolated. It is artificial for the school to separate what life unites. Outside of school there is no separation between natural facts and human action; the understanding of natural facts, principles, and processes are necessary for social activities to go on. For the school to rupture this intimate association of the natural and the human breaks the continuity of the student's mental development, deprives him of the normal motive for interest in his studies, and makes him feel an indescribable unreality in them. Instead, education should aim at cross-fertilizing the sciences and the humanities. And the pedagogical problem of doing so is simpler than that of keeping the two apart, as we shall see.

(2) The way science has been taught has tended to keep man and nature apart. Science has been taught as a body of logically arranged subject-matter distinct from the interests of life. The reason for so doing has been blind tradition, not a conscious dualistic philosophy. The colleges introduce their students as would-be experts into segregated scientific subject matter, and the high schools imitate the colleges. The student beginning science should begin with his daily experiences; instead, he is offered a choice between "nature study" and "science" as a body of technically organized subject matter. The "nature study" is miscellaneous, is presented haphazardly, and leads nowhere in particular. The "science" is cut off from daily life. And so it results that a large part of the teaching of science is comparatively ineffective.

There are two classes of students of science, the few who will be specialists and the many who will not be. The many are concerned with the effect of science upon their understanding of their daily environment and upon their mental habits; they need to be more alert, more open-minded, more inclined to accept ideas only tentatively until they are tested in the crucible of experiment. For all such students it is certainly ill-advised to start them off with technically organized subject matter. They achieve only a smattering which is too superficial to be scientific and too technical to be practical. But how about the few who will be experts? Even here the procedure described is questionable. They would probably make a better finish if they had a better start. Of course all who have the disposition and the ability to become scientific experts should have the chance to do so. They may end by learning what other experts already know and by adding to such knowledge, but they might better begin by experiencing science.

So to begin is easier to-day than ever before. Ordinary experience should be utilized to secure an advance into science. Scientific material and method should be kept connected with familiar human interests. This is easy to do in our day because the usual experience of everybody in civilized communities is now intimately associated with industrial processes and results, which, in turn, are so many cases of science in action. Illustrations of science in action within the experience of most persons are the steam engine, both stationary and traction, the gasoline engine, the automobile, the telegraph, the telephone, the electric motor, the radio, and the airplane. Children may see scientific achievements in both the business occupations and the household pursuits of their parents, in the maintenance of health, and in the sights of the street. Such experiences can be utilized to stimulate interest in scientific principles. What is the starting point in scientific instruction? Obviously not to teach things labeled "science." Rather to utilize the familiar in directing observation and experiment. Let pupils learn to know some fundamental principles in their familiar practical workings.

Here the old question meets us, is it better to study "pure" or "applied" science? Pure science is held to be cultural, while applied science is held to be practical. This view is mistaken. A subject is cultural in proportion as it has meaning; the more meaning the more culture. And meaning is a matter of connections; you see the meanings of a thing in proportion as you see its connections. Pure science deals with physical, technical, connections. Applied science adds the human and the economic connections. Thus the cultural value of science is enhanced when it is both pure and applied. And the more important thing is that the fact is grasped in its human, social connections, that is, in its function in life. This makes the study of science humanistic, and bridges the gap between the physical and social studies.

This is the place to note too that there is a "humanism" that is not humanistic. The right sort of science is humanistic; the wrong sort of "humanities" is not humanistic. The wrong sort is that which pursues its interests apart from social well-being. The true humanism is inbued with an intelligent sense of human interests. Social interest is in its deepest meaning identical with moral interest, and this social-moral interest is necessarily supreme with man. Any study, whether physical or social, deserves to be considered "humane" only when it increases concern for the values of life, produces sensitiveness to social well-being, and develops ability to promote the public good. Instead, a specious humanism gives a knowledge *about* man, such as his past, his documented records, his literature, and his languages. Such a store of facts readily degenerates into a miser's accumulation, and the pedant, missing the meaning in the affairs of life, comes to pride himself on what he has. Such pedantic occupations as his have the letter without the spirit of real activity; they are on the level with the "busy work" of children; they are as technical as any accumulation of scientific details; they do not enlarge the imaginative vision of life. Physical and social studies have alike to learn the lesson of genuine humanism.

(3) We may point a contrast here by referring to the limits of Greek humanism. Not even the culture of the Greeks, could we attain it by studying our "humanities," would give us the true humanism. Despite the acuteness of the social observations and speculations of the Greek thinkers, they regarded Greek civilization as self-inclosed and self-sufficient; they did not suspect that its future was at the mercy of the despised "barbarians!" Within the Greek community the humanistic spirit was native and intense, but narrow; there was higher culture but it was based on the labor of slaves and

economic serfs,—classes necessary to the state but not genuine parts of it, as Aristotle declared. This ancient Greek humanism failed to consider economic and industrial conditions. It was thus one-sided. Its culture inevitably represented the intellectual and moral outlook of the ruling class. Such culture is aristocratic, emphasizing class distinctions, and the conservative standards of the past. It does not represent common fundamental interests, it does not aim to extend the range of human values.

(4) The industrial revolution has given us a different world from that of the Greeks, necessitating a democratic culture. This revolution is due to applied science. It has brought different peoples in close contact through colonization and commerce. One nation may still look down upon another but it can no longer harbor the delusion that its career is decided wholly within itself. Further, agricultural serfdom has been abolished. A new class of more or less organized factory laborers with political rights has been created; this class claims a responsible rôle in the control of industry; these claims receive sympathetic attention from many of the well-to-do; economic class barriers are breaking down. The new democratic culture is to be conveyed through the educational use of industrial activities. This is not so much an attack upon the narrow culture of the past; it is a wider way of making the culture of the classes more solid and the culture of the masses more genuine. Technical scientific studies and refining literary studies are opposed to each other to-day because an industrial democracy and a literary aristocracy are opposed to each other. If society is to be unified in a true democracy, education must unify the physical and social studies.

Comment. We pause not for praise but for appraisal. The matters not specifically mentioned receive our tacit support.

Studies are here held to be usually divided into the physical and the social. This is the historic division into the sciences and the humanities. It falls in with the distinction between nature and man. This division can be profitably sub-divided. Among the sciences there are the physical and the natural. The physical sciences include physics and chemistry. The natural sciences include biology and related studies. The social studies may also be sub-divided into the humanistic and the social sciences. The humanities include languages and literatures. The social sciences include history, sociology, and economics. A division into these four groups is carried out in the new reorganization of the curriculum at the University of Chicago. At the very time that Dr. Dewey proposes a monism of studies to overcome the dualism of the physical and the social, a new pluralism appears on the scene. Here are two counter tendencies in the curriculum,—toward greater unification, and toward greater diversification. The advance of science favors specialization and so diversification of studies. Yet a mental unification is necessary for a large life of adjustment to one's world. And certainly a social unity is gradually being attained by a zig-zag course. It is philosophy that says unify; it is science that says divide.

What will the educational outcome be? Probably the curriculum will continue to be divided in Junior High School, High School, and College, where the project method meets increasing difficulty. Possibly the curriculum will be much more unified in the lower grades where the project method works best. But to offset the disunion of the higher curriculum, more stress will be laid upon the inter-connection of all subjects, and the unifying study of philosophy will receive more attention. That all subjects may be cross-fertilized to mutual advantage is perhaps obvious. The British scientists, like J. Arthur Thomson, often show a wide literary background.

The text argues for the unity of man and nature as a basis for the unity of the social and physical studies. This unity may very well exist but hardly on the naturalistic ground advocated. The two arguments adduced are evolution and pragmatism. The doctrine of evolution is still a doctrine, an hypothesis, or, at most, a theory, accepted it is true by most leading scientists to-day. Still, it is not yet a principle or a fact, the demonstration of which would be convincing to all. Furthermore, as a theory, it still requires a philosophy beyond biology. Biology as a science tries to answer the question whether man came from some preëxistent animal, and, if so, how. Philosophy tries to answer the question *why*. Whatever biology says, its answer is not final, though it may be true as far as it goes. The text goes no further than biology on the question of the origin of man. But all the typical philosophies have their answer as to the why of evolution. Among the variants there is a theory of theistic evolution which does not make man a child of nature except as nature itself is a dependent child of a Supreme Person.

The experimental method of inquiry, which is the same as the pragmatic method of Dr. Dewey, does not really make man one with nature, though it claims so to do. It is admitted that the means are nature's, but the ends are man's. If nature has means without ends, and man has ends without means, here is a dualism indeed. A real unity would assign ends also to nature and means also to man. This Dr. Dewey does not do. Until it is done, dualism remains. It can hardly be done on a naturalistic basis. It has been done on an idealistic basis which regards both nature and man as having both ends and means in themselves. Nature realized an end in the appearance of man, and man has some physical means in his own physique as well as in his powers of both practical and abstract thinking. We conclude on this point that the dualism between man and nature has not been overcome on the grounds indicated but might be overcome on a different basis.

We may refer also to the possible danger of applying the experimental method to the social questions. With gravest difficulty can we experiment with the marriage rate, the birth rate, the death rate, and the fundamental virtues of truth-speaking and respect for personality. Some social questions are already settled in principle. There is no occasion to call every social virtue and attitude into question. The race has learned much by unconscious experimentation. Society can ill afford to start afresh in testing by conscious experiment what the race has already well established by unconscious experiment.

A last point concerns the distinction between pure and applied science. That made in the text is between the technical and the practical, meaning by "practical" the human and the economic. In this sense applied science may well have the richer culture. But there is another distinction possible, as seen before. Pure science is disinterested, applied science is interested in consequences. In this sense the pure scientist is not thinking of applications, he is in love with the discovery of truth for its own sake; the applied scientist is not thinking of advancing human knowledge, he is thinking of making use of what is already known. The pure scientist is following an intrinsic interest, the ultimate results of which for society are extrinsic to him. His is the culture of truth. The applied scientist uses the results of the intrinsic interest of the pure scientist; these become instruments to his ends. Some industrial companies, practical, money-making, man-serving concerns, employ some high-salaried men just to do pure research, not to solve practical problems at all. Some of the most striking recent discoveries have so arisen. While some of these discoveries are immediately useful, some are not. Here is a type of pure science that fully justifies itself, because it satisfies the intrinsic interest of the investigator, and because it furnishes a supply of knowledge greater than the practical demand for it. Our conclusion on this point is that there is a form of pure science, and so a form of culture, that does not have to be harnessed to solving practical problems, and that nevertheless justifies itself.

CHAPTER XXII

THE INDIVIDUAL AND THE WORLD

1. Mind as Purely Individual

Exposition. In this chapter there is the consideration of another dualism to be overcome. It is the dualism between mind and matter.

We have been considering three other dualisms, viz., labor and leisure, the intellectual and the practical, and the physical and the social. These dualisms have served to split up undesirably our curriculum into separate studies, which have thus both reflected and perpetuated objectionable social divisions. These dualisms have influenced not only practical education but also theoretical philosophy. They have been formulated in dualistic philosophies, opposing body to mind, practice to theory, and mechanism to teleology. The culminating dualism of all is that between the individual mind and the world. And note that if individual minds are sharply demarcated from the world, they are also sharply demarcated from each other.

In treating this dualism we will first use the historical or genetic mode of approach, as hitherto. Then the preferred mode of viewing mind will be presented, and this will be followed by certain objectionable educational and social implications of the dualistic view of mind and its world, with their correctives.

It was first in the early modern period that mind was conceived as purely individual. During the barbarian, the Greek, and the mediæval periods, it was not so. In the barbarian period the individual was most humble in his attitude toward truth; it was divinely revealed; it was received on authority of the medicine man or the priest by the individual, whose business it was to understand it and follow it. Beliefs were transmitted by custom. No one supposed that the belief of the individual could be a personal matter.

In the Greek period too the individual mind was not identified with a personal self, and so the personal self was not identified with a private self-consciousness. Rather, the individual mind was a channel through which a universal and divine intelligence operated. The individual was not the true knower; the true knower was the "Reason" which operated through the individual. There was thus a universal Reason thinking in and through the individual mind. The soul to Plato was one of the universal and essential "ideas." There was a universal and rational element in the soul of man, according to Aristotle. It was this element in man which was immortal. With this element of rationality within him, the individual interfered to the detriment of truth and at his personal peril; conceit, error, and opinion, as substitutes for true knowledge, came from the individual who did not follow the universal reason. The Greeks observed acutely and alertly; they thought freely, almost to the point of irresponsible speculations. Their theory of the universal in the individual was not a restraint upon their thinking. One thing, however, they lacked: the experimental method. And so the knowing of individuals lacked social control; it could not be checked up by the findings of other inquirers. Lacking such a check, individual thinkers could not be held to intellectual responsibility. Results that in our day would have to stand the test of experimentation by others were then accepted for no better reason than their æsthetic consistency, their agreeable quality, or the prestige of their authors. So, in sum, in the Greek days the individual mind had a universal metaphysical element in it but lacked a social check. It was well that the individual was not conceived as private but it was ill that he was conceived as universal instead of as social.

In the mediæval period, influenced by Aristotle, the rule still was to regard the individual as the channel through which the divine intelligence operated. Here was a religious individualism containing a universal or "real" element. The salvation of the individual soul was the deepest concern of of life. Latent in this individualism was the implication that the individual was a private self. In the later middle ages this latent individualism came to the surface as a heresy. It was formulated in the philosophy of "nominalism." This philosophy dropped out of sight the universal element in the individual. It held that the structure of knowledge was built up within the individual by his own mental acts. The "universals" of orthodoxy were only "names" (cf. Roscellinus). Here is a private intellectual individualism without either divine or experimental control. It was well that the individual lost the alleged universal element within him, but ill that he construed his individuality privately and without social control.

It was but a step intellectually to Protestantism and the right of private judgment in interpreting divine revelation. In the same sixteenth century which saw the rise of Protestantism, and thereafter, came reënforcements to private individualism from the spheres of politics and economics. Economic competition arose between individual states. In this early modern period the times were ripe for an emphasis upon the rights and duties of the individual in achieving knowledge for himself. Finally, the full-fledged but narrow view arose that knowledge is won wholly through personal and private experience. But mind was conceived as the source of knowledge and as the possessor of knowledge, and so mind was held to be wholly individual. The reaction was on against authority in all spheres of life; the struggle was intense in behalf of freedom of inquiry and action; it was carried on against great odds; it led to extreme emphasis upon personal observation and ideas. An educational reform was launched on the new basis. Montaigne, Bacon, Locke, and other "realists," vehemently denounced all learning acquired on hearsay; even a true belief was not knowledge unless it had grown up in and been tested by personal experience. The effect was to isolate individual mind and set it apart from the world to be known. The rejection of external authority in interpreting divine revelation or in transmitting approved racial experience was well, but the isolation of the knowing mind from the known world was ill.

At this point the problem of knowledge becomes acute and "epistemology" takes up the tale. Epistemology is that branch of philosophy which deals with the theory of knowledge. It had a great development just now. And naturally so. If the individual and his world are two separate and distinct realities, how can the one know the other? How can the other affect the one? How can the two so become one that valid knowledge is possible at all? A regrettable dualism was driving philosophy headlong onto the barren rocks of false epistemologies. Some of their desperate solutions are the following: we can not know the world as it really is but only the impressions it makes upon the mind (phenomenalism); there is no world beyond the individual mind (subjective idealism); knowledge is only a certain association between mental states (associationism); the inner world of "consciousness" is more truly and immediately known than anything else (introspectionism). We are not here concerned with the truth of any of these "isms,—" they all rest upon a false setting of the problem. But we are concerned to note that such widely accepted counsels of despair are speaking evidence of the extent to which mind had been set over against the world of realities. What began as a desirable practical individualism, struggling for greater freedom of thought in action, ended in a regrettable philosophic subjectivism.

In sum, the individual was one with his world in the periods of barbarianism, Hellenism, and mediæval "realism," which continued the tradition of Plato and Aristotle. The individual began to be separated from his world in the periods of mediæval "nominalism," Protestantism, French skepticism, and English empiricism. Our own view is that the individual is indeed one with his world, but not on the bases hitherto suggested. The sense in which the individual is one with his world will be presented in our next section.

Comment. This section as it stands is one of the most confusing in the book. The reason is that the discussion is so highly concentrated and presupposes so much history of philosophy. The unbewildered student of Dr. Dewey's text needs to have a large background in history, in the history of philosophy, and in the history of education. Like Browning, Dewey compliments (or ignores) his readers by presupposing that they know what he is writing about. Besides, in this particular section the reader is puzzled to know at times how the views presented are related to Dr. Dewey's own views. These difficulties the expositor has sought to clarify by some additions and interpretations.

We will not at this point consider any element of truth in the rejected epistemologies. Dr. Dewey himself passes them by with the phrase: "desperate solutions." His method is not to solve old problems, but to outgrow them. He refers to them here only to point a moral against dualism and to adorn its tale.

But looking at the historic review itself, one is told that private individualism is "comparatively modern," beginning in fact with the mediæval nominalists. This late origin of the idea somewhat disposes the reader in advance to reject it, and doubtless is intended so to do. But the fact is, the story as told omits three earlier and striking illustrations of individualism, meaning by individualism the privacy and independence of the person in his relation to his world.

The first illustration is that of the Greek Sophists. They were individualists indeed. They did not agree among themselves; they did not accept custom as standard for either action or thought. Protagoras held that the individual man was the measure of all things, both of things that are and of things that are not. Gorgias taught that nothing exists; if anything did exist, we could never know it; if we could know it, we could not communicate our knowledge. It was this individualism which, by rejecting all authority, set Socrates and also Plato and Aristotle to work. We refer to it not to accept it but to recognize it, and to indicate that modern philosophic subjectivisms have Hellenic precedent, as indeed the "Summary" on p. 356 indicates.

The second illustration is even earlier. It is somewhat noteworthy that Dr. Dewey's historic reviews,—his characteristic mode of approaching an issue, do not include Hebrew and early Christian thinking. In the Hebrew prophets of the eighth century and following there is distinct individualism. So much so that orthodox Judaism has regularly followed Moses instead of those prophets. Reference is made to Amos, Hosea, Isaiah, Jeremiah, and Ezekiel. Especially in Ezekiel is social responsibility rejected and individual responsibility promulgated. "The soul that sinneth, it shall die: the son shall not bear the iniquity of the father, neither shall the father bear the iniquity of the son; the righteousness of the righteous shall be upon him, and the wickedness of the wicked shall be upon him" (Ezek. 18: 20). In these views the individual emerges from the social group as a distinct moral entity.

The "religious individualism" of the mediæval period is not original. It but carries on the Christian view of the first century as the latter carries on the prophetic view of the earlier centuries. Jesus taught the infinite worth of the individual soul and its distinct survival of bodily death. His emphasis on the immortality of the soul differed from that of Plato and Aristotle in that they were thinking of the soul as rational while he was thinking of it as personal. Here is the very view whose date is assigned by our text to a period ten centuries later. Whoever rejects the personality and the privacy of the self can not do so on the ground of the late origin of the view.

A fourth illustration may be adduced, though not in the direct line of descent of Western thought. About the time of Ezekiel an unknown personality in India, named Kapila, was developing the Sankhya philosophy. The very term "Sankhya" means "connected with number." The Sankhya system teaches the absolute distinction of matter and spirit. Besides, the number of souls is boundless. Here is a qualitative dualism and a quantitative pluralism; that is, the kinds of reality are two, and of one kind there is an unlimited number of instances. In this system individual minds are demarcated not only from the world but also from each other.

In sum, these historic illustrations show that the conception of the mind as purely individual is ancient; it is Hellenic, Hebraic, and Indian; and it can not be rejected on the ground that it arose in the early modern period through the unfortunate translation of acceptable practical individualism into objectionable theoretical subjectivism. If rejected at all, it must be on other than historic grounds. Meantime, there is considerable ground for holding that the universe itself is a Self and selves (Personalism), or even a Self of selves, including the realm of physical nature (Objective Idealism).

2. Individual Mind as the Agent of Reorganization

Exposition. The individual mind should be conceived as the agent of reorganization of the world. This is our position. Before stating it in detail, we will first continue the historic approach to the question, taking up the argument where it was left at the end of the preceding section. We there saw the failure of the epistemological philosophies to overcome the dualism between the mind and its world. We will now study in some detail the parallel failure of the moral philosophies to do the same. There are four of these.

The problem is, what connections will unite a separated individual with his fellows? How can actions proceeding from separate moral individuals be controlled in the interest of the public? How can an egoistic consciousness act altruistically?

The problem itself is set by a moral individualism, by the separation of different conscious centers of life, by the notion that a person's consciousness is wholly private, self-inclosed, like an island, intrinsically independent of everyone else.

There are four typical ways in which moral philosophies have dealt with this problem, all of which are rejected, because the problem itself is non-existent, there being really no such separated selves. These four ways are those of (i) the religious authoritarian; (ii) the French rationalist; (iii) the English utilitarian; and (iv) the German objective idealist.

(i) Religious authoritarianism. This view is an ancient survivor under modern conditions. The progress of events has extorted some concessions and compromises. In principle this view would have the individual guided by external authority. Individual deviations from authority are suspect, leading to disturbance, revolt, and corruption. In the physical sciences, like mathematics, physics, and astronomy, and in the resulting technical inventions, intellectualism and individualism are tolerated; this however as a matter of fact, not of principle. In the biological sciences territory is yielded only grudgingly under the pressure of accomplished fact. But no intellectual individualism is allowed in the moral sciences,—in social, legal, and political matters. Here dogma is still to be supreme; individual observation and speculation are beset by unpassable limits; certain binding and eternal truths have been made known by divine revelation, intuition, or the wisdom of the forefathers. The efforts of misguided individuals to transgress these boundaries are the cause of the social evils. There is a sacred domain of truth to be protected from the inroads of individual disbelief.

Looking at the educational results of this "authority" theory, emphasis is put on the authority of book and teacher, and individual variation is discouraged. But past history has demonstrated that responsible inquiry, not authority, widens and secures human good.

(ii) French rationalism. This is a form of abstract intellectualism. The reason is trusted to guide separated individuals into social living. It sets up a formal logical faculty. This faculty of reason is endowed with the power to influence conduct directly. It deals wholly with general and impersonal formulas. It says: "Be reasonable as individuals and you will harmonize socially." This power of reason is set up as judge in distinction from all tradition, all history, and all concrete subject matter.

This philosophy has rendered valuable social service. It successfully opposed doctrines based on mere tradition and class interest. It accustomed man to free discussion. It brought beliefs to the bar of reason. It made for clear and orderly exposition. In all these ways it undermined prejudice, superstition, and brute force.

Though serviceable, it is an inadequate philosophy of social conduct. It was more successful socially in the destruction of old falsities than in the construction of new ties. It was impotent to suggest specific aims and methods. It was formal and empty. It conceived reason as complete in itself apart from subject matter. It was hostile toward historical institutions. It disregarded the powerful influences in life of habit, instinct, and emotion. Bare logic is important in arranging and criticizing existing subject matter, but it can not imitate the spider and spin new subject matter out of itself.

There is a significant educational correlate to this abstract rationalism. It is trust in ready-made rules, in general principles, to secure agreement among pupils, without seeing to it that their ideas and attitudes really do agree.

(iii) English utilitarianism. This moral philosophy is based on the view that the intelligent self-interest of each leads to the common social interest of all. It says: "Act with intelligent regard for self, and society will be unified." Law, government, prisons, education, and trade were all invoked to make the principle work. Self-regarding action was not to offend others. To be happy oneself, one must not interfere with others and even consider their welfare. Chief emphasis was put on trade: to satisfy one's own wants, to gain profit, one must supply some commodity of service to others. To get pleasure for oneself, one must give pleasure to others. Here is a moral individualism with a social emphasis.

This philosophy too rendered genuine service. It recognized the values of conscious life. It judged institutions by their contributions to life. It also helped to rescue work, industry, and machinery from the contempt long poured upon them by a leisure class. In thus stressing values and the worth of work it promoted a wider and more democratic concern about social welfare.

But this philosophy too, though valuable, was inadequate. It was tainted by the narrowness of its primary premise: that every individual is selfish, that he acts only from self-regarding motives, that he is seeking only to get pleasure and avoid pain, that all altruism is veiled egoism, that all generosity and sympathy are indirect ways of securing one's own comfort. It thus rested social union upon external calculations. Of it Carlyle could contemptuously say that it was "anarchy plus a constable," recognizing only a "cash nexus" among men. Mental life is not a self-inclosed thing; it is an attempt to redirect common concerns. Deny this, and the weakness of atomic individualism appears.

Educationally, the equivalents of utilitarianism are too obvious in the school uses of pleasurable rewards and painful penalties.

(iv) German objective idealism. This view began with French rationalism but did not end there. Descartes and his French successors separated the reason of the individual from the reason of the divine mind. German thought, as in Hegel, made a synthesis of the two. "The real is the rational." Reason is absolute. An absolute reason is not purely formal and empty like the reason of rationalism; it includes all content within itself. Thus, nature is embodied reason. And history is the progressive unfolding of reason in man. The organized state expresses objective reason. Historical institutions are idealized as embodiments of an immanent universal mind. An individual loses his eccentric individuality and becomes rational only as he absorbs into himself the rationality embodied in nature and in social institutions. Thus freedom is not an initial gift; it is an achievement. The problem is not to control individual freedom in the interest of social unity, but to achieve individual freedom through accord with objective reason. This philosophy is usually called objective or absolute idealism; for educational purposes it might better be called institutional idealism.

This philosophy too rendered valuable service. It helped powerfully to rescue early nineteenth century thinking in France and England from isolated individualism. It left less to individual logical conviction, less to *laissez faire,* less to the workings of private self-interest. It made the organized state more constructively interested in public welfare, bringing intelligence to bear upon the conduct of affairs. It made for efficient organization,—more so than any previously mentioned type of philosophy. It promoted freedom of inquiry into all natural and historical phenomena. And it accentuated the need of national education in a corporate state.

And yet, with all its values, it was an inadequate moral philosophy. It reinstated the principle of authority. It made no provision for experimenting with established social institutions. Political democracy was foreign to it,—that political democracy which believes in the right of the individual to share in re-adapting even the fundamental constitution of society.

Educationally this view survives in the emphasis placed on the existing social institutions and on the importance of bringing individuals into conformity with them.

From these inadequate philosophies we turn to our own view that the individual mind should be conceived not as a private self but as the agent of reorganizing the world. Once this mind, as we saw, was conceived as public, but in a submissive way. Then it became conceived as private and submissive. We conceive it as public and active. This philosophy we may call experimentalism.

The individualism that came to a head in post-renaissance social and philosophical movements was really practical. It was misread by the epistemologists as theoretical. The mediæval nominalists, the renaissance humanists, and the religious protestants were not absurdly striving to be free *from* nature and society; they were reasonably striving to be free *in* nature and society. They wanted not private isolation from the world but intimate connection with the world. They wanted to change the world of things and men. They wanted greater freedom to observe conditions and to apply ideas. They wanted their beliefs to come not by tradition but at first hand. They wanted to unite with their fellows for more effective mutual influence. They were really practicing the theory of mind which we hold. Epistemological dualism, so far from being a transcript of that movement of practical individualism, was really a perversion of it.

Those practical individualists were really experimental thinkers. Knowledge to them was more than accumulated past opinions, more even than correct opinion when accepted on authority. Imposed dogma is not truth. The mind does more than formally acquiesce. The method of knowing is not deductive but experimental and inductive. So they held, and rightly. They were ceasing to be mediæval, they were becoming modern. They were being thrown by social conditions upon their own resources; such social conditions were the rise of free cities; the development of travel, of exploration, and of commerce; and the use of new methods of production and distribution of commodities.

Not that these practical reformers invented the inductive experimental method; they widened the scope of its application. Men had always used, though somewhat blindly, an inductive method in dealing with their immediate practical concerns. Nature's processes have to be observed, ideas concerning them have to be checked, if men would be practically successful in such matters as agriculture, manufacture, and architecture. Even here undue reliance was placed on blind custom. And, as we saw (Chapter XX), this observational experimental method was restricted to matters of practice and was excluded from matters of theory.

What the genuine reformers of science, like Roger and Francis Bacon, Galileo, Descartes, and others, really did was to ascertain the facts about nature by methods analogous to those used in successful farming, manufacturing, and building. A just interpretation would have recognized mind here as an agent and would have emphasized the right of the individual to test authoritative beliefs and to gain personal knowledge. Instead, a false interpretation isolated individuals from their world and, in theory, even from each other; not discerning that such a rupture in continuity denied in advance the possibility of success in their practical endeavors to shape men and things.

As a matter of fact, the conception of mind as a purely isolated possession is at the very antipodes of the truth. The individual gradually acquires a mind of his own. This he does through social intercourse, through sharing in activities embodying beliefs, through growing up in a social medium. Living and acting in a social medium of accepted meanings and values, his own responses gain meaning and become intelligent. He *achieves* a mind to the degree in which the life he shares embodies knowledge; there is no separated mind, and, if there were, it could not build up knowledge anew on its own account. This always has been so, and always must be so. The mind of the individual is continuous with nature and with man. It is the instrument of changing one's environment.

Yet this much we must grant to the subjectivist. There is a distinction between knowledge which is objective and thinking which is subjective. Knowledge is impersonal, thinking is personal. Knowledge is that which is taken for granted, settled, disposed of, established, under control, no longer needing to be thought about; it is certain, assured. Knowledge is more than a feeling of certainty, a sentiment; it is a practical attitude, a readiness to act without reserve or quibble. Of course one may be mistaken; what is *called* knowledge, fact, or truth at a given time may not *be* such. In contrast with knowledge, thinking starts, as we have seen, from doubt or uncertainty. It marks an inquiring, hunting, searching attitude; it lacks the knowing attitude of mastery and possession. Thinking is critical, it reorganizes our convictions about things, it revises and extends knowledge.

This distinction between knowing and thinking has been illustrated in the last few centuries. They have been typically a period of revision of beliefs. Men set out from what had passed as knowledge; they critically investigated its grounds; they noted exceptions; they brought to light new data, inconsistent with old beliefs, by using new appliances. They did not throw away all transmitted beliefs; they did not start afresh upon the basis of their exclusive sensations and ideas. They could not have done so, if they had wished; if they could have done so, the only outcome would have been general imbecility. Their work was piecemeal, a retail business; one problem was tackled at a time. They also used their imaginations to conceive a different world from that in which their forefathers had trusted. The sum of all the revisions amounted to nothing less than an intellectual revolution, a reorganization of prior intellectual habitudes, a new conception of the world. This was infinitely more efficient than a cutting loose from all past connections would have been. It was the effect of thinking upon what was accepted as knowledge.

This result suggests the rôle of the individual in knowledge: to reconstruct accepted beliefs. Every *new* idea must have its origin in an individual, and new ideas are doubtless always sprouting. They are not encouraged, however, by a custom-governed society. Being deviations from current belief, the tendency is to suppress them. The thinker is suspect; to persist in thinking is generally fatal. Science has had its martyrs, Socrates and Bruno, no less than religion. Even under a relaxed censorship, new ideas may lack appliances for their elaboration; the thinker may lack material support; whence his ideas remain mere fancies, aimless speculations, romantic castles in the air. The modern scientific revolution was not easily secured. It meant freedom of observation and imagination; these had to be fought for; many individuals suffered for their intellectual independence. Modern European society first permitted, and then encouraged, at least in some fields, individual deviations from prescribed custom. Social fashion came to tolerate, or even decree, research, discovery, and inventions.

Thus, the meaning in the intellectual transition from mediæval, religious authority to modern, scientific investigation is the pivotal influence of the individual mind; thus beliefs are reconstructed; thus the continuity of the individual mind with the world of nature and fellowman is maintained. This is the true theory of mind in the individual; this is intellectual individualism, the attitude of critical revision of former beliefs as indispensable to progress. When the individual mind sets out to transform customary beliefs so as to win general conviction, there is no opposition between the individual and the social. Just as conformity is the agency of social conservation, so variation from habit is the agency of social progress. Knowledge as tested belief does not arise within a separated individual; it arises when an individual seeks to improve a social situation.

We have already noted how this true intellectual individualism was mistakenly formulated as a moral individualism, with the resulting problem of bringing individuals together who had first been unwarrantably separated, and the four improvised methods of solution for the artificial problem thus created. It remains next for us to note the educational equivalents of individual mind as a reorganizing agency.

Comment. The history of modern, ethical philosophy in outline is packed in these nine pages; small wonder it is tough reading for the uninitiated. The discussion would have been more concrete had some additional names been included; such as among the French, Voltaire, Condillac, Helvétius, Lamettrie, Diderot, Holbach, Cabanis, and Rousseau; among the British, Shaftesbury, Samuel Clarke, Hutcheson, Adam Smith, William Paley, Bentham, and Mandeville; and among the Germans, Fichte, Schelling, Schlegel, Oken, Krause, as well as Hegel. Of course such a list of names is still more perplexing, unless they are followed up in a history of the subject (cf. Weber and Perry, *History of Philosophy*; Sidgwick, *History of Ethics*).

As an illustration of the authoritarian point of view rejected by our author as a solution of the ethical conflict between the individual and society, and as showing the current, vigorous vitality of that view, the following quotation will serve: "If education is the development of all the capacity of man, the perfecting of man, then we boldly assert that the only real educator in the world to-day is the Catholic Church. For she alone understands the meaning, value, and fullness of life. During these four years your Alma Mater has given you a sound education. She has been enabled to impart it to you because she has the scientific method. She is the daughter of a still greater mother, the Church, the mother of true liberty, the mother of the arts and sciences."[1]

The author finds something valuable in each of the philosophies reviewed except authoritarianism. This view upholds the principle of authority in its conflict with individual freedom. Authoritarianism alone is indeed unduly repressive of individuality. But individualism alone is unduly subversive of authority. This is another dualism between authority

[1] Father Denis P. Coleman in a Baccalaureate Sermon, quoted in *The New York Times,* June 15, 1931.

and individuality. Here, however, our author does not synthesize the two, he wipes out one and leaves the other alone. The past, he holds, has no authority over the present; its lessons are only hypotheses to be tried out under new and changed conditions. But some lessons and discoveries of the past abide as true, and have the authority of truth, such as, the worth of personality, the obligation to be unselfish and intelligent, and the multiplication table. Dr. Dewey himself holds that true individuality is social, and acknowledges the supreme authority of the scientific method.[1] It is clear that what is required is not the elimination of authority, but its proper synthesis with individuality.

Such a synthesis can be effected in both theory and practice, though not easily. The exact difficulty consists in determining which propositions are true. Once that is done, such true propositions have authority over the individual, over his thinking, his taste, and his conduct. He violates them at the price of lessened personality; he follows them with the reward of heightened personality. One develops an actual self out of a potential self only as he assimilates the experience of the race; in time his assimilation may lead on to origination. So the synthesizing formula is this: Authority is to be upheld when its principles are true; individuality is to be asserted against false propositions, whether in theory or practice. Individual freedom is lost by rejecting true authority or by accepting untrue authority. Freedom is not the absence of truth, it is conformity to truth.

Which propositions then are true? And when is a proposition true? Here all the rejected epistemologies come trooping back again. In vain do we reject epistemology, claiming that the problem of knowledge is outgrown. Dr. Dewey himself rejects the historic epistemologies only in the name of an instrumental epistemology. For ourselves those propositions are true which adequately represent fact; they do not have

1 Cf. *The Quest for Certainty*, Chapter IX.

to wait to be true till they successfully control fact; and there are true propositions.

Now concerning Dr. Dewey's own epistemology, that knowledge is successful control of events, that the individual mind is only an agent of reorganization, there are two things to note. The first is that the individual mind does indeed effect changes in the course of physical and social events; it is an agent of reorganization; it is in a measure a directing and controlling influence. Unless it were a useful phase of organic life, it is hard to see why it should have emerged at all in the course of evolution.

The second thing is that the individual mind is more than an agent of reorganization. It is a conscious centre of existence; it is a private self; it is a responsible being; it is a moral agent; it is a source of æsthetic enjoyment. Dr. Dewey's view is depersonalizing; it denies the private personal self. But the evidence for such is ineluctable. We are more sure of sound sensations than of air vibrations; of sight sensations than of ether vibrations; of awareness than of the specific object of which we are aware; of what we meant to say than of what we said. There may be behavior without an observer, but there can be no observation of behavior without an observer. There may be action without a self, but no conduct without a self. The issue hinges precisely on whether the individual mind is public or private. The bodily responses alone are public; all the mental processes are private. They are private, not in the sense that they can not be inferred more or less exactly by an observer, but in the sense that they are not felt by any external observer whatsoever. They occur as the felt experiences of one person only. You, not I, think your thoughts, feel your emotions, make your decisions. The occurrence and the awareness of these processes are private. This is not to deny the influence of environment on the self or the influence of the self on the environment; it is to affirm the privacy of one's awareness. In one sense it is true that we all live in the same world; this means that there is a subjective world of individual consciousness forever closed to all others. You can tell me how you feel and think and decide, but I can not feel your feeling or think your thinking, or decide your decision. As Morris Cohen writes: "To recognize a deliberate lie is to recognize what goes on in the mind of another." And again: ". . . we can not fully understand or conduct human life without some introspection."[1] The personal pronoun "I" refers to a different subject in every case. Education is more than the reorganization of public experience; it is the right cultivation of personalities in both their public and private aspects.

3. Educational Equivalents

Exposition. There are educational equivalents of the philosophies rejected above and of the philosophy accepted. Detailed educational counterparts of the rejected philosophies will not be given. Suffice it to say in general that the school has both exhibited clearly and suffered keenly from the false philosophies which oppose individual freedom to social control. Thus, individual methods of learning have been set over against social action; the social motive and the social atmosphere for learning have been lacking; the method of instruction has been separated from the method of government; slight opportunity has been afforded individual variations; learning has been a carrying over of presented material into a purely individual consciousness; learning, through lack of the social factor, has not socialized the emotional and mental disposition of pupils. In contrast with the effects of a dualistic philosophy dividing the individual from his world, social control enters into the very process of learning under the influence of that unitary philosophy which makes knowledge a phase of active undertakings involving mutual exchange between individuals.

[1] Cohen, M. R., *Reason and Nature,* New York, 1931, pp. 317, 318.

Further educational consequences of the accepted philosophy will now be given in some detail. These all center in the conception of true freedom. There are two mistaken views of freedom, held alike by upholders and opponents of freedom in school. One of these identifies freedom with the absence of social direction, and the other identifies it with the absence of restraint of physical movement. Neither of these is that true freedom which involves both social direction and physical unconstraint. True freedom concerns the conditions which enable an individual to make his own special contribution to a group interest. An individual is truly free whose mental attitude is socially guided as he partakes of group activities. His acts are not authoritatively dictated. So far as the mental phase of behavior is concerned, freedom means essentially the part played by personal thinking in learning, viz., intellectual initiative, independent observation, judicious invention, foreseen consequences, and ingenious adaptation of means to secure them. This is the phase of individual freedom in the social and physical process of learning. It is internal to the process. Discipline and "government" often have to do regrettably with the external side of conduct alone; then, by reaction against such practices, freedom is mistakenly supposed to be the absence of such external restraint. Really, freedom, like other general ideas, refers to the quality of mind expressed in action. There is no real opposition between a supposed mind within and the act without. Freedom belongs to both combined aspects of one process, not to each or to either separately.

On the physical side of behavior, freedom thus means opportunity for unconstrained physical movements. Realizing a problem, undertaking the needed observations, performing the experiments to test the suggested ideas, are all hindered by enforced quietude. There is a physical element in the much-vaunted "self-activity" in education; it is not merely internal, excluding the free use of sensory and motor organs. At certain times little perceptible overt activity is needed, as, for instance, when one is far enough advanced to learn from print or other symbols, or when one is elaborating the implications of an idea preliminary to acting upon it. But completed self-activity includes investigation and experimentation with things, materials, and appliances.

It is a mistake to suppose that to be free one must be alone. Working alone is a matter of detail, working with a group is a matter of principle. There is no inherent opposition between working as an individual, and working with others. To suppose that a child must work alone to be free and to develop his individuality is to measure individuality by distance and so to reduce it to something physical. Certain capacities of the individual are brought out only under the stimulus of associating with others. But this is not to deny that there is a time to be alone and to be let alone. Children, like grown persons, require it to secure calm and concentration.

What does respect for individuality in education really mean? Two things: the pupil is to do his own thinking, and his own responding. The pupil is to do his own thinking, have his own problem, follow his own purpose, make his own observations, do his own reflecting, frame and test his own suggestions. Only so can what he already knows be amplified and rectified. The phrase "thinking for oneself" is a pleonasm; unless one does it for oneself, it is not thinking. Digesting one's food is an individual matter; thinking is no less so.

The pupil is also to do his own responding. Pupils vary in point of view, in the appeal objects make to them, and in their mode of attack. Such variations are not to be suppressed; there should not be uniformity in method of study or in recitation. When such variations are suppressed, many harmful results ensue, such as, mental confusion, artificiality, the destruction of originality, the undermining of confidence in one's own mental operations; and either docile subjection to others or else a running wild of ideas. Individuality in learning is recognized out of school; not to recognize it in school is harmful, more so than when the whole community was governed by custom. It is admitted that systematic scientific advance began when individuals were first allowed and then encouraged to respond to subject matter in their own characteristic way.

But an objector may say, pupils in school are not capable of originating, and so they should be confined to appropriating and reproducing. The reply is twofold.

(i) We are concerned with originality of attitude, not of product. Originality of attitude is the unforced response of one's own individuality. The conditions of learning should be such that to the learner, if not to the advanced student, there is genuine discovery. Measured by product, not attitude, no one expects the young to make original discoveries. The facts and principles embodied in the sciences of nature and man are as yet beyond them.

(ii) But even young pupils react in unfamiliar ways to subject matter already familiar to others. Things strike them freshly, they attack a topic in an unexpected way; they may thus surprise even the most experienced teacher. Such unanticipated responses are to be welcomed. Instead, too often, they are brushed aside as irrelevant, and pupils are held to rehearsing material exactly as conceived by the older person. Both pupil and teacher suffer in consequence; the originality of the pupil goes unused; teaching ceases to be educative to the teacher, he does not get new points of view, he fails to experience intellectual companionship, at most he simply improves his technique. Teaching and learning thus become conventional and mechanical, with accompanying nervous strain on both sides.

The stages of learning are three; action, quiet, and action again. The period of quiet is shorter with the young and longer with the old. But even the old do not stop short of the final action. For the young there is an initial period of general and conspicuous organic action. For the old there is a later time for using what has been apprehended. Between these two periods the mature student seems inactive; he projects his new topic on a large familiar background; random physical experimentation is reduced; activity is specialized; energies are confined to nerve channels, to eyes, and vocal organs; there is intense mental concentration. Obviously such quiet is no model for the young who still have to find their intellectual way about.

The mind and body are thus united in acquiring knowledge. When education recognizes this fact, it is not necessary to insist upon the need of external freedom. That person is free who by thinking enlarges his knowledge and refines his beliefs. Secure the conditions favorable to effective thinking, and freedom will take care of itself. That individual is intellectually free who has a question which piques his curiosity, which leads him eagerly to acquire the information helping him to cope with it, and who has at command the equipment needed for the answer. Such a person's initiative and imaginative vision will be called into play, his impulses and habits will be thereby controlled; and his own purposes will direct his acts. He is adapted to life in a democratic society. Without intellectual freedom in studying and learning, there is seeming attention, docility, memorizing, and reproducing; these partake of intellectual servility. Such intellectual subjection fits the masses into a society where they are expected not to have ideas or aims of their own but to take orders from the few set in authority; it is not adapted to a democracy. In a conservative society, conformity to usage is the ideal; in a progressive society individual variations as the means of social growth are precious.

Comment. This section seems to admit the existence of "a purely individual conciousness" (p. 352) which the previous section denies, though the quoted phrase may refer to a false notion. Furthermore, it allows that one may properly at times work alone. Also, that the student may be without obvious overt action at one stage of his work. Also, that freedom is essentially personal thinking. The individual mind which was cast out the front door in the two preceding sections seems to have returned by the back door in the last section. The only surviving feature in the denial of individual mind is the insistence that the body is always united with the mind in acquiring knowledge. Since few thinkers have ever held that in our present experience the mind can operate without the body and brain, this contention may well be admitted. The mind has a body, yes; but the mind is not a body. The mind has its social relations, yes; but the mind is not its social relations.

Concerning freedom. The view presented is that freedom resides in the set of physical and social conditions allowing effective thinking to go on. This is intellectual freedom. There is no discussion of moral freedom, or the freedom of the individual as a self-determining agent. Here the omission is consistent with the denial of the private, personal, self. Personality is not here presented as a fundamental category. Individuality is allowed not to a private mind, but to the thinking organism in its physical and social environment. The individual is not held to be free to choose. He is also not held to be free to think or not to think as he chooses. He is held to be free in his thinking when unconstrained physically and guided socially. Freedom is thus lack of constraint on thinking.

Such freedom might just as well be called determinism. Wrong conditions constrain thinking; right conditions liberate thinking. In either case the thinking is determined by the conditions. There is no indication that men may voluntarily set to work to improve the conditions. Such would be moral freedom. That man has such freedom has been strongly denied by the determinists of all ages, and as strongly affirmed by the libertarians.[1] That such freedom exists accords with the deliverance of personal consciousness, with the very will to deny it, with the moral sense of mankind, and with the

[1] Cf. the writer's volume: *Free Will and Human Responsibility*, The Macmillan Company.

recognition of intelligence as directive and of action as deliberate. We are not free to do all things; we are free to do some things. Among the educational applications of this view are the following: education is not so much the transformation of experience as the transformation of personality; educating is not so much changing conditions as changing pupils; the control of children may be direct through personal appeal as well as indirect through an impersonal appeal; ethical instruction may be intellectual, direct, and systematic as well as practical, indirect, and incidental; action may be controlled by an idea as well as by a group situation; the categories of duty and obligation may be stressed as well as the categories of sociality and interest; the conception of immortality is permissible as well as the importance of the present.

It should also be noted that the views of the text would educate a society of leaders, not a society of leaders and followers. In the progressive democratic society described each individual is to be an intellectual aristocrat; he does not accept solutions, he finds them; he does not follow the ideas of others; he develops his own ideas and tests them for himself either alone or in a group situation. Each member of the group leads, nobody follows. If anybody follows by accepting the opinions of others without testing them out for himself, it is not recognized in the text. Each member of the group is his own authority. It may well be questioned whether a progressive, democratic society so conceived would be practicable. It would be highly individualistic. It might fall to pieces through its centrifugal forces.

Three suggestions occur to us in this connection. One is that of Professor James, previously mentioned, that the function of education in a democracy is to enable us to select our leaders. This view distinctly implies a few leaders and many followers. A second view is that of President Eliot who urged that a democracy needs to develop confidence in the expert. This again implies a few leaders in each field of knowledge or action and many followers. A third view is that of Ross L. Finney who holds that our democracy is suffering from an excess of individualism and that the remedy is more "passive mentation," and "regimentation of mind" of the many while the colleges develop real leadership among the few.[1] With the suggestions of Professor James and President Eliot we concur but at the suggestion of Professor Finney we demur in so far as any denial of opportunity might be involved in it, though agreeing that even in a democratic society, or especially in it, there must be the progress of all through the expert leadership of the few and the intelligent followership of the many. Dr. Dewey's system would make leaders; would it make followers? And if everybody leads, who is to follow? And whither go we? "For we are suffering from a bankruptcy of followership no less than from a bankruptcy of leadership."[2]

[1] Cf. Finney, R. L., *A Sociological Philosophy of Education*, New York, 1928.

[2] President Glenn Frank, quoted in *The New York Times*, June 22, 1931.

CHAPTER XXIII

VOCATIONAL ASPECTS OF EDUCATION

1. The Meaning of Vocation

Exposition. What we are now going to say may arouse incredibility, but it is none the less true: vocational education is the focus of present conflicts in philosophic theories. Vocational and cultural education are antithetic to each other. "Liberal culture" as an historic term has been linked to the notions of leisure, of purely contemplative knowledge, and of a spiritual activity not involving the active use of the organs of the body. The term "culture" too has latterly been linked with a purely private refinement, a cultivation of certain individual conscious attitudes; it has been an escape from any direction given to it by society and a solace for the necessity of rendering service to society. In contrast, vocational education has been regarded as concrete, practical, physical, even pecuniary.

Recall our discussions of previous dualisms: leisure and labor, theory and practice, mind and body, mental states and the world. They all culminate in this antithesis between culture and vocation. So, significant philosophical issues, though using remote and general terms, do find their focus in the problem of vocational education.

Now we are going to defend the position that education should centre around vocation. To avoid the impression of narrow practicality in such a view, we must at once define vocation. A vocation is life activities so directed that their consequences are significant to oneself and useful to one's associates. Synonyms for vocation are career and occupation. These are all concrete terms for continuity between one's activities and society. They include becoming an artist of any kind, a specialist in science, an effective citizen, as well as engaging in business or one of the professions, to say nothing of mechanical labor. Any one of these may be a gainful pursuit. Vocations include but are not limited to occupations producing tangible commodities. No one of these is opposed to culture or leisure. With any one of these culture and leisure may be associated. What vocation does exclude is, on the personal side, aimlessness, capriciousness, lack of achievement, and, on the social side, idle display and parasitic dependence. Vocation is consistent with culture but inconsistent with having nothing useful one can do. Culture is consistent with vocation but inconsistent with doing nothing personally significant or socially useful.

So vocations are not limited to producing material commodities. Neither is one person limited to one vocation. Such restricted specialism is impossible. Nothing could be more absurd than to try to educate individuals to follow only one line of activity. The notions that each individual should have only one vocation and that each vocation should have its own education are objectionable on two counts, (i) each individual has of necessity a variety of callings, and (ii) any one occupation isolated from other interests loses its meanings. To each of these points special attention will be given.

(i) Every individual should be intelligently effective in a variety of callings. One of these he has in common with a few; the others he has in common with all. But they are no less callings on that account, especially when the vocational phases of one's education are being considered. For illustration, take the artist. No one is just an artist and nothing else; the more he is only an artist the less is he a human being; to be just an artist is to be a kind of monstrosity. In addition, the artist must be, at some period of his life, a member of a family; he must have friends and companions; he must support himself (or be parasitically supported by others) and so have business dealings; he is a member of some political party, and so on. His callings are many; we *name* his vocation from his distinctive calling.

(ii) One's social efficiency in one's calling is dependent upon its association with other callings. When isolated from other interests, one's occupation loses its meaning and becomes routine, just keeping busy. Consider the artist again. If his artistry is to be more than a technical accomplishment, he must have experience, he must *live*. The content of his art can not be found within his art; it must be found in what he suffers and enjoys in other relationships. And this suffering and enjoying again depends upon how alert and sympathetic his interests are. The same is true of any other calling. Every distinctive, specialized vocation tends through habit to become too dominant, too exclusive, too absorbing. This leads to emphasis on skill at the expense of meaning. So far from fostering this tendency, education should safeguard against it. So far from educating exclusively for one's distinctive calling, we should educate for all one's callings, that is, for all one's personally significant and socially useful activities. Such education is culturally vocational. It is far from being narrowly practical and utilitarian.

Comment. Three things are noteworthy here. One is this further illustration of the use of a familiar term with an unfamiliar meaning. Usually by vocation we mean the occupation by which one earns his living. It is commonly recognized that one's vocation is not his only interest. Among his other interests are his health, his character, his enjoyment of art, his social relations, his knowledge, and his religion. These all affect the success of his vocation, but they are not his vocation. The definition given in the text extends the usual meaning of one's vocation to cover all his personally significant and socially useful activities; one's vocation is to be usefully human. Of course one has the right to define the terms he uses. In this case the effect of the meaning given the term is so to widen it that vocational education will be equivalent to liberal and vocational education. This is to beg the question at issue by initial definition. The only activities excluded by the definition of vocation would be the personally insignificant and the socially useless. Only an education for these would be non-vocational. And for such an education there is no call. So all education, by definition, becomes vocational. This obscures the real issue, which is, may some personally significant activities not be socially useful? May some knowledge be worth while on its own account without solving any social problem? May there be an education for leisure that is not an education for work? Of course, if one's vocation is defined as being fully human, then all education is vocational, without quarrel. But when "vocational" includes everything worthy and excludes nothing worthy, it has ceased to be meaningful and useful as a term.

A second related thing. We have just seen the definition is too broad, including too many of the worthy interests of life. It is also too broad in excluding from the definition some unworthy interests in life. There are socially useless vocations, such as racketeering, rum-running, boot-legging, burglary, banditry, dope-peddling, "Mrs. Warren's profession," and the like. Any one of the social vices may be used as a business, a vocation, an occupation. One may have a career of crime. These are all vocations in the sense that they are ways of making a living. Our government caught Al Capone, not because he had no business or because it was dishonest, but because he had not paid his income-tax on his ill-gotten gains. The price of making all culture vocational by a definition is flight from the reality of unworthy vocations. This fault of not recognizing distinctions appears also in handling the conceptions of "experience" and "life."[1] "Education through first-hand experience" means little that is valuable till it is recognized that some experience is bad. "The school is life" means little that is valuable till it is recognized that some life should not be in the school. Dr. Dewey himself is less amenable to this criticism than some of his followers.

[1] Cf. Cohen, Morris, *Reason and Nature*, pp. 450 and ff.

A third thing. The position taken in the text would seem logically to oppose any scheme of vocational education based on a specific analysis of the jobs available in society with a curriculum set up to prepare for each.[1] Is such opposition practical?

2. The Place of Vocational Aims in Education

Exposition. Conceive vocational aims broadly enough, and their place in education is basic. The content of one's vocation is varied, but it is all connected. Any particular calling should be projected upon a broad background. Having these things in mind, we shall now consider education for one's distinctive career in life.

In this discussion three principles will guide us, viz., one's occupation harmonizes his individual capacity with his social service; the best way to learn is *through* occupations; and the only adequate way to train *for* occupations is *through* occupations. Special consideration will be given to each of these principles.

(1) To find out what one is fitted to do and to secure an opportunity to do it,—that is the key to happiness. Such an occupation balances individual capacity and social service. Failure to discover one's true business in life, to drift, or to be forced into an uncongenial calling, is tragic,—nothing is more tragic. The right occupation for any person means simply that his aptitudes are in adequate play, working with the minimum of friction and the maximum of satisfaction, and yielding one's best service to the other members of a community.

Two illustrations of this principle of balance between individual capacity and social service will be given, a positive one from Plato and a negative one from slavery. As we saw (Chapter VII, § 3), Plato asserted it was the business of education to discover what each person is good for, to train him

[1] Cf. Snedden, D., *Towards Better Educations*, New York, 1931.

for it, that he might thus serve society most harmoniously. This is the fundamental principle of a philosophy of education. In laying down this principle Plato was not in error. His error was in unduly limiting the number of socially useful vocations and thus limiting the infinite variety of individual capacities.

Slave labor, too, is generally believed to be ultimately wasteful, even economically. And this for two reasons, viz., the stimulus under slavery is not sufficient to direct the energies of slaves, and, slaves being confined to prescribed callings, much talent remains unavailable to the community. Here are wastage and dead loss. The noteworthy thing is that results similar to these of slavery happen whenever an individual does not find himself in his work. His real energies are undirected and his real talent is not applied. And no one can find himself completely when vocations are looked upon with contempt and when a conventional and non-vocational ideal of culture, essentially the same for all, is maintained. One's vocation both cultivates and utilizes one's capacities. Herein is happiness, to find your work and to work your find.

(2) The best way to learn is *through* occupations. An occupation is a continuous activity having a purpose. No other method combines within itself so many of the factors conducive to learning. Thus, being a foe to passive receptivity, it calls instincts and habits into play; aiming at results, it has an end in view; having an end in view, the activity can be neither routine nor capricious; the movement being progressive, leading from one stage to another, there are required at each stage, observation, ingenuity, and thought to overcome obstacles and to discover and readapt means of execution. Conditions should allow the activity itself, not its external product, to be the aim. So pursued, an occupation fulfills the requirements laid down earlier for aims, interest, and thinking (See Chapters VIII, X, and XII).

A vocation is an occupation. As occupation is the best way to learn, so also is vocation. A vocation is necessarily an organizing principle for information, knowledge, ideas, and intellectual growth, causing different experiences and facts to fall into order with one another, providing an axis running through an immense diversity of detail. One's vocation is a constant stimulus to note and to correlate pertinent material, motivating both one's gathering and retaining of relevant information. "The vocation acts as both magnet to attract and glue to hold" (p. 362). So it is with lawyer, physician, chemist, parent, and locally interested citizen.

Furthermore, knowledge so organized is vital, it has reference to needs. Being expressed in action and readjusted in action, it never becomes stagnant. Being knit under the stress of one's occupation, it is solid and effective. Consider by way of contrast any selection and arrangement of facts consciously worked out for purely abstract ends; it is formal, superficial, and cold. The best way to learn, then, is for children through occupations, and, for adults, through occupation.

(3) Training *for* occupations is training *through* occupations. This is the only adequate way. The educative process is its own end, we saw (Chapter VI). The way to prepare for the future is to make the most of the present. These principles apply in full force to the vocational phases of education. The dominant vocation of all persons at all times is living itself, that is, intellectual and moral growth. This fact is naked and unconcealed in childhood and youth, with their relative freedom from economic stress.

So, education should not be a strict preparation for some pre-determined future occupation. Such an education injures the possibilities of present development and thereby reduces the adequacy of preparation for the right employment in the future. Instead, all the earlier preparation for a vocation should be indirect. Pupils prepare indirectly for their future vocations by engaging in those occupations indicated by their needs and interests at the time. Only so can educator and educand genuinely discover those personal aptitudes indicating a later proper choice of a specialized pursuit.

Moreover, the discovery of aptitude is itself a *constant* process, not an accomplished fact. While growth continues, new capacities are being discovered. To assume that one's life work is chosen once for all is conventional and arbitrary. Suppose, for example, one discoveries he has an interest in the intellectual and social matters having to do with engineering and so makes that his calling. His decision determines only in outline the field for his further growth; it is a map, roughly sketched, to direct his further activities. He has discovered his profession in the sense in which Columbus discovered America,—by touching its shores. Future detailed and extensive explorations remain to be made.

A few words about "vocational guidance." The aim should be a flexible attitude of readjustment. This, in effect, is a choice of a new and further calling. Vocational guidance should not lead up to a definitive, irretrievable, and complete choice. If it does, both education and vocation are likely to be rigid; further growth is hampered; the person concerned will be left in a permanently subordinate position, executing the intelligent directions of those having a more flexible and readjustable calling. Adults have to be watchful lest their callings shut down on them and fossilize them; how much more should the vocational preparation of youth engage them in the continuous reorganizing of aims and methods! At this point vocational counsellors must be careful.

There is an important social aspect to this question of a free or fixed training for a free or fixed calling. The prevention of the development of freedom and responsibility is often a conscious object in an autocratically managed society; a few do the planning and ordering, the many follow directions and are deliberately confined to narrow and prescribed channels. Thus we have a master class and a subject class. The scheme inures to the prestige and profit of the master class, but it confines the opportunities for learning through experience of that class and limits the development of the subject class. In both ways, as we have previously seen

(Chapter XIX, § 2), the life of the society as a whole is hampered. A fixed training for a fixed vocation may develop a machine-like, routine, skill; it may also develop distaste, aversion, and carelessness; it will not develop alert observation and ingenious planning which make an occupation intellectually rewarding.

Comment. There are several observations to be made here. The first concerns the two meanings of the term "occupation." The first is any continuous purposeful activity, the second is one's vocation or calling in life. The first of the three principles, which states that one's occupation balances individual capacity with social service, uses the term in the second sense. The second principle, which says the best way to learn is through occupations, uses the term in both senses at the same time. The third principle, which says that training *for* occupations is training *through* occupations, uses the term the first instance in the second sense and the second instance in both senses. The three principles might be stated in one as follows: one's vocation in life harmonizes him with society, organizes his experience, and is best prepared for first by purposeful activities and then by practicing the vocation itself.

The second thing to note is that the principle of training for occupations through occupations has both a logical and a temporal limitation. Logically, it is limited by the fact that much enjoyable and useful knowledge is acquired without the aid of purposeful activities at all, but by such means as reading, being read to, having questions answered, and hearing stories told. Thus, a child of seven may converse intelligently about prehistoric animals, such as the dinosaur, pterodactyl, and eohippus. Of course, it is an aid in clarifying ideas, if he can also draw and model these creatures. The temporal limitation is that there comes a time when one prepares for medicine, law, and chemistry by going to a professional school in which one gives up his childhood purposeful activities but is not yet practicing his profession. His education is distinctly preparatory. Only under the now discarded apprenticeship system did one learn to follow a profession by following it.

A third observation is that under these conceptions life becomes vocationalized. It may be with a broad background, but nevertheless it does. The man may bring much to his vocation, but he is no bigger than it is. A supplementary conception would allow a man to have an avocation as well as a vocation, a hobby as well as a job. Some of our most serviceable men have such hobbies. One of the greatest teachers and finest scholars of our age, the Assyriologist, R. W. Rogers, had a number of hobbies. He collected canes, pocket-knives, precious stones, stamps, and Johnsonia; he was a printer, a violinist, and a rosarian.[1] He was a more efficient and more human worker because of his avocational interests.

Again, from the list of vocations one misses the greatest of all,—that of being oneself, one's own unreduplicable self. Most of the service we can render society can be as well or better rendered by some other person. But no other person can be myself for me. Here is a centre of conscious experience uniquely felt as belonging only to myself. What I say to myself, lay upon myself, the way I feel toward myself, the kind of experiences I allow and forbid myself, here is a vocation behind, in, and through one's service to society. My self is much more than my distinctive aptitude; it is all my aptitudes, attitudes, and ideas as phases of a single self-conscious existence.

Finally, it helps us to realize the positivistic significance of Dr. Dewey's philosophy to note that he refers to one's calling now as something one can make and now as something one can choose. It is represented as determined by the aptitude of the individual. There is nothing objective or cosmic or externally teleological about one's calling. There is another view, that one's calling is a call, involving some cosmic

[1] Cf. Thompson, W. J., "Professor Robert William Rogers," *Methodist Review*, May–June, 1931.

intention. It is found in the "call to the ministry," but not there only. Many leaders have felt it. So Joan of Arc, at eighteen, raised the siege of Orleans and led her king to his coronation in Rheims. So George Washington freed his country. If such an interpretation can not be positively affirmed to be correct, neither can it be denied as incorrect. So to interpret the universe in relation to the individual is to add a quality and a value to life and a dynamic to social service not otherwise available.

3. Present Opportunities and Dangers

Exposition. The present opportunities include making vocations cultural and the present dangers include perpetuating class distinctions by trade education. In this section we will discuss these matters in some detail. In doing so we will come near to the heart of our educational philosophy.

The first thing to observe is that education, historically speaking, has actually been vocational, at least in fact, if not in name. This is true both of the masses and the classes.

(i) Consider the education of the masses. It has always been distinctly utilitarian. It was called apprenticeship, or else just learning from experience, rather than education. The three R's were the tools used in labor. The schools were devoted to these tools because reading, writing, and figuring were the common elements used in all kinds of work. There were two phases to this apprenticeship type of education: the in-school and the out-of-school. The two supplemented each other. The in-school phase was narrow and formal. The out-of-school phase was working in some special line under orders. Such education of the masses was vocational and was intended to be so. The objection to it is not that it was vocational but that it was narrowly so.

(ii) The education of the dominant classes was likewise essentially vocational, at least to a considerable extent. The pursuits of the dominant classes have been ruling and enjoying. They were vocations, professional in character, but by chance they were not called so. The occupations that were called vocations or employments involved manual labor, working for keep or for its money equivalent, or rendering personal service to specific persons. A corresponding tradition grew up. It divided society into those with callings and those without callings. Those without callings or employments were the classes. Those with employments were the masses. The masses were contemned by the classes as rendering service to specific employers. It was not recognized that the classes were also rendering service to the ultimate employer, the community. This traditional distinction is still at the bottom of our not recognizing the education of the classes as vocational. But it is so none the less.

Let us consider some illustrations of the false distinctions between a utilitarian education for the employed masses and a supposed non-utilitarian education for the allegedly unemployed classes. Once the profession of the surgeon and the physician ranked almost as low as that of the valet and the barber. Why? Partly, forsooth, because it had to deal with the body, and partly because it was direct service to another individual for pay. Among the vocations, education for which is really vocational, though supposed to be liberal, we may list the following: directing political or economic concerns, in peace or war; display, the adornment of the person; social or other leadership; spending money; teaching; research; conspicuous idleness; and literary pursuits. Higher education in the past, wherever not under the thumb of tradition, has actually given preparation for all these employments, though unconsciously so. Higher education to-day is doing the same thing; it is for a certain class (albeit smaller than formerly), mainly preparing for engaging effectively in the pursuits indicated. In its advanced work higher education is engaged largely in training for the calling of teaching and special research. Yet such education has been strangely regarded as non-vocational and even as peculiarly cultural.

Peculiar superstition! Literary training is especially enthralled by this superstition. It fits for writing newspaper editorials which, in turn, advocate a cultural education and oppose a practical education! So with articles and books in behalf of humane, non-vocational, education,—written by persons educationally trained for their work. Teachers trained for their profession will argue against the encroachments of a specialized education, calling their own liberal. It is all a conventional, social pattern, this regarding of the business of the classes as liberal, this overlooking of the cultural possibilities of the employments of the masses.

In our own time there is a conscious emphasis on vocational education, a disposition to make explicit and deliberate vocational aims previously implicit and unconscious. It is the most important aspect of current educational theory and practice. It is so because it builds education upon occupations and suggests the needed type of school reform. It is worth while to consider the causes of this movement. We may enumerate five of these.

First, democracies are coming to recognize the dignity of labor, whether manual or commercial. There is an increased esteem for tangible services rendered to society; "service" is a much-lauded moral ideal. Labor is extolled. Society supports men and women intellectually and economically; theory is demanding that they do something in return. One is socially responsible for the use of his time and capacity; this is more generally recognized than formerly. Lives of conspicuous idle display are still lived; they receive still much admiration and envy; they are condemned by the better moral sentiment. If labor is esteemed, vocational education must be.

Second, the industrial vocations have come to the front in the last century and a half. A hereditary landed gentry has been displaced. The immediate directors of social affairs are now the manufacturer, the banker, and the captain of industry. Manufacturing and commerce, once domestic, local, incidental, are now world-wide, engaging the best energies of an increasingly large number of persons. The problem of social readjustment to changing conditions, always present, is now openly industrial; it has to do with capital and labor. How is schooling to be related to this new industrial life? That question will not down to-day. The great increase in the social importance of conspicuous industrial processes will not allow it. Our education is inherited from a different set of social conditions; it is challenged by modern industrialism; it faces new problems inescapably. A new conception of vocational, including industrial, education, is imperative.

Third, the machine age can and should provide the worker with intellectual emancipation; actually it is making him an appendage to the machine he tends; the school must come to the rescue. To develop these ideas somewhat, we note again, as oft before, that modern industry has ceased to be empirical and has become scientific. Once its procedure was handed down by custom, rule-of-thumb; now its technique is technological; its machinery is devised by mathematics, physics, chemistry, bacteriology, and the other sciences. Manufacture has become "machinofacture." The economic revolution brought about by transfering industry from the home to the factory, from the hand to the machine, set problems for science, thus creating intellectual respect for the machine. And science reciprocated with compound interest, giving solutions for problems and a cultural background for mechanical operations. Thus industry has acquired "infinitely greater intellectual content and infinitely larger cultural possibilities" than it had formerly.

But what is the condition of the laborer? Lacking this background, workers sink inevitably to the status of tools of machines they operate. The worker must adjust himself to his machine. He lacks a tool he can use to his own purpose. In this respect he is in worse estate than the worker under the old régime. Those craftsmen did not belong to their tools; they were approximately equal in knowledge and outlook;

they developed personal ingenuity within at least a narrow range. The old worker used a tool; the modern worker is a tool. Actually, the age of machine production for world-wide markets is less educative for the masses than was the age of hand production for local markets.

Intellectual possibilities greater, intellectual attainments smaller! Such is our situation for the many in our modern machine age. The solution? The school! The demand is imperative. Education must acquaint workers with the scientific and social bases and bearings of their pursuits. The new school must carry the burden of realizing the intellectual possibilities inhering in modern work. This means vocational education.

Fourth, though it may fall strangely upon our ears, the school shop is a laboratory where knowledge is made. Under the influence of modern science, the pursuit of knowledge is experimental; it is less dependent upon literary tradition, less associated with dialectics and symbols. Industrial occupations now present more of the content of science than formerly; they also embody the method of science. In the school shop the chief conscious concern of the student is insight; any intellectual interest aroused by a problem may be followed up. Where laboratory and shop are conventionally separated in schools, knowledge is made in the laboratory and applied in the shop. The social bearings of a scientific principle are emphasized in the shop. With many pupils a livelier interest is stimulated by the shop. The worker in the laboratory produces knowledge; the ordinary worker in the factory at present is under pressure to produce profit. It is for industrial occupations in the school to produce knowledge in the scientific way through controlling materials successfully.

Fifth, and finally, through industry we learn. Modern psychology has shown us about learning in general and childhood learning in particular. It emphasizes the radical importance of native unlearned tendencies to explore, to experiment, to try. It shows that learning is not the work of a ready-made mind. Most remarkable of all, it reveals mind itself as an organization of native capacities into activities having significance. Younger pupils play; older pupils play and work; both are engaged in the educative development of raw native activities. The passage from play to work should be gradual; the play spirit of enjoying the activity for its own sake should be carried forward into work; no radical change of attitude should occur; the reorganization should be continuous and in behalf of greater control with greater reference to the outcome of the activity. All this obviously falls in line with the increased importance of occupations in life. By occupation we learn and by occupation we live.

Thus, in these five ways has come about in our day a conscious emphasis upon vocational, that is, occupational, education. The reader will remark how this argument resumes our previous contentions. The arguments for vocational educational summarize our philosophy of education. And the reader will now be prepared for our reconstructive suggestion: *our schools should become occupational.* This is the key to the present educational situation. The reconstruction of our educational system will have to be gradual. The occupations used should typify the social callings. A change of both materials and methods is involved. The intellectual and moral content of the occupations is to be brought out. What is wanted is the intelligent development of consecutive and cumulative activities. Text books are only auxiliaries, though necessary indeed. All literary and dialectical methods must be relegated to the rank of aids in guiding the ongoing process.

In the proposed reform of schools, which would make all education occupational, there is a grave danger to be avoided. It is that vocational education will be interpreted in theory and practice as trade education. Vocational education is the use of occupations for intellectual and moral purposes. Trade education is a means of securing technical efficiency in specialized future pursuits. Vocational education utilizes the factors of industry to make school life more active, more meaningful, more connected with out-of-school experience. Trade education gives a technical preparation for industries and professions as they now operate. Existing industrial conditions are not to be reproduced in the school; the school is not to be made into an adjunct of manufacture and commerce. The transformation needed will not be easy. One standing danger is that education will perpetuate the older traditions for a select few. Another is that it will adjust itself to the newer economic conditions on the basis of acquiescence. That would be calamitous, for our newer economic conditions, our present industrial régime, are defective, unrationalized, and unsocialized. Education should not perpetuate the existing industrial, social order, it should transform it.

A narrow trade education obstructs all social progress and all educational reform. It splits our education and our society. It transmits into a nominally democratic society the older divisions of labor and leisure, of menial service and culture, of body and mind, of directed and directive classes. It discounts the scientific and human connections of industrial materials and processes. Such intellectual and historic connections are regarded in narrow trade circles as waste time, not "practical," suitable for the leisure class with superior economic resources, even as dangerous to the interests of the controlling class through the possible arousing of ambition "beyond the station" of directed workers. We require not a vocationalist but a cultivated vocationalist as the outcome of our transformed school and social order.

Why not perpetuate the existing order? Its greatest evil is not poverty and its suffering, but callings, without any personal appeal, pursued for money. Sentimentally viewed, that sounds harsh. Actually, however, such callings are bad for laborers and capitalists. Laborers are constantly provoked to aversion, ill-will, and a desire to slight and evade; neither their hearts nor their minds are in their work. The capitalists are much better off in worldly goods; they are in excessive, or even monopolistic, control of the activities of the workers; but they are shut off from equal and general social intercourse; they try to bridge the distance separating them from others by impressive force, superior possession, and idle enjoyment; they are stimulated to pursue indulgence and display. Thus, at present, both intellectual and emotional limitations characterize both the employed and the employing class. The employed, not being interested in what they are doing, are looking for a money reward; the employers are looking for profit and power. The interest in wages gets restricted expression in certain direct muscular movements. The interest in private profit or personal power gets expression in greater intellectual initiation, in a larger survey of conditions, and in directing and combining a large number of diverse factors. None the less, since such work of the directors does not contemplate its social bearings, intelligence is inevitably limited to technical, non-humane, non-liberal channels. In fact, the economically unfortunate, not having experienced the hardening effects of a one-sided control of the affairs of others, have often a more sympathetic and humane disposition than their employers.

A narrowly conceived scheme of vocational education would perpetuate this division. It would take its stand on the feudal dogma of social predestination, it would assume that some are to continue to be wage earners, it would aim simply to give them greater technical efficiency by means of trade education. There is no objection to technical proficiency *per se;* it is often sadly lacking; it is desirable both for producing better goods at less cost and for securing the greater happiness of the worker, no one caring for what he can only half do. But there is a vast difference between efficiency in carrying out the plans of others in one's immediate work and efficiency in forming one's own plans with insight into their social bearings. Trade education perpetuates the existing economic order; vocational education would transform it.

Into what? It is not difficult to provide a formal answer. The desired society is one in which each individual has work; this work is congenial because based on aptitudes; the worker's interest is uncoërced and intelligent; each person's work makes the lives of others better worth living; it accordingly makes the ties binding persons together more perceptible. The ideal society is a worker's society. The variety of workers is numberless. We are far from such a social state; literally we may never arrive at it. But the quality of social changes already made lies in this direction; resources for its realization are more ample than ever; given the intelligent will, no insuperable obstacles stand in the way.

Upon what does its successful realization depend? More upon suitable educational methods than anything else. The desired change is in the quality of mental disposition. This is a change to be wrought by education. Not that mind and character can be changed by instruction and exhortation, apart from changes in industrial and political conditions. That would not be education; nor would it involve the true idea of mind and character, which are really attitudes of participative response in social affairs. But the method is to produce in schools a typical projection of the society we want to realize; and, by forming minds in such a school, to modify gradually the larger and more recalcitrant features of adult society.

The solution of the social problem is the same as the solution of the educational problem: a cultural occupation. Those in a position to make their wishes good, will demand a liberalized occupation for youth. This will give them directive power.

What would such a cultural or liberalized vocation include? At least four things, viz., (1) instruction in the historic background of present conditions; (2) training in science, to give intelligent initiative in dealing with the materials and agencies of production; (3) the study of economics, civics, and politics, to bring the future worker into touch with current problems and methods of progress; and (4) training the powers of re-adaptation to changing conditions, so that future workers would not be blindly subject to any imposed fate.

This ideal has to contend with two things, the inertia of educational tradition and the opposition of the captains of industry, who realize that such an educational system, if made general, would threaten their ability to exploit others. Such opposition is an encouragement to those believing in a better order; it presages a more equitable and enlightened economic arrangement, giving evidence, as it does, of the dependence of society upon the school. A vocational education is to be promoted which does not subject youth to the present system but which utilizes the scientific and social factors of the present system to develop an intelligence that is courageous, practical, and executive.

The new school will utilize industrial life to develop mind and character. In modern industrial life there are enough scientific content and method and enough social intercourse to allow this. The right educational use of modern industrialism would so affect intelligence and interest as to modify, through legislative and administrative agencies, the present evils of that system. Social sympathy is increasing; it is now a somewhat blind philanthropic sentiment; the occupational school would turn it to constructive account. Industrial workers would share in social control and so become masters of their industrial fate.

Vocational education is a crucial problem to-day. The reason is that it concentrates in a specific issue two fundamental questions, viz., Is intelligence better exercised apart from, or within, activities putting nature to human use? Is culture best secured under egoistic, or social, conditions? Readers of our previous eight chapters will have no doubt of our rejecting the former alternatives, and accepting the latter.

Comment. Here we reach the climax of Dr. Dewey's educational philosophy. The new things here are the synthesis of the old things and their application to the specific problem of vocational education.

It is evident that Dr. Dewey's prime interests are scientific rather than humanistic, social rather than personal, economic rather than literary, and naturalistic rather than transcendental. It seems not to be given to any thinker to be adequately synthetic of all the values of life. This suggests the logical demand for an absolute knower.

To be more specific, past education of the classes and the masses can be claimed as vocational in character only by universalizing the meaning of "vocation" to include all activities of life pursued with a purpose. To enlarge the denotation of a term in this way is to make it less meaningful. A term that covers everything means nothing. Instead of calling past conceptions of liberal education really vocational, it would probably be clearer to define education as the acquisition of the art of living completely, and then distinguish within this art vocational and non-vocational elements. Certainly in the past, Plato and Aristotle, the Renaissance humanists, the English universities, and the American colleges, to go no further, thought they knew the difference between a liberal and a vocational education. It was the difference between living, which was broad, and earning a living, which was narrow, always recognizing that earning a living was one phase of living. It was the difference in attitude between pursuing truth for the joy of the pursuit and possessing and pursuing truth to use it in solving the problems arising in daily life. Thus, a man who studies mathematics because he loves it, pursues the study liberally; one who studies it to become a mechanical engineer pursues it vocationally. There are these two types of attitude. In some persons they may be combined. It would not do to say that in all persons they should be combined. A later generation may very well apply vocationally what an earlier generation acquired liberally. In any case, man loves knowledge on its own account, and will have some of it. As Sheldon says: "Nor can the pure æsthetic delight of knowing be abolished by apotheosis of experimental sociology;

it is as intense and persistent as the gregarious impulse which Western democracy glorifies.''[1]

What Dr. Dewey is really denying is the right of any person to enjoy leisure at the expense of another person's labor. This can be admitted at once as an ethical right and as a plank in a platform of social reform without confusing the historic meanings of the terms ''liberal'' and ''vocational.'' What Dr. Dewey is really demanding is that all workers be given the cultural backgrounds of their occupations. This too can at once be accepted without implying, however, that the only culture worth having is this vocationalized culture.

It will be noted also that again in this section there is the double meaning attaching to the term ''occupation.'' The first meaning is purposeful activities of any sort pursued by children or adults; the second meaning is one's distinctive service to society based on aptitude. The occupations of young children are not occupations in the second sense of the term. But the use of the single term with a double meaning allows reference to the occupational school as the solution of the social problem. It is held that by occupations children learn best and by an occupation adults learn best. It is also held that children educated in an occupational school will as adults reform society, calling legislation to their aid.

Both of these positions deserve comment. That children learn in an occupational (or ''activity'') school is indisputable; that they learn best in this type of school is dubious, seeing the gaps and lack of system in knowledge so acquired; that they should learn only by using occupational methods is deniable, seeing the many modes of learning besides the ''project,'' such as, reading for interest, hearing stories, seeing pictures, asking questions, etc. The same school may wisely have ''listening,'' as well as ''doing,'' features.

That the occupational school will reform society in time is doubtful. The reasons are that the socially unified school, even

[1] Sheldon, W. H., ''Professor Dewey, the Protagonist of Democracy,'' *The Journal of Philosophy*, XVIII, p. 314.

if it generally existed, would be surrounded by a divided society; that children are perhaps more influenced by community standards than by school standards (it will be recalled that Plato sent the elders away from the society he would reform); that children would have difficulty in transferring their social school attitudes to adult life; that schools usually reflect societies rather than change them; and that societies have usually been changed by adults with radical attitudes not acquired in school. Societies have used schools for their own ends; schools have not revolutionized societies. A study of social revolutions indicates that the movement got under way by adult initiative, was established by adult initiative, and then used the schools to perpetuate itself during the coming generations. Dr. Dewey proposes nothing less than an economic revolution; he then calls upon the occupational school to accomplish it. The recommended means are probably inadequate to the desired end. Social changes come rather by the adult population changing the school than by the school changing the adult population. There are those who claim that teaching morals in the schools of France for two generations made the morale of the French army in the World War. This seems far-fetched. Others claim that the teaching of temperance in the American public schools brought about prohibition. At most it could have been only one among many causes. This is not to minimize the social significance of the work done in schools; it is to evaluate it. Schools usually lag behind the needs of the social situation; rarely do they keep abreast of them; never, practically, have they anticipated them. In this connection a profitable study might be made of the causes of the American Revolution, the French Revolution, the Russian Revolution, and the recent Spanish Revolution. To what extent were the schools a factor?

How then is social reform to come about, if not through the school? Social reforms eventuate through the attitudes of adults. These attitudes are affected only in part by earlier schooling. They are affected mainly by the institutions and affairs of society to which men are related, viz., the home, the state, newspapers, libraries, the church, scientific advances, the economic life, the recreational life, the economic and social trends in neighboring societies, and geographical influences. The problem of directing these changes is enormous. Even the notion of doing so consciously is recent, *e.g.*, the Russian "five-year plan." Hitherto, the race has met, somewhat empirically, one emergency after another as it arose. Only the few prophets and saviors of the race have had a social plan for all. Their vision has aided and inspired their followers. In short, social changes are due to the attitudes of adults, which themselves have many complex causes.

It is at this point that some critics of Dr. Dewey say he has a method but not a program. It is the scientific method of experimentation, not a program of any kind of "ism." He believes in independent political action without commitment to any platform or party. This is too vague to command votes. He is at the head of the "Peoples' Lobby," which is not an organ of Socialism, though its work is socialistic.

The critics of Dr. Dewey who say he has a method but not a program are not fair to him, like those who say he has a methodology but not a metaphysics. Methodology involves metaphysics, a method involves a program. His method of occupational activities leads to his program of an ideal society: one in which every person is employed, in accord with his own aptitude, in rendering useful service to society. Let us look at this outcome. It is a community of workers at once highly individualized through following one's aptitude and highly socialized through rendering useful service. The work done by the individual may be of any kind that expresses his talent and at the same time binds him to his fellows. The implied limitation is that one is not to engage in isolating activities; one is not to work without increasing the value of life for others.

The elements of value recognized in this workers' community are history, science, economics, civics, politics, and readaptability. Health, literature, and art are omitted from the stated list, but perhaps implied. A leisure class is intentionally excluded, though it is implied that those who labor may enjoy leisure. Philosophical speculation concerning matters beyond social experience is intentionally excluded, though philosophy as the study of social conflicts remains by implication. Religion, as prayer, praise, or worship of any transcendent Being, is intentionally excluded, though religion as social passion remains by implication.

Just here the following comments would seem to be in order. A greater recognition in this ideal of human society should be accorded the problem of health, the enjoyment of literature and art for their own sake, the wise use of leisure time, the impulse of man to speculate concerning the unexperienced, and man's religious need of the Infinite. The picture as drawn in the text for man's ideal society and his preparation for membership in it is singularly drab, dour, unimaginative, and unappealing. It is stark naturalism untouched by emotion; it is man lifting himself into sociality by the might of his own intelligent control of nature; it is Comte's positivism without his love and worship of man. Contrast Dewey's transformed vocationalized society with Plato's *Republic,* More's *Utopia,* Bacon's *New Atlantis,* Campanella's *City of the Sun,* Harrington's *Oceana,* Bellamy's *Looking Backward,* Wells' *New Worlds for Old.* The new and dubious thing is the supremacy of the scientific method in the educational process as the means of transforming a competitive industrialism into a coöperative community; the lost arts are *a priori* thinking and worship. Philosophy becomes sociology and religion becomes science. This proposed reconstruction of experience enriches the values of living in certain scientific and social ways but impoverishes it in many personal, philosophical, and religious ways. Man has lost his self and his God, but he still has left his own adaptive behavior and that of his fellow organisms.

PART IV

THE PHILOSOPHY OF EDUCATION

CHAPTER XXIV

PHILOSOPHY OF EDUCATION

1. A Critical Review

Exposition. In this section we will seek to unify the previous argument and so reveal our philosophy of education as it has been in action. We have been dealing with the philosophy of education, but there has been as yet no explicit consideration of its nature and no definition of philosophy. We will first introduce the subject by giving a summarizing account of the logical order implied in the previous discussions; this will bring out the philosophical issues involved. Following this section we will give and discuss our notion of philosophy. This final part of our whole inquiry will be concluded by two chapters dealing with knowledge and morals. Philosophical terms will there be used. The different theories of these two important matters will be discussed as they are implied in the practical operation of varying educational ideals.

The prior chapters fall logically into three parts, as follows:

I. The first six chapters deal with education as a social need and function. They outline the general features of education as the process whereby social groups maintain their continuous existence. Education renews the meanings of experience through a transmissive process. This process is partly incidental to the ordinary companionship of youth and adults and partly deliberately instituted to effect the continuity of earlier and later societies. This transmissive process leads to the growth and the control of both the immature individuals and their social group. It is not commonly recognized that the group grows as well as the individual. This formal consideration takes no account of the quality of the social group, of the *kind* of society aiming at perpetuating itself through education.

Some social groups are conservative and aim simply at the preservation of established customs under the control of a superior class. Others are intentionally progressive, aim at a greater variety of mutually shared interests, allow greater freedom to their constituent members, and feel the need of securing in individuals a consciously socialized interest. Such progressive societies have the democratic quality. The democratic criterion was adopted in the further analysis of education.

II. The succeeding eleven chapters were devoted to the detailed study of that education appropriate to the development of a democratic community. The democratic school and the democratic society have the same ideal: the reorganization of experience so as to enrich its recognized meaning and increase the capacity of individuals to act as the directive guardians of its reorganization. From this democratic standpoint the character, principles, and unity of subject matter and method were then outlined. Method in study and learning is just consciously reorganizing the subject matter of experience.

III. The following six chapters dealt with the present limitations in realizing the democratic ideal in school and society. Incidental criticisms were directed at contrasting, non-democratic principles. The obstacles to democracy have a common root in the notion that experience consists of a variety of segregated interests; that each interest has its own independent value, material, and method; that each interest checks every other; that thus a kind of "balance of power" is formed in education.

What assumptions underlie these segregations? On the practical, social side, these segregations were found to have their cause in the divisions of society into marked-off classes and groups, thus obstructing full and flexible social interaction. On the intellectual side, these ruptures in social continuity appear as antitheses, such as labor and leisure, practical and intellectual, nature and man, individuality and association, vocation and culture.

These different issues have their counterparts in the chief problems of classical philosophy, such as spirit and matter, mind and body, mind and nature, the individual and society, etc. All these dualisms rest upon the fundamental assumption of the isolation of mind from some physical activity, whether of bodily organs, material appliances, or natural objects.

Such being the root of the trouble, a different philosophy, our own, was indicated. The origin, place, and function of mind is *in* an activity controlling the environment. This is our characteristic philosophical position. It is in harmony with the conceptions of Part I, such as, the biological continuity of man and nature, of his impulses and tendencies with natural energies; the dependence of mental growth upon participating in common purposeful activities; the influence of the uses made of nature upon society; the necessity of utilizing individual variations in a progressive society; the intrinsic continuity of means and ends; and the recognition of thinking as perceiving and testing the meanings of behavior. These conceptions are inconsistent with all dualistic philosophies; they are consistent with the experimental humanism which sees human intelligence as the purposive reorganization of experience through action.

Comment. The review in this section is "critical" in the sense of discerning, discriminating, not in the sense of weighing and evaluating. It is an aid in understanding the continuity of the preceding argument. Our division of the Table of Contents into parts is based on this section.

Though done by the author himself, the review does not do justice to the richness of the content of the preceding twenty-three chapters. Among the neglected viewpoints are the necessity of education, educating as directing the process of growth, the dependence of discipline on interest, the five stages of reflective thinking, the spirit of play in work, the causal relation of geography to history, the logical division of subject matter and the psychological mode of teaching, the basic rôle of vocational aims, together with the penetrating criticisms of education as preparation, as unfolding, as formal discipline, as conservative, and as natural development. One rarely meets such concentrated expressions of thought, such meaning-laden sentences, such brief and weighty observations. Occasionally in the summaries at the end of the chapters a new phrase not appearing in the previous sections will open a long vista of thought. Our own comments on the successive chapters have followed the argument and have been critical in the evaluating sense of the term, not omitting the appreciative.

2. The Nature of Philosophy

Exposition. Our task now is to make explicit the idea of philosophy implicit in all our preceding discussions. We shall see that philosophy, truly viewed, is resolving the conflicts arising in social life. We have hitherto presented philosophy in terms of the problems with which it deals. These problems all arise in the difficulties of social life. The genesis of philosophy is social. The lineaments of social practice reappear in philosophical systems. It is the quality of current experience which determines what men already think about nature, themselves, and the reality supposed to include or govern both. The philosophical problems whose solutions record the social practices of the period are such as these: the relations of mind and matter; of soul and body; of humanity and physical nature; of the individual and society; of knowing and doing; of theory and practice,—just such matters as have engaged our attention.

It is generally recognized that one of the most significant social enterprises is education. Since social practice gives rise to philosophical theory, it is suggestive that it was the pressure of educational questions among the Athenians that gave rise to European philosophy. As philosophy is understood to-day, it began with the Sophists of Greece. Prior speculations of the Greeks in Asia Minor and Italy belong rather to the history of science than to the history of philosophy. True, these speculations are recorded in our histories of philosophy but the topics are scientific, such as how the things of nature are made and changed. Those thinkers dealt with the action of nature, not the conduct of man. Succeeding these natural philosophers were the Sophists, travelling teachers, who applied the methods and results of the earlier thinkers to the problems of human conduct. Their story is worth following in some detail.

The Sophists were the first body of professional educators in Europe. They instructed the youth, for pay, in virtue, politics, and the management of household and city. Philosophy began to deal with the relation of the individual to some group, some comprehensive class, some universal, such as nature, or tradition. The Sophists raised many such questions, among them, the following: Can virtue be learned? Can approved excellence in any line be learned? What is learning? What is knowledge? Is knowledge acquired through the senses, or through a logically disciplined reason, or through apprenticeship in some specific form of doing? How is *coming* to know possible? that is, how can a transition be made from ignorance to wisdom, from privation to fullness, from defect to perfection, from "non-being to being?" Is change, becoming, development, really possible? If so, how? And especially, how is instruction related to virtue? How is knowledge related to action? Virtue dwelling in action, how is reason related to action? How is theory related to practice? Is the activity of reason the noblest attribute of man? Is purely intellectual activity the highest excellence? Are the virtues of neighborliness and citizenship secondary? Or, is intellectual knowledge empty and vain pretense? Does it demoralize character and destroy the social ties of community life? Is the only true and moral life gained through obedience to custom? Is the new education, setting up a rival standard to tradition, an enemy to good citizenship?

These clever questions all originally had practical bearings on education. The stream of European philosophical thought arose as a theory of educational procedure. This fact is eloquent witness to the intimate connection of philosophy and education. True it is that in the course of two or three generations these questions were cut loose from their original educational setting and were discussed on their own account. Thus came about what never should have happened, viz., philosophy became an independent branch of inquiry into matters of theory apart from practice. The objectional classical tradition in philosophy began.[1]

However, it is from the situation of the Sophists that the conception of a philosophy of education is to be reached. The origin and purpose of educational practice and philosophical theory are the same, viz., how to form right mental and moral habits respecting the problems of nature and the current social difficulties of man. Philosophy, rightly viewed, is just a general theory of education. The philosophy of education is simply a formulation of the problems involved in securing these socially useful mental and moral habits. It is far from being the external application of a set of ready-made ideas to an alien educational practice.

Thus appears the intimate connection between philosophy and education. They are reciprocally serviceable. Education saves philosophy from the artificial and makes it vital; philosophy saves education from routine and makes it socially effective. To amplify these views somewhat, we note that education is interested in the human, in distinction from the technical, significance of philosophical discussions. A philosophical theory which makes no difference in educational practice must be artificial. The student of philosophy needs warning not to take it as so much nimble or severe intellectual ex-

[1] Cf. Dewey, *Reconstruction in Philosophy*, New York, 1920.

ercise or as something said by philosophers that is of concern to them alone. Philosophic issues really formulate life situations; this is apparent when we ask, to what mental disposition do they correspond? What differences in educational practice do they make? The educational point of view enables the student to see philosophical problems in the practical social settings where they arise, thrive, are at home, and make a difference. Philosophy audits past experience; philosophy's program of values must affect conduct; the alternative is for philosophy to remain verbal, symbolic, or a sentimental indulgence for a few, or mere arbitrary dogma. Philosophy indicates what social changes are desirable; education produces the mental and moral attitudes necessary to bring about these changes. In doing so education calls to its aid public agitation, propaganda, and legislative and administrative action; these all help to modify attitudes.

But these methods are less effective because used with adults whose habits are already set; the education of youth in school has a fairer and freer field. Philosophy is helpless to execute its own program of values without education. Philosophy constructs values intellectually, but it has no Aladdin's lamp to summon them into immediate existence. As in the mechanical arts the sciences utilize the energies of things for recognized aims, so in the educative arts philosophy utilizes the energies of youth to realize the values of life. Education is the laboratory of philosophy; here its distinctions are made concrete and tested.

In these many ways education saves philosophy from the artificial and makes it vital. On the other hand, philosophy provides education with a broad and comprehensive survey of its place in modern life. This is its business. Thus it animates the aims and methods of education, and so saves the business of schooling from becoming a routine empirical affair.

Philosophy has disguised its social origin. Why? Because philosophers have become a specialized class; they use a technical language; they forget the vocabulary in which widespread social difficulties are stated as felt. So philosophy, thus cut off from its social roots, becomes, as one German philosopher said, "the systematic misuse of a terminology invented for that very purpose." In the following paragraphs we will endeavor to reëstablish its human connections.

From its nature as surveying conflicts in social situations, philosophy has generally been defined in terms of totality, generality, and ultimateness. Such terms have been and are applied both to its subject matter and to its method. However, as we shall see, they should be applied only to the attitudes of philosophers themselves. There is nothing total, general, or ultimate about the subject matter or the method of philosophy; there are, however, certain attitudes describable in these terms.

Consider subject matter. Philosophy has mistakenly been an attempt to gather together the varied details of the world into a system. Some of these systems reduce the many details of reality to a small number of ultimate principles; this is "pluralism." Some reduce the number of ultimate principles down to two; this is "dualism." And some reduce these two to unity; this is "monism." But any such completeness and finality are out of the question as applied to subject matter. The very nature of human experience as an ongoing, changing process forbids it. If any subject matter is to be regarded, though loosely, as total, general, complete, ultimate, final, it would be science, not philosophy. Science reports the particular facts discovered about the world. It is for science to say which generalizations about the world are tenable. For anything about the world approaching completeness and finality we go, not to philosophy, but to mathematics, physics, chemistry, biology, anthropology, history, and the like.

It is just here that the distinction between science and philosophy comes in. Subject matter and method are matters of science, not philosophy; it is science that knows; it is science that has the method leading to knowledge. But attitudes and dispositions toward the world of nature and man as disclosed by science are matters of philosophy. In short, science gives us the facts and the generalizations about our world; philosophy gives us our outlooks, attitudes, and dispositions toward our world. Philosophy knows nothing science does not know; philosophy has no method science does not have; but philosophy governs attitudes and conduct. It is in the attitudes of men, not in subject matter or method, that philosophy seeks totality, generality, and finality. It is our outlook upon experience that philosophy would have as unified, consistent, and complete as possible.

From another angle, philosophy gives the community the ends it is to realize and science provides the means. Without ends philosophically determined, science is indifferent whether its discoveries are used to cure or to spread disease, to sustain or to destroy life. In relation to science, philosophy has the double task of criticizing existing ends and of anticipating future ends; it criticizes existing ends by rejecting those that are obsolete because of new scientific resources, and those that are only sentimental because of the lack of scientific resources for realizing them. It anticipates the future ends or values which specialized science is likely to make possible.

From still another angle, in science we know and in philosophy we think. Science gives us knowledge, grounded knowledge. It represents objects which have been settled, ordered, disposed of rationally. It is a record of accomplished facts. Its reference is retrospective when its work is done. It furnishes solutions by trying, by action. Philosophy is not so. It is thinking; that is, prospective in reference. It is occasioned by unsettlement, it aims to overcome a disturbance. Philosophy is thinking what responsive attitude the known demands of us, exacts from us. It is an idea of what is possible. Like all thinking, it is hypothetical. It assigns something to be tried, to be done. It defines difficulties and suggests methods of meeting them, but it does not furnish solutions. It asks questions and suggests possible answers, without answering. Philosophy is thus, in part at least, thinking which has become conscious of itself, which has generalized its place, function, and value in experience.

In emphasizing philosophy as the responsive attitude appropriate to the solution, we return to the etymological meaning of the term: the love of wisdom. Philosophy, taken seriously, signifies achieving wisdom concerning the conduct of life. Examples of this are many; the ancient schools of philosophy were organized ways of living, tenets led to conduct; philosophy was the handmaid of theology to the Roman church of the middle ages; philosophy is frequently associated with religious interests; philosophy is associated with political struggles in national crises. Thus, philosophy is characterized by a direct and intimate outlook on life.

What, then, to be specific, does totality mean in philosophy? Not a quantitative summation of facts and generalizations about the world. That is hopeless of attainment, and it would be science, if attained. Totality as a trait in the philosophical disposition means readaptive continuity, that is, the carrying on of former habitual acts with the new adaptations to changing circumstances necessary to life and growth. It means keeping the balance between many diverse acts, each borrowing significance from, and lending significance to, every other act. Thus the philosophic disposition means in part an open-mindedness and sensitivity to new impressions, together with concentration and responsibility in connecting them. Totality or readaptive continuity, means *consistency* in response to diverse events. Consistency in response, however, is not identity in response; identity in response would mean maladjustment in a world in which the same thing does not happen twice.

How does the demand for a "total" attitude arise? The interests in life are various; they often conflict; these conflicts need to be integrated; they are integrated in action; because of this need of integration the demand for the attitude of totality arises. Some interests are superficial, gliding readily into one another; no need for philosophy is felt. Other interests are not sufficiently organized or widespread to come into conflict with each other; again, there is no felt need for philosophy. But consider such conflicts as these: science and religion, economics and æsthetics, conservatism and progressivism, order and freedom, institutionalism and individuality. In all these cases there is a need to discover some more comprehensive point of view, bringing divergencies together, and recovering consistency, or continuity, of experience.

There are homespun philosophies and there are systematic philosophies. When the area of the struggling interests is limited, when the clashes may be settled by an individual for himself, a person works out his own rough accommodations, genuine and often adequate. Such are homespun philosophies. But the discrepant claims of different ideals of conduct sometimes affect the community as a whole. Then the need for readjustment is general, and systems of philosophy arise to meet the need.

Related to this attitude of totality is the attitude of philosophic calm and endurance in the face of difficulty and loss, a power even to bear pain without complaint. This meaning is a tribute to the influence of the Stoics. It is not an attribute of philosophy in general; some philosophers are not stoical. But the wholeness characteristic of philosophy is the power to extract the meaning from pain, to learn from unpleasant experiences, and so to go on learning more. In so far as Stoicism means this, it is justified in any philosophy.

The philosophic disposition, we said, was characterized by totality, finality, and generality. Consider finality or ultimateness, and generality next. Taken literally and applied to subject matter, they are absurd pretensions, indicating insanity. There is no final philosophy; experience is never ended and exhausted. But there is a final attitude; it is the disposition to go below the surface, to penetrate to deeper levels of meanings, to find out the connections of any object or event, and to keep everlastingly at it.

Likewise, it is not philosophy but science, as we saw, which deals with generalities about the world. But the philosophic attitude is general; that is, it is averse to taking anything as isolated, it tries to place an act in its context, thus discovering its significance. In sum, then, philosophy is the disposition of man to solve social conflicts ("totality"), to go on solving them ("finality"), and to solve them thoroughly ("generality").

Certain objections are often brought against philosophies. Among the objections are these: individual speculation plays too large a part in them; controversial diversities characterize them; and the same old questions, differently stated, occupy them. All these objections do characterize, more or less, historic philosophies. These objections are explained by the traits of disposition just considered; so they are objections not so much to philosophy as to human nature itself and to the world in which it is set. If there are genuine uncertainties in life, as there are, and if the same predicaments in life recur in different social contexts, as they do, then we should expect philosophies to show speculative, controversial, and repetitious features. When the conflict of interests is embodied in different sets of persons, there are different diagnoses of the cause of the conflict and different prescriptions for handling it, and so arise divergent, competing philosophies. With respect to what has happened, evidence brings agreement and certainty; the thing itself is sure; this is science. But with respect to what has not happened, to what is wise to do in a complicated social situation, the thing itself is still indeterminate, and discussion, with diverging opinions, is inevitable; this is philosophy.

Take the conflict of the classes and the masses; the classes live at ease with their possessions; the masses struggle for existence, being dispossessed. One can not expect these groups to have the same philosophy of life, the same fundamental disposition toward the world. That would argue either insincerity or superficiality. The needs and possibilities of life will not seem the same to an industrial and commercial community, like America, as to an æsthetic and industrially unenterprising country, like ancient Greece. A political crisis will not meet the same mental response from a social group with a fairly continuous history, like England, as from one which has felt the shock of abrupt breaks, like France. Even if the same data were presented to such conflicting groups, they would be evaluated differently. But the same data can not be presented to such struggling groups; the data are not the same; the different sorts of experience attending the different types of life prevent the data from being the same. Conflicting interests inevitably make conflicting philosophies. That philosophies of life conflict is no objection to philosophy but to our human life in our natural world.

Objection is also made, we saw, to the fact that philosophies seem to be repeatedly occupied with different statements of the same old problems. There is a similarity in problems. But this is more so in appearance than in fact; old discussions, instead of being dropped, are brought over into the contemporary perplexities; this gives a specious sense of familiarity. There is, however, a real similarity in philosophical problems; it is due to the fact that the fundamental predicaments of life do recur in changed social and scientific contexts. There are certain unchanging aspects to philosophy's changing problems.

Looking back over the argument, we noted that education is the practical art of forming the mental and moral disposition appropriate to social need; that philosophy is the intellectual account of the characteristics of the disposition appropriate to social need. Thus it is evident how philosophy is the general theory of education; it assigns the large tasks education must accomplish. So the three reconstructions of philosophy, education, and society go hand in hand. The dominant fact of the present time is the thorough-going changes of our social life. These social changes accompany the advance of science, the industrial revolution, and the development of democracy. These changes reveal the need for educational reconstruction. Such sweeping practical changes can be met only by educational reformation. And educational reconstruction reveals the need for philosophical reconstruction, involving a reconsideration of the basic ideas of traditional philosophical systems. Thus men are led to ask, what ideas and ideals are implicit in these social changes? And what revisions of the ideas and ideals inherited from older and unlike cultures do they require? The order is from science, to industry, to democracy, to education, to philosophy. These questions have engaged us incidentally throughout the whole book and explicitly in the last few chapters. They are the now familiar problems of mind and body, man and nature, the individual and society, theory and practice, and the like.

Two things still remain for us to do in the concluding chapters. One is to state our philosophy of knowledge. The other is to state our philosophy of morals. In doing each thing we shall only sum up our prior discussions.

Comment. Here we have the longest, with one exception (Chapter XII, § I), as well as the most important, section in the book. In it occur many of the characteristic positions of Dr. Dewey's philosophy, such as, the social origin of philosophy; the social subject matter of philosophy; the rejection of the classical European tradition in philosophy; the identification of the method of philosophical thinking with that of scientific or reflective thinking; the uncertainties of experiences; the ongoing process of experience; philosophy as the general theory of education; the basic influence of science in changing society; the need for reconstruction of our industrial and undemocratic society, of our inherited feudal education, and of our aristocratic Grecian philosophy. The later writings of Dr. Dewey have enlarged some of these germinal thoughts. Evidently here is material, not for paragraphs, but for volumes, of comment.

Dr. Dewey is not an Herbartian in his educational philosophy, far from it, but he has Herbart's conception of the relation of philosophy to education. Before Dr. Dewey's day,

Herbart was sometimes described as the greatest philosopher among educators and the greatest educator among philosophers. He held that philosophical theories must be put to the educational test. He was thus led to reject Kant's doctrine of transcendental freedom. Herbart, however, did not limit philosophy to formulating the interests of social life. He was a pluralistic realist in philosophy, not an experimental humanist.

There is also a modified Hegelianism in Dr. Dewey's conception of philosophy. Once Dr. Dewey was an absolutist, but is so no longer. Hegel held that the method of philosophy is the reconciliation of opposites, that the truth is to be found in the whole, that over against a static thesis stands a dynamic antithesis leading to an organic synthesis. Dr. Dewey likewise holds that philosophy seeks to comprehend and unify a conflict of interests. The method is Hegel's; the difference is that Hegel applies his method to all phases of reality and to reality itself, while Dewey applies his only to social struggles. Thus, Dr. Dewey has inherited from educational and philosophical systems which he rejects.

It is noteworthy that in the list given (p. 378) of the philosophical problems that have puzzled mankind, Dr. Dewey includes his own and omits those of philosophies he rejects. His own philosophy is epistemological, and ethical or social, or he intends it so to be (note the titles of the two following chapters). He does not intend his philosophy to be metaphysical (though a metaphysics is implied) and so raise questions about the nature of being, the order of being, and man's relation to the whole of reality. He rejects these problems of ontology and cosmology as non-philosophical, and so omits them from his list.

But the interesting thing here is that it takes a metaphysics to reject a metaphysics. Ontology creeps in. The following statements and phrases disclose ontological views: ". . . completeness and finality are out of the question. The very nature of experience as ongoing, changing process forbids . . . the hopeless task of quantitative summation. . . . Finality does not mean, however, that experience is ended and exhausted. . . . If there are genuine uncertainties in life . . ." (pp. 379, 380, 382). These fragments suggest that it is self-contradictory for philosophy to rule out ontology. The defense of the denial of metaphysics is itself metaphysical. These statements in their context imply the rejection of an Absolute whose knowledge is complete and whose experience is comprehensive. The displacement of the Absolute leads to its replacement by an ongoing, precarious, exhaustless, naturalistic process. Such a view can be defended or opposed only by re-instating the conception of philosophy as metaphysical.

Such generalizations as those quoted about the universe are not scientific; they lack proof; they can not be tested in action. They are philosophical, not in the social or attitudinal sense, but in the metaphysical sense. A recent sympathetic expositor [1] of Dr. Dewey's philosophy holds that he has a metaphysics, in defending him against the charge of being only a methodologist. Cohen shows that method is indefinable apart from the reality dealt with.[2] If these views are correct, Dr. Dewey's rejection of metaphysics, his "reconstruction in philosophy," his limitation of the subject matter of philosophy to social conflicts, his interpretation of the traits of philosophy as human attitudes, go for naught as facts; they become only emphases; the question remains, which metaphysics? And must not the final Solver be above the battle?

The view that Thales, Anaximander, Anaximines, Anaxagoras, Heracleitus, Parmenides, and other pre-Sophist thinkers were early scientists and not philosophers is correct only if Dr. Dewey's view of philosophy as having to do, not with nature, but with society and human attitudes, is accepted. But this limitation on philosophy can not be taken literally,

1 Childs, J. L., *Education and the Philosophy of Experimentalism*, New York, 1931.
2 Cohen, Morris, *Reason and Nature*, New York, 1931.

since Dr. Dewey himself has written a volume on *Experience and Nature.*

The appreciation of the pragmatist for the Sophist is significant. (The term Sophist as a proper noun referring to certain Greek teachers is only a designation here.) The Sophists are appreciated as being the originators of true philosophy, without ancestors and with but few worthy successors. They saw philosophy in its educational origin. Following them philosophy cut loose unfortunately from social questions. Further affinities between pragmatists and the Greek Sophists are emphasis upon the individual; upon attitudes, temperament, and disposition; upon the doctrine of change; upon the rejection of tradition, custom, and external authority; upon the relativity of truth; upon the futility of speculation; and upon the lack of absolute moral standards. Dr. Dewey differs from Protagoras in emphasizing the socializing of the mental and moral disposition of the individual through conjoint activities. It should be noted that some of the questions apparently attributed to the Sophists (pp. 385–386) were really asked by contemporaries and successors of theirs.

The views are expressed that science gives us generalizations about the world, that philosophy has been mistakenly supposed to have generality, that generality in philosophy properly refers to the disposition to place an act in its context. But these views as stated are not consistently maintained in the discussion. It is suggested that philosophy is thinking which has "generalized" its own work in experience. Also it is explicitly stated that philosophy may be defined as a "general" theory of education. Apparently there is the generality in philosophy as subject matter which is denied it. One possible reconciliation would be that these generalizations are really scientific and not philosophical. Another would be that they are limited to human experience and are not universal. The latter is probably preferable.

It should also be noted that the distinction made in the text between ends or values as determined by philosophy, and means of realizing them as determined by science, is surrendered in the later volume, *The Quest for Certainty.*

Without being personal, one may apply the traits of philosophy as described by Dr. Dewey to his own philosophy. Is his attitude general, final, total, in the senses as stated? The first two, yes. The last one, no. His philosophy lacks the total comprehensive, complete outlook on experience. He illustrates one of his own views that philosophy takes sides and not his other view that philosophy keeps the balance between sides. His bias is on the side of the scientific as against the languages and literature; he does not recognize the *a priori,* and the transcendental element in thinking; he does not care for speculative philosophy; he does not acknowledge the experience of the mystic; he is not interested with another pragmatist, William James, in "the varieties of religious experience." In these respects his philosophy does not exemplify the disposition of "totality." Whose philosophy does?

In the light of these comments we may feel the need of a larger definition of philosophy than "a general theory of education." Is it not a general theory of the universe? including life and education? And if any scientist gives us this, has he not become a philosopher, dealing with the whole, and no longer with a part? Perhaps we feel too the need of a larger definition of the philosophy of education than an account of the formation of habits needed by society: "only an explicit formulation of the problems of the formation of right mental and moral habitudes in respect to the difficulties of contemporary social life" (p. 386). Is it not an interpretation of the meaning of education in the light of a general theory of the universe? Such definitions of the nature of philosophy and of the philosophy of education would seem to allow more of the balance, inclusiveness, and totality of viewpoint which Dr. Dewey ascribes to the philosophical disposition.

CHAPTER XXV

THEORIES OF KNOWLEDGE

1. Continuity *versus* Dualism

Exposition. As indicated in the previous chapter, we shall now undertake a brief discussion in more philosophical terms of the antithetical theories of knowledge implied in different educational ideals as they operate in practice. It will be a summary of our prior discussions with respect to this topic. Theories of knowledge are commonly referred to as epistemology. In the title of this section "continuity" means that knowing is the way one experience gives meaning to and control of another experience. This view we accept. "Dualism" as a theory of knowledge means there is some separation between the knower and the thing known. This view we reject, in line with our previous rejection of all dualisms. If S is the subject that knows and O is the object that is known, then the first diagram would illustrate the theory of continuity in knowing and the second the theory of dualism.

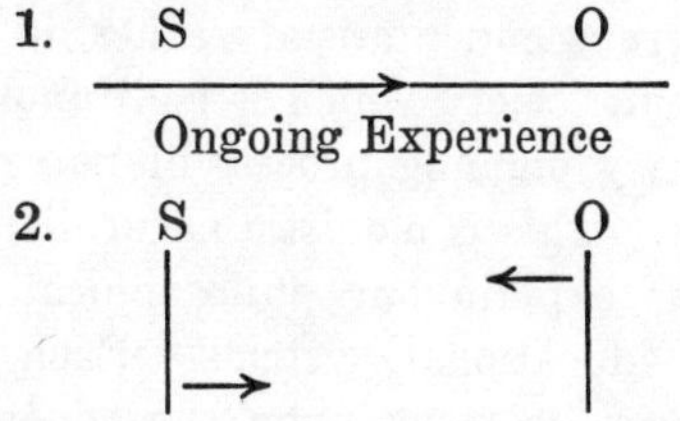

In presenting the theme of this section, the various dualisms in the theories of knowing, with their educational equivalents, will first engage us, and then three reasons will be given for rejecting all these dualisms in favor of the theory of continuity.

All dualistic theories of knowledge agree in one fundamental respect: they imply certain basic divisions, separations, antitheses. The origin of these divisions is social. We think differently about knowledge because we are aristocratic or democratic. The subject is divided from the object of knowing because hard walls mark off social groups from each other or even classes within a group. These walls separate rich and poor, men and women, noble and baseborn, ruler and ruled. Such social barriers mean the lack of fluent and free intercourse, the setting up of different types of life-experience, each with its own isolated subject matter, aims, and values. Such divided social conditions are, and must be, formulated in dualistic philosophies, in case philosophy is to be a sincere account of human experience.

But unitary or monistic philosophies, in form at least, sometimes arise under divided social conditions, like that of Spinoza. This seems to constitue a difficulty. What is the explanation? It is because such philosophy takes wings unto itself and flies away from human experience to some transcendental realm; it appeals to something higher than anything found in experience. Such monistic theories deny dualism in name but restore it in fact; they too make a division between things of this world as appearances and things of that inaccessible world as realities. We too deny dualism, but not in the name of transcendentalism, rather in the name of democracy in human society which is continuous with, and a phase of, the unitary ongoing process of nature which is all the reality there is. This is monistic naturalism.

Social conditions explain our philosophical systems; they also explain our educational systems. Each old and new social division leaves its mark upon the educational system, which becomes a deposit of various purposes and procedures. The outcome is the objectionable, check and balance, segregation of values previously described (Chapter XVIII, § 3).

We will now exhibit some dualisms in the theory of knowing with their educational equivalents. There are five of these, viz., the empirical and the rational, the particular and the universal, learning as result and as process, passivity and activity in knowing, and the intellect and emotions.

Empirical knowing is opposed to rational knowing. Empirical is lower, rational is higher. Socially, the working class intelligence is empirical; the leisure class intelligence is rational. Working class intelligence is concerned with the means of living, leisure class intelligence is concerned with the pursuit of learning. Empirical knowing is connected with everyday affairs, serves the purpose of ordinary individuals lacking intellectual pursuits, enables them to work with their immediate physical environment to satisfy their wants. Such knowing is depreciated, perhaps despised, as lacking cultural meaning. Rational knowing is not so; it is supposed to touch the ultimate reality intellectually, to be pursued for its own sake, to terminate properly in purely theoretical insight, and not to be debased by practical application in behavior. It is like Plato's vision of the good, Aristotle's God thinking his own thoughts, and the mediæval saint's beatific vision.

A parallel opposition is that between the particular and the universal, experience and reason. Experience is held to be an aggregate of isolated particulars; acquaintance must be made separately with each of them. Reason is supposed to deal with universals, general principles, laws; these lie above the welter of concrete details. These dualisms are precipitated in education. Illustrating the one view, the pupil is supposed to learn a lot of items of specific information, each standing by itself. Geography, as often taught, exemplifies this view in practice. Illustrating the other view, the pupil is supposed to learn a certain number of laws and general relationships. Mathematics, beyond the fundamental operations, illustrates this view in practice. Geography and mathematics, facts and principles, two independent worlds!

There are two antithetic senses of the term "learning." These senses correspond to the division of society into the two classes of those who are subject to authority and those who are free to advance. For those subject to authority, learning is the sum total of what is known; it is handed down in books and by learned men; it is something external, an accumulation of cognitions, like commodities in a warehouse; it is an objective body of truth, existing ready-made somewhere. And study? It is the way the mind draws on the knowledge in storage. On the other hand, for those free to advance, learning is what the individual *does* when he studies; it is an active personally conducted affair; it is purely subjective, internal, psychical. There is a ready-made mind, equipped with a faculty of knowing, which, strange to say, it is often loath to will to exercise. Objective truth, subjective mind! This dualism appears in education in the separation, often touched upon already, between subject matter, as something objective to be learned, and method, as something subjective to be used in learning.

Then there is the dualism between passivity and activity in knowing. The division in society is that between those who are controlled by direct concern with practical things, and so are passive, and those who are free to pursue culture for themselves, and so are active. Empirical, particular, physical things are often supposed to be known by passively receiving impressions, by the mind being stamped with them, consciousness receiving them through the sense organs. On the contrary, rational knowledge, that is, knowledge of spiritual things, is supposed to spring from self-activity, activity initiated within the mind, activity carried on all the better for being kept remote from all sullying touch of the senses and external objects. In education, a fair expression of this distinction is that between sense training, object lessons, laboratory demonstrations, representing passivity, and pure ideas contained in books and appropriated by an output of mental energy. Miraculous!

Another dualism, still current, is that between the emotions and the intellect. The reader may supply the social division which it reflects. The emotions are conceived to be purely private, personal, supplying a disturbing heat, turning inward to considerations of personal profit and loss. The single emotion that might perhaps affect the work of pure intelligence is that of intellectual curiosity. On the other hand, the intellect, intelligence free from emotional influence, apprehends facts and truths, it is a pure light, turning outward and upward to truth. The pupil has a mind much as his clothes have a pocket. Corresponding to this dualistic view of emotions and intellect, we see in education a systematic depreciation of interest as emotional, and a preference for intellectual things. But lo! Most pupils have to be induced in practice by extraneous, irrelevant rewards and penalties to apply their minds to the truths to be known. Professional educators decry the appeal to interest but dignifiedly uphold the need to rely upon examinations, marks, promotions and demotions, prizes, and time-honored rewards and punishments. They reject intrinsic interest and appeal to extrinsic. What a spectacle! "The effect of this situation in crippling the teacher's sense of humor has not received the attention which it deserves" (p. 391).

All these five instances of separations of the features of experience culminate in the one between doing and knowing, practice and theory, body as means and mind as end. The source of this culminating dualism is, as we saw, the division of society into the laboring and leisure classes, the one working with their muscles for material sustenance, the other, free from economic pressure, devoting themselves to the expressive arts and directing others. The educational evils springing from this separation need not be re-stated.

So we turn at once to an account of the forces making dualism untenable in society, philosophy, and education, and so establishing continuity instead. There are three of these, viz., the connection of mental activity with the nervous system, the doctrine of evolution, and the experimental method. These forces will now be summarized.

(i) Physiology and physiological psychology have shown the connection of mental activity with the activity of the nervous system. The older dualism of soul and body is no longer possible. The recognition of the connection of mental and nervous activity has given rise to a new dualism, that between the brain and the rest of the body. This too is not tenable. The nervous system is not apart from the body, neither is the brain apart from the nervous system. The purpose of the nervous system as a specialized mechanism is to keep all bodily activities working together. It is not isolated from them, it is the means whereby they interact. The organ of knowing is not isolated from the organs of response. Stimulus determines response and, something not usually recognized, response determines the succeeding stimulus. Thus a reciprocal adjustment is affected between the stimuli received from the environment and the responses directed upon the environment. It is the brain whose function as an organ it is to effect this reciprocal adjustment between stimulus and response. It is the brain that constantly reorganizes activity so as to maintain its continuity. It is the brain that modifies coming action to meet the requirements of past action.

This matter is important. Let us illustrate it. Consider the carpenter at work sawing a board. Each motor response is adjusted to what the senses report concerning the board and at the same time the motor response shapes the next sensory stimulus. The stroke of the saw is motor, it changes the board somewhat, thus the next sight stimulus is changed. And so on. The carpenter's work is continuous, not a routine repetition of the same ineffective motion, nor yet a random activity without a cumulative effect. It is continuous, consecutive, concentrated because each earlier act prepares the way for later acts while later acts reckon with the results of earlier acts. Here is the basis of all responsibility. What is true of the carpenter and his board is true of the etcher and his plate, and of any case of a consecutive activity. Thus, knowing is connected with the nervous system and the nervous system readjusts activity continuously to meet new conditions. In sum, knowing is not something isolated from all activity, complete on its own account, but it has to do with reorganizing activity.

(ii) Biology, with its discovery of evolution, clinches this lesson. The doctrine of evolution teaches the continuity of simpler with more complex organic forms till man is reached. This is its philosophic significance. The mutual adjustment of organism and environment is obvious in the simplest organic structures; here evolution begins; anything called mind is at a minimum. Activity becomes more complex; a greater number of factors in space and time are coördinated by it; intelligence has a larger span of the future to forecast and plan for, and so plays a more and more marked rôle. The living creature, including man, is a part of the world, sharing its fortunes, leading a precarious existence, surviving at all only as it is intellectually at one with the things about it, forecasting the consequences of the present, shaping its own responses accordingly. The living experiencing organism is an intimate participant in the changes in its world. If so, knowing is a mode of participating, valuable only as it is effective; it is not something complete in itself, it is not the idle view of an unconcerned spectator.

(iii) The experimental method has transformed our theory of knowledge. It confirms the view of knowledge implied by both physiological psychology and biological evolution. It is the method of getting knowledge, that is, of discovery. It is the method of knowing that we know, that is, of proof. It is the method of separating knowledge from opinion.

The experimental method is as old as man and as new as recent scientific procedure. The savage used it; for him to try was to try his luck; so we call his efforts magic. The modern scientist uses it; for him to try is to try his ideas; so we call his efforts science. As a practical device, the experimental method is as old as life; as a scientific resource it is as new as Galileo and Darwin.

It has two sides. On the one hand, it means that thinking without testing is not knowing. Testing involves physical changes. The physical changes confirm or negate the prior conceptions, ideas, beliefs. Without such specific confirmatory or else refutatory physical changes, our beliefs are not knowledge; they are hypotheses, theories, suggestions, guesses; these are important indeed, but they are to be held only tentatively and to be utilized as guides to experiments. We may know that we believe, but we do not know that our beliefs are true.

On the other hand, it means that thinking with testing is knowing. It is knowing that our hypothesis is true, or else false. Thus thinking is of avail; it is of avail in proportion as anticipation rests on observation; valuable prognosis rests on thorough diagnosis. Experimenting is not reacting blindly; it notes consequences; it uses consequences in predicting. It is intelligence that observes and anticipates, then tries, and checks by results. Thus does the experimental method treat the material resources and obstacles confronting us. In sum, nothing short of the scientific method gives us knowledge, and the scientific method does give us knowledge.

Two generalities here are in order about the experimental method. Observations may be various, hypotheses may be many; a certain surplus activity is an unescapable factor in all our behavior; it is the experiment that reduces possibilities to actuality. A related thing: our failures teach us too. We learn the ideas that will not work in that situation. The surplus possibilities are reduced by so much. A seriously thoughtful experiment, though unsuccessful in confirming the hypotheses, is fruitful.

The experimental method, then, is a systematized means of making knowledge. Its significance is generally regarded as belonging to technical, physical fields. It is not surprising, because of its newness, that men have not recognized its full scope. It applies equally well to social and moral matters.

It may take a long time to recognize that it does so. Men still want the crutch of dogma and authoritative beliefs; this relieves them of the trouble of thinking and of the responsibility of acting as they think. They tend to confine their thinking to choosing between the rival systems of dogma.

Turning to the schools for an application. John Stuart Mill was right, they are better adapted to making disciples than inquirers. They have been governed by literary, dialectic, and authoritative methods. These methods form beliefs, they do not make knowledge. Experimentation outlaws such methods. The influence of the experimental method is advancing; it will change our theory of knowing; a changed theory of knowing will change our school methods. The schools adopting the scientific method will be actively concerned with things and persons, aiming to increase man's knowledge of things in space and events in time. These results will eventuate when dualism as a theory of knowledge is surrendered and continuity is accepted.

Comment. Among the prominent ideas in this summarizing section deserving special comment are the social origin and nature of philosophy, the social and educational equivalents of the epistemological dualisms, the validity of the conclusions of physiological psychology, the philosophy of evolution, the adequacy of the experimental method, and the practicability of schools devoted to the experimental method. Here is material for experimentation! But Dr. Dewey uses the literary and dialectic methods which he decries, not the experimental method which he praises, in advocating his views. He does not go into the laboratory and experiment; he goes into his study and writes a book advocating the experimental method. If his aim is to "make knowledge," his method is not in accord with his theory. If his theory is correct, then he has made for us, not knowledge, but more beliefs. Besides, having stated his beliefs, he is transmitting them with whatever authority attaches to his great reputation.

Following his example, not his theory, we will reason together about these things. Such reasoning may assist us in reaching conviction, if not knowledge.

From divisions in society to dualism in epistemology is a far cry. It suggests that philosophy is another expression of the class struggle, that thought, arising in the strife of parties, can not rise above the strife. But it is to be noted that naturalistic theories of knowledge, similar to that of continuity, have arisen when society was under the strain of class division, *e.g.*, in the cases of Democritus and Lucretius. Also that monistic theories of knowledge have arisen under conditions of social strife and religious prejudice, as those of Leibniz and Spinoza. Their flight from social reality may be construed as a flight to ontological reality. Also, that dualistic theories of knowledge have arisen under the identical social and economic conditions that condition Dr. Dewey's philosophy, like those of Montague [1] and Lovejoy.[2] Also, that Dr. Dewey holds our society with its surviving divisions is only nominally democratic, and yet it gives rise to his philosophy of continuity. These examples and others that might be cited suggest that dualistic epistemologies and divided societies are rather independent variables.

Then there is the notion that experience knows, one experience giving meaning to another experience, one experience controlling another experience. This is even less personal than the doctrine of James that "the thoughts are the thinkers." James at least had "a stream of consciousness." Dewey has only a stream of experience. James left sensations intact, of which one could be introspectively aware. Dewey leaves only the organism making flexible responses to environmental stimuli. After losing its "soul," modern psychology lost "consciousness," but it still has its "behavior," though it is in danger of losing its head and becoming physiology. Modern behavioristic psychology saith, "What shall it profit

1 Montague, W. P., *The Ways of Knowing*, New York, 1925.
2 Lovejoy, A. O., *The Revolt against Dualism*, New York, 1930.

a man if he gain the whole world of rational knowledge and lose his own behavior?"

It is both reason and critical common sense to recognize that experience can not know anything, though it may be known; that to know experience involves a knower and a known; that the knower is a subject and the known is an object, that the knower in the case of man is a conscious being; that man is conscious of himself as different from that which he knows; that knowledge intends an opposite unless it is directed toward itself; and that language has a meaning when it says "methinks," or "I think." Man is a self, a spirit, a conscious thinker; as Descartes said, a *res cogitans*. The way to overcome dualism, if dualism should be overcome, is not to wipe out the distinction between the knower and the known, not by reducing mind to a type of response. Epistemological dualism remains. It can be overcome by an ontological monism, a theory of reality as unity, in which the same substance, whatever it be, is at the bottom of both knower and known. When it is recognized that the self of man can know itself, we have the clue. In this experience knower and known are both phases of one unitary experience. The self of man may suggest to us the solution of the great problem of the unity of the world despite epistemological dualism. The world is one and knowledge has two phases, in case there is an Absolute experience which knows itself as the all-inclusive reality.

In the first part of this section the social origins and educational equivalents of the dualisms in the theory of knowledge seem far-fetched and not well worked out. In the case of one of the dualisms, that between intellect and emotions, the social origin is not indicated at all. One might supply it, however, and say with Plato that the intellect represents the ruling class and the emotions the working masses. But this dualism is said to be "current." Then the intellect might illustrate the industrial overlords and the emotions their economic slaves. But pointing out such a remote parallel, not to mention the compliment to the overlords, is far from proving that the epistemological dualism is the effect of the economic class war. But the argument requires this. It might only be that the opposition arose through the fact that the intellect grasps facts and relations coldly through insight and the emotions lay hold on truth warmly through intuition, or sensing the whole of a situation. In the discussion of the same dualism it is not clear what the school equivalent is for pure intellect as distinct from the emotions.

The old working hypothesis of physiological psychology was: no psychosis without neurosis. This meant that all mental states or processes had corresponding physiological states or processes. It was an hypothesis, not an affirmation. No one has proved it yet by laboratory methods. It is still a defensible position that some mental processes have no exactly corresponding physiological processes. For example, who knows the physiological difference between the concept of virtue and the concept of truth? What is the difference in the functioning of the brain when one thinks of time and eternity? We know more about sensations than about their stimuli, more about abstract concepts than about their brain equivalents. But be that as it may, the position taken in the text is the affirmation, not the hypothesis, that psychosis is neurosis. If the concept of matter were still in vogue, this would be called materialism. But since nature in the light of modern physics can no longer be regarded as matter, this position is naturalism. What saves it from being mechanism and behaviorism is the recognition that the responses of the organism are adaptive. Just how the carpenter's organism works successfully without the mental image of the future box his board is to help make is not clear. Aristotle recognized four classes of causes: the material cause, the wood of which the box is made; the efficient cause, the maker of the box; the formal cause, the pattern by which the box is made; and the final cause, the purpose for which the box is made. The text recognizes the material and the efficient cause. It does not recognize the formal and the final cause. The brain does the directing and the brain is called "machinery." It is difficult to see how machinery can either conceive a pattern or execute a purpose. But machinery easily embodies both; it is made by a pattern and it fulfills a purpose.

The text makes clearer what mind does than what mind is. It holds that it is what it does. But in the state of awareness, in the state of knowing what it does, the mind is different from what it does in manipulating objects.

It is easier to deny that mind is adaptive behavior than it is to say how mind and brain and nervous system are related. Recurring to the figure of machinery, it is clear that machinery may embody a pattern and fulfill a purpose. The body is machinery. It embodies a pattern, meets a need, and fulfills a purpose. It would be better to say that the mind *has* a body than that it *is* the body. We may refer again to the fact that, in addition to Dewey's theory of naturalistic continuity, many other theories purport to state the relationship of mind and body, such as, the Cartesian dualism, Haeckel's materialistic monism, Huxley's epi-phenomenalism, Fechner's psychophysical parallelism, Spencer's agnostic monism, Schelling's theory of identity, Hegel's idealistic monism, and James' "release" theory.[1] Dewey's theory is no more proven than any of the others. It too remains in the field of philosophic speculation, it too is a belief unproven as yet by experiment.

Concerning the doctrine of evolution, its "philosophic significance" is said to lie "precisely in its emphasis upon continuity of simpler and more complex organic forms" (p. 392). Here is a statement about nature which is said to have philosophic significance. But in the preceding chapter, such statements were said to be scientific, and only statements about mental and moral habitudes were allowed to be philosophic. The author here uses the term "philosophic" in a wider sense than his previous discussion of its meaning allows. The usage is preferable to the definition.

[1] Cf. Laird, John, *Our Minds and Their Bodies*, London, 1925.

A scientific statement of evolution, whether or not called philosophic, is not the philosophical significance of the doctrine. Philosophy evaluates the assumptions, and interprets the findings, of science.

To begin with, the hypothesis of evolution has become a theory, and the theory has become a "doctrine," but the doctrine has not become either a principle or a fact. This is not to deny the doctrine, it is to deny that the doctrine has been proven by experimentation. It is still a belief, a philosophy, not knowledge, not science, if we accept Dr. Dewey's own account of the experimental method. Evolution may be experimentally demonstrated sometime but it has not been.

Never mind, let it be assumed to be true that man has descended from some lower form of organic creature, not from the anthropoids but from some common ancestor of the anthropoids and man. What does it mean? Here is a one-way, irreversible series of growth with one product, or by-product, man, able to grasp the process conceptually. To what is it due? Chance? Necessity? The unknowable? Emergence of the novel? Purpose? Could chance explain such adaptations as the male and female bodies? Could impersonal necessity explain the appearance of personality? Is appeal to the unknowable both a surrender of the problem and self-contradictory? Is emergence of the novel another name for chance combinations? Is Purpose the only adequate category to explain a series of such cumulative growth as evolution suggests? And if Purpose, what kind, immanent or transcendent?

Our aim in asking these questions is not to consider the possible answers to them, but to suggest that the doctrine of evolution, if accepted, still requires a philosophy.[1] The text questionably identifies the philosophy of evolution with its science and then equally questionably concludes the knower is not an onlooker or a spectator but only a participator. The knower might well be both a spectator of his past, else he could

[1] Cf. Howison, G. H., *The Limits of Evolution*, New York, 1905.

not frame the doctrine of evolution, and a participator in his present, else he could not survive, and also an anticipator of his future, else he could not suitably prepare for it. There is something about thinking, and knowing, and knowing that one knows, that transcends the naturalistic process.

Concerning the adequacy of the experimental method as defined, let us note three limitations. There are types of knowledge which the experimental method does not give, there are truths which require no further experimentation, and there are unsuspected regions to which it may be applied. We know that all events must occur in time, that all material objects must exist in space, that nothing occurs without a cause. No experimentation has ever proven such universal and indeed necessary propositions, nor indeed can. We know those propositions are true because that is the way we must think and we cannot think otherwise. Such knowledge is not derived experimentally but is *a priori,* as Kant showed. Experiment is not necessary to prove that some events occur in time, that some objects occupy space, and that some occurrences have causes; observation without controlling conditions is enough; and no observation, with or without experiment, can ever give either universality or necessity to propositions. Experiment is observation under conditions controlling the occurrence of the event observed.

Again, there are truths which the experimental method does not give. If all the angles of a triangle in Euclidean space are equal to two right angles, and this figure is a triangle in Euclidean space, then the angles of this figure are equal to two right angles. And, if all capitalistic orders are doomed, and ours is a capitalistic order, then ours is doomed. In general, a greater truth contains a lesser truth. This is not experimentalism, it is deduction. Experiment may have contributed in cases to the establishment of one or both of the premises, but it need not have done so. In sum, there is *a priori* knowledge and there is deductive knowledge, and neither is the effect of experimenting.

There are truths which require no further experimenting. Such truths are to be found in both physical and social realms. One does not need to experiment further with the relations of numbers expressed in the multiplication table; it is enough to know them as they are. The rate of motion of bodies in space may change but the fact that bodies move in space does not change. And there are presumably changeless laws of motion within certain limits of space. Some things stay fixed in mathematics and physics. There is an element of static stability in our changing physical universe represented by the ideal of fact, principle, law.

In the social realm too there is the law written in the nature of man that there shall be law. Human laws change, the fact of human law does not change. Such a proposition has formal truth. It is better that human interests should be mutual than competitive. Such a proposition has material truth; it would be as difficult as useless to prove it experimentally. It is better to be unselfish than selfish; here is a moral constant; the experience of the race supports it; it requires no further experimental proof. It would be both cynical and false to say the race had learned nothing morally in the course of its long experience; it would be both useless and injurious to begin experimenting with the moral inheritance of the race. The wickedness and righteousness of man is laboratory enough for observational purposes without further experimentation. There are physical and social truths that are acceptable without further experimental proof. The younger generation should profit by the mistakes of the older generation, not repeat them to learn for themselves they are mistakes.

Also, be it noted, there are unsuspected regions to which the experimental method may be applied. The experimental method involves the having of a real problem in experience whose data are carefully observed, concerning which an hypothesis is formulated and tested. It involves confidence in the method, not in the outcome. There is always some outcome. One may use the experimental method in the devotional life.[1] There are conditions to be met in effective devotions as elsewhere, hypotheses may be proven, and truths discovered. With the solidity of the material universe surrendered by modern physics, with the incoming of the doctrine of energy as universal, with the recognition of the directive agency of man as a part of the universe, the personal experimental proof of spiritual factors in the world is not inconceivable. And even if such proof were "inconceivable," that would be no objection to trying the experimental method. Darwin often tried what he called "fool's experiments."

Concerning the practicability of making all our schools experimental in method one may observe that such a procedure unduly calls into question what the race already knows, it neglects the transmissive function of education, and it is not necessary so to do in order to cultivate individuality, share interests, and establish democracy. Some problems having been solved, it is not necessary or desirable that the schools should be devoted only to problem solving; some of their time may well be spent in learning what others have found out, in appreciating it, and in laying adequate foundations for adding to it. That there should be some schools, both private and public, devoted to experimental education goes without saying. The careful study of all schools should render them, in effect, experiment stations. Some experimental schools might well try out the exclusive use of the experimental method in gaining knowledge. But that all schools should utilize only the experimental method of acquiring knowledge is neither practical, nor necessary, nor desirable.

2. Schools of Method

Exposition. The title refers to divergent theories concerning the method of knowing. Our own theory is pragmatism.

[1] Cf. Wieman, H. N., *Religious Experience and the Scientific Method,* New York, 1926.

In this section our own view will be stated in some detail, together with the opposing views and their social origins.

Now the function of knowledge is to make one experience freely available in other experiences. Knowledge works differently from habit, knowledge functions in new situations, habit in old situations. Habit means the formation of a disposition to act easily and effectively in similar situations. It thus makes one experience available in subsequent experiences, but not "freely." It works successfully within its own limits. Its limits are that it has no prevision of change, and so it often leads one astray, or comes between a person and his task. The mechanic's skill, if based on habit alone, deserts him when the unexpected happens to the machine. Habit supplies a fixed method of attacking a problem. Knowledge makes allowance for change of conditions, for novelty. Knowledge uses or modifies habits according to old or new conditions. The mechanic who knows the machine can take care of the unexpected. Knowledge allows one to select from habitual modes of attacking problems the one most suitable to the specific problem.

To take an extreme example of the working of habit and knowledge. The savage and the astronomer see a comet. The savage has habits but not knowledge; the astronomer has knowledge and habits. Savages frighten wild animals and their enemies by shrieks, beating on gongs, brandishing weapons, etc. The comet appears to threaten them. They react in the same way to scare off the comet. They fall back on habit, thus exhibiting the limitations of habit. The only reason the astronomer does not take the comet in some analogously absurd way is his knowledge; he apprehends the comet, not as an isolated immediate occurrence, but in its connections with other objects and events, placing it in the astronomical system. Thus the attitude of the astronomer is freer than that of the savage.

Knowledge approaches an object from any one of the angles provided by its connections. Knowledge gets at a new event, not directly, but indirectly, by resourcefulness, ingenuity, and inventiveness. An ideally perfect knowledge would have such a network of interconnections from past experience that always some point of advantage would be available for attacking a new problem.

Knowledge is the general and free use of former experiences in new situations. It has two aspects, one of control, and one of meaning (cf. p. 90 of the text). The power of control is the more tangible. Experience is controlled by knowledge. What efficient habits are in specific cases, genuine knowledge is in every case. What can not be managed directly by habit may be managed indirectly by knowledge; barriers between ourselves and undesirable consequences may be interposed by knowledge; what can not be overcome may be avoided by knowledge. Thus experience is controlled.

Further, the meaning of experience is increased by knowledge. There is a minimum of experienced significance in habitual, or routine, responses, and in capricious, or random, responses; there is no mental reward. But with increase of knowledge there is increase of meaning, increase in the perception of connections, increase in the selection of suitable habits of response; there is great mental reward. Knowledge leads to felt meanings even in one's failure to control experience.

There is a difference between the content and the reference of knowledge. The content of knowledge is past, the reference of knowledge is future. The content of knowledge is what has happened, is finished, settled, sure. The knowledge of a physician is what he has found out by study of what others have learned and by personal acquaintance. The reference of knowledge is future, prospective. Thus knowledge furnishes the means of understanding what is still going on, what is still to be done. The physician's knowledge supplies resources to interpret the unknown before him, filling out the partial facts with suggested phenomena, thus leading to diagnosis, prognosis, and prescription. This is why what he has learned is still knowledge; he uses it in understanding and controlling disease.

Knowledge apart from use ceases to be knowledge. It may be forgotten entirely. Or, it may become an object of æsthetic contemplation, affording emotional satisfaction as its symmetry and order are surveyed. The same sort of joy comes from viewing a finished picture or a well composed landscape. It is not the subject matter but its harmonious organization that yields the satisfaction. Indeed, the subject matter might be wholly invented, a play of fancy. But this contemplative attitude is æsthetic, not intellectual; we have here art, not knowledge; but such emotional satisfaction is legitimate.

The reference of knowledge is to the future. The applicability of knowledge to the world is not to the past; that is impossible, the past is gone. The applicability of knowledge is to what is still going on, the unsettled in the moving scene in which we are implicated. Why then do we regard statements about the irrevocable past as knowledge? Why do we ignore the prospective reference of knowledge? Because we assume the continuity of past and future, we assume the knowledge of the past is as a matter of course helpful in forecasting the future and in giving it meaning. We ignore the prospective because it is so irretrievably implied in the retrospective.

This is the pragmatic theory of knowing. What is its essence? The continuity of knowing with a purposeful activity modifying the environment. Knowledge is both something possessed and an act. Knowledge as something possessed consists of all the habits that render our action intelligent, the dispositions we consciously use in understanding present happenings, our intellectual resources enabling us to adapt our environment to our needs and our aims and desires to our environment. It is not just something of which we are now conscious. Knowledge as an act is using our dispositions in solving our perplexities; this it does by perceiving the connections between ourselves and our world.

Thus pragmatism is democracy in epistemology. In the pragmatic theory of knowledge, one experience is made freely available in giving control and meaning to another, there is continuity between the knower and the known. In democracy there is likewise free interchange and social continuity. It is democracy in society which has developed the pragmatic theory of knowledge.

And what is the educational equivalent of democracy in society and pragmatism in epistemology? Once again, the acquisition of knowledge in schools through activities carried on in a social medium. Real knowledge fructifies the ongoing experience of pupils associated in common enterprises.

But pragmatism is one of many schools of method. The method of knowing accepted by pragmatism has proved most effective in achieving knowledge. The deviations from this theory will now be considered. Such consideration may render clearer the true place of knowledge in experience. Many of these devious theories have already been criticized in discussing previously some educational problem.

Like the various systems of philosophy, the various schools of method of knowing all originate in the strife of social systems. Epistemologies exhibit an explicit formulation of traits implicit in one-sided, cut-off, segments of experience, betraying the barriers to intercourse which prevent the experience of one class from being supplemented and enriched by that of other classes.

Just as democracy leads to pragmatism, so those who are concerned with progress in changing received beliefs, like the Sophists, are individualistic in knowing, while those whose chief business it is to conserve received truth and withstand change, like Plato, emphasize the universal factor in knowing. Those who deal with utilities apart from the ends they serve, like laborers, are practical empiricists, while those who enjoy the contemplation of a realm of meanings they did not help produce, like the mediæval scholastics, are practical rationalists. Those who come into direct contact with things, having to adapt their immediate activities to them, like Helvétius, are realists, while those who isolate the meanings of these things and put them in a religious or so-called spiritual world aloof from things, like J. Royce, are idealists. And so we might go on to show the social origin of other types of epistemology. For such more specific treatment we will select scholasticism, sensationalism, and rationalism.

Socially speaking, scholasticism arose when it was needed. There was a vast amount of material accepted on authority; it had been handed down from church councils and decrees. It needed systematizing. It came to be increasingly felt that it needed the sanction of the human reason. The defining, systematizing, and rationalizing of this material is scholasticism. The meaning of the subject matter itself was so great to the scholastic doctors that the scholastic method was vital to them.

Under modern conditions the scholastic method means for most persons a general form of knowing divorced from any particular subject matter; it is logic-chopping without objective in experience, making distinctions, definitions, divisions, and classifications for the mere sake of making them. "Formal logic" is essentially the scholastic method generalized; it views thought as a purely psychical activity having its own forms; these forms are applied to any material as a seal is stamped on any plastic stuff. Turning to the work of our schools, the doctrine of formal discipline in education is the natural counterpart of the scholastic method.

Sensationalism and rationalism are contrasting theories of the method of knowing. Sensationalism emphasizes the particular, bare facts, without the general; rationalism emphasizes the general, bare relations, without the particular. The mistake of each is to do without the other, and the mistake of both is failing to see that the function of both senses and thought is to reorganize experience, to apply the old to the new, to maintain the continuity of life.

In real knowledge, as we have presented it, there is both a particularizing function of the senses and a generalizing function of thought. A confused problematic situation can be cleared up only by resolving it into details, and defining the details sharply. These specified details, facts, qualities, constitute the elements of the problem; they are fragmentary, partial, lacking meaning; they are particulars. But these particulars are to be given meaning. Our task is to discover their connections and to recombine them. Old and available knowledge is useful in mastering new particulars. Such application of the old to the new, introducing connection into the unconnected, is general in function. Any fact used to give meaning to the elements of a new experience is general. "Reason" is just bringing the old to bear in perceiving the significance of the new. The reasonable person is habitually open to seeing a new event, not as isolated, but in its connection with man's common experience. In genuine knowing there is both the particularizing of the senses and the generalizing of the reason. Without the particulars of sense there is no material for knowing, no intellectual growth; without the use of reason in placing these particulars in the meaningful context of past experience, particulars are only exciting or irritating. Thus does the pragmatic theory of knowledge modify and supplement sensationalism and rationalism.

The non-pragmatic theories of knowledge fail to use the old in understanding and controlling the new; they miss the prospective reference of knowledge; they are led to deny that the application is a part of the knowing; they regard knowledge as complete in itself apart from its use. This omission vitiates those theories, and vitiates the practices they sponsor in our schools. Recall those practices. "The acquisition of knowledge" is the appropriation of subject matter stored in books; it is as xerophilous as a cactus; it might as well be about Mars or the land of nowhere; it lacks fruitful connection with the ongoing experience of the pupils. Such canned information may have been knowledge to the canners; it is only embalmed relics to live pupils. Information becomes knowledge only when it fertilizes the individual's own life.

Comment. Here at last is the heart of Dr. Dewey's pragmatic philosophy. That there is merit, virility, tang in it is unquestionable. The true ideas are held to be those that work successfully in controlling experience; knowing is held to be the understanding and the control of experience. Pragmatism is held to be socially democratic and educationally experimental. Competing epistemologies are held to be socially divisive and educationally sterile. What shall we say to these things? Several things.

(1) In this section knowing is contrasted with habit. Knowing is flexible, habit is rigid. This account makes all habits "passive" and so opposes the theory of "active" habits earlier accepted (Chapter 4, § 2). This, however, may be an inconsistency only in nomenclature, what is there called active habits being here called knowing.

(2) Knowing is presented as involving a general function in carrying over old meanings into new situations. If accepted, this view contradicts the notion of education held by some as specific habit formation and allows for transfer of training, though rejecting the theory of formal discipline. If the faculty psychology underlying the theory of formal discipline is omitted, there is but slight difference between formal discipline and transfer of training.

(3) It is recognized that knowledge can be divorced from use. It is held that such knowledge then ceases to be knowledge and may become an object of æsthetic contemplation, a source of "legitimate" emotional satisfaction. This is culture in the old sense. It is here allowed as a phase of æsthetic appreciation. It is not culture then that is denied, nor its legitimacy, but that it is any longer knowledge. It appeared earlier that culture as an educational aim was legitimate only as it ministered to social efficiency (Chapter IX, § 3). Of the

two positions it would seem the later one enlarges life more, recognizes the right of unpractical beauty to exist, and so is preferable. Beauty, if not truth, is allowed to be a consummatory experience.

(4) Since all knowledge is held to have a prospective reference, there is no knowledge of the past unless it is used. What then is the status of unused knowledge about the past? Of knowledge that enters into no hypothesis for controlling the present passing experience? It loses its status as knowledge. It is either forgotten or it becomes information. Losing its status as knowledge, it loses also its status as truth. No true statement can be made about the past unless thereby some problem is being solved. What happens to the status of unused truths about the past? They become dry records, the fossilized remains of truth. Since this view allows information as unused knowledge to remain, and allows the legitimacy of emotional satisfaction in unused knowledge, it may after all amount to no more than the sense in which the term knowledge is to be used. The contraction of knowledge to the field of use is the expansion of information in the field of art. But the information must have symmetrical and orderly arrangement. On this principle one could not cut out the "dead wood" in the curriculum unless it were first shown not to be an object of æsthetic contemplation. But this is not the intended conclusion of the argument for school reform. The root of the difficulty is that in logic Dr. Dewey is a pragmatist but in æsthetics he is not; truth must work but beauty need not.

(5) Democracy is given the credit for the social origin of pragmatism. This is a difficult position to maintain for three reasons. First, there are advocates of democracy who are not pragmatists but realists, like Perry, or idealists, like Hocking. Second, the pragmatic method is more obviously derived from science, especially the biological sciences. It is biology that regards the mind as a useful characteristic of the organism. Dr. Dewey himself has been much influenced by Darwin[1] and

[1] Cf. Dewey, *The Influence of Darwin*, New York, 1910.

the method of the experimental sciences. And third, the pragmatic theory of knowing is individual, the earlier experiences freely influencing the later; but the theory of democracy is social, the experiences of one person freely influencing those of another. It seems a *tour de force* to assign pragmatism in epistemology to democracy in society.

(6) There is a close parallel between Herbart's doctrine of apperception and application and Dewey's doctrine of the two aspects of knowledge as giving meaning and control. By apperception, according to Herbart, the new is understood by means of the old. By one aspect of knowledge, according to Dewey, the new is understood by means of the old. By application, according to Herbart, a new problem is solved in the light of previous conclusions. By the other aspect of knowledge, according to Dewey, a new experience is controlled by the foregoing experiences. In both Herbart and Dewey, the old helps in understanding the new and the new modifies the old. What then is the difference? In Herbart the idea is basic and feelings and acts secondary; in Dewey the act is basic and feelings and ideas secondary. In Herbart the teacher communicates ideas; in Dewey the teacher guides activities. In Herbart the "problem" comes as the last step in an intellectual process; in Dewey it comes as the first step in an experimental process. Herbart is an intellectualist; Dewey is a voluntarist.

(7) What we want to know about pragmatism is, is it true? There are two views of the meaning of truth. One is the pragmatic view that the ideas which on the whole and in the long run solve our problems best are true. They are not true because they represent reality correctly but they are true because they control reality successfully. Ideas are true because they work. It is the successful working of an idea that constitutes its truth. The other view is that true ideas represent the situation correctly. The proposition, the sun shines, is true because the sun does shine. A true proposition states what is so. It is only a question of fact. There is no ques-

tion of making the sun shine, or controlling the shining of the sun, but only of the fact whether the sun shines. Truth is the agreement of statement with fact. Ideas are not true because they work; they work, if they work at all, because they are true. This view is held by realists and idealists alike. Realists and idealists differ, not in their theory of truth, but in their theory of reality.

How shall we decide between these two views of truth? It is partly a philosopher's logomachy. The pragmatists call truth what the non-pragmatists call the effect of truth. The non-pragmatists call truth what the pragmatist denies can ever take place, holding that no static proposition can ever correctly represent a fluid fact. "The sun shines" means the sun emitted light beams eight minutes ago. But, say the non-pragmatists, some facts are not fluid, and so on, back and forth.

We might begin by applying pragmatism to pragmatism. Does it work? The answer is, to some it does and to some it does not. Pragmatism works with the pragmatists and does not work with the non-pragmatists. Thus, pragmatism lacks a workable criterion of truth, landing us hopelessly in individualism, re-instating the position of Protagoras that man is the measure of all things. A successful working of the pragmatic theory of truth would include the general recognition and acceptance of it. This is lacking. The theory falls by its own standard. Or, maybe it has not had time yet to win its way.

But possibly pragmatism is the view that men ought to accept, whether they do or not? Why? Because it is the true view. But this sets up the non-pragmatic standard of truth. It could be the true view which men ought to accept, whether they do or not, only because it correctly states the case. And this is the non-pragmatic standard. There is no ought in the pragmatic theory of truth, requiring men to accept it. There is an intellectual obligation to know and accept the truth in the non-pragmatic theory.

Strictly interpreted, the pragmatic theory means the pursuit, but not the possession, of truth. The situation changing constantly, the ideas controlling it must change constantly, and so the truth is no sooner determined than it is dissolved again. "One never descends twice into the same river," said Heracleitus. Dr. Dewey admits this; knowledge ceases to be knowledge unless it is being used ever afresh in solving new problems.

A bit of the dialectic so offensive to the pragmatist. Dialectic insists on consistency in thinking. The pragmatic theory that truth is constantly changing is itself held to be a truth that does not change. The theory is self-contradictory. The truth that does not change is so because it correctly represents a situation, even a changing situation.

But there are cases in which two different sets of ideas will work equally well, in which it makes no difference to the outcome which set of ideas is held. A clever thief substitutes a copy for an original painting of an old master. The owner never knows the difference and goes on believing he owns an original. Is his belief true? Or, if the substitution is later detected, was his belief true while it lasted? and became false after the detection? His satisfaction was the same with the substitute as with the original until the discovery. A bank employee misappropriates funds, using them in profitable stock speculation; he replaces the funds taken; assume he does not risk it again; his act is undetected; the bank officials go on believing his honesty never lapsed. Is their belief true? Suppose the "perfect crime" were committed. There is no clue. Many different persons may each be guilty. One of them, A, is. But there is no evidence. No one theory works better than any other. Is the theory that A did it true or false? Most persons would probably say the theory that A did it is true, though it could not be known to be true. Here the appeal is not to workability of the idea but to its agreement with fact. Consider the case of the "useful fiction" described by Plato,[1] that the earth is the common mother of all and that all are brothers, which future generations might believe. Suppose this "royal lie" worked increasingly well in the state. Would that make it the truth?

Many other illustrations could be given of the difficulty in accepting the pragmatic theory of truth.[2] Turning to education, we may allow the acquisition of knowledge in schools by means of activities carried on in a social medium without excluding other methods of knowing. If knowing is agreement with reality as well as controlling situations, and if there are legitimate satisfactions in such knowing, then our schools may continue to stress knowledge for its own sake and non-occupational modes of acquiring it. It is a good thing for our pupils to know what has worked, what is so, as well as what may be tried. Our viewpoint does not exclude from the schools the pragmatic method of trying and seeing but supplements it with the tried and true.

In sum, we question the democratic origin of pragmatism, its adequacy as an epistemology, and its exclusive adoption by our schools.

[1] *Republic*, III, 414 C.

[2] Cf. Hocking, W. E., *Types of Philosophy*, Chapter X, New York, 1929.

CHAPTER XXVI

THEORIES OF MORALS

1. The Inner and the Outer

Exposition. The establishment of character is a comprehensive aim of school instruction and discipline. This is the commonplace of educational theory. Some conceptions of the relation of intelligence to character hamper the realization of the aim. We should be on our guard against such, looking out at the same time for the conditions that allow the realization of the aim. Morality is concerned with conduct. If mind is separated from activity, it is separated from conduct. A dualistic theory of mind and action leads to a dualistic theory of morals. And a dualistic theory of morals leads to, justifies, and idealizes certain objectionable practices employed in moral training. In this chapter we will undertake a brief critical discussion of the situation, showing the social origin of dualistic theories of morality, how the opposition is to be overcome in theory, and how moral character is to be formed in our schools.

The inner motive and the outer act, really inseparable, have been opposed to each other. The course of activity is split by this dualistic theory into the inner spiritual and the outer physical, into the inner motive of action and the outer consequences of acting, into even the inner character and the outer conduct. One ethical theory identifies morality with the inner state of mind; another, with the outer act and its results. This division is a culmination of the dualisms previously considered of mind and the world, soul and body, and end and means.

Let us show the unity and the continuity of inner and outer in the process of experience. Take the case of a man considering jumping across a ditch. If he were sure he could make it, he would jump; if he were sure he could not make it, he would not try. But he is not sure and so he considers, doubts, hesitates, is in suspense. During this time is only mental activity going on? No; energy is being redistributed within the organism preparatory to jumping or not; his eyes measure the width of the ditch; he feels his available energy by tightening his muscles; he looks about for other ways to cross; he reflects upon the importance of getting across. The initial activity is these tensions and adjustments within the organism. During the hesitant period consciousness is accentuated, his own attitudes, powers, wishes are to the front, but incipient activity is not lacking. The conscious recognition of the surging personal factors is a part of the whole temporally developing activity. The conscious phase of the continuous activity may be distinguished as mental; this does not mean it exists separately; it only means that the activity is still indeterminate and formative. There is not first a mental process without the body and then a bodily process without the mind. There is one continuous behavior process from an uncertain, divided, hesitating stage to an overt, determinate, complete stage. When the initial tensions and adjustments within the organism are coördinated into a unified attitude, the organism as a whole acts; he jumps or he doesn't.

So it is with all deliberate action, or conduct. It is action with a purpose; it involves a consciously foreseen end, and a mental weighing of the case for and against; it involves conscious longing for the end. Deliberation takes time. During this time there is bodily activity without overt action. There can not be overt action yet because the deliberating person does not know what to do; he postpones definite action; deliberation passes into decision, and bodily adjustments end in action. They are not two things but two phases of one thing.

When in doubt about what to do, we deliberate. When our instincts and habits are blocked by novel conditions, we are thrown back upon ourselves. We reorganize our attitudes before making action definite and irretrievable. Our organic resources need to be adapted to new situations, unless we try to drive through like an unreflecting brute. Our conscious processes, observations, thoughts, wishes, aversions, these represent inchoate, nascent activities. This important function issues in specific, efficient acts. We think when action is blocked; we think to start suitable action. We do not act to think, we think to act.

The nascent activities represented by thought are important. These budding organic readjustments are our sole escape from blind impulse and routine habits; they are activities having a new meaning in the process of development.

The proper rôle of mind is thus to guide a continuous activity, especially when it is blocked. But this rôle of mind is not always maintained. It sometimes builds castles in the air. When? Under the following circumstances: the blocking of the successful activity causes aversion and a desire for something different; the imagination is stimulated; it may run loose, yielding immediate emotional satisfaction; the air castles are built as a substitute for actual achievement; the pains of real thinking are avoided; an imaginary world is built up in mind; overt action exhibits acquiescence instead of struggle. Thus comes the breach between thought and conduct. The breach is then reflected in the dualistic theories separating mind as inner from conduct and its consequences as outer. What never should have occurred is used falsely to justify a theory.

Such a break between thought and conduct does not occur in persons with disciplined dispositions. With these the imagined picture aids observation and recollection to find a way out of the practical difficulty; the imagined objects are checked practically; if not realizable under present conditions, they are discarded; the emotions are drafted off in buildings on the earth.

Thus are divisions between inner and outer made and avoided in the lives of individuals. But such divisions also occur socially on a large scale. The early centuries of Christianity and the later eighteenth and early nineteenth centuries in Germany threw the reflective classes back upon themselves. The ethics of Stoicism, Monasticism, and Kantianism emphasize the motive; the ethics of Hedonism, or Utilitarianism, emphasize, by reaction, the deed and its consequences. The Stoics, the monks, and Kant could not have the outer world like they wanted it; so they took refuge in the inner world. They took a kind of revenge upon the alien, hostile environment by contemning it, by giving it a bad name. They complimented their own imaginings by calling them both more real and more ideal than the despised outer world. The inner cultivation of ideals was regarded as the essence of morality. The external world of activity was conceived as morally indifferent. The motive was everything, though effecting nothing. Kant insisted upon the good will as the sole moral good; the good will was regarded as complete in itself, apart from action and its consequences in the world. Hegel too, not being able to change institutions, rationalized them, idealizing them as the embodiment of reason.

The internal morality of "meaning well" led to a natural reaction. The idea of having a good disposition without regard to what comes of it was rejected. Instead it was said that the important thing morally is what a man does, the changes he effects and their consequences. Conduct, results, are what count; they afford the sole measure of morality. Inner morality was attacked as sentimental, arbitrary, dogmatic, and subjective. It gave men leave to dignify any dogma congenial to their self-interest by calling it an ideal of conscience, or to protect any caprice occurring to the imagination by calling it an intuition. This reaction against the morality of inner motive in favor of the morality of outer conduct was known as hedonism, or utilitarianism.

Ordinary morality is likely to be an inconsistent compromise of both views. The same is true of the schoolroom. On one hand, the individual is to have certain valued states of feeling; he must "mean well," his intentions must be good. If these conditions are met, he may be relieved of full responsibility for the results. On the other hand, certain things must be done to meet the convenience and requirements of others. The individual must do the work, have his nose held to the grindstone, obey, form useful habits, learn self-control. The individual's interest and intelligence in doing these things are not invoked. The effects of this externalism upon attitudes are unconsidered. The virtue is in the doing. Thus the two sides of a continuous single moral process fall apart in school and in life.

The remedy? The prior discussion has indicated the way to avoid both evils. Let individuals be occupied in progressively cumulative undertakings engaging their interest and requiring their reflection. Here they both do something outwardly and feel and think inwardly. The disposition of desire and thinking becomes an organic factor in overt conduct. The student should engage in a consecutive activity embodying his own interest; a definite result is to be obtained; routine habit will not suffice; capricious improvising will not do; dictated directions are happily absent; conscious purpose, desire, and reflection rise inevitably; the inner is the spirit of the outer; the outer embodies the inner; the outer and the inner are at one.

Comment. In the case of a man planning to lie, instead of jumping a ditch, the unity and continuity of inner and outer, earlier and later, are not so obvious. There is a division in consciousness between the knowledge of the truth and the plan to lie. Supposably there is a conflict in the body between the tendencies to tell the truth and to lie. In the case of a multiple personality, like Dr. Jekyll and Mr. Hyde, the unity and continuity of behavior is still further disturbed. The different personalities within the same organism alternate; successive states of the same personality are continuous with each other but are discontinuous with the alternating personality. In the case of a deranged personality there is but little unity and continuity left. These test illustrations do not prove there is an inner without an outer; they prove that successive behavior is not always continuous. In case it could be shown that there are ideas without neurosis, a pure, non-physical inner world would be established. This is as hard to do as to prove that all ideas are dependent on neurosis. James remarks: "We do not in the least explain the *nature* of thought by affirming this dependence."[1]

But there is an outer without an inner. The analysis given is of deliberate, purposeful, voluntary action. Involuntary acts of all kinds lack the inner motive. Some reflexes, like the contraction of the pupil of the eye in the light, are even unaccompanied by feeling tone or sensation. "The development of organic forms begins . . . where anything which can be called mind is at a minimum" (p. 393). The discussion in the text is concerned with moral, not sub-moral, action.

The discussion does not really avoid dualism. The psychical phase of experience is asserted to be distinguishable from the physical; they are not then identical. "Our conscious thoughts . . . represent inchoate, nascent activities." The word "represent" carries the whole mind and body problem. What is its meaning? The discussion clearly allows two phases of the ongoing experience. "We may distinguish, of course, the more explicitly conscious phase of the continuous activity as mental or psychical" (p. 403). What is denied is the separation of the inner and outer; they are asserted to be distinguishable; then a kind of dualism remains as the two phases of experience. If the inner is not identical with the outer, if the inner has been growing from more to more through the ages, there is no logical warrant for engaging the mind always with occupations whence it arose. Progress might consist in freeing it more and more from material occupations and

[1] *Psychology*, p. 6.

physical activities. This occurs, for example, in the composition of poetry, or in conceptualizing the values of life, or in building a social Utopia, or in constructing an intellectual system of the universe.

In this connection, why not take an occasional mental holiday and, with Dr. Felix Adler, build a few castles in Spain? Certainly not as a flight from reality but as an imaginative release from the humdrum of reality. There is much compensation in mental fiction. It is a form of recreation. Unless a person imaginatively idealizes, he may not have much to realize. The dreamers of the world have often done nothing, sometimes they have built castles on the earth. Necessitous living will usually bring us back to reality from our air castles. Children may properly have more fancies than adults. Only the do-nothing can not afford to yield now and then to moulding this scheme of things more to his heart's desire.

The discussion of the social origins of ethical theories is very vague and general. It does not summarize any preceding discussion. It, consistently with other arguments, affirms the thesis that philosophical systems reflect social conditions. No doubt the author has much in mind here he does not express. Marcus Aurelius was a Stoic, and one of the greatest, most active, and best of the Roman emperors; he did not take refuge in his own state of mind. The monks flew from social corruption but they took refuge not in a state of mind but in a monastery which, despite admitted weaknesses, was one of the most influential social institutions of the middle ages, being a combination agricultural station, hostelry, apothecary shop, bookstore, library, school, and church. Simeon Stylites, though a hermit, and so coming nearer leading the inner instead of the inner-outer life, still from the top of his sixty-foot pillow engaged in political and ecclesiastical pursuits and instructed his disciples. One would welcome details as to how the social conditions in Germany so checked the expression of ideals in action that Immanuel Kant became an ethical rigorist. The social origin of hedonism and utilitarianism is not given at all. Hedonism makes pleasure the highest good; utilitarianism, being more social, makes the greatest good of the greatest number the *summum bonum.* It is suggested they are reactions against the preceding views which cover two millenia. But hedonism existed in Greece prior to any one of the views it is said to be a reaction against. Evidently the topic of the social origin of ethical theories is complex.[1]

The question remains as to what the student who has been guided in engaging, physical occupations in school is going to do when he meets the world as it is. The following is one illustration: ". . . a mill owner complained that one of O'Neill's graduates had asked to change jobs two weeks from the time that he was set on an uncongenial task. O'Neill asked if this had ever happened before. The mill owner said, 'Not in sixty years of operation of that mill.' O'Neill said that he was glad his school was beginning to produce results."[2] Will the environment be changed to make all tasks congenial? Will pupils have to be trained to perform some uncongenial tasks? Will something of both take place?

2. The Opposition of Duty and Interest

Exposition. If one acts from a sense of duty, he is commonly supposed not to be interested in what he has to do. This is another moral dualism to be overcome. One who acts from a sense of duty is really always interested in what he does. There should be no conflict between the two.

Yet there is probably no antithesis in moral discussion set up more often than that between acting from "principle," which is approved, and acting from interest, or self-interest, which is reproved. To act from a sense of duty, from principle, is to act, it is said, disinterestedly, according to a general,

[1] Cf. Dewey and Tufts, *Ethics*, Part I (Written by Dr. Tufts), New York, 1910.

[2] Washburne and Stearns, *New Schools in the Old World*, p. 59, New York, 1926.

unswerving, moral law, above all personal considerations. To act from interest is, according to the allegation, to act selfishly, with one's personal profit in view, according to the changing expediency of the moment. A false idea of interest underlies this opposition. Though it has already been criticized (Chapter X), some ethical aspects of the question will now be considered.

We should distinguish between "interest" and "self-interest." All action, even from principle, involves interest; some action does not involve self-interest. Those who say all men act only from selfish motives mistakenly identify interest and self-interest. Their argument is: All deliberate action is motivated by interest; acting from principle is deliberate action; therefore, acting from principle is motivated by self-interest. The premises are sound; the conclusion is false, the term "interest" being used in two senses, the fallacy being that of "four terms." The supporters of acting from a sense of duty reply: Generous action is without self-interest; some men act generously; therefore, some men act without interest. Again, the premises are true and the conclusion false, for the same reason.

The truth is that all men are motivated by interest but some men are not motivated by self-interest. The error lies in the two meanings of interest, in a false notion of the relation of interest to the self. Interests are the motives of the self but some interests are not selfish.

Take the example of a physician in a plague. He stays and does his duty, not because he lacks interest but because he lacks self-interest. He is more interested in doing what his profession requires of him than in saving his own life. When he began his career, he may not have thought of a pestilence, may not have identified himself with such dangerous service. But, supposing he has a growing self, he willingly adopts the unanticipated risks involved in his vocation as integral portions of his activity. The larger self includes unforeseen relationships. The physician acts from no other "principle" than the aim of his practice,—the care for the diseased. It is a distortion of facts to say that his interest is self-interest, that his service is selfish. The good physician thus finds his self, his wider self, *in* his work, despite personal dangers; if he ran away through preference for personal safety, he would find his self, his narrower self, in running away. He would be interested not in healing the sick but in saving his own life. Thus, all action is from interest; some interests expand the self and some limit it; the self is its interests.

Both sides to this controversy between duty and interest mistake this relation of interest to the self; both assume that the self is a fixed and isolated quantity prior to action; both set up a rigid dilemma between acting from self-interest and acting without interest. As a consequence, acting from interest is interpreted to mean acting from self-interest, to get fame, power, approbation, profit, or pleasure. This cynical depreciation of human nature leads by reaction to the equally untenable view that noble action is without any interest at all; untenable, because it must be plain to an unbiased judgment that a man would not do what he is doing unless he were interested in it. The self is not ready-made, it is in process of continuous making through actions chosen. Recognize this, and the situation clears. There is no separation between interest and self. Interests in objects and acts are not means to the self as end. Self and interest are two names for the same fact. The self is revealed and measured in the kinds and amounts of interests taken in things. Interest means the active *identity* of a self with an object; acting from principle and acting from interest are the same; bear this in mind and the whole alleged dilemma falls to the ground. The mistaken argument and the reply may be stated as follows: If you act for yourself, you have self-interest; and if you act for an object, you have no interest. But either you act for yourself or for an object, and so you either have self-interest or no interest. To which the adequate reply, though not the only one, is that one may escape between the horns of the dilemma;

the minor premise does not exhaust the alternatives; another alternative is: You act for some object with which you identify yourself. In this case one can have an interest without self-interest.

We may look at the whole controversy from the standpoint of unselfishness. This virtue does not mean lack of interest; it does not mean selflessness; it does mean a self interested in the whole situation and expanding to meet it. A machine lacks interest, it is indifferent. A selfless act lacks virile character. An unselfish act is neither indifferent nor pale. It is an expansive and inclusive interest. These two features of expansiveness and inclusiveness are intimately associated. Expansiveness means that the generous, or unselfish, self readjusts its *past* ideas of itself to take in new consequences of one's vocation as they become perceptible. Inclusiveness means that the generous self, not drawing a line between itself and its world, consciously identifies itself with the *full* range of ties involved in its activity. The growing self is unselfish.

So there is no abiding conflict between "principle" and "interest"; there may, however, be a transitional conflict; it comes in crises of readjustment between the old self and the new situation; the crises may be slight or great. The conflict then is between the interest one has in following habit or the interest one has in readjusting habit. The latter interest is "principle." Habit means ease in action; there is a tendency to identify the self with its habits. Readjusting a habit involves disagreeable effort; a man has deliberately to hold himself to it; modifying his habit is unpleasant; the mind naturally turns away with aversion or irritation from the unexpected, disturbing thing. One's duty having been done in the past without facing the new disagreeable situation, why do so now? This is a temptation between interest and principle. To yield to the temptation is to narrow and isolate the self, treating it as complete; it is the selfish refusal to expand one's self. Any set habit may bring this temptation.

In this conflict between interest in following an old easy habit and effort in readjusting to a new trying circumstance, to act from principle is to act upon the *principle of one's chosen course of action;* it is not to act upon the favorable *circumstances* which have attended it hitherto. In such an emergency to act from principle is not to act upon something abstract, some duty at large. The principle is just another name for the continuity of the activity itself; it is not what justifies an activity. A gangster acts upon principle in continuing to be a gangster, even when it involves more killings than anticipated. If any activity is shown to be undesirable by its consequences, "to act upon principle" is to make a bad situation worse. In this case "interest" in following a past bad habit is in conflict with the "principle" of continuity in action involving worse effects. A man who prides himself upon acting from "principle" is likely really to be acting from "interest"; he insists on having his own way without learning from experience what is the better way; he acts from habit instead of expanding to meet a new situation; he fancies that having his own way is justified by some abstract principle without recognizing that his habit, really his selfish interest, is his "principle" and that it itself needs justification. Really to act from principle is to act generously, expansively, inclusively.

The secret of doing one's duty is to be interested in what one is doing. Duties are the specific acts needed for fulfilling any function, performing one's "offices," doing one's job. Genuine interest in one's job enables a man to stand discouragement, to withstand obstacles, to take the lean with the fat, even to make an interest out of overcoming distractions.

It is the same way in school, assuming it is an occupational school. Interest keeps the pupil working. Interest in the continuous development of the occupation as a whole overcomes temporary diversions and unpleasant obstacles. In the absence of a growing, significant activity, interest fails; to appeal to "principle" in such cases is purely verbal, or a form of obstinate pride, or extraneous motivation in dignified clothes. Of course there are times when momentary interest ceases, attention flags, and hard stretches lie ahead. What is the necessary reënforcement? Not loyalty to duty in the abstract but interest in one's occupation.

Comment. The pedagogy of this section is as soft as any in Dewey, yet there are hard places in it. We must examine it with care, as the issues are important.

(1) Let us note first that there is no *ought* in this ethics, no universal binding moral principles, no obligatory duties, no rapturous apostrophe with Kant to the starry heavens above and the moral law within, no clear universal distinction between the right and the wrong. Instead there are preferences of the individual, there are contrasts between growing and limited selves and there is interest in one's occupation. The most used string on Dr. Dewey's harp is "occupation" and the most played tune is "continuity."

But, really, is there no ought? Any individual has received more than he has given; he has received life, capacities, and opportunities; he has given a measure of service, and in the giving he has received more. He owes a debt for what he has received; he owes it to his family and his fellows; perhaps he owes it to a spiritual universe which made him a spirit. What he owes is his *ought;* his debt is what is due; what is due is his duty. The obligation is binding whether he is interested in paying it or not; if he is interested in paying it, in a measure he discharges his obligation; if not, he remains the worse debtor.

(2) Interest is presented as the adequate motivation of work. "Yet to an unbiased judgment it would appear plain that a man must be interested in what he is doing or he would not do it" (p. 408). This overstates the case. Work done under coërcion is not done through the motive of interest in the work; it is done through fear of the consequences of not doing it or through hope of the reward of doing it, that is, it is done through extrinsic motivation of some kind. Such work is ap-

parently not contemplated in the statement. Probably most of the world's work is actually done under extrinsic motivation in whole or in part. Such work can be brought under the statement quoted only by recognizing that there are extrinsic as well as intrinsic interests.

(3) The self is presented as identical with interest. "In fact, self and interest are two names for the same fact" (p. 408). This is confusing. The self *has* interest but *is* not interest. Interest is the emotional attraction an actual or ideal object has for the self. The self is more than all the interests it has, actual and potential; it is a conscious centre of experience; it has not only interests but also ideas and choices. The whole self not only feels interests but also, of course, thinks and purposes. These phases of experience are recognized in other portions of the text. They need to be associated with interests as possessions of the self. This does not mean the self is isolated from its world, nor does it mean the self is identical with its world, but it means the self is related to its world.

(4) The conflict between interest and effort reappears in the discussion, and this time effort wins. Interest sides with agreeable habit and effort sides with disagreeable readjustment. "It is the nature of a readjusting of habit to involve an effort which is disagreeable—something to which a man has deliberately to hold himself" (p. 409). Why, one asks, does the effortful readjustment in line with principle against interest take place? It is acknowledged that it does take place. And it is claimed that effort is needed to win out against interest. It sounds strange in this pedagogy which has consistently maintained hitherto that effort is due to interest. A possible solution is that the conflict is between an immediate interest in following habit and a remote interest in carrying through fully one's activity. In this case the remote interest requires effort to win out against the easy immediate interest. The apostles of effort could hardly ask for more. The facts of the moral life have here won a delayed victory for effort.

The paragraph on "crises of readjustment" really allows what the section as a whole is intended to deny, that is, a real conflict between interest and principle. The conflict is called "transitional." But since everything is transitional in this philosophy, the conflict might as well be called perpetual. Old habits always have to be adjusted to meet new situations; interest is said to support the old habit; principle is said to support the new demand. In this case the opposition remains as a dualism. There is another aspect to the crises of readjustment between old habits and new situations not here recognized. The old habit may be better than the new demand. "When in Rome, do as the Romans do," is a maxim whose following should depend on what the Romans do. In this case the conflict might be between an old principle and a new interest. When the things that interest us are wrong, whether old or new, it is principle that should win, with or against immediate interest, against or with the new.

In sum, the ideal is to have no conflict between duty and interest, to be interested in doing right at whatever cost. But the ideal is never attained, though ever functioning, and so the conflict between duty and interest remains. The opposition between them ceases at infinity.

3. Intelligence and Character

Exposition. Here is another dualism in the moral life; some intelligent people are said to lack character; some good people are said to lack intelligence; really intelligence and character are to be regarded as two phases of one practical activity. Let us see how.

Here is a noteworthy and frequent paradox in ethical discussions: the moral is, and is not, the rational. The one view identifies the moral with the rational; ultimate moral intuitions proceed from reason; even the only proper moral motive, according to Kant, is supplied by the practical reason. Socrates, and Plato too, identified virtue and knowledge, tracing the doing of evil to ignorance of the good.

...moral with the non-rational; ...ve nothing to do with the ...nce is constantly underestimated, even deliberately depreciated; moral knowledge is held to be a thing apart, conscience being thought of as radically different from consciousness. It is said that a man often knows the good and does the bad, that the bad man lacks, not knowledge, but habituation and motive. Even Aristotle at once attacked Plato's teaching on the ground that virtue is an art, like medicine, in which practical experience in handling diseases and remedies is better than theoretical knowledge without practice.

The issue in the paradox turns on what is meant by knowledge, or the rational. The paradox is resolvable in this way: the moral is to know the good, the moral is not to know about the good. Ideas about morality are not moral ideas. What then are these two meanings of knowledge?

According to one view, knowledge is intimate, vital, personal realization, a conviction gained and tested in experience. Thus we know that sugar is sweet and quinine bitter, thus we sit on chairs rather than stoves, carry umbrellas in the rain, and consult a doctor when ill. Knowledge of this kind finds direct issue in conduct.

According to the other view, so-called knowledge is used to denote a devitalized, remote information, a second-hand, symbolic recognition that people generally believe so and so. Of course this kind of knowledge finds no direct issue in conduct, does not profoundly affect character.

Aristotle's objection to Plato mistook the first meaning of knowledge for the second. Plato taught a man could not know the good theoretically except as he had first experienced it practically; that he could not acquire such knowledge from either books or others; that it was achieved through years of habituation, discipline, education; that it was the final, culminating grace of a mature experience of life. Because of Aristotle's emphasis on virtue as a habit, he would have agreed with Plato, if he had understood him. Intelligence functioning is character.

Knowledge of the good affects character; knowledge about the good need not affect character. The good when experienced is felt as desirable, as sugar when tasted is sensed as sweet; without such experienced satisfaction, "good" is an empty term. Knowledge about good deeds in which others believe might lead one to perform such deeds to win approbation, or to appear to be in agreement, but not through personal loyalty to such beliefs.

Turning to the significance of these views for our schools, we note first that, on the basis of a dualism between intelligence and character, moral education is practically hopeless. Character is set up as the supreme end of education in school; the acquiring of knowledge, the development of understanding, occupy the chief part of the time in school. If the two things are separated, the problem of moral education in school is insoluble.

Again, direct moral instruction in schools is ineffective.[1] Having divorced the general work of the school from character formation, this is a fatuous attempt to bridge the gap. Such catechetical instruction gives lessons in what other people think about virtues and duties. It could be of value only if the pupils already had a sympathetic, dignified regard for the sentiments of others; without such regard it might as well be information about the mountains of Asia; with a servile regard, it increases dependence upon others, throwing upon those in authority the responsibility for conduct. Direct instruction in morals is effective only in autocratic social groups where the few control the many; its effectiveness here is due to its reënforcement by the whole régime of which it is an incident. The expectation of similar results from lessons about morals in a democratic society is sentimental magic.

Learning and reciting from books in school has little influence on life out of school. It influences that conduct which

[1] Cf. Dewey, *Moral Principles in Education,* Boston, 1909.

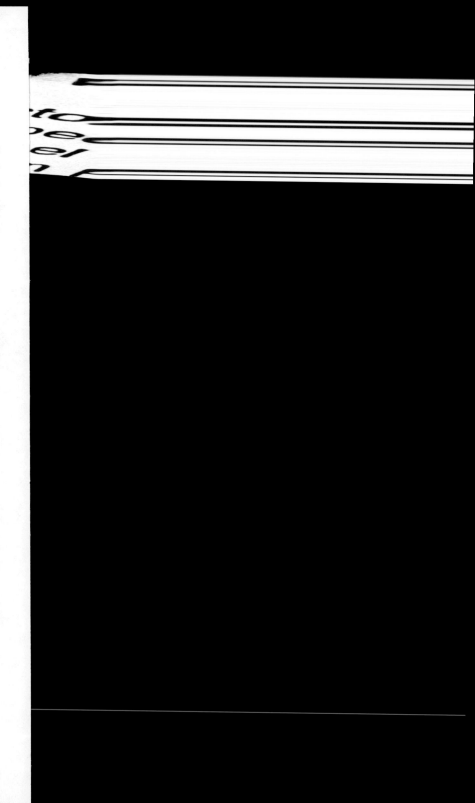

reproduces statements at the demand of others. Su tainment is indeed divorced from general, moral cond it is not knowledge worthy of high esteem. What is learning and reciting from books is true of knowledge o isolated, technical specialty; it modifies conduct, but only its own narrow line. The acquisition of mere school studies has only a technical worth.

In contrast with the preceding restrictions, first-hand knowledge does affect conduct significantly. The way to secure knowledge is the same as the way to form character. There is vital connection between knowledge and activity. Genuine knowledge is acquired in connection with one's system of impulsive and habitual activities. The knowledge of dynamite is only verbally the same to the safe-cracker and the chemist; actually it is different, having a different import, through being knit into a different system of aims and habits. When we learn through activities, knowledge functions in guiding activities. The qualities of mind involved in learning from experience are all intrinsically moral: open-mindedness, single-mindedness, sincerity, breadth of outlook, thoroughness, and responsibility for the consequences of accepted ideas. These intellectual attitudes do not lead to conformity to external authority. Such conformity reduces morals to a dead, machine-like, undesirable routine. Such external morality is unsuited to a democratic society dependent on personal initiative. Acquire knowledge in the right way, and right character will be acquired in the self-same process.

And, again, what is this right way to acquire knowledge? Through purposeful occupations involving social coöperation. As we saw, subject matter proceeds from direct activity having an immediate aim; then, geography and history enlarge the meaning of subject matter beyond the immediate; and then, subject matter is scientifically organized (Chapter XIV, § 2). Subject matter so treated never loses vital connection with activity. Knowledge so acquired under social conditions is moral, though it may not so be regarded. It builds up a social interest through the process of learning together; it confers the intelligence necessary to make that social interest practically effective. Representing standard factors in social life, acquired under conditions where their social significance is realized, the studies in the curriculum initiate the pupils into social values, feed moral interest, and develop moral insight.

Comment. Here is a discussion of character without recognition of the unique and signal function of conscience. All that is said about conscience is that it is mistakenly "thought of as something radically different from consciousness" (p. 411). Its work is apparently identical with the perception of undesirable consequences flowing from a certain line of action. It is not distinguished from an intellectual judgment concerning the true and the false or from the æsthetic judgment concerning the beautiful and the ugly. But there is in man a moral judgment concerning the right and the wrong. This moral sense belongs to man as man; its form is the same in all men: "this is right, I ought to do it, and this is wrong, I ought not to do it"; its content varies with the social heredity and the individual training. It is a precious possession. Cultivated carefully, it becomes both sensitive and discerning; abused, it first rebels and then becomes callous. Enlightened, it is man's safest guide in conduct. It has been praised by the wise as "celestial fire" and prized by all. Though flexible, it is not temporizing; though changing in content, it is permanent in form; though often a feeble ray, it lights the step ahead. If uninstructed, unbending, and unsympathetic, it leads into many evils. It is properly developed only by doing the right one sees and trying to see the right to do.

The position is accepted by Dr. Dewey that, in the sense of Socrates and Plato, knowledge is virtue. But we face the fact that a man with fifty years of a good life to his credit may go wrong. He has knowledge of the experienced satisfactions of virtue. Yet, he lapses in virtue. Why? Because of the pleasures of wrong-doing, first imagined, then dwelt upon, then rationalized, then yielded to. It is possible that Aristotle, the "mind," as Plato called him, of his Academy, understood Plato's position perfectly but did not accept it. Socrates and Plato were both intellectual determinists; they held that ideas determine conduct. Aristotle saw something new and different. He taught that both goodness and badness are within our power, that ". . . the man of self-control, knowing his lusts to be wrong, refuses by the influence of reason, to follow their suggestions."[1] Aristotle thus gave first distinct recognition in Western philosophy to the volitional aspect of consciousness. A man may know, in the habitual, experiential, vital sense of the term, what the right is, and yet after long deliberation decide to do the wrong. The lacking element is that he does not adequately love the right. By doing the wrong, he enlarges his moral knowledge, but it is his knowledge of evil.

This brings us to observe that the discussion sets up no adequate distinction between, no working criterion of, good and evil. "Moral knowledge" is implied always to be knowledge of the right. But moral knowledge of the wrong may result from exactly the same prescription: "What is learned and employed in an occupation having an aim and involving cooperation with others is moral knowledge, whether consciously so regarded or not" (p. 414). A band of racketeers meet the conditions. Any school of thieves is an occupational school. The prescription for forming character applies equally to good and bad character. What then is the difference between the two and the criterion by which to judge? The discussion lacks both clarity and precision at this point. And it is a matter concerning which teachers, who also flounder in this realm, should know. The way out, in line with preceding views of the author, probably is the insistence that the social occupations be such as to unify and not divide society.

[1] *Ethics,* VII, 1.

4. The Social and the Moral

Exposition. There is no moral experience that is not also social and no social experience that is not also moral; the two are phases of the same experience. The idea of education set forth previously is designed to avoid all dualisms. The dualisms in the theory of morals already considered, between the inner motive and the outer conduct, between action from duty and from interest, between intelligence and character, all come from taking morals too narrowly. Morals are taken too narrowly in two ways. On the one side, they are given a sentimental, goody-goody turn without effective ability to do what is socially needed. On the other side, they are limited to a list of definitely stated acts through over-emphasis on convention and tradition.

Really, morals are as broad as our human relationships. The moral and the social quality of conduct are identical. All our acts are actually or potentially social, even those not thought of as social at the time of performance. Why? Every act modifies disposition by the law of habit; it sets up a certain inclination and desire; the habit thus strengthened may at any time directly and perceptibly influence others.

Morals concern the whole character of man, not just certain traits. The whole character is the man himself in all his concrete makeup and manifestations. Certain traits are so obviously social that they are called "moral" emphatically, such as, truthfulness, honesty, chastity, amiability, etc. This should not mean that they are all of morals or that they are isolated, or exclusive of other traits; it means only that they are central in morals, more central than other attitudes, and so carry other attitudes with them. There are thousands of these other attitudes which we do not explicitly recognize, which perhaps are even unnamed. To isolate such central traits and designate them virtues is like taking the skeleton for the living body; the skeleton is certainly important, not in itself, but in the support it gives the organs of the body, making possible their integrated, effective activity. To possess virtue is not to cultivate a few nameable and exclusive traits; "it means to be fully and adequately what one is capable of becoming through association with others in all the offices of life" (p. 415).

Its social spirit is the measure of the worth of the school. This is the import of our earlier chapters regarding the social function of education. The administration, the curriculum, the methods of instruction have worth in proportion to their social spirit. The great threatening danger to the school, the great enemy of effective moral training, is the absence of conditions making possible a permeating social spirit. There are two conditions which make possible the active presence of this spirit.

The first of these is, the school must itself be a community life. Social perceptions and interests can be developed only in a social medium. In a genuinely social medium there is give and take in building up a common experience. Any one who has learned language can gather informational statements about things in relative isolation, but realizing the *meaning* of the linguistic signs is another matter, involving a context of work and play in association with others. A plea has been made in this book for continued constructive activities because they afford an opportunity for this social atmosphere. Here we have a school, not set apart from life as a place for learning lessons about life, but a miniature social group where study and growth are incidents of present shared experience. Playgrounds, shops, workrooms, laboratories, both direct the natural, active tendencies of youth and involve intercourse, communication, and coöperation. These all extend the perception of social connections.

Second, life and learning in school should be continuous with that out of school, with free interplay between the two, with numerous points of contact between the social interests of the two. The school is now too often an isolated institution; the reason is the absence of a social atmosphere in and out of school which develops a felt need for learning and so makes learning itself a reward; it is this isolation of the school which makes its lessons inapplicable to life and infertile in character. A monastery does not represent or typify the world beyond its walls, yet there is a spirit of companionship and of shared activity in it. A school like that is conceivable; inside there would be developed a social concern and understanding but these would not carry over and be available outside. There is a proverbial separation, even opposition, of town and gown. Academic seclusion is cultivated, sites for institutions remote from populous centres are chosen. The culture of the past is so fostered as to generate a reminiscent social spirit, making an individual feel more at home in the life of other days than in his own; a professedly cultural education peculiarly runs this risk; an idealized past becomes the comforting refuge of the spirit, present day concerns being found sordid and unworthy of attention. All these things operate to isolate the school from life.

All the aims and values desirable in education are moral. A narrow, moralistic view of morals is responsible for the failure to recognize this truth. Discipline, natural development, culture, and social efficiency, are both educational values and moral traits. They are marks of a worthy member of that society which it is the business of education to further. "It is not enough for a man to be good, he must be good for something." This something is living socially, so that getting from living and contributing to living balance each other. What he gets and gives materially is not external possessions; at its best it is opportunities and means for the development of conscious life; at less than this it is not getting and giving at all, but shifting the position of things in space, like stirring water and sand with a stick. But what, as a human being with desires, emotions, and ideas, he receives and gives is a more intense, disciplined, and expanding realization of meanings, that is, a widening and deepening of conscious life, which is a continual beginning afresh. Such values as discipline, culture, social efficiency, personal refinement, improvement of character are not things by themselves; they are but phases of a growing capacity nobly to share in such a balanced, give-and-take, experience. To maintain that capacity is the essence of morals. And education is not a mere means to such a life; it is such a life.

Comment. To identify the moral and the social quality of conduct is confusing; it is as confusing as to identify oneself with others. After all, there are the personal and the social aspects of experience. They may not be separable in fact; they are so in thought. The moral side of life is the personal, how one thinks and feels and purposes. These may have their physiological accompaniments. When these personal ideas, feelings, and purposes express themselves overtly in acts affecting others, they become social. Man's social relations are reciprocally related to his moral life.

The definition of virtue as given is as follows: "To possess virtue . . . means to be fully and adequately what one is capable of becoming through association with others in all the offices of life" (p. 415). This definition appears to cover too much. One is capable of becoming an enemy, or a friend, to man. The definition lacks a criterion to distinguish good from evil. In case the meaning of good is read into the statement by understanding some such word as "proper" or "correct" before "association," then the question is, what does the addition mean? This involves the initial question as to the meaning of virtue. Perhaps the missing word that should be supplied is "democratic." If so, who could qualify under the definition as possessing virtue? It is probably better to define virtue in terms of pursuit rather than possession; virtue then would be the quality of seeking to know the best to do, and of doing the best one knows, in specific situations.

As one envisages the occupational school community, it lacks certain features of worthy life. There are playgrounds, shops, workrooms, and laboratories. These may be supposed to provide for health, knowledge, character, and vocation. Is one ever allowed to observe and enjoy for himself the wonders and beauties of nature? Is there a cozy corner in a library where one may read for pleasure? Is there an art gallery where one may enjoy a work of beauty for what it says to the observer? Is there a quiet study where one may compose a poem or a piece of music? Is there a chapel where one or a group may go for meditation, prayer, praise, and worship? Is there any place for doing nothing in particular? Perhaps so, but these things are not specified in any analysis of the work and play school. And they suggest real values of common human experience.

It is said the school life should represent or typify that of the world. This proposal makes the school social but no more progressive than the society the school represents. There are three conceivable relations of the school to any given civilization, viz., it might be behind it, abreast of it, or ahead of it. The proposal would keep the school abreast of civilization. But education is said to transform, not to conform. This it could do only by keeping ahead of civilization, and so typifying an ideal, not an actual, society. But this would make the school discontinuous with life and continuous with an ideal. Human society is not what it ought to be. Should the school then typify life as it is or as it ought to be? Dr. Dewey's view is that the school should typify the best in current life as a projection of the coming democracy. This makes the school discontinuous with life below the best. The doctrine that the school is continuous with life, that education is life, is too vague to be practical. The school should be continuous with the good life, and education should be realizing the values of the good life. And the good life is progress toward the ideal, is the finite seeking to embody the Infinite, of which democracy might very well be a social expression.

The inclusion of discipline (twice), natural development, culture (twice), and personal refinement, along with social efficiency and improvement of character, among the educational aims and values (p. 417) throws a light backward. Dr.

Dewey does not mean to reject discipline, but only discipline without immediate interest; nor natural development, but only natural development in an unsocial atmosphere; nor culture, but only culture that is inefficient; nor personal refinement, but only personal refinement that is unsocial. All of these values as isolated, he rejects; all as integrated in a social ongoing process, he accepts.

L'ENVOI

Probably no one can read these last pages of Dr. Dewey understandingly without being quietly thrilled by them, without getting something of the socialized attitude here described, without being moved to act as he suggests and himself does. One of my students remarked, "Dr. Dewey is a genius, as yeast enabling humanity to rise." With St. Paul he rejects an abundance of things as the secret of the good life. With St. James he rejects fine sentiments without corresponding deeds. With Leigh Hunt he writes at the head of the list the one who loves his fellowman.

Dr. Dewey's thinking is not theistic. He writes: "The universe of moral and spiritual values exists only in the sentimentalism that generates them."[1] And again: "The demand of righteousness for reverence does not depend upon the ability to prove the existence of an antecedent Being who is righteous."[2] For theism there is a corresponding substitute on the practical side in his social passion, and on the intellectual side in his recognition in man of those forces working for rationality, beauty, and goodness. And he knows what he is omitting, for it was once his. He does not give us here in detail the naturalistic, cosmic setting[3] for his philosophy of education, and he gives us only by implication his view that sociality toward man and piety toward nature ade-

1 Dewey, "Is Nature Good?" *Hibbert Journal,* Vol. VII, p. 827.
2 Dewey, *The Quest for Certainty,* p. 304.
3 Cf. Dewey, *Experience and Nature,* New York, 1925.

quately cover man's religious experience.[1] At this point many will feel the widest and deepest conscious life can not be secured apart from the sense of man's continuity with an Infinite life, and that such a sense is necessary to secure the dynamic to live the good life. Others will feel too grateful to Dr. Dewey for what he has given to criticize him for what he has omitted. All sympathetic, discerning students will recognize his deep sincerity, his intellectual candor, his ripe scholarship, his penetrative insight, his social vision, and his practical dynamic, along with some regret that his writings are not more readable. To assess his views is itself a form of appreciation.

One misses in this volume a theory of feeling. There are theories of knowledge and of morals but none of feeling. There is a recognition of the imagination as the medium of appreciation, there is a recognition of the place of art in life. These things involve feeling. There are many references to the emotions of man. They are associated with the active responses to the environment. They are not to be opposed dualistically to the intellect. But any treatment of the feelings in relation to beauty, corresponding to the treatment of knowing in relation to sciences and to the treatment of action in relation to morality, is lacking, be it said regretfully.

One also misses adequate recognition of health education. Only one short, though strong, paragraph (p. 134) is devoted to the subject.

The home as an educational institution is neglected. There is no reference to it at all in the comprehensive fifteen page index. In the body of the discussion the methods of the pioneer community are praised, and school contacts with all social institutions are urged, but there is nothing about education for worthy membership in the modern home, nothing about interest in home decoration, nothing about preparation for parenthood, nothing about the art of spending, etc.

[1] Cf. Dewey, *The Quest for Certainty*, New York, 1929.

There is likewise no adequate recognition of education for leisure. There is such strenuous objection to a leisure class and to the dualism of labor and leisure that there is failure to recognize the importance of educating for free time. Leisure appears rather as self-expression in labor than as time off the job to be enjoyed.

With all the emphatic rejection of dualisms in the interest of continuity, there still remains a certain division in aims. Does education aim at individual growth or at social efficiency? Or, is it such individual growth as makes one socially efficient? Is the method of education the intelligent guidance of activities or is it social coöperation? Or, is it social coöperation in the intelligent guidance of activities? Is growth for the sake of more growth or is it for the sake of democracy? Or, is growth of the individual a phase of the democratic process? The emphases in different portions of the book are not shown to be continuous with each other. Geyer feels this difficulty which he expresses as follows: "The two distinct aims or ends which seem to be set up for education in Dr. Dewey's outline are on the one hand a preparation for sharing and improving the community life, and on the other a growth of the child's powers simply for the sake of growth."[1]

The failure to appreciate the significance of personality is one of the striking features of this philosophy. Education is concerned with teachers, pupils, parents, manual workers, lawyers, doctors, ministers, business men and women, and society composed of such, no two individuals being the same. Yet the discussion hinges not on the worth of personality but on the democratic type of experience. And it is personalities who have experience. It is almost as though democracy and individuality were so read as to omit personality. Sheldon states the case strongly: "Personality is, and forever ought

[1] Geyer, Denton L., "The Wavering Aim of Education in Dewey's Educational Philosophy," *Education,* XXXVII, p. 484.

to be, a mighty force; and the social democratic heaven of equal development would reduce personality to nothingness."[1]

Pragmatism is here presented as at one with the scientific method and also as democracy in epistemology. It is held to be at one with the scientific method in limiting thinking to proving hypotheses, and it is held to be democracy in epistemology in allowing earlier experiences freely to modify later ones. In view of these claims, it should be noted that pragmatism is not alone among modern philosophies in accepting the scientific method and in providing a theory of democracy. As Creighton says: "Pragmatism has no exclusive claim to be a philosophy of democracy, or a philosophy which is open-eyed to the results and methods of the sciences. I make this remark because writers of this school frequently convey the opposite assumption."[2]

The naturalistic view of intelligence is both inadequate in itself and insufficient as a basis of school procedure. It is inadequate in itself because the course of nature is not its own object; yet it is the object of intelligence. Dr. Dewey has himself written a book about it. It is insufficient in schools because the guiding of physical activities intelligently, even in a social medium, limits the formation and free play of both intellectual and ethical ideals, without which full mental and moral development is not possible. As Creighton observes: "The description of intelligence exclusively in terms of 'planning,' 'reorganizing,' 'reconstituting,' 'purposive activity' may be necessary to bring it under a naturalistic category, but it is surely a caricature even of the imperfect life of reason that ordinary individuals realize."[3] The same objection to instrumentalism is expressed by Marie Swabey as follows: "Whereas it is the merest platitude to assert that our biological makeup has something to do with the character of

[1] Sheldon, W. H., "Professor Dewey the Protagonist of Democracy," *The Journal of Philosophy,* XVIII, p. 484.

[2] Creighton, J. E., Review of "Democracy and Education," *Philosophical Review,* XXV, p. 739.

[3] *Ibid.,* p. 741.

our thinking, it is the extremest dogmatism to claim that all thought finally expresses nothing but an activity of adjustment on the part of the organism to its surroundings."[1]

On the insufficiency of the naturalistic theory of intelligence in school work, the following judgment of a school man is significant and interesting: "Dewey is still a formal disciplinarian to the extent that he believes, with much faith, that work with the hands in complex situations will provide, with no definite planning on the part of the teacher, for all the important intellectual and character traits."[2]

These summary views of the work as a whole lead us to remark that Dr. Dewey is a philosopher of revolt. Some of his emphases are one-sided and extreme. Many of the things he stands for in method can be accepted; many of the things he stands against have value in them. The acceptance of scientific technique is not inconsistent with other philosophies of the universe. His revolt against formality in education is, and of right ought to be, successful. He is last in line of those educational reformers who would make the school a pleasant place in which children may grow. Ahead of him stand, to name no others, Vittorino, Luther, Comenius, Rousseau, Pestalozzi, Mann, and Froebel. Dewey is the prophet[3] of the experimental method in an age burdened with the problems of science, industrialism, and incipient democracy. The company of those hearing his voice is vast and increasing. We have tried to take heed how we hear.

1 Swabey, M. C., *Logic and Nature,* New York, 1930, p. vii.

2 Gainsburg, Joseph C., "Evaluation of the Dewey School," unpublished paper.

3 Cf. Slosson, E. E., *Six Major Prophets,* Boston, 1917.

INDEX